Worlds of Political Economy

Also by Martin Daunton

HOUSE AND HOME IN THE VICTORIAN CITY: Working-class Housing, 1850–1914

ROYAL MAIL: The Post Office since 1840

PROGRESS AND POVERTY: An Economic and Social History of Britain, 1700–1850

CHARITY, SELF-INTEREST AND WELFARE IN THE ENGLISH PAST

EMPIRE AND OTHERS: British Encounters with Indigenous Peoples, 1600–1850

THE CAMBRIDGE URBAN HISTORY OF BRITAIN, VOLUME III, 1840–1950

TRUSTING LEVIATHAN: The Politics of Taxation in Britain, 1799–1914

THE POLITICS OF CONSUMPTION: Material Culture and Citizenship in Europe and America

JUST TAXES: The Politics of Taxation in Britain, 1914–1979

Also by Frank Trentmann

MARKETS IN HISTORICAL CONTEXTS: Ideas and Politics in the Modern World

PARADOXES OF CIVIL SOCIETY: New Perspectives on the Evolution of Civil Society in Modern Britain and Germany

CRITIQUES OF CAPITAL IN MODERN BRITAIN AND AMERICA: Transatlantic Exchanges

CIVIL SOCIETY: A Reader in History, Theory and Global Politics

Worlds of Political Economy

Knowledge and Power in the Nineteenth and Twentieth Centuries

Edited by

Martin Daunton and Frank Trentmann

palgrave
macmillan

First published 2004 by
PALGRAVE MACMILLAN
Houndmills, Basingstoke, Hampshire RG21 6XS and
175 Fifth Avenue, New York, N.Y. 10010
Companies and representatives throughout the world.

PALGRAVE MACMILLAN is the global academic imprint of the Palgrave Macmillan division of St. Martin's Press, LLC and of Palgrave Macmillan Ltd. Macmillan® is a registered trademark in the United States, United Kingdom and other countries. Palgrave is a registered trademark in the European Union and other countries.

ISBN 1–4039–3218–2 hardback

This book is printed on paper suitable for recycling and made from fully managed and sustained forest sources.

A catalogue record for this book is available from the British Library.

Library of Congress Cataloging-in-Publication Data

Worlds of political economy : knowledge and power in the nineteenth and twentieth centuries / edited by Martin Daunton and Frank Trentmann.
p. cm.
"Most of the contributions to this volume arise from an international symposium held in September 2002 at Churchill College, University of Cambridge" – preface.
Includes bibliographical references and index.
ISBN 1–4039–3218–2 (alk. paper)
1. Economics – History – 19th century – Congresses.
2. Economics – History – 20th century – Congresses.
3. Economics – Political aspects – Congresses. 4. Economic policy – Congresses. I. Daunton, M. J. (Martin J.) II. Trentmann, Frank.

HB85.W67 2004
330′.09′034—dc22 2004050534

10 9 8 7 6 5 4 3 2 1
13 12 11 10 09 08 07 06 05 04

Printed and bound in Great Britain by
Antony Rowe Ltd, Chippenham and Eastbourne.

Contents

Preface

Most of the contributions to this volume arise from an international symposium held in September 2002 at Churchill College, University of Cambridge. The conference was made possible through the generous support of the Ellen MacArthur and George Macaulay Trevelyan Funds of the Faculty of History, University of Cambridge, and we wish to record our gratitude to the Managers of these Funds for making possible a stimulating and productive meeting. We would also like to thank authors for developing their papers in the light of discussions in order to develop a shared project in thinking about a new history of political economy. Unfortunately, it was not possible to include all the papers presented at the conference, but participants' thoughts and comments over the two days have influenced the shaping of this volume. For discussion and comments we are particularly grateful to William Ashworth, Cristoph Conrad, Dinah Copelman, Margot Finn, Matthew Hilton, Julian Hoppit, Joshua Getzler, Craig Muldrew, Marta Petrusewicz, Gareth Stedman Jones, Pat Thane, Keith Tribe, Hans van de Ven and Donald Winch. Many thanks also to Newgen Imaging Systems for copy editing and to Laura Bevir for preparing the index.

Martin Daunton
Frank Trentmann

Notes on Contributors

Timothy Alborn teaches modern British history at Lehman College, City University of New York. His publications include *Conceiving Companies: Joint-Stock Politics in Victorian England* (1998).

Sunil Amrith is a lecturer in imperial history at the University of Cambridge. He is completing a dissertation on 'The United Nations and Public Health in Asia, 1940–1960'.

Martin Daunton is professor of economic history at the University of Cambridge and Master of Trinity Hall. He has published widely in modern social and economic history. His most recent publications include *Progress and Poverty: An Economic and Social History of Britain, 1700–1850* (Oxford, 1995), *Trusting Leviathan: The Politics of British Taxation, 1793–1914* (Cambridge, 2001) and *Just Taxes: The Politics of British Taxation, 1914–1979* (Cambridge, 2002).

S.M. den Otter is associate professor of history at Queen's University, Canada. She works on social theory and debates about Empire in Victorian Britain. She is the author of *The British Idealists* (Oxford, 1996).

Sheldon Garon is professor of history at Princeton University. He has worked widely on twentieth-century Japan in a comparative perspective. He is the author of *State and Labor in Modern Japan* (Berkeley, 1987) and *Molding Japanese Minds: The State in Everyday Life* (1997).

Heath Pearson teaches economic history and the history of economics at the University of California-Berkeley. He is the author of *Origins of Law and Economics: The Economists' New Science of Law, 1830–1930* (Cambridge, 1997).

E.G. Reisz is completing a PhD at the University of Cambridge on 'Rubber in the British Empire: Technical Knowledge, Economic Ideology and Global Trade, 1843–1934'. Her research covers the history of agricultural science and the relationship between economic knowledge and power in the British empire.

Willibald Steinmetz is professor of modern history at the Universität Bielefeld. He has worked on political language and on a social and cultural history of labour law. He is the author of *Das Sagbare und das*

Machbare: Zum Wandel politischer Handlungsspielräume – England 1780–1867 (Stuttgart, 1993) and, most recently, has edited *Private Law and Social Inequality in the Industrial Age: Comparing Legal Cultures in Britain, France, Germany, and the United States* (Oxford, 2000).

Francois-David Todd is currently completing a Cambridge PhD on the emergence of the free trade/protectionist controversy in nineteenth-century France. He wrote the new French translation of J.M. Keynes, *The Economic Consequences of the Peace.*

J. Adam Tooze teaches modern German and European history at the University of Cambridge. He is the author of *Statistics and the German State, 1900–1945: The Making of Modern Economic Knowledge* (Cambridge, 2001) and is completing a new economic history of Nazi Germany for Penguin.

John Toye is a visiting professor at the University of Oxford. He has worked on the political economy of development and is author of *Dilemmas of Development* (Oxford, 1993) and *Keynes on Population* (Oxford, 2000).

Richard Toye is a lecturer in history at Homerton College, Cambridge. He is the author of *The Labour Party and the Planned Economy, 1831–1951* (2003) and co-author, with John Toye, of *The Intellectual History of the United Nations* (2004).

Frank Trentmann teaches modern history at Birkbeck College, London, and is the director of the Cultures of Consumption research programme (ESRC and AHRB). He is the editor of *Paradoxes of Civil Society* (Oxford and New York, 2000/2003) and (with Mark Bevir) of *Markets in Historical Contexts: Ideas and Politics in the Modern World* (Cambridge, 2004).

1
Worlds of Political Economy: Knowledge, Practices and Contestation

Frank Trentmann and Martin Daunton

Political economy has been a central component in the making of modern societies since the commercial and industrial revolutions of the eighteenth century. It provided a dominant knowledge regime for understanding and managing economic relations, and for informing a system of practices and policies moulding cultural life and political power in state and civil society. Walter Bagehot, writing in 1876, 100 years after the publication of Adam Smith's *Wealth of Nations*, had little doubt about the 'wonderful effect' of 'political economy'. As he put it, with the emphasis appropriate to the editor of *The Economist*, 'The life of almost every one in England – perhaps of every one – is different and better in consequence of it. The whole commercial policy of the country is not so much founded on it as instinct with it … . No other form of political philosophy has ever had one-thousandth part of the influence on us; its teachings have settled down into the common sense of the nation, and have become irreversible.'[1] Bagehot was giving a patriotic rendering of a distinctly British embrace of what is often called 'classical' political economy: '[i]deas which are paradoxes everywhere else in the world are accepted axioms here'. Yet, under different names and with different intellectual, social, and political overtones, versions of political economy everywhere shaped modern knowledge, practices, and power relations, from *economie sociale* to historical *Staatswissenschaft* and Marxism, from imperial ecology to transnational savings movements, from civil society to international organizations, and from evangelical religion to popular (and often radical) political economy.

This volume is an effort at retrieval, an attempt to explore these broad and diverse worlds of political economy that have largely been expunged from economics textbooks and from the histories of economic ideas. The standard account proposes a fall of political economy and rise of a more abstract and individualistic approach to economic analysis from the close of the nineteenth century, with renewed calls for a revival of political economy since the 1960s. These have produced Marxist, radical and institutionalist critiques of liberal economics, which had become the dominant mode of discourse and applied practice in the course of the twentieth century. Political economy – in these new heterodox schools – focuses on the political and institutional settings of economic life, and sought to reassert the role of political power and interests vis-à-vis liberal representations of economic individualism. This volume is an intervention in this debate. It supports the political repositioning of economic subjects but also moves beyond the radical and institutionalist approaches. Instead of viewing the relationship between economics and political economy as one of the rise and fall between two rival and mutually exclusive systems of knowledge, as in the standard account, the volume here reclaims their historical interdependence. Rather than presenting a view of the advancing differentiation of economic life from other parts of modern society, culture, and politics, the new political economy advocated here explores the large and often neglected universe of economic knowledge and practices, and the way the two have shaped each other.

Worlds of Political Economy makes three related contributions to a new study of political economy. First, it argues that knowledge or ideas cannot be treated on their own, as in established *Dogmengeschichte* or a high intellectual history of economic thought,[2] but must be reconnected to fields of practice. Here we can learn from the debate about text and context in the literature on political thought.[3] Economics formed only a small part of the richer world of economic knowledge; indeed, until the second half of the twentieth century, economists themselves were deeply embedded in moral and popular practices and milieus, ranging from fiction and advice books to evangelical religion and popular science.[4] Yet these worlds have all too often been either flattened by grand narratives of theoretical revolutions in economics with their focus on analytical watersheds, such as the marginalist revolution of the 1880s, Keynesianism in the 1930s, or lost altogether in a triumphalist neoliberalism of the 1970s/80s, where the increasingly hegemonic analytical appeal of rational choice models silenced the rich cultural, social and ethical dimensions of political economy in the past.

Second, this volume's attention to the practical and contested workings of economic knowledge draws attention to the changing appeal, location and use of political economy in civil society as well as the state. Development studies and Marxism, and the renewed interest in the state in historical sociology in the 1970s and 1980s revived the use of the term 'political economy' in a new sense, a claim to reassert politics, power and interests in response to the dominance of the rational, utility-maximizing economic man of liberal economics. Yet in this work, the focus – some would say fixation – lay firmly on state institutions and public policy making, resulting in a vast literature with titles such as *The Political Economy of Foreign Investment in Mexico, The Political Economy of Land Reforms, The Political Economy of Coal*, or more corporatist inquiries into interest groups' capturing of the power of the state.[5] At their best, these studies revealed the uses and generation of economic knowledge by states in domestic and international relations, highlighting, for example, the different propensity of different state institutions to employ and maintain economic ideas and expertise, and the diverse and different degrees of entrance for new theories like Keynesianism into the corridors of state power in the mid-twentieth century.[6]

Nevertheless, Bagehot recognized in his observation that political economy was more than just economic theory and more than just economic policy affecting relations between state and market. It was about ideas and practices shaping collective identity and power relations, in his words 'the common sense of the nation', or what would now be called culture and national identity. Indeed, for much of the nineteenth and even twentieth century, as the chapters in this volume will show, political economy was a central field of cultural as well as economic knowledge. Some of that authority derived from its relation to the state – after all, Smith defined political economy as a 'branch of the science of a statesman or legislator'.[7] Commerce, taxation and development were crucial here, subjects that were, of course, understood and acted upon in different ways depending on different types of state formation. Yet to pursue this question simply by turning to the state for answers is to ignore more interesting historical questions. For political economy was more than statecraft, and before the onset of academic professionalization and institutional power in the early and mid-twentieth century, its authenticity and legitimacy were derived from multiple, competing sources and used different genres of communication. Attempts to understand and regulate market failure in mid-Victorian Britain, for example, were partly energized by a culture of associational life, as Alborn's discussion of company law highlights.[8] Its authority was ultimately cultural: economic knowledge and its popularization had a base and resonance outside the state in civil society, with its network of associations, popular forms of communication and education, and an infinite number of schemes of social and self-improvement.

Even at a high, more exclusive level – we can think here of the Political Economy Club or the British Economic Association (founded in 1890) – most bodies were dominated by professional, commercial and political experts (lawyers, bankers, statesmen and journalists), rather than by those intellectuals whose main identity and expertise was that of economic theorists.[9] At a more general level, it is also necessary to consider the vast popular turn to political economy amongst social reformers, population writers and public health officials, popular Free Traders, or the co-operative movement in and beyond Europe. Much focus has been on the initial rise of this wave of popular knowledge in the early and mid-nineteenth century, but, arguably, it crested in the early twentieth century, pushed by the expansion of mass politics and education. Thus, for example, the Anti-Corn Law League in Britain in the early 1840s organized 800 public lectures and distributed 9 million items of publications a year.[10] By 1910, by contrast, one Free Trade campaigning body alone held over 5000 meetings, from small towns to sea-side resorts, in which the superior principles of Free Trade were popularly and entertainingly disseminated, while protectionist opponents mobilized the new media of film, records and speaking postcards.[11] Political economy was public engagement and entertainment. And it was a popular course in working-class education and self-improvement; 52 per cent of Workers' Educational Association classes studied economics and economic history in 1913, a proportion that remained 32 per cent a decade later.[12] Nor was the popular communication of economic knowledge a peculiarly British phenomenon, whatever its distinctly liberal patriotic flavour. Trade and fiscal policy in other European countries were also prisms through which national power and social improvement were evaluated. As Todd shows in his discussion of French commercial debates after the Napoleonic period, it is misleading to project back in time a purer economistic duality between liberal Free Trade and conservative protectionism as it emerged later in modern trade theory.[13] Few politicians, capitalists, and economic writers occupied such neat and exclusive camps. Rather concern for liberty went hand in hand with a dose of agreed regulation of trade while protection, as a traditional form of benevolence was underpinned by an organic representation of interdependent interests.

Both the generation of knowledge and its employment in the policy-making process, then, occurred in a larger, pre-existing cultural universe of ideas, values and language. It is unwise to presume that the professionalization of economics at the turn of the twentieth century immediately or automatically put an end to this cultural situatedness of economic knowledge. The dissemination and contestation of practical economic knowledge about the progress of wages and prices, exports and imports, for example, were a staple of popular politics as well as state discussion before and after the First World War.[14] As Tooze convincingly argues for inter-war Germany, it is problematic to view the following decades as creating a divide between politics and economics.[15] A narrow focus on economics as professional knowledge in university departments unduly distracts from the many new and broader channels and outlets for economic knowledge in political debate, including parties' new research offices, expanding economic reporting in newspapers, and economic institutes. Whatever the growing divorce between economic and political thought in university departments, and the declining number of chairs which carried that explicit job description, the two continued to flow in and out of each other in public political life. Indeed, it could be argued that, far from ushering in a decline of deliberative politics, the new journalism was part of a media expansion that broadened the worlds of political economy. Clearly, this was a hybrid world, with different genres of communication for different audiences – the *Economist*, the *Statist*, and later the *Financial Times* and *Wall Street Journal*. Bagehot, not a formally trained economist, and editor of the *Economist* in the mid-Victorian period, saw his mission as spreading the principles of political economy. Likewise, George Paish, a practical, self-trained expert on trade and financial statistics was an advisor to the Treasury and Board of Trade in the early twentieth century.[16] This hybridity, however, may be more usefully viewed as a continuation of nineteenth-century trends in the popular expansion of political economy in advice literature, religious sermons, and theatrical productions, than as a sharp break. Early nineteenth-century journals and reviews provided an umbrella and shared context for erudite discussions of political economy, next to articles on science and literature.[17] To understand the ebb and flow of the worlds of political economy, and their changing salience and reception, it is wise to broaden the view beyond the corridors of state power and beyond the intellectual canon of economics to civil society, law and communication.

The third and final general contribution of this volume is to explore the transnational flows and barriers to the generation and contestation of political economy. 'Worlds', in a literal sense, here draws attention to the transnational dynamics of transmission. Once again, intellectual history and state-centred approaches have tended to favour a nation-state perspective, be it to contrast different national schools of economic thought (British liberal vs German national economics; analytical vs historical, and so forth) or to compare states' use and development of economic ideas and expertise. Yet, many of these states were not nation-states but imperial formations and, as such, involved – indeed, required – the exportation of knowledge and authority. As we shall see, this often involved a constructive dialogue with different practices of economic knowledge on the ground. In other words, by their nature of being imperial, many modern societies were themselves hybrid composites of different cultures of knowledge and practice. Furthermore, nation-states were not sealed containers but competitive contributors to a transnational exchange network of ideas and practices of development. Political economy provided a common currency in this transnational flow.

In one seminal approach introduced by Alexander Gerschenkron, this mode of exchange is seen as late developing states observing front-runners in the development game, and adopting strategies of imitation or leapfrogging.[18] This volume, by contrast, proceeds with a different geographic and temporal design that is less linear and more circular and porous. In the worlds of political economy, core and periphery were often part of a mutually interactive and creative relationship, rather than those of actor and passive recipient. As with the transatlantic exchange of social reform ideas at the turn of the twentieth century,[19] the transnational flow of economic knowledge proceeded in multiple, reciprocal directions. As Sheldon Garon's chapter on the transnational dynamic of savings campaigns shows, late modernizers like Japan not only contributed to and developed but also took political knowledge from more advanced industrial societies.[20] Similarly, as den Otter shows, administrators and jurists in imperial India, did not simply impose the political economy they had taken with them from the metropole, but adapted and revised their knowledge in practical encounters with different cultures of the colonial economy.[21] More generally, the uses and status of political economy were never pure and it cannot be understood on its own terms, for it often stood in productive tension with other rival forms and institutions of knowledge. Within national societies as well as within international organizations, this dynamic relationship between economic knowledge and other forms of knowledge created relationships that were sometimes symbiotic and sometimes conflicting between political economy, law, ecology and public health.

So far we have pursued two shifts: first, from a seemingly autonomous world of ideas to the mutual interaction between knowledge and practice; second, from a state-centred perspective to areas of civil society, Empire and transnational relations. Together these turn attention to the points of contestation that shaped political economy. Contests over political economy – its substantive meanings, its socio-political scope, its institutional home, and its authoritative spokespersons and users – impinged on vital conduits of power and identity. Max Weber recognized that liberal economists did not stand in an objective relationship with the material world around them observing it in a neutral fashion, but were entangled in the shaping and reproduction of this world through the application of their knowledge.[22] This point can be generalized beyond the question of the value neutrality of academic inquiry, to the many other ways in which popular economic knowledge has helped to shape the 'real' make-up of political economy. Hence, we are always speaking of political economy in two ways that need to be related through the interaction of idea and practice: political economy as a system of ideas, value, meanings; and knowledge in relation to the construction as well as observation of political economy in terms of the material relationship between state, market and civil society. The everyday life of imperial power in this double sense hinged on political economy, just as much as did the modernization of Japan, the popular perception (and anxieties) of economic crises and political possibilities in Weimar Germany, or the social improvement of groups in civil society. At the same time, the scope and cultural purchase of political economy were not constant, but varied in different contexts and time periods. The history of economics and the state's relation to economic knowledge are part of this equation; they cannot explain it. To understand the changing historical significance of political economy, this volume argues, it is necessary to trace its generation, diffusion and contestation. To do so, the frame for analysing political economy needs to include both the political uses and meanings of economic knowledge and the influence of economic knowledge on political and institutional practices. The chapters to follow are case studies exploring the three approaches laid out above.

Reviving political economy

This volume is a historically informed contribution to the revival of interest in political economy developed since the late 1960s by Marxist, post-Keynesian and heterodox economists. By the mid-twentieth century 'political economy', as understood in the nineteenth century, had virtually become extinct. Although some chairs of political economy have nominally survived, as at Cambridge, and some might still move back and forth when talking about the subject between economics and some appreciation of political constraints on policy choice and behaviour,[23] in effect the mid-twentieth century were dark days for the broader subject, for a discourse with a proud pedigree of intellectual forefathers, and for its popular mission in the eighteenth and nineteenth centuries. What had happened? We need to distinguish here between several distinct long-term trends in the intellectual trajectories of economic knowledge, the professionalization of knowledge, its institutionalization, and the shifting dynamics and contours of popular everyday life and knowledge. And these, in turn, need to be connected to the changing semantic fields of economics and political economy. It is from here that a new more historically informed retrieval of political economy suggested in this volume will become apparent.

One prominent approach is to distinguish between the following conceptions of political economy as revived from the 1960s: Marxist radical economics; institutionalist economics; historical economics; system theorists; neoclassical public choice.[24] Whereas the former four approaches offer distinctive ways of embedding economic processes in social, political or institutional spheres, the last approach reflects the increasingly ambitious project of recent neoclassical economics to subject all social phenomena to market-based models of interpretation. Whatever the merits of public choice theory informing the latter project, the so-called 'economic imperialism' of the neoclassical model has certainly structured the way in which the current battle is conducted over what counts as 'political economy' and who owns it. And, inevitably, this has coloured and distorted current advocates' conceptions of the historical fortunes and misfortunes of their subject. One prominent narrative that has emerged is to imagine a sharp break between the lineage of political economy (Smith, Ricardo, Mill) and a subsequent differentiation of an increasingly refined, separate analytical model of economics (Jevons, Marshall, Walras and Menger all the way to Keynes and monetarists). This narrative, in short, deduces the decline of political economy from the well-known paradigm shift towards marginalism in the 1880s, often seen as the root evil of 'economic imperialism' with its model of rational economic man. Thus, for example, recent advocates for an interdisciplinary revival of political economy have argued that the two sisters, politics and economics, were 'formally split in the late nineteenth century'.[25] True, this is the period when Alfred Marshall sought to professionalize 'economics', with its distinct text book (his *Principles of Economics*), and its own undergraduate courses (the tripos of economics at Cambridge in 1903). Yet, this hardly amounted to a differentiation of economic knowledge in general, turning its back to politics, nor the enthronment of the rational utility-maximizing individual at the expense of all other moral, psychological and biological considerations. Moreover, it is a teleological account of economic theory with a strong Anglo-American bias that ignores the resilience of historical, institutional and radical economics in many parts of the world after the turn of the twentieth century.

Much of the popular imagery of economics today as a 'dismal science' comes from its critics in the past, a view that was a staple as in Ruskin's critique of J. S. Mill. Today's writers seeking to disseminate their own version of political economy would do well to distinguish between such polemical accounts and the political and cultural cross-fertilization of economic knowledge that persisted. Neither during the heyday of classical nor of neoclassical economics is it possible to draw a stark dichotomy between schools of 'market' and 'culture' supposedly inhabited by economists and their critics. A critique of markets continued to be generated from within political economy. Mill, for instance, developed a strong view of the environmental limits of market societies. Rather than seeing economics and their moral-political critics as two mutually exclusive clubs, it may be more appropriate to view them as standing in a constructive dialogue. Economic knowledge was not only internally generated within its own frame of analysis but responded constructively to critiques produced by other knowledge forms, such as in Marshall's ethical liberal economics which responded to Ruskin's romantic critique.[26]

It is important not to read back the purer economistic versions that have come to dominate economic analysis onto the mindset of their intellectual forefathers. Marshall's consumer, for example, was not a simple machine with given preferences responding to laws of supply and demand, but an active individual whose wants were changing and driven by his activities: a socio-psychological need for distinction was imperative.[27] Instead of projecting key analytical categories into the past, the new history of political economy advocated here asks about the historical processes that created and shaped economic units of analysis, like the 'consumer', which, far from being universal or self-evident, only became a distinct category for social groups, institutions, and writers in the course of the nineteenth century, and then with greater prominence in some societies than in others.[28] Well into the twentieth century, economists – including neoclassical economists – worked with organic, multi-layered social models of human actors, their nature and motivations. As Heath Pearson notes in this volume, the writings of Alfred Marshall, the founding father of economics, were thick with considerations of other-regarding actions, sympathy and benevolence.[29]

Rather than seeing a bifurcation between selfish individual man favoured by a model of neoclassical economics gaining power in some nations (Britain and later the United States) and visions of *economie social* or historical economics preserving their foothold in France, Germany and elsewhere, Pearson's inquiry reveals a shared international culture of altruism informing different economic theorists at the turn of the twentieth century.[30]

While we therefore welcome the recent revival of interest in political economy, we also argue that the current institutional and radical versions that are set up in opposition to neoclassical economics are insufficiently historicized, holding out ideal-typical distinctions between these schools that draw attention away from the workings of hybrid forms of economic knowledge in the past and from the cultural and social embeddedness of dominant or orthodox forms of economic ideas. Put differently, recent proponents of political economy have constructed a convenient history of their disempowerment by neoclassical economics in the mid-twentieth century that closes the door to historical inquiry almost as quickly as it has opened it by all too happily accepting a much longer narrative of differentiation between politics and economics since the 1880s. This volume argues that this is an unfortunate and altogether debatable view of the role economic knowledge continued to play in society, culture and politics. Fixation on canonical authors can easily distract from broader worlds of political economy. Rather than starting from the assumption that the marginalist paradigm shift of the 1880s must have led to a differentiation of politics and economics, this volume proceeds from a more open, historical line of inquiry asking how political economy functioned in key social and international settings; how it continued to be generated, by what groups, with what meanings and for what aims, objects, and audiences, and in co-operation or conflict with what neighbouring fields of knowledge.

A historically sensitive new political economy, then, needs to situate the changing status of the discipline of political economy in a broader interpretation of the relationship between economic knowledge and practice over time. Central questions in this relationship concern when and how different forms of knowledge stood in tension or in symbiosis; the changing political uses and institutional location of economic knowledge; the patterns of diffusion of economic ideas, data and values, their modes of transmission or blockage; and the place of political economy in nation-state and transnational developments.

Tensions and symbiosis

Economic knowledge does not exist as the only form of knowledge, but operates in relation to other types of knowledge. In addition to tracing the internal development of intellectual traditions – the task of the history of economic thought – it is also crucial to explore the sometimes competing and conflicting, sometimes symbiotic relationships which economic knowledge develops with other knowledge forms. Knowledge, information and ideas are generated and used in a competitive arena, and seek the attention of social groups, public bodies and international organizations. Like any other knowledge, economic knowledge can rarely claim an undisputed monopoly, and where it has managed to obtain influence, it requires social work to preserve its influence by either keeping rival knowledge claims and experts at bay or by solidifying the symbiotic relationship to adjacent forms of knowledge.

The officials of the imperial state or the bureaucrats of international organizations were besieged by siren voices offering different passages through the rocks of economic policy. To whom were they to listen? In part, they were guided by their own sense of political expediency and self-preservation. But the economists who were seeking to make their voices heard might either form an alliance with other forms of knowledge and intellectual authority, or seek to challenge the claims of these rivals to speak on economic matters. Economic knowledge therefore stood in tension or symbiosis with adjacent disciplines depending on the precise historical circumstances. In colonial India, forests were contested by the native populations and the Raj. Notions of property rights were deeply contested throughout the colonial world and a prime site where law and economics collided or worked together depending on different contexts and traditions.[31] Economists were also in tension, as Reisz indicates, with ecologists and foresters.[32] The property rights of native peoples might be threatened because of their perceived 'uneconomic' use of their resources – but ecologists also began to argue that capitalist owners destroyed ecological resources and long-term benefits. Forest legislation, like property regimes more generally, provided an arena for competing forms of knowledge that sought the attention of officials and politicians. Law intruded into these debates, sometimes as an ally of political economists seeking to weaken the restraints on a free market in land and its product, and sometimes as a restraint on what was seen as an unequal and inequitable attack on valid claims by the occupiers of land.

The story of tension and symbiosis between law and economics is also found in Steinmetz's account of legal disputes on restraint of trade in Germany and Britain from 1870 to the First World War.[33] Should individuals have freedom to make a contract – or should they be given freedom to enter into trade, which would mean that contracts in restraint of trade should be struck down? The question was one which puzzled lawyers and economists in both countries – but were they arguing in autonomous intellectual spheres, did they take account of each other's approaches to reach mutual understanding, or were they in tension? Much the same issue arises in the case of medical knowledge. As Amrith shows in his chapter, debates over public health in the United Nations raised the old spectre of Malthusian crisis which had alarmed British governments in the early nineteenth century and the Raj in the later nineteenth century.[34] Would the interventions of public health programmes run by the World Health Organisation provide the path to prosperity by ending the waste of resources by disease, so raising productivity and allowing economic growth based on social justice? Or were doctors simply threatening a further slide into poverty as population growth outstripped resources? Why save people from malaria only for them to starve? Perhaps a better answer was to mobilize doctors in a different way, to control births. Economic and medical programmes competed for legitimacy and for funding, responding to each other's arguments and shifting their ground as appropriate. Even when the battle was won or lost, and a particular programme was rejected or accepted, economic ideas then encountered everyday practices, where working knowledge of family or communal behaviour was needed. Colonial officials or the local medical officers might soon find that responses to various economic incentives were not as expected or intended – and the question arose of whether to change behaviour or to amend policies. For men on the ground, facing immediate dilemmas of authority and consent, the answer was often the latter.

The institutional location of economic knowledge

Much of the literature on modern economic thought is about economists written by economists or economic historians, that is by university people and (mainly) for university people. For a new history of political economy as outlined above it is wise to take a broader institutional view of the subject. For economists in universities are only a small, and at many times insignificant group in the generation, dissemination, and contestation of economic knowledge. Even in Britain at the turn of the nineteenth and twentieth centuries, which is often seen as the core of the intellectual and institutional expansion of the new marginalist economics, the new method was actually marginal in a cultural sense – it was far from dominant. In 1894, the British Association for the Advancement of Science issued a blazing indictment of economic training, concluding that it 'was difficult to imagine a more complete indifference to the *scientific study* of Economics than that displayed at the present time.'[35] Indeed, Marshall, the very doyen of the discipline, had immense difficulties attracting students to his new course. Contemporaries found things were much better in America and continental Europe where economically trained experts occupied crucial positions in the civil service and where economic analysis was a central component of social and political investigation broadly defined.

Yet, it is dangerous to overdo the contrast between national systems. As Adam Tooze's chapter shows,[36] next to the German civil service – long dominated by the patronage, vision and students of the leading historical economist Gustav Schmoller – and the German university (also located within the state system), there was a host of alternative, commercial and party–political networks of knowledge generation and communication, from expanding forms of economic journalism to new statistical services, and party and trades-union in-house research groups. Looking beyond established and recognized institutional bodies, then, suggests some more general transnational trends that complicate a simple division between statist and civil society-oriented knowledge systems. Political economy had an important presence in the imperial state. Civil servants in British India had ingested a heavy dose of political economic training at Haileybury, and Malthus had a continued influence on reactions to famine in the Raj.[37] In Britain, too, newspapers like *The Economist* or *The Manchester Guardian* had played seminal functions in creating new economic experts as well as in communicating facts, ideas and representations of the economy. J.A. Hobson, the heretical progressive economist, wrote for the latter in the late nineteenth-century; W. Layton, the editor of the former in the 1920s, used his authority as an expert in domestic and international debates. Liberal party organizations followed Conservative tariff reform bodies in the Edwardian period in setting up in-house researchers and authors on particular trades. The Trades Union Congress started its own (admittedly small) economic research department in the early 1920s. The late nineteenth-century transatlantic network of buyers' leagues and consumer leagues generated a mass of information on working conditions, prices and shop hours, a process that considerably expanded with the development of the larger and more technocratic American consumer bodies in the inter-war years, like Consumers' Research and Consumers Union, which became the models for many later consumer organizations elsewhere. More than any other social reform movement and institutional network, Home Economics, with its expanding curriculum and growing foothold in secondary and college education, expanded the economic knowledge horizons (and political demands) of men and women in the first half of the twentieth century.[38] From a marketing direction, the proliferation of commercial and academic market research organizations mainly took shape outside established universities, although this did not prevent marketing research from leaving its imprint on public policy and the theoretical development of economics in mid-nineteenth century.[39]

Institutions, then, play an important role for understanding the substance, flow and limits of economic knowledge. To this extent, the new institutional economics has a point. But it is the actors, and the values and meanings they mobilize or contest through institutions, not rigorous pre-determined structures, that are of primary concern. Institutional structures shape the room for manoeuvre, the capacities for fighting the battle again or in a different way, but do not ordain the outcome. The Toyes' analysis of the United Nations is a case in point, where heterodox ideas emerged, despite the desire of bureaucrats to close off debates.[40] Economists knew how to work within its diffuse structure, in a way they were less able to do in the World Bank with its stricter control by leading industrial countries. There had been a similar contrast between the British and American state in response to the new economic ideas of the 1930s: the tighter hold of the Treasury and its firmly entrenched mandarins meant that newer ideas had a harder task than in the United States, with a less entrenched civil service and a more diffuse power structure.[41] Of course, academic economics has its own institutional structures which made it more or less easy to secure an authoritative status for opinions. Access to the pages of prestigious journals was controlled by editors who might be averse to new ideas; appointment committees might define certain approaches as inappropriate and unacceptable. Professionalization was not a simple, beneficial process as it appears in some accounts: it was also about the gradual exclusion of heterodoxy, whether of radical or often female voices.

But this is to flirt with pre-determined outcomes according to structures. For government institutions, like the Treasury, could be attacked from without through mobilizing public opinion, through the insidious work of intellectual criticism in academic journals and its popularization in the press. New economic ideas emerged from what might now be called think-tanks, from the Fabian Society to the Institute of Economic Affairs, which challenged the dominance of the current orthodoxy within the academy. Are politicians influenced by the ideas of economics – or is it rather that politicians turn to economists for the intellectual authority to justify actions and policies taken for other reasons, as has been the case with recent neo-liberal policies in America, Europe and Asia? Economic ideas will only be adopted when transmitted through a wider cultural process of diffusion and connected to a language through which the economy and economic behaviour is understood. The international hegemony of state power means that this process of diffusion is not a free or neutral powerless process equally open to all participants, but likewise, international hegemons, like the United States or the British empire before it, do not exert or export policies and knowledges outside this cultural process, which is always open to contestation and revision.

Diffusion of knowledge: transmission, blockages and systems of cultural provisioning

One critique of neoclassical theory and modelling made by recent advocates of political economy – a critique that can be traced back to late nineteenth-century historical economists and institutionalists as well as to more popular movements, like home economics – has been that a narrow focus on questions of utility-maximization fails to grasp the more organic societal configuration of economic life. Instead of reducing economic questions to ones of the efficient allocation of resources, one call has been to think in terms of 'social provisioning'.[42] Another critical voice has focused on the way in which mainstream economics itself 'is pitifully inadequate with respect to the more traditional factors commonly treated within its own discipline in comprehending the economics of consumption itself (the nature and sources of technology etc.)'.[43] Instead it calls for a 'system of provision' approach in which consumer choice is itself the changing product of the social and economic processes that are connected to particular commodities, their production, distribution and consumption. More generally, historians and sociologists have re-embedded markets as historically changing ideas and practices of social co-ordination.[44] Taking these discussions further to inquire into the diffusion of economic knowledge, we can inquire into cultural modes of provision, that is the values, ideas and genres of communication that disseminate and shape political economy in different social settings at different times.

Of course, economists have recognized asymmetry of information, imperfect knowledge and bounded rationality. But these qualifications ultimately all point back to an essential economic individualism. Here we want to step back from the attempt of economists to understand what forms of information and reasoning goes into individual decisions of choice or utility-maximization, in order to raise a more cultural question about how information circulates in the first place: what are its limits and exclusions, how does it reach some parts of society but not others, percolating into some political debates but being sidelined in others? In addition to asking about how markets come into being, then, the question becomes a more open historical one that asks what sort of knowledge about economic processes actually circulates. The existence of market society does not automatically tell us about the system of cultural provision of knowledge and communication through which members of that society obtain their views of the economy.

If economic knowledge can be said to be competing with other forms of knowledge, the marketplace for ideas also involves different genres and processes of dissemination. These concern discursive tropes through which ideas or data acquire social purchase as well as social and media bodies through which such ideas and discourses are disseminated, and the popular acts of reception through which actors, listeners and viewers make sense of these ideas and 'facts'.

The ways in which genres of communication and knowledge in terms of ideas and substantive meaning interact have been an important theme especially for sociological and historical inquiries into the transformation of knowledge in early modern science and print culture.[45] The understanding of modern economic knowledge has benefited far less from this literature. Statistics, it has been shown, transformed the visual representation of economic data and economic processes, as well as the generation of facts that were assigned new authoritative status.[46] Clearly, the supply and demand curve that have become a ubiquitous sign of economic literacy in classrooms, corporate boardrooms, and media-screens all over the world structured economic understanding and not just recorded data. Yet the algebraic–graphic turn of economics also created new problems for experts and politicians seeking to utilize this newly packaged and steadily expanding information in persuading voters or mobilizing party supporters or social movements.[47] Instead of charting the story of twentieth-century economics in terms of a perpetually refined analytical model, from the perspective of communication we may rather see it as the growing asymmetry between ever more sophisticated tools and ever richer data, on the one hand, and a growing need to communicate economic knowledge in accessible manner in an age of mass democracy and mass propaganda, indeed to modulate economic behaviour in accordance with the imperatives of economic policy.

One answer to this challenge can be found in the recycling and adaptation of older images and genres of economic knowledge to communicate appropriate ways of viewing and responding to more complex modern economic challenges. In Britain, Labour supporters after the Second World War explained the predicament of the national economy and their economic policy towards balance of trade and payments in terms of 'good housekeeping': the government was likened to 'the good housewife [who] shares out the food fairly', looks after her family, house, and garden, and balances her incoming money and outgoing expenses.[48] In nationalist but also liberal economics, mass mobilizations of supporters continued to translate complex economic processes into an organic image of the family. Representations of the economy were therefore gendered and also involved generational images of independence/dependence. In the massive campaigns and exhibitions to promote the purchase of national products in early twentieth-century China, for example, economic decision-making was portrayed in terms of the national family. Women's consumption choices were represented simultaneously as alternative forms of military defence and tied to child-bearing activities.[49] Similarly in the West, versions of economic imperialism, like the tariff reform movement in Edwardian Britain, portrayed the state of the economy through a gendered representation of male breadwinners losing their independence, civic virtue and social standing as *pater familias* thanks to the inflow of cheap goods and immigrant labour in a Free Trade system.[50] Such gendered models were not only discursive phenomena but had significant legacies on welfare state structures and social relations; in Britain, in contrast to France, social provision in the twentieth century centred on the male breadwinner.[51] It is dangerous, however, to contrast such organic or gendered renderings of the economy in conservative or nationalist traditions with supposedly purer, more modern or rational knowledge in liberal political economy. For contemporary Free Trade, popular politics was equally keen to reduce complex economic questions into easily manageable, culturally loaded stereotypes (the white loaf vs the black loaf), and to invoke the healthy family unit as a symbol of the superior workings of its own policy.

Conclusion

Together the chapters in this volume are explorations in a new history of political economy. Instead of a linear, synthetic narrative, they open up shared themes and problems that have all too often been submerged or eliminated altogether in accounts driven by the expansion of the modern state, interest group formation, or the evolution of economic theory from classical, to neoclassical to Keynesian and monetarist models. Instead of a footnote, or a subject best left to 'soft' disciplines, the chapters assembled here take the broader cultural formation and significance of political economy as their starting point. As with science or any other body of ideas, economic ideas and knowledges, too, need to be reconnected to their broad fields of practice, including everyday practices, working knowledge, and the generation of cultural values in civil society – as well as at the level of state departments or in economics' textbooks. By doing so, the volume helps to problematize a story of professionalization that has been viewed primarily from within the professionalized communities and agencies of economists themselves. For most of the modern period, however, economic knowledge had far deeper and diffuse roots in many arenas of public life; economic writers were working within this larger culture of political economy, not apart from or above it. The diffuse and complex popular resonance of political economy means that, prior to the development of more abstract free-standing theoretical models, economic knowledge stood in a constructive field of engagement with other forms of knowledge – constructive both in the sense of being able to mobilize symbiotic relationships as well as in the sense of having to respond to rival claims of authority and legitimacy from other forms of knowledge. As this volume shows, these exchanges and encounters operated not only within nation-states but also across and between them, producing a transnational transfer of ideas and practices. Our understanding of the current dynamics and limits of globalization will be much assisted by a greater emphasis on this broad set of social and cultural knowledges and practices and their transnational workings that have shaped the worlds of political economy in the past.

Notes

1. Walter Bagehot, 'The Postulates of English Political Economy', in Richard Holt Hutton (ed.), *Economic Studies* (London: Longmans, Green & Co., 7th edn, 1908), p. 1.
2. Dennis O'Brien, *The Classical Economists* (Oxford: Clarendon Press, 1975); Douglas A. Irwin, *Against The Tide: An Intellectual History of Free Trade* (Princeton, NJ and Chichester: Princeton University Press, 1996).

3. James Tully (ed.), *Meaning and Context: Quentin Skinner and His Critics* (Cambridge: Polity Press, 1987); J.G.A. Pocock, *Virtue, Commerce, and History: Essays on Political Thought and History, Chiefly in the Eighteenth Century* (Cambridge: Cambridge University Press, 1985); Stefan Collini, Donald Winch, John Burrow, *That Noble Science of Politics: A Study in Nineteenth-Century Intellectual History* (Cambridge: Cambridge University Press, 1983); Mark Bevir, *The Logic of the History of Ideas* (Cambridge: Cambridge University Press, 1999), for critical discussion.
4. Philip Connell, *Romanticism, Economics and the Question of 'Culture'* (Oxford: Oxford University Press, 2001); Margot C. Finn, *The Character of Credit: Personal Debt in English Culture, 1740–1914* (Cambridge: Cambridge University Press, 2003); Clare Pettitt, *Intellectual Property and the Victorian Novel* (Oxford: Oxford University Press, 2004). Anna Gambles, *Protection and Politics: Conservative Economic Discourse, 1815–1852* (Woodbridge, England and Rochester, NY: Boydell Press, 1999); Boyd Hilton, *The Age of Atonement: The Influence of Anglicanism on Social and Economic Thought 1785–1865* (Oxford: Clarendon Press, 1986); Philip Mirowski, *More Heat than Light: Economics as Social Physics: Physics as Nature's Economics* (Cambridge: Cambridge University Press, 1989); Crosbie Smith, *The Science of Energy: A Cultural History of Energy Physics in Victorian Britain* (London: Athlone, 1998).
5. Van R. Whiting, Jr, *The Political Economy of Foreign Investment in Mexico: Nationalism, Liberalism, and Constraints on Choice* (Baltimore, MD: Johns Hopkins University Press, 1991); G. Thimmaiah and Abdul Aziz, *The Political Economy of Land Reforms* (New Delhi: Ashish Publishing House, 1984); Ferdinand E. Banks, *The Political Economy of Coal* (Lexington, MA: Lexington Books, 1985); Peter B. Evans, Dietrich Rueschemeyer, Theda Skocpol (eds), *Bringing the State Back In* (Cambridge: Cambridge University Press, 1985); Charles S. Maier, *In Search of Stability: Explorations in Historical Political Economy* (Cambridge: Cambridge University Press, 1987); Suzanne Berger (ed.), *Organizing Interests in Western Europe: Pluralism, Corporatism and the Transformation of Politics* (Cambridge: Cambridge University Press, 1981).
6. Mary O. Furner and Barry Supple (eds), *The State and Economic Knowledge: The American and British Experiences* (Cambridge: Woodrow Wilson International Center for Scholars and Cambridge University Press, 1990); Peter A. Hall (ed.), *The Political Power of Economic Ideas: Keynesianism Across Nations* (Princeton, NJ: Princeton University Press, 1989). Robert Gilpin with the assistance of Jean M. Gilpin, *The Political Economy of International Relations* (Princeton, NJ: Princeton University Press, 1987).
7. Adam Smith, *The Glasgow Edition of the Works and Correspondence of Adam Smith: Vol. 2: An Inquiry into the Nature and Causes of the Wealth of Nations:* edited by W.B. Todd (text), R.H. Campbell and A.S. Skinner (general) (Indianapolis: Liberty Press, 1981), Book IV, introd., para 1.
8. Alborn, Chapter 5 in this volume.
9. In the British Economic Associations in 1891, only 86 of the 501 members came from universities, compared with 113 from business, 51 from law and 48 from banking. Keith Tribe, 'Political Economy and the Science of Economics in Victorian Britain', in Martin Daunton (ed.), *The Organization of Knowledge in Victorian Britain* (Oxford University Press for the British Academy, 2005).

10. Paul A. Pickering and Alex Tyrrell, *The People's Bread: A History of the Anti-Corn Law League* (London and New York: Leicester University Press, 2000), pp. 20–2.
11. Frank Trentmann, 'National Identity and Consumer Politics: Free Trade and Tariff Reform', in Patrick O'Brien and Donald Winch (eds), *The Political Economy of British Historical Experience, 1688–1914* (Oxford: Oxford University Press, 2002), esp. pp. 229–35; Frank Trentmann, 'Vergangenheit, Zukunft und die Inszenierung von Wirklichkeiten: Politische Ökonomie und Politische Kommunikation in Großbritannien zu Beginn des 20. Jahrhunderts', in Hartmut Berghoff and Jakob Vogel (eds), *Wirtschaftsgeschichte als Kulturgeschichte: Dimensionen eines Perspektivenwechsels* (Frankfurt am Main: Campus Verlag, 2004), pp. 405–434.
12. Jonathan Rose, *The Intellectual Life of the British Working Classes* (London and New Haven: Yale University Press, 2001), p. 274.
13. Todd, Chapter 3 in this volume.
14. Christoph Nonn, *Verbraucherprotest und Parteiensystem im wilhelminischen Deutschland* (Düsseldorf: Droste, 1996); Alan Milward, 'Tariffs as Constitutions', in Susan Strange and Roger Tooze (eds), *The International Politics of Surplus Capacity: Competition for Market Shares in the World Recession* (London: Allen & Unwin, 1981).
15. Tooze, Chapter 9 in this volume.
16. Martin Daunton, *Trusting Leviathan: the Politics of Taxation in Britain, 1799–1914* (Cambridge: Cambridge University Press, 2001), pp. 361f.
17. On the idea of a common context, see Robert Young, 'Natural Theology, Victorian Periodicals and the Fragmentation of a Common Context', in his *Darwin's Metaphor: Nature's Place in Victorian Culture* (Cambridge: Cambridge University Press, 1985), pp.126–63, 265–71.
18. Alexander Gerschenkron, *Economic Backwardness in Historical Perspective: A Book of Essays* (Cambridge, MA: Belknap Press of Harvard University Press, 1962).
19. Daniel T. Rodgers, *Atlantic Crossings: Social Politics in a Progressive Age* (Cambridge, MA and London: Belknap Press of Harvard University Press, 1998).
20. Garon, Chapter 8 in this volume.
21. Den Otter, Chapter 4 in this volume; and see also Sandra den Otter, 'Freedom of Contract, the Market and Imperial Law-Making', in Mark Bevir and Frank Trentmann (eds), *Critiques of Capital in Modern Britain and America* (Houndmills and New York: Palgrave Macmillan, 2002), pp. 49–72.
22. Max Weber, 'Der Sinn der "Wertfreiheit" der soziologischen und oekonomischen Wissenschaften' [1917] in Johannes Winckelmann (ed.), *Gesammelte Aufsätze zur Wissenschaftslehre* (Tübingen: J.C.B. Mohr, 1985), pp. 536f.
23. Peter Groenewegen, 'Political Economy', 'Economics', in John Eatwell, Murray Milgate and Peter Newman (eds), *The New Palgrave: A Dictionary of Economics:* Vol. 3 (New York: Stockton Press, 1987), pp. 904–7.
24. For these groups, see David K. Whynes (ed.), *What is Political Economy?: Eight Perspectives* (Oxford: Blackwell, 1984); Bruno S. Frey, *Modern Political Economy* (Oxford: Martin Robertson, 1978); and, most recently, the historical perspectives by Alfred Bürgin and Thomas Maissen, 'Zum Begriff der politischen Ökonomie heute', *Geschichte und Gesellschaft*, 25, 2 (April–June 1999), pp. 177–200; Berghoff and Vogel, *Wirtschaftsgeschichte als Kulturgeschichte.* See also the proliferation of recent journals, such as *Review of Political Economy* (1989 on) and *Review of International Political Economy* (1993 on).

25. J.S. Banks and E.A. Hanushek (eds), *Modern Political Economy: Old Topics, New Directions* (Cambridge: Cambridge University Press, 1995), p. 1, cit. in Bürgin and Maissen, 'Zum Begriff der politischen Ökonomie heute', p. 185.
26. Donald Winch, 'Thinking Green, Nineteenth-Century Style: John Stuart Mill and John Ruskin', in Mark Bevir and Frank Trentmann (eds), *Markets in Historical Contexts: Ideas and Politics in the Modern World* (Cambridge: Cambridge University Press, 2004), pp. 105–28.
27. Alfred Marshall, *Principles of Economics*, ed. and annotated by C.W. Guillebaud (London: Macmillan for the Royal Economic Society, 9th [variorum] edn, 1961), Vol. 1, Book III, ch. ii. G.M. Peter Swann, 'Marshall's Consumer as an Innovator' in Sheila C. Dow and Peter E. Earl (eds), *Economic Organization and Economic Knowledge*, Vol. 1 (Cheltenham: Edward Elgar, 1999), pp. 98–118.
28. Frank Trentmann, 'The Genealogy of the Modern Consumer: Meanings, Identities, and Political Synapses', in John Brewer and Frank Trentmann (eds), *Consuming Cultures, Global Perspectives* (Berg: Oxford and New York, 2005) ch. 2.
29. Pearson, Chapter 2 in this volume.
30. Rather than being overwhelmed or crushed by the new institutional science of economics, many of these traditions migrated productively to neighbouring disciplines and methods, including economic history, economic anthropology, geography and sociology. See, for example, Karl Polanyi, *The Great Transformation: The Political and Economic Origins of our Time* (New York: Farrar & Rinehart, 1944); Theda Skocpol (ed.), *Vision and Method in Historical Sociology* (Cambridge: Cambridge University Press, 1984); Marshall Sahlins, *Stone Age Economics* (Chicago: Aldine-Atherton, 1972); Terence K. Hopkins and Immanuel Wallerstein, *World Systems Analysis: Theory and Methodology* (Beverly Hills and London: Sage, 1982); Fernand Braudel, *Civilization and Capitalism: 15th–18th Century: Vol. 2: The Wheels of Commerce*, trans. by Sian Reynolds (London: Phoenix, 2001); M.M. Postan, *The Medieval Economy and Society: An Economic History of Britain in the Middle Ages* (London: Weidenfeld and Nicolson, 1972).
31. See, for example, Henry Reynolds, *The Law of the Land* (Ringwood, Victoria: Penguin, 1987); P.G. Robb, *Ancient Rights and Future Comfort: Bihar, the Bengal Tenancy Act of 1885 and British Rule in India* (Richmond: James Currie, 1987) and P. Karsten, *Between Law and Custom: High and Low Legal Cultures in the Lands of the British Diaspora: The United States, Canada, Australia, and New Zealand 1600–1990* (Cambridge: Cambridge University Press, 2002).
32. Reisz, Chapter 6 in this volume.
33. Steinmetz, Chapter 7 in this volume.
34. Amrith, Chapter 10 in this volume.
35. *Report of the Proceedings of the British Association for the Advancement of Science* (London: 1894), p. 391, cit. in Donald Winch, 'Economic Knowledge and Government in Britain', in Furner and Supple (eds), *State and Economic Knowledge*, p. 50.
36. Tooze, Chapter 9 in this volume.
37. Mike Davis, *Late Victorian Holocausts: El Niño Famines and the Making of the Third World* (London: Verso, 2000).
38. See especially the influence of John Dewey on approaches to the consumer in the large home economics' movement in inter-war America, Hazel Kyrk, *Economic Problems of the Family* (1929; New York and London: Harper & Bros., 1933); in France, see the work of Charles Gide, *Cours*

d'économie politique, trans. as *Political Economy* from the 3rd edn (1913) by Constance A.M. Archibald under direction of William Sharp (London: G.G. Harrap, 1924); in Britain, J.A. Hobson, *The Evolution of Modern Capitalism: A Study of Machine Production* (London: 1897 edn). See Trentmann, 'Genealogy of the Modern Consumer'.
39. See Christoph Conrad, 'Observer les consommateurs', in *Le Mouvement Social*, 206 (Jan–March 2004), pp. 17–39.
40. John Toye and Richard Toye, Chapter 11 in this volume.
41. Furner and Supple, *State and Economic Knowledge*.
42. W.M. Dugger, 'Redefining Economics: From Market Allocation to Social Provisioning', in Charles J. Whalen (ed.), *Political Economy for the 21st Century: Contemporary Views on the Trend of Economics* (Armonk, NY and London: M.E. Sharpe, 1996), pp. 31–43.
43. Ben Fine, *The World of Consumption: The Material and Cultural Revisited* (London: Routledge, 2nd edn, 2003), esp. pp. 79–124, cited at xi.
44. Bevir and Trentmann (eds), *Markets in Historical Contexts*; William M. Reddy, *The Rise of Market Culture: The Textile Trade and French Society, 1750–1900* (Cambridge: Cambridge University Press, 1984); Craig Muldrew, *The Economy of Obligation: The Culture of Credit and Social Relations in Early Modern England* (Basingstoke: Macmillan, 1998); Margot Finn, *Character of Credit* (Cambridge: Cambridge University Press, 2003).
45. Peter Burke, *A Social History of Knowledge: From Gutenberg to Diderot* (Cambridge: Polity, 2000) with further discussion and references. Steven Shapin, *A Social History of Truth: Civility and Science in Seventeenth-Century England* (Chicago: University of Chicago Press, 1994); Mary Poovey, *A History of the Modern Fact: Problems of Knowledge in the Sciences of Wealth and Society* (Chicago and London: University of Chicago Press, 1998).
46. J. Adam Tooze, *Statistics and the German State, 1900–1945: The Making of Modern Economic Knowledge* (Cambridge: Cambridge University Press, 2001).
47. Clearly, the algebraic mathematical mode of analysis was only one amongst many forms of representations, from statistical flow models in the inter-war years to energy-based, mechanistic and biological models in the nineteenth century; Tooze, *Statistics and the German State*; Philip Mirowski (ed.), *Natural Images in Economic Thought: 'Markets Read in Tooth and Claw'* (Cambridge and New York: Cambridge University Press, 1994); Smith, *Science of Energy*; F.Y. Edgeworth, *Mathematical Psychics and Further Papers on Political Economy*, ed. by Peter Newman (1877/1882; Oxford: Oxford University Press, 2003).
48. A.E. Oram, *Labour's Good Housekeeping* (London: Co-operative Party, 1950), cit. in Frank Trentmann, 'Bread, Milk and Democracy: Consumption and Citizenship in Twentieth-Century Britain', in Martin Daunton and Matthew Hilton (eds), *The Politics of Consumption: Material Culture and Citizenship in Europe and America* (Oxford and New York: Berg, 2001), p. 157.
49. Karl Gerth, *China Made: Consumer Culture and the Creation of the Nation* (Cambridge, MA: Harvard University Asia Center, Distributed by Harvard University Press, 2003), ch. 7. For European examples, see Victoria de Grazia, *The Culture of Consent: Mass Organization of Leisure in Fascist Italy* (Cambridge: Cambridge University Press, 1981); Ina Zweiniger-Bargielowska, *Austerity in Britain: Rationing, Controls, and Consumption, 1939–1955* (Oxford: Oxford University Press, 2000).

50. Trentmann, 'National Identity', 'Politische Kommunikation'; and for the masculine attributes in Conservative popular politics, see Jon Lawrence, *Speaking for the People: Party, Language, and Popular Politics in England, 1867–1914* (Cambridge and New York: Cambridge University Press, 1998).
51. Susan Pedersen, *Family, Dependence, and the Origins of the Welfare State: Britain and France, 1914–1945* (Cambridge: Cambridge University Press, 1993).

2
Economics and Altruism at the *Fin de Siècle*

Heath Pearson

What drives the little dynamo that is Economic Man? The founders of political economy as a distinct discipline appear to have entertained few doubts as to the answer. This discipline, like the older science of statecraft from whence it emerged, would accept the human animal in its fallen state and move on from there: benevolence, charity, public spirit and suchlike were childish things to be put away, leaving only prudent self-interest as the prime mover of economic action.

As sweeping historical generalizations go, the one just stated is fairly robust. Few would challenge its applicability to the likes of Boisguilbert, Cantillon, Mandeville, Steuart or Quesnay. I would include Adam Smith in the list, and cite in support his authorship of a *Theory of Moral Sentiments* alongside the *Wealth of Nations*. For here we have a scholar who, when writing at length in the vein of moral philosophy, defended stoutly the notion of an inborn trait of sympathy; and yet this same man, when writing at even greater length in the conceit of political economy, dropped all mention of it. Instead we are left with such memorable epigrams as

> It is not from the benevolence of the butcher, the brewer, or the baker, that we expect our dinner, but from their regard to their own interest. We address ourselves, not to their humanity but to their self-love, and never talk to them of our own necessities but of their advantages.[1]

Even Steuart gave more ground to benevolence than is to be found in the *Wealth of Nations*! Of all the nice solutions to the 'Adam Smith Problem' (i.e. the apparently incongruous visions of human nature expressed in his two major works) that have been offered over the years, none is as appealing as the simple notion that here was a man who knew one discourse from another, and who trimmed his analytical sails accordingly. For our purposes the point is that already by the end of the eighteenth century, political economy was defining itself as a science of enlightened self-interest.

Racing ahead to the turn of the twenty-first century, we find that not a great deal has changed. To be sure, the concept of altruism has found a place in advanced economic theory; and the authors of basic treatises are typically coy – when not simply silent – on the question of why it is that we go to work in the morning. But odd indeed would be the student who emerged from lectures on the widget market, the Prisoner's Dilemma or the Coase Theorem without the notion that economic agents, by definition, treat one another with the purest instrumentalism.

So much for ancient history and current events. What of the *fin de siècle* that fell roughly midway between them, in the late nineteenth century? Interpolation is generally less dangerous than extrapolation, but I will argue here that it too can mislead. Specifically, I will show that several of the most prominent theorists of that day were at pains to set 'altruism' – increasingly termed as such, but also gestured at with older terms denoting a preference for the well-being of others – alongside self-interest as a principle of economic psychology. Towards this end we shall traverse a broad geographic arc, beginning in Berlin and proceeding to Vienna, Lausanne, Paris and the two Cambridges.

Gustav Schmoller (1838–1917)

Berlin is the place to start a search for any antinomian trend in late-nineteenth-century economic thought. The city's university in particular – a young institution at the heart of Europe's youngest nation-state – was less invested in traditional modes of thought than its peers. And among Berlin's economists, who better to interrogate than Gustav Schmoller, the thrusting doyen of the 'younger historical school' and the scourge of all reductionism? Here surely was a man who would have no truck with the drastic simplifications of *homo oeconomicus*, such as Carl Menger had lately been purveying from his base in Vienna. On the other hand, though, such a magpie-in-scholar's-clothing would have little to offer by way of alternative, since that too would entail a degree of abstraction and generalization. Thus it is fortunate for our purposes that this standard caricature of the man is wrong: for all his monographic zeal and his scruples about deductive reason, Schmoller felt that he too had a theoretical vocation, one that would place psychological wisdom at the heart of economic science. As a founder of the *Verein für Sozialpolitik* (Association for Social Policy, a prominent scholarly society dedicated to social reform) and a leading proponent of 'ethical' economics, moreover, the problem of man's capacity for moral action may have had special poignancy for him.

Schmoller's meditations on this subject predated his arrival in Berlin. As early as 1874 he was acknowledging egoism as 'one of the poles of human life', but he insisted that its practical meaning was ever shaped by 'the constant process of humanity's psychological evolution'. 'The concrete, the decisive question', he declared, 'is how this drive is modified, at specific moments and in specific contexts, by the cultural experience of the millennia'.[2] Such a question does not admit of ready answer, of course, but it is to Schmoller's credit that once he finally collected his thoughts in an *Outline of Economic Theory* (1901–04) the problem featured quite prominently. Indeed, one is tempted to say that the *Outline* was structured much as the *Wealth of Nations* might have been, were the Adam Smith Problem truly the non-problem that is often supposed. Following a few pages of conceptual definition, the *Outline* launched into an extended treatment of social psychology and moral evolution. In it the human ego was given pride of place, but Schmoller hastened to add that among social beings pure egoism is quickly compromised: from the earliest stages of evolution, 'constant and irresistible psychic interaction' had given rise to 'common feelings, mutual understanding, and mutual accommodation, as well as external insularity'. What resulted were what Schmoller sometimes called 'circles of consciousness' (*Bewußtseinskreise*), sets of reflexive proclivities towards altruistic behaviour within the group. Far from a notional or historical curiosity, this phenomenon of group solidarity was a cornerstone of all economic organizations: 'no family, no workplace, no large enterprise, no market can exist that does not rest upon a distinctive, unitary *Bewußtseinskreis*, upon certain feelings of sympathy and common interest, of amicability and agreeability'.[3]

Altruism thus was held to spring from subconscious interpersonal magnetism; but Schmoller also emphasized the role of conscious moral deliberation within the human mind. Here too he followed the lead of Adam Smith the moral philosopher, even going so far as to introduce the concept of an 'impartial and always fully informed spectator' as the link between judgement of others and judgement of self. The result was a simple moral code known to civilizations the world over: 'Assert and perfect yourself; love your neighbour as yourself; give to each his own; feel like a member of the group to which you belong; be humble before

God, self-assured yet modest before humankind'.[4] Unlike Adam Smith the political economist, though, Schmoller insisted openly on the importance of such moral self-command (*Sittlichkeit*) in the creation and circulation of wealth. It was altogether too appealing, he opined, to see the modern economy as a system driven by impersonal forces – endowments, technology, markets, self-interest – and thereby to miss its deeper roots in 'feelings that are transformed over the course of spiritual and moral evolution, in ethicised urges, in a well-ordered co-operation between natural and higher (i.e. essentially ethical) feelings, in virtues and habits which spring from moral life in a community'.[5]

Adolph Wagner (1835–1917)

A comparison of Schmoller and Adolph Wagner yields many similarities. Colleagues in the Berlin economics faculty, in the Prussian Upper Chamber, and at the forefront of the *Verein für Sozialpolitik*, they must have crossed paths regularly. Though Schmoller's views carried more weight at the education ministry – he was often accused of wielding peremptory powers over all economics appointments in Prussia – Wagner's influence extended further into the imperial chancellory and among the large number of foreign students who came to Berlin for the latest economic wisdom.[6] To what end? By reputation Wagner was more a theorist and less a moralist than Schmoller, and yet he too saw fit to feature altruism among the determinants of economic action.

Like Schmoller, Wagner's interest in economic psychology dated back at least to the 1870s, in his case to a two-and-a-half-page excursus on 'Man's Economic Nature' in the first edition of his influential *Textbook of Political Economy*.[7] By the time of the definitive third edition of this treatise, now renamed *Foundation of Political Economy* (1892–94), the discussion had ballooned to 67 closely typeset pages. There Wagner declared as error the tendency of 'British economics' to feature self-interest exclusively, and deemed it a cardinal task of future economic theory to avoid it.[8] His own approach to the problem was to reaffirm that human action must be viewed holistically, while at the same time distinguishing five distinct motives behind it. Four of these were variants on the principle of self-interest. The fifth was awkwardly denominated as the *unegoistisches Leitmotiv*; more helpfully, this he resolved in turn into the familiar altruistic motives of love and conscience.[9] These motivational categories were carried over into Wagner's far lengthier taxonomy of economic organization, which he based on a trio of distinct 'principles', namely the private (*privatwirtschaftlich*), the collective (*gemeinwirtschaftlich*) and the charitable (*caritativ*). The fifth, altruistic, motive played a role in each of each of these: a modest and subsidiary one in the private economy, a more significant one in the collective economy, and of course the dominant role in the charitable economy.[10]

Wagner was too much a theoretician to be reckoned among the so-called 'historical' school of German economists, and yet he did share their penchant for the telling empirical example. Many of these offered practical confirmation of the economic role he ascribed to altruistic motivation. For instance, behind the economy of ancient Greece he saw the 'bonds of love and sympathy' between master and slave as a key organizing force; the profound difference of the Hellenistic world, in turn, and of the imperial Roman economy of which it became a part, was due largely to the growing importance of egoistic motives.[11] Europe's Middle Ages witnessed a resurgence of economic altruism, as evidenced in the extensive system of poor relief and in the profound ethic of devotion that permeated both private and public service; the guild system, in particular, he saw as a fine mechanism for channelling human energies into unselfish action.[12] Modernity, not unlike late classical civilization, had strengthened the force of pure (pecuniary) egoism at the expense of impure forms such as the quest for honour, and especially at the expense of unselfish motives.[13] But all was not lost. Switzerland, Britain and the United States were managing to preserve an economic organization based in large part on a civic ideal of *caritas*, while the recent outpourings of charitable aid to soldiers and veterans had demonstrated that this virtue lived on in imperial Germany as well. The Catholic church and Jewish synagogues promoted benevolent acts among co-religionists. And above all, contemporary industrialists were once again venturing beyond the call of contract, to engage in 'acts of common benefice' (*gemeinnützige Leistungen*) on behalf of their employees. Indeed so prominent was this trend, Wagner noted wryly, that even economic theorists were beginning to address it.[14]

The foregoing observations say something about the role of altruism in *fin-de-siècle* economics, but they also suggest that Adolph Wagner may have been misunderstood to a degree. As against the theoretical proposition most closely associated with his name – that the economic remit of the bureaucratic state is destined to grow at the expense of civil society – a more precise formulation may be in order. The purely individual principle of economic organization was receding from its recent peak, and was being replaced by two other principles working in tandem: the collective principle, invoked where necessary, and the charitable one, invoked where possible.

Eugen von Philippovich (1858–1917)

Unlike Schmoller or Wagner, whose posthumous fame was and remains appreciable, the name Philippovich is now shrouded in obscurity. This would have come as a surprise to his contemporaries: long-time professor at Vienna's famous economics faculty, politically prominent as well as the author of the most widely assigned economics textbook in the German-speaking world over a quarter century, surely he could have hoped for more? Again unlike his counterparts in Berlin, Philippovich's views on the place of ego and alter in economics evolved with his personal development. As befitted Carl Menger's reputedly favourite student, the young Philippovich espoused his mentor's vision of an 'exact' economic theory that, while never denying outright the existence of diverse motives to human action, refused on principle to muddy the analytical waters by taking them into consideration. Thus in an inaugural lecture on economic method delivered at the age of 27, Philippovich saw fit to adduce repeatedly the presence of altruistic impulses to social action, and yet he insisted on methodological grounds that such behaviour 'does not fall within the domain of the economic sciences'.[15]

Philippovich's tender age seems significant in this regard, as does the fact that his inauguration was not in Austria but rather in the German Empire, at Freiburg. His eight years at that university (1885–93) coincided, it seems, with an emerging taste for the politics of social reform as well as for the more pluralistic economic psychology that was now the norm in German discourse. By age 30 he too was sitting on the executive council of the *Verein für Sozialpolitik*, and would soon carry that perspective to his activities as a member of the Baden state assembly. In 1893 Philippovich returned as full professor to Vienna and to more theoretical concerns, but the imprint of his German sojourn proved lasting. He maintained his links to the *Verein*, served briefly in the Lower Austrian assembly and for a decade in the Austrian Upper Chamber, and generally served, in the words of one historian, as 'a powerful moral and pedagogical influence on hundreds of young academics, journalists, and government bureaucrats'.[16]

What does this personal arc tell us of Philippovich's evolution as an economic theorist? Perhaps not much, but it is suggestive; and the fact remains that his later writings acknowledged altruistic motivation in a manner quite inconsistent with his youthful strictures. So much is clear from another inaugural speech he gave 20 years after the first, upon taking up the rectorship of the University of Vienna, titled 'Individual Responsibility and Mutual Aid in Economic Life'. Relationships of mutual aid, according to Philippovich, emerged not only as self-interested alliances of convenience but also – as for Petr Kropotkin, an early theorist of evolutionary altruism whose *Mutual Aid* (1902) was an obvious inspiration for the speech – reflected deep-seated 'feelings of community' within families, tribes and races. Thus Kropotkin, despite his misguided anarchist conclusions, had quite rightly observed that no community subsists on self-reliance alone, and furthermore that, 'as far as the economy is concerned, from the early origins of society the individual has been able to shoulder his responsibility only with the help of organisations of mutual aid'.[17] The significance of this insight for high theory Philippovich made clear two years later, in a contribution to a *Festschrift* for Schmoller, when he criticized explicitly the self-interest assumption of classical theory. Notwithstanding its manifest virtues, this assumption

> shows us nevertheless only the operation of a *single* condition of social life. How human relationships shape themselves *within* these bounds no longer depends upon economic evaluation, but rather follows from the moral ordering of life. To have shown this, and to have made it the basis of human action in society and state, is the merit of that change which has been brought about through the infusion of socio-political ideas into economics.[18]

Whatever the momentary interest of inaugural lectures and memorial volumes, it must be to his best-selling textbook, the *Outline of Political Economy*, which went through 18 editions between 1893 and 1923, that we look to for Philippovich's true manifesto. And here he made clear just how far he had come from Menger's knee. That he saw fit to include in his theoretical survey a section on economic motives is telling, as is the plurality of motives that he adduced there. Alongside the ubiquitous principle of self-interest, '*altruistic, charitable* factors, the feelings of community, of brotherly love and mutual aid, can also be effective forces in the construction of an economic organisation'. In the first place, altruism worked an impact by inspiring the creation of new economic units such as philanthropic foundations. Moreover it could affect economic outcomes by modulating the degree and manner in which agents pursued their various objectives. And last but not least, it helped to determine the distribution of income and expenditures in society.[19]

Léon Walras (1834–1910)

By contrast with Philippovich, the renown of Léon Walras has only grown during the century since his death. But his very claim to great fame makes him seem an unlikely candidate for inclusion in our survey. After all, the main thing he is remembered for – in most minds, the only thing – is his contribution to the mathematical modelling of competitive general equilibrium, an approach to economic theory that is rich in insight but bereft of psychological nuance. Were he alive today Walras would no doubt welcome his fame, and yet regret its failure to match his artistic, scholarly and political ambitions, which had been manifold. He was, for one thing, a romantic and something of a bohemian. A teenager in 1848, he later styled himself as 'one of those youths whom the February Revolution had united, heads and hearts, into a movement'; then at age 24 he published a sentimental *Bildungsroman* that capped (or more precisely, ended) an aspiring literary career.[20] For another thing, he was a lifelong proponent of social reform in general and the co-operative movement in particular. In his thirties and still unable to find an academic post, Walras had briefly edited and published a journal devoted to co-operation, and had even served as managing director of a bank for co-operatives; both enterprises failed under his watch. After finally establishing himself at the University of Lausanne, Walras continued to structure his economic thought around the tripartite division of what he inherited from his father: 'pure political economy', on which his posthumous fame is founded, but also 'applied political economy' and 'social economy'. All three branches were in his teaching curriculum, and each became the subject of a substantial treatise. He devoted far more energy to exploring the first of these, but there is reason to believe that he saw it as ultimately subservient to the richer problematics of the latter two. As he wrote to Augustin Cournot in 1874, '*économie pure* is nothing but the theory of social wealth. In order to proceed to *économie politique appliquée* and *économie sociale*, one must introduce the physiological and psychological man, individual and moral. Rest assured that I will keep this element well in mind.'[21]

In what did this psychological man consist? Self-interest, of course, but not only that. In his *Studies in Social Economy* (1896) Walras praised

> the faculty that crowns our human sensibility with love, with amity, with the affection that joins us to our kin, with charity, with enthusiasm for the homeland and for humanity. ... Such, gentlemen, are the results of observation. They establish the existence of a series of intimate phenomena which are not self-interested ideas – nor volitions, nor sensations, nor sentiments – but rather disinterested emotions.[22]

Altruism was not merely extant and morally desirable, it was economically necessary:

> We can be sure that industry calls rigorously for [individual] mores, and that economic society calls rigorously for moral society. ... We know that if man is capable of a division of labour, this is on condition of being a moral being; and we know that if man is a moral being, this is in order to be capable of a division of labour. ... Thus for peoples as for individuals, the moral order and the economic order, far from mutual exclusion, appeal to, sustain, and fortify one another.

'Truth be told', he concluded, 'man could in no way exist without the disinterested emotions of sympathetic and aesthetic love'. It was therefore a great boon of nature that these were exactly the personal qualities to which a free division of labour tended to give rise.[23] The same points were made more briefly in his *Studies in Applied Political Economy* (1898).[24] Strange utterances indeed from a man who is now remembered for conceptualizing the economy as a set of logical algorithms, but very much in keeping with the man and his times.

Charles Gide (1847–1932)

Gide was, in his way, one of the most influential social scientists in the Paris of his day. Consider the testimony of Joseph Schumpeter, a man never accused of excessive generosity towards his peers:

> Charles Gide cannot occupy any great place in a history of analysis but played a most useful and most creditable role all the same. He was an all-round leader, free from prejudice, in sympathy with all that was going on, and made by nature for imparting this sympathy to others.[25]

As a professor at the University of Paris, the École Nationale des Ponts et Chaussées, and ultimately the Collège de France; as co-editor of the *Revue d'Économie Politique* for 45 years after founding it in 1887; and as the author of two highly successful textbooks in economic theory and the history of economic thought, Gide did not want for opportunities to shape the parameters of political economy.

'Solidarity' and 'co-operation' were the most important concepts in Gide's economic lexicon. Some biographers have traced this turn of mind to his deep roots in French Huguenot culture, and not without reason.[26] But it is just as plausible to see in it a plain reflection of Charles Fourier, the 'utopian' socialist to whose thought Gide was exposed as a schoolboy in his small Midi hometown, and whom Gide held in open reverence throughout his professional life. Fourier, it will be recalled, foretold a social and economic revolution founded upon secessionist communities. Among other marvels, these communities would be so geared as to cultivate the innate human capacity for intimacy, sympathy and of course co-operation. It is in the light of this Fourierist tendency that we should interpret Gide's brief first intervention in the question of economic motives, in an 1882 critique of Catholic 'social' economics published in the *Journal des Économistes*. On the one hand, he shared these reformists' vision of a day when all men would be perfectly 'charitable and disinterested', as the gospels advised. 'But on that day', he went on, 'if it ever arrives, political economy will be rendered useless: humanity, in effect, will have lost its terrestrial nature'.[27] What Gide did not go on to say at that juncture, but would make abundantly clear in later years, was that he envisioned another, piecemeal and terrestrial road to moral improvement, one based not so much on perfect virtue as on group solidarity.

By the early 1890s Gide was able to speak of a veritable fashion for the idea of solidarity among natural scientists and social theorists; his contribution would be to introduce the idea into political economy.[28] As he warned students early in his *Course in Political Economy* (published in ten editions, 1909–30),

> The error of the classical school was not at all that of excessive use of the abstract method, but only that of having too often taken abstraction and hypothesis for reality. For example, having postulated its *homo oeconomicus* motivated solely by self-interest – which it had every right to do – [the classical school came] to believe in his real existence, and no longer saw anyone but him in the economic world.[29]

In future this stick-man of self-interest would have to be fleshed out with a greater appreciation for the power of sociability, affection, even love. Gide made this point forcefully in an 1898 contribution to Britain's *Economic Journal*:

> Observation and history do assuredly reveal this principle of love functioning in the world, under a thousand different shapes, side by side with the principle of hedonism. Let no one, therefore, say that we are creating chimaeras. Contrariwise, it is the *homo oeconomicus*

> who is the chimaera! Economists have no doubt a right to imagine and to study him, as a naturalist may study the skeleton hung on a wire in his laboratory. But leave the right to study the real man, the concrete man, the sociable man, the living man![30]

And indeed he saw reason for hope, for man and for economic theory. In a 1912 speech he hailed the rise to prominence of a new acquisitive motive, namely the desire for wealth as a means to help others; in support of this view he cited recent acts of grand philanthropy, and especially the proliferation of modest co-operative associations. Economists were watching these solidaristic institutions pierce through the hard crust of industrial society

> like snowdrops after a long winter, following a thaw; for there has been a sort of thaw within political economy, within the science of wealth such as it had emerged from the hands of the first economists – brilliant and clear as crystal, but as frigid and rigid as crystal as well. Its hard and keen edges have been softened by a new breeze.[31]

We may never know whether Gide's vision was ultimately that of the Calvinist congregation or the Fourierist phalanstery, or some fusion of the two. But it does seem certain that he saw that new dispensation in the offing.

Alfred Marshall (1842–1924)

The person of Alfred Marshall gathered together many of the threads that run through this story, and the story of nineteenth-century altruism in general. Like Gide, he was raised in an environment of stern and earnest piety, and yet held the utopian socialists in high regard, asserting that they 'knew something about the hidden springs of human action of which the economists took no account'.[32] Like Philippovich, his academic training imparted skills of formal analysis that he would later downplay. Like Schmoller he cultivated an interest in psychology, evolution and their interrelations.[33] Like Wagner, he was crucial to the international dissemination of economic ideas. Like both Germans, he lived in the shadow of idealist philosophy. (Unlike theirs, Marshall's association was voluntary and far more enthusiastic; he even described Kant as 'the only man I ever worshipped'.[34]) Like all of them, he was a public intellectual and a well-published author. To this heady mixture he added one that was distinctive. At Cambridge, as at no university on the Continent, economists typically emerged from the Moral Sciences curriculum, where the nature and prospects of ethical behaviour were of course a central concern.

In about 1868, during the time when he still sensed his primary calling to be in psychology, Marshall composed a lecture titled 'Ye Machine', in which he (rather after the fashion of La Mettrie and Condorcet) described a fictive mechanism that his audience was obviously intended to interpret as a metaphor for the perfected human organism. The machine would be, among other things, profoundly sympathetic towards its fellows:

> For instance, suppose it perceived that the other Machine were in want of coal; this would suggest the idea of more coal being put into it, and thus the idea, and hence the action, of putting more coal into it. And the association might be so strong as to be effectual in spite of the opposition which might be raised internally if it had to take the coal out of its own reservoir.

Lest the import of the metaphor be lost, 'I ought incidentally to call attention to the power of Natural Selection in preserving those races in which the principle of sympathy was most powerful, and thus increasing the pleasure attached to the idea of another's pleasure.'[35]

This abstract position was carried over directly into Marshall's economic analyses. In 'The Present Position of Economics' (1885), he announced that 'wherever we get a glimpse of the economic man he is not selfish. On the contrary he is generally hard at work saving capital chiefly for the benefit of others.'[36] This became a major theme in his epoch-making *Principles of Economics* (1890, revised up to 1920), in the introduction to which he declared that

> ethical forces are among those of which the economist has to take account. Attempts have indeed been made to construct an abstract science with regard to the actions of an 'economic man', who is under no ethical influences and who pursues pecuniary gain warily and energetically, but mechanically and selfishly. But they have not been successful, nor even thoroughly carried out. For they have never really treated the economic man as perfectly selfish: no one could be relied on better to endure toil and sacrifice with the unselfish desire to make provision for his family; and his normal motives have always been tacitly assumed to include the family affections. But if they include these, why should they not include all other altruistic

> motives the action of which is so far uniform in any class at any time and place, that it can be reduced to general rule? There seems to be no reason; and in the present book normal action is taken to be that which may be expected, under certain conditions, from the members of an industrial group; and no attempt is made to exclude the influence of any motives, the action of which is regular, merely because they are altruistic. If the book has any special character of its own, that may perhaps be said to lie in the prominence which it gives to this and other applications of the Principle of Continuity.[37]

Marshall's many revisions changed the manner in which he expressed his views on altruism, but the essential teaching remained intact, if not enhanced. In the first edition, for example, he wrote that

> It is sometimes said that economists regard it as 'natural' or 'normal', and in some sense even right, that man should be governed only by selfish motives; this opinion may however be dismissed at once as a popular error, which finds no support in the teaching or practise of the best economists. But again it is said that the scope of economics is limited to the consideration of those actions which are governed by self-regarding, if not by selfish motives. This view also seems to be mistaken; but there is so much authority for it that it requires to be carefully examined.[38]

In the second edition (1891) the foregoing passage was replaced with an assertion that if the classical economists had stated more clearly that money was not man's primary motive, but merely as convenient measure of man's motives,

> they would have escaped many grievous misrepresentations; and the splendid teachings of Carlyle and Ruskin as to the right aims of human endeavour and the right uses of wealth, would not then have been marred by bitter attacks on economics, based on the mistaken belief that that science had no concern with any motive except the selfish desire for wealth, or even that it inculcated a policy of sordid selfishness.[39]

Then in the third edition (1895) he appended a further statement to the effect that economists

> deal with man as he is: not with an abstract or 'economic' man; but a man of flesh and blood. They deal with a man who is largely influenced

> by egoistic motives in his business life to a great extent with reference to them; but who is also neither above vanity and recklessness, nor below delight in doing his work well for its own sake, or in sacrificing himself for the good of his family, his neighbours, or his country; a man who is not below the love of a virtuous life for its own sake.[40]

In keeping with these forthright precepts, the *Principles* was littered with specific observations of unselfish behaviour among animals, within families, tribes and firms, by voters and public officeholders; and as a latent potentiality, unselfishness was a centrepiece of Marshall's 1907 article on 'The Social Possibilities of Economic Chivalry'.

F.W. Taussig (1859–1940)

Though his Missouri origins were an ocean and a half-continent away from the European mainstream of economic thought, Frank Taussig was no frontier naïf. Himself the son of German immigrants, the young Taussig had joined the throng of aspiring economists converging on Prussia's universities – in his case Berlin, where he developed a lifelong sympathy for Adolph Wagner and his ideas.[41] Upon his return from Europe Taussig settled at Harvard University, where he completed his doctorate and embarked on a 52-year academic career. Such was his standing that Schumpeter, his junior colleague, hailed him not only as a formidable theorist, but also as 'one of the greatest teachers of economics who ever lived'.[42] Taussig's influence extended well beyond his own classroom, thanks to the *Quarterly Journal of Economics*, which he edited from 1896 to 1936, and to his *Principles of Economics* (1911, in print through 1945), which became the standard American textbook along the lines of Marshall's *Principles*, Gide's *Principles*, and Philippovich's *Grundriss*. In short, here is a man befitting the august company in which we have placed him.

It must be said that Taussig's *Principles* belonged to the twentieth century in a way that the other textbooks did not: lacking any explicit statement regarding economic motivation, it nevertheless broadcast an implicit message that self-interest reigned alone. But elsewhere he addressed the question squarely, and with the same upshot as we have come to expect from his generation. In his 1905 presidential address to the American Economic Association (AEA), for instance, titled 'The Love of Wealth and the Public Service', Taussig warned that 'in enumerating and classifying economic motives, we must not forget the altruistic impulse. Whether or no it be innate, and whatever its origin, its existence and influence are patent.' No mere theoretical curiosum, he cited this stock of philanthropy and public spirit as a significant resource in the solution of the day's social ills.[43]

Taussig returned to these themes at some length in his 1915 book *Inventors and Money-Makers: Lectures on Some Relations Between Economics and Psychology*, which reprinted his public remarks at Brown University's sesquicentennial celebration. The fourth and final of the lectures carried the title 'Altruism; The Instinct of Devotion'. 'It is most curious', he mused aloud, 'that the earlier economists ignored so completely the existence of the instinct of devotion, or if they did not quite ignore it, brushed it aside with something like impatience'.[44] Such neglect was no longer tenable, not least in light of the rise of the modern business corporation, which had divorced ownership from control and thus had come to depend utterly on 'a sense of duty, on social solidarity'.[45] This solidarity was destined to grow stronger still:

> the striking phenomenon in our modern world, and especially in our United States, is the widening range of this gregarious feeling, the consciousness that we are all, even though less than kin, yet something of kind. I will not say that human nature has altered during the last century; the biologists would promptly challenge the assertion. But the conditions of the environment have altered, under multiform and mysterious influences, combining to bring an unmistakable strengthening of those traits which go with the wider self. A stronger sense of social sympathy enfolds us all. This was the great moving force in the social legislation of the nineteenth century; probably it will be a force of even greater power in the present century.[46]

What is truly curious, one is left to conclude, is the fact that Taussig saw fit to share these vital insights with his learned colleagues at the AEA, and with the assembled public at a festive occasion, but not with the many thousands of students who depended on his *Principles* for enlightenment. It is a Frank Taussig Problem that Smith himself might have appreciated.

Lessons from history?

In conclusion, we may reasonably ask what 'lessons' emerge from the historical facts that are now in evidence. I would like to suggest four of them. The first lesson, most relevant to the concerns of practising economists, is that there is nothing intrinsic or necessary about the axiomatic status of self-interest in most contemporary theory, unless one cares to define the term so broadly that it loses all meaning. Or perhaps more precisely: Every economist has an indefeasible right to define the discipline's remit as he or she sees fit, but no definition that excludes altruistic motives can claim the mantle of historical continuity. By the same token, the growing number of theorists who acknowledge an altruistic motive are not exploring *terra incognita* so much as they are bringing modern tools and sensibilities back to exotic landscapes that a previous generation knew well. From the shared rhetoric of the economists we have surveyed it is clear that altruism was nowhere near the status of settled *orthodoxy*, but from their collective stature it is equally clear that it was no longer quite *heterodoxy* either.

Historians will likelier seek out a second lesson, an answer to the question why the *fin de siècle* – and, as I have argued elsewhere,[47] the entire century between Waterloo and Sarajevo – proved so amenable to the penetration of altruistic psychology into economic theory. Was it that these economists, or the age they lived in, were themselves more benevolent that their predecessors and successors? Possibly, but I have my doubts, and anyway I would despair of ever proving it to the sceptic's satisfaction. Instead I would argue a subtler and less sanguine tack. On the one hand, it does seem clear that these economists were exceptional in their degree of social engagement: for all their achievements in the study and at the lectern, they nevertheless made heroic commitments to political movements, governmental institutions, professional organizations, social-reform associations and the personal lives of their students. We may reasonably speculate that such lives of extroversion and interaction served to heighten their appreciation for the multifarious and protean nature of interpersonal relations.

On the other hand, that same century witnessed a flurry of thinking about altruism that might even deserve the term 'intellectual fashion'. The preceding age of Enlightenment was an intensely humanitarian one, and yet its tendency, especially in its French and English heartlands, was to view man as a self-regarding entity, a creature of simple pleasures and pains. Counterintuitive, clear-eyed elegance was the order of the day, as witness the continuity between Machiavelli, Hobbes, Larochefoucauld, Locke, Mandeville, Beccaria, La Mettrie, Helvétius, Paley, Bentham and many other thinkers of lesser renown.[48] Victor Cousin sensed this fact – and its historical contingency – as early as 1828, when he instructed his students at the Sorbonne to identify the preceding century with 'the philosophy of sensation and of selfishness', as a time when Helvétius was fêted as 'a man who has told the secret of all the world'. 'No', he went on, 'surely this is *not* the secret of all the world; it is not the secret of humanity and of all the epochs of history; but it is very true, that it *was* the secret of that epoch, and of almost all the world in the eighteenth century.'[49]

If the intellectual aesthetic of the eighteenth century may fairly be termed neoclassical, then the nineteenth can be contrasted as neo-Baroque. Now the preference was for verisimilitude, even at the cost of simplicity and elegance, and emotional depth in particular was commuted from vice to virtue. It is conventional to acknowledge this in the field of *belles lettres*, with the emergence of Romanticism, and perhaps also in the theological ascent of Pietism and Evangelicalism. But the writ of this new sensibility ran further, into moral philosophy and the emergent fields of psychology, sociology and ethology; in each of these endeavours we see a fundamental reorientation from simplicity to complexity, and from egoism to altruism.[50] Comte (who coined the term), Gall, Schopenhauer, Spencer, Hazlitt, Giddings, Durkheim, Tolstoy and many others gave it a prominence that is without parallel today. Even Nietzsche and Marx were paying it a backhanded tribute when they derided the 'slave morality' or 'bourgeois sentimentality' of their age; perhaps the importance of the superego in Freud's mature thought reflects a similarly grudging acknowledgement. In many of these systems, political economy bore a special onus – or in the case of Marx, at least, a special credit – as the branch of thought that was least susceptible to its blandishments. So dire was the state of affairs that an 1894 survey of London's lending libraries reported John Ruskin, whose *Unto This Last* (1862) had excoriated political economy for its psychological and ethical impoverishment, as the single most popular author *in that discipline!*[51] In so far as the economists themselves cared to be seen as friends of man and modernity, and to remain masters of their collective fate, they had a vital interest in adapting to these new currents.

A third lesson, relevant to the concerns of both historians and economists, concerns strategies for social co-ordination in an imperfect world. Contemporary debates on economic policy often presume a market-or-state dichotomy, meaning that co-ordination problems must be solved either through competitive individualism or through coercive collectivism, or perhaps through some *ad hoc* amalgam of the two. A superficial reading of the history of normative economics suggests that this dichotomy characterized the *fin de siècle* as well, where laissez-faire liberalism and state socialism confronted one another across a vast and empty ideological chasm. Wise economists know that this dichotomy is a false one, and wise historians know that there were plenty of wise (or at the very least, imaginative) economists in the nineteenth century.[52] This chapter confirms that wisdom: in every case we have inspected – even that of Wagner, whose name is now so closely associated with neo-étatism – there ran alongside the theoretical assertion of altruism a patently normative vindication of civil society, and of its capacity to meet life's challenges through free association. It might take the form of individual charity, philanthropic or religious foundations, producer or consumer co-operatives, credit unions, friendly societies or even modern corporations, but in each case the point was that sociability itself might cure modern society's ills.

The final lesson to be learned is one of humility before the future's imponderability. We all know the dangers of extrapolation, and yet we cannot resist it when the signs are propitious. The case in point is these celebrated economists, all of whom, it seems, looked forward to a future in which altruism would grow only stronger in economic theory as in economic reality. A glance into the twentieth century shows how mistaken these expectations were. Economics was gradually reconceived in such a way that an assertion of altruism would come to be viewed as false or, worse, simply beside the point. This is not the place to speculate as to the ultimate sources of this sea change in economic theory, except to note its likely roots in a yearning for formal closure and predictive determinacy. For however strong the conviction that altruism played a vital role in economic phenomena, none of the theorists we have surveyed would have dared postulate it as a universal constant. It could only be a variable, and an idiosyncratic one at that. To affirm it thus amounted to an admission that economics would ever remain an art rather than a science, and this would not do.

The process of expurgation was already underway in the nineteenth century, for example in Francis Y. Edgeworth's influential tract on *Mathematical Psychics* (1883). This book has been held up as a seminal contribution to the economics of altruism,[53] but I am inclined to see it more as the beginning of the end. My assessment hinges on the fact that *Mathematical Psychics* consists of two clearly distinct sections. The first section, largely reprinted from earlier articles in the philosophical journal *Mind*, contains Edgeworth's famous presentation of a utilitarian calculus based on interdependent utility functions – altruism, in a word. But these articles were written at a time when Edgeworth was aspiring to a career in philosophy, and they contain no mention of political economy or its specific concerns. The second section, newly composed for this publication, was devoted to what he called the 'Economical Calculus', but it contained no exploration of altruistic motives. To the contrary, the section opens with the dictum that 'The first principle of Economics is that every agent is actuated only by self-interest.' In so far as economic agents were in reality motivated by 'sympathy with each other's interests', he held that they were emphatically '*not* "economic" agents'.[54] In later years, once Edgeworth had established himself as a pioneer in neoclassical economics and his stillborn career as a moral philosopher was forgotten, it was only natural to view *Mathematical Psychics* as a contribution to the economics of altruism. Edgeworth himself, though he remained convinced of his early utilitarian ethics, never broached the topic again.

Edgeworth's real contribution to our storyline is as an early harbinger of things to come: as an economist who never denied altruism (quite the contrary, in this case), but who firmly refused to admit it into his discipline. Unlike Philippovich, who faced the same quandary at about the same juncture in his career, Edgeworth chose the path of parsimony. And unlike Walras, who similarly posited a 'pure' economic theory presupposing self-interested interaction, Edgeworth never again emerged from Plato's cave into the phenomenal world. One suspects that the old guard accepted this trend too readily. Gide, for instance, felt so confident of his brief that he dismissed with Gallic nonchalance the various attempts underway to rebuild economic theory as hedonic calculus. 'Banish co-operation, if you will, from the domain of pure political economy; without there remains a world, a greater world. That world shall be ours.'[55] In retrospect, the best we can say is that he was half-right.

Acknowledgements

My thanks to Richard Adelstein, Thomas Brady, Thomas Dixon, Negley Harte, Ian McLean, Elliot Neaman and participants at the 'Worlds of Political Economy' conference at Cambridge University for close readings and useful suggestions on this and earlier drafts.

Notes

1. Adam Smith, *An Inquiry into the Nature and Causes of the Wealth of Nations* (1776), I.ii.2.
2. Gustav Schmoller, *Über einige Grundfragen des Rechts und der Volkswirtschaft* (Jena: Mauke, 1875), pp. 37–8; see also his 'Menger und Dilthey: Zur Methodologie der Staats-und Sozialwissenschaften' (1883), reprinted in *Zur Literaturgeschichte der Staats- und Sozialwissenschaften* (Leipzig: Duncker & Humblot, 1888), pp. 281–2.
3. Gustav Schmoller, *Grundriß der allgemeinen Volkswirtschaftslehre* (Leipzig: Duncker & Humblot, 1901–04), vol. 1, pp. 10, 19.

4. Schmoller, *Grundriß*, vol. 1, pp. 42–3.
5. Schmoller, *Grundriß*, vol. 1, pp. 59–60.
6. Wagner was particularly popular among American students. See Benny Carlson, 'Wagner's Legacy in America: Re-Opening Farnham's Inquiry', *Journal of the History of Economic Thought* 21 (1999), pp. 289–310.
7. Adolph Wagner and Erwin Nasse, *Lehrbuch der politischen Oekonomie* (Leipzig, 1876). Technically this tome was a revision of Karl Heinrich Rau's standard textbook of the same name, first published in 1828.
8. Adolph Wagner, *Grundlegung der politischen Oekonomie* (Leipzig: Winter, 3rd edn, 1892–94), vol. 1, p. 136.
9. Wagner, *Grundlegung*, vol. 1, pp. 115–20.
10. Wagner, *Grundlegung*, vol. 1, pp. 776–8, 784–6, 806, 854.
11. Wagner, *Grundlegung*, vol. 1, p. 122; vol. 2, p. 64.
12. Wagner, *Grundlegung*, vol. 1, pp. 127, 779; vol. 2, p. 65.
13. Wagner, *Grundlegung*, vol. 1, pp. 122, 125–7.
14. Wagner, *Grundlegung*, vol. 1, pp. 779, 844–7.
15. Eugen von Philippovich, *Über Aufgabe und Methode der politischen Ökonomie* (Freiburg i.B.: Mohr, 1886), p. 42.
16. John W. Boyer, 'Freud, Marriage, and Late Viennese Liberalism: A Commentary from 1905', *Journal of Modern History* 50 (1978), p. 77. Consequently 'almost all of the social Liberal associational groups in Vienna after 1895 were established by friends or disciples of Philippovich' (p. 78).
17. Philippovich, 'Individuelle Verantwortlichkeit und gegenseitige Hilfe im Wirtschaftsleben', *Zeitschrift für Volkswirtschaft, Sozialpolitik, und Verwaltung* 14 (1905), p. 560, also p. 566.
18. Philippovich, 'Das Eindringen der sozialpolitischen Ideen in die Literatur', in *Die Entwicklung der deutschen Volkswirtschaftslehre im neunzehnten Jahrhundert* (Leipzig: Duncker & Humblot, 1908), vol. 2, pp. XXXI, 51.
19. Philippovich, *Grundriß der politischen Oekonomie* (Tübingen: Mohr, 6th edn, 1906), vol. 1, p. 106.
20. See Albert Jolink, *The Evolutionist Economics of Léon Walras* (London: Routledge, 1996), pp. 36–7, 152.
21. Léon Walras, *Correspondence of Léon Walras and Related Papers* (ed.), William Jaffé (Amsterdam: North-Holland, 1965), vol. 1, p. 252. Needless to say, when it came to allocating his energies he did not in fact keep this hierarchy in mind. As he acknowledged privately in 1887, 'je reste avant tout un homme de science pure'.
22. Walras, *Études d'économie sociale (Théorie de la repartition de la richesse sociale)* (Lausanne: Rouge, definitive edn, 1936), pp. 108–9. This section of the book (pp. 25–171) reprinted lectures delivered in 1867–68; the book as a whole was originally intended for publication in 1882 (*Correspondence*, vol. 1, pp. 606, 711).
23. Walras, *Études d'économie sociale*, pp. 131–42.
24. Walras, *Études d'économie politique appliquée (Théorie de la production de la richesse sociale)* (Lausanne: Rouge, definitive edn, 1936), pp. 457–62.
25. Joseph Schumpeter, *A History of Economic Analysis* (Oxford: Oxford University Press, 1954), p. 843.
26. See, for example, his comments in 'L'idée de solidarité, en tant que program économique', *Revue internationale de sociologie* 1 (1893), esp. pp. 389, 393.

27. Charles Gide, 'Les doctrines économiques de M. Charles Périn', *Journal des Économistes* (June 1882), reprinted in *Les oeuvres de Charles Gide* (ed.), Marc Penin (Paris: Harmattan, 1999), vol. 1, p. 295.
28. Gide, 'L'idée de solidarité'. Prominent among his cited authorities were Émile Durkheim, Wilhelm Wundt and Alfred Fouillée.
29. Gide, *Cours d'économie politique* (Paris: Récueil Sirey, 9th edn, 1925–26), vol. 1, pp. 23–4. Or more pointedly elsewhere: when economics clings too tightly to the axiom of hedonism it approaches geometry, which wags have defined as 'a science which consists in reasoning correctly about forms that are false' ('Has Co-operation Introduced a New Principle into Economics?' *Economic Journal* 8 (1898), p. 495).
30. Gide, 'Has Co-operation?', p. 504.
31. Gide, 'Le matérialisme et l'économie politique', *Revue d'économie politique* 26 (1912), pp. 144–5. The speech was also reprinted in *Le matérialisme actuel* (1913), pp. 84–105. See also his 'Co-operation', in R.H. Inglis (ed.) Palgrave *Dictionary of Political Economy* (London: Macmillan, 1894–99), vol. 3, p. 444; and his *Principes d'économie politique*, 3rd edn, translated *Principles of Political Economy* (Boston: Heath, 1892), p. 23.
32. Alfred Marshall, 'The Present Position of Economics' (1885), reprinted in *Memorials of Alfred Marshall*, ed. A.C. Pigou (London: Macmillan, 1925), p. 156.
33. Marshall had once planned to be a psychologist, and switched to economics only around age 30. Intriguingly, he noted some months before his death that 'If I had time to live my life over again, I should have devoted it to Psychology. Economics has too little to do with ideals.' Quoted in Peter Groenewegen, *A Soaring Eagle: Alfred Marshall, 1842–1924* (Aldershot: Elgar, 1995), p. 127.
34. Quoted in J.M. Keynes, 'Alfred Marshall, 1842–1924', in A.C. Pigou (ed.), *Memorials of Alfred Marshall* (London: Macmillan, 1925), p. 7; see also Groenewegen, *Soaring Eagle*, p. 130.
35. Marshall, 'Ye Machine' (*c.*1868), reprinted in *Research in the History of Economic Thought and Methodology* Archival Supplement 4 (Greenwich, CT: JAI Press, 1994), pp. 129–30.
36. Marshall, 'Present Position,' p. 160. This point had already been alluded to in the preface to the second edition of his *Economics of Industry* (London: Macmillan, 2nd edn, 1881), p. vi, and was all but repeated in his *Principles of Economics* (London: Macmillan, 9th [variorum] edn, 1961), p. 187.
37. Marshall, *Principles*, 1st edn (1890), p. vi.
38. Marshall, *Principles*, 1st edn, p. 79.
39. Marshall, *Principles*, 8th edn, p. 22.
40. Marshall, *Principles*, 8th edn, pp. 26–7.
41. See Joseph Schumpeter *et al.*, 'Frank William Taussig'. *Quarterly Journal of Economics* 55 (May 1941), p. 340. Taussig himself credited his teacher Wagner with 'great stimulus – new points of view' (Carlson, 'Wagner's Legacy,' p. 300).
42. Schumpeter, *History of Economic Analysis*, p. 870.
43. F.W. Taussig, 'The Love of Wealth and the Public Service', *Publications of the American Economic Association*, ser. 3, 7, 1 (1905), pp. 11–12.
44. Taussig, *Inventors and Money-Makers: Lectures on Some Relations Between Economics and Psychology Delivered at Brown University in Connection with the*

Celebration of the 150th Anniversary of the Foundation of the University (New York: Macmillan, 1915), p. 103.

45. Taussig, 'The Love of Wealth', Taussig, *Inventors and Money-Makers*, p. 131.
46. Taussig, *Inventors and Money-Makers*, pp. 133–4. Like Walras, he cited the work of the sociologist Franklin Giddings in particular in this regard.
47. Heath Pearson, 'Not Master in its Own House: Ego and Alter in Economic Orthodoxy, 1776–1914', manuscript, 2002. Briefer efforts in this vein include Philippe Fontaine, 'Making Use of the Past: Theorists and Historians on the Economics of Altruism', *European Journal of the History of Economic Thought* 7 (2000), pp. 407–22; David A. Collard, 'Edgeworth's Propositions on Altruism', *Economic Journal* 85 (1975), pp. 355–60; and Ian Steedman, 'Rationality, Economic Man and Altruism in P.H. Wicksteed's *Common Sense of Political Economy*', in his *From Exploitation to Altruism* (Cambridge: Polity, 1989), pp. 185–204.
48. For a deeper reading of the historical roots of Enlightenment anthropology see Stephen Holmes, 'The Secret History of Self-Interest', in Jane J. Mansbridge, *Beyond Self-Interest* (ed.) (Chicago: University of Chicago Press, 1990), pp. 167–86; Milton L. Myers, *The Soul of Modern Economic Man: Ideas of Self-Interest, Thomas Hobbes to Adam Smith* (Chicago: University of Chicago Press, 1983); and Albert O. Hirschman, *The Passions and the Interests: Political Arguments for Capitalism before its Triumph* (Princeton: Princeton University Press, 1977).
49. Victor Cousin, *Introduction à l'histoire de la philosophie* (1828), translated *Introduction to the History of Philosophy* (Boston, MA: Hilliard, 1832), p. 82.
50. One may invoke here the authority of Stefan Collini, *Public Moralists: Political Thought and Intellectual Life in Britain, 1850–1930* (Oxford: Clarendon Press, 1991), pp. 65–7, 87, who has concluded that the Victorians' repute of celebrating self-interest is undeserved, and that ' "living for others" was less likely to be trumpeted as an ideal in the eighteenth century, "rational self-love" had a harder time of it in the nineteenth'. See also Walter E. Houghton, *The Victorian Frame of Mind, 1830–1870* (New Haven CT: Yale University Press, 1957), pp. 273–81. More recent explorations of this theme include Thomas Dixon, 'The Invention of Altruism: Auguste Comte's *Positive Polity* and Respectable Unbelief in Victorian Britain', in David Knight and Matthew Eddy (eds), *Science And Belief: From Natural Philosophy to Natural Science* (Aldershot: Ashgate, 2004); Thomas Dixon, 'Herbert Spencer and Altruism: The Sternness and Kindness of a Victorian Moralist', in Greta Jones (ed.), *Herbert Spencer, 1820–1903: Founding Father of Modern Sociology* (London: Galton Institute, 2004); and Abigail Lustig, 'Ants and the Nature of Nature in Auguste Forel, Erich Wasmann, and William Morton Wheeler', in Lorraine Daston and Fernando Vidal (eds), *The Moral Authority of Nature* (Chicago: University of Chicago Press, 2004), pp. 282–307.
51. 'What London Reads', *London*, 2 (10 April 1894), p. 243. This survey would not have disappointed Ruskin himself, of course, as he had always intended *Unto This Last* as a contribution to political economy as well as a broadside against its current practice.
52. The standard reference is J.S. Mill's chapter 'On the Probably Futurity of the Labouring Classes', in his *Principles of Political Economy*. For German analogues see Rüdiger vom Bruch (ed.), *Weder Kommunismus noch Kapitalismus: Bürgerliche Sozialreform in Deutschland vom Vormärz bis zur Ära Adenauer*

(Munich: Beck, 1985); and Erik Grimmer-Solem, *The Rise of Historical Economics and Social Reform in Germany, 1864–1894* (Oxford: Clarendon, 2003).

53. See especially David A. Collard, 'Edgeworth's Propositions on Altruism', *Economic Journal* 85 (1975), pp. 355–60; and his *Altruism and Economy: A Study in Non-Selfish Economics* (Oxford: Oxford University Press, 1978), pp. 60–4.
54. Edgeworth, *Mathematical Psychics: An Essay on the Application of Mathematics to the Moral Sciences* (London: Paul, 1881), pp. 16, 53. Something very comparable might be said of Philip Wicksteed's *The Common Sense of Political Economy* (1910), or even of Pareto's *Manuale di economia politica* (Milan, 1906).
55. Gide, 'Has Co-operation?', p. 504.

3
Before Free Trade: Commercial Discourse and Politics in Early Nineteenth-century France

Francois-David Todd

Early nineteenth-century France has been viewed as a battleground between modern versions of free trade and protection. In this view, French debates and policies acted out the new canon of economic thinking about commerce that had played a seminal role in the formation and export of liberal political economy developed in the first industrial nation, Great Britain. In contrast to modern free trade, Restoration France saw the establishment of a highly restrictive trade regime. This 'protecting system' remained in place, with only minor modifications, until the conclusion of the Cobden–Chevalier Treaty with Britain in 1860.[1]

The restrictive policies of the early Restoration have been viewed as a victory of 'ultra-protectionism' over free trade with negative consequences for France's modernization. High tariffs and prohibitions have been castigated for slowing down French economic growth and described as the result of interest groups' pressures and/or 'protectionist prejudices'.[2] Reappraisals of this standard view of French commercial policy have been few and unsatisfactory. The main work on the Restoration period gives an anachronistic interpretation of this policy as a 'project of development', revealing higher levels of growth and its contribution to industrialization.[3]

This chapter offers an alternative narrative, focusing on the intellectual and cultural context that shaped commercial policies. Rent-seeking interests certainly played an important part. Yet they exerted pressure in a specific environment, that is, a set of prevailing ideas and assumptions about economic phenomenon and policies. It is this environment that allowed their pressure to be effective. Such an alternative narrative requires that more attention be paid to language.[4] Economic discussions stood in relation to the political and social conditions in post-Napoleonic France, namely, an experiment in constitutional monarchy and the social domination of *notables*. Instead of being separated, several levels of economic ideas and knowledge interacted with each other. I shall distinguish three main levels of economic ideas and debates: analytical knowledge (theoretical treatises and elaborate pamphlets), practical knowledge (parliamentary debates, producers' petitions and pamphlets) and concrete practices (as expressed in archival sources on the repression of smuggling).[5]

In the early nineteenth century neither the free trade vs protectionism controversy, nor organized lobbies had yet fully emerged. Rather than an opposition between two ideologies, freedom and state intervention, debates on the regulation of trade at the time were a contest amongst the three 'interests' constituting society: agriculture, manufactures and commerce. Represented by political and economic notabilities, each interest endeavoured to obtain the maximum protection. Protection often implied the granting of trade restrictions, but it could also mean refusing them. Moreover, far from being purely economic, protection was also intended to preserve society from moral and political decay. This intellectual and cultural environment made the adoption of a policy other than strong barriers to foreign imports impossible. Free trade remained, in practice, inconceivable.

This chapter highlights three major features of the early Restoration discussions on trade policy. First, it stresses the continuity with *Ancien Régime* economic controversies. Second, it examines the prevalence of a specific discourse on trade policy, which combined economic arguments with moral, social and political considerations. This discourse promoted a paternalist conception not only of economic policy, but also of society and polity. Through trade restrictions, the upper layers of society proclaimed their benevolence and asserted a hierarchical order. 'Protection' relied on several complementary types of economic knowledge, particularly on mercantilist ideas and an organic representation of society, combined in varying proportions according to the level of debate. Third, it shows that public opponents to protection were few and far between. This opposition did not promote a coherent alternative economic project. To a large extent, it may be construed as a defence of individual rights, based on moral, social and political grounds.

The persistence of *Ancien Régime* economic ideas

Despite the revolutionary upheaval, French society and economy underwent only limited change between 1789 and 1815. A structural shift occurred with the decline of the Atlantic economy and the rise of the industrial north-east. However, in 1814, the income per head and the urbanization rate had barely regained their pre-1789 levels.[6] Material continuity was reinforced by the restored monarchy's conscious attempt to 'renew the chain of time'.[7] Although the restoration was not a simple re-enactment of the *Ancien Régime*, a large fraction of the old elite returned to power and many traditional practices were reinstated. This prolonged the national reconciliation begun under Napoleon, only tilting the balance further in favour of the old France.

Against this backdrop, it is hardly surprising that many economic debates of the eighteenth century were still alive or revived in the early Restoration. Usually associated with the reign of Louis XV, discussions on the free circulation of grain continued in 1814–17. As in the 1760s, the freedom of internal circulation was propounded by most publicists and state officials. It was reasserted by the law of 2 December 1814 in a concert of praise. As in the 1760s, however, free circulation was hindered in practice by numerous riots and action by state officials. Again as in the 1760s, exports abroad were the main bone of contention amongst officials and publicists. The law of 2 December 1814 eventually struck a compromise, with exports free of duty up to a price-limit, and fully prohibited beyond that limit.[8] A pervading nostalgia for the economy of the *Ancien Régime* resulted in attempts to restore old institutions and flows of exchange. The opportunity to re-establish guilds continued to be discussed until the early 1820s.[9] The 1814 decrease in colonial tariffs and the 1816 interdiction to import colonial goods 'by land' were intended to resuscitate the trade with the Caribbean and hence the prosperity of the Atlantic ports. The re-establishment in 1814 of Marseilles' *franchise*, a word highly evocative of *Ancien Régime* practices, was meant to revive the lucrative trade with the Levant. Both projects achieved only limited results; in fact, Marseilles' *franchise* was repealed as early as 1817.

Dominant ideas and concepts were also reminiscent of seventeenth- and eighteenth-century discussions. A number of words and expressions had retained their older, sometimes ambiguous meaning. *Economistes*, for instance, still designated the Physiocrats.[10] As in the controversy on the grain trade under Louis XV, both opponents to, and proponents of, trade restrictions believed to stand against monopoly, stemming either from state regulation or the hoarding of goods by merchants.[11] Similarly, *liberté du commerce* should not be misconstrued as the contemporary equivalent of *libre-échange*. Scholars of seventeenth- and eighteenth-century debates have stressed that the advocates of *liberté du commerce* or 'free trade' in early modern France and England were frequently supporters of trade restrictions on imports and exports.[12] In the aftermath of the Napoleonic wars, defenders of high tariffs and prohibitions strove to maintain a meaning of 'liberté' that was compatible with trade restrictions. They were adamant that *liberté* was not *licence.* Only *liberté absolue, indéfinie* or *illimitée,* in their view, was objectionable. They backed their claims with definitions provided by eighteenth-century authors, such as Jean-François Melon or Charles de Montesquieu, frequently quoting the latter's statement: 'Liberty of commerce is not a faculty granted to traders to do what they want; this would instead be the servitude of commerce.'[13] The meaning of *liberté du commerce* overlapped with that of *liberté d'industrie,* that is, the freedom to enter a trade. In any case, freedom of trade was not conceived of as the opposite of protection. The maxim *liberté et protection,* first recorded in the late seventeenth-century and very popular in eighteenth-century France, had not disappeared from discussions. The circular sent to chambers of commerce in June 1814 concluded: 'Liberty within, protection without, such are the principles that will be applied to commerce.'[14] The object of the debate on *liberté du commerce* was not to embrace or reject freedom, but, as for other public freedoms, to define its proper limits.

In addition to borrowing eighteenth-century language, contenders in early Restoration commercial debates constantly cited eighteenth-century authors. The Physiocrats, together with the French (Melon, François Véron de Forbonnais) and British (James Steuart) mercantilists, remained important references. Adam Smith had already acquired a privileged status and *The Wealth of Nations* surpassed all other works for the number of references. Indeed, many treatises were described by their authors as vulgarisations (Jean-Baptiste Say) or criticisms (Charles Ganilh, François Ferrier) of Smith's masterpiece.[15] Yet, beyond the most sophisticated economic literature, his name seldom appeared. If lower levels of debate, that is, parliamentary debates, pamphlets and petitions, are taken into account, the most commonly cited author was Montesquieu. For many contemporaries, his recommendations in books XX, XXI and XXII, of *L'Esprit des lois,* which extolled the virtues of commerce and, at the same time, advocated trade restrictions, seemed to embody a conventional wisdom on these issues. Many pamphlets, for and against prohibitions, began with an epigraph borrowed from *L'Esprit des lois.*[16] Ferrier, a major defender of prohibitions, paid Montesquieu a lengthy homage in his treatise.[17] Deputies quoted him during parliamentary debates.[18] In his *Traité d'économie politique,* Say made a scathing attack on his economic ideas.[19] The persistence of eighteenth-century economic ideas in post-Napoleonic France may thus be interpreted as a lag in the diffusion of economic knowledge, combined with the mediation of non-economist authors like Montesquieu.

The structure of debate equally retained many features of the *Ancien Régime*. Commercial discussions remained confined to the uppermost layers of French society. Most writings on the subject were too sophisticated to allow for more than a select audience. The number of books and pamphlets printed confirms this hypothesis: a sampling, formed by the 17 publications on trade policy declared between 1 September 1816 and 1 April 1819 at the *Librairie*, the branch of the Ministry of the Interior responsible for publishing, gives an average number of 841 copies.[20] This figure suggests that the readership did not extend beyond the elite. The extraordinary length of parliamentary debates also points to a pattern of intense discussions limited to privileged groups. During the 1814 session, as a new political regime was being established following 25 years of revolution and wars, deputies dedicated 20 per cent of their work to this issue. For the period 1814–22, this share reached 7.3 per cent, probably the most discussed item after the budget.[21] Yet, parliamentary chambers during the Restoration only represented a small fraction of French society. The members of the upper chamber were hereditary Peers, while deputies were designated by less than 100,000 electors, out of a population of 30 million.

The press echoed these debates only faintly. In a sample of seven newspapers for the periods October–November 1814 and March–April 1916, only one article dealt with trade restrictions, plus eight shorter news items.[22] As the author of that single article emphasized, the subject only interested the 'enlightened share of the public that deals with themes of general utility'.[23] Debates on trade policy were not fully transmitted in the public sphere. The vast majority of French society did not engage in the controversy, with the sole means of expression at its disposal being petitions and smuggling. Petitions reflected a submission to the prevailing order, smuggling its rejection. The structure of commercial debates remained traditional: at its core stood an official economic order, and, on its margins, subversive forms of protest, whether by philosophers or smugglers.

Protection

According to the prevailing discourse associated with this official economic order, trade policy was not a matter of controversy but of reconciliation. Between 1814 and 1822, 12 laws dealing with the regulation of trade were passed and the topic occupied an important share of deputies' time. Nevertheless, the subject was not contentious. These laws were adopted by an overwhelming majority.[24] Consensus in the chambers suggests that parliamentary debates were more the celebration of a political, social, moral and economic order than a genuine controversy. The chief concern of deputies was to protect and reconcile the 'interests' constituting society, under the paternal authority of the monarchical state.[25]

Claims by these interests were collected through petitions. Petitions were couched in a highly deferential language akin to the phrasing of *Ancien Régime* fiscal petitions or *doléances*.[26] Most of these supplications were mediated by chambers of commerce, consultative chambers of arts and manufactures and two national *Conseils Généraux*, one for manufactures and one for commerce. All these institutions occupied an ambiguous status: they wielded public power, but their members, chosen through a complicated process combining election, co-optation and nomination by the government, were not salaried by the State and remained primarily manufacturers or merchants. These chambers and councils were the main providers of economic information for the state. Deputies and state officials repeatedly insisted on the necessity to follow their advice. They may be considered to epitomize the symbiotic relationship between state and society promoted by the prevailing discourse.

Responding to prayers, the state was to allay sufferings by granting 'protection', presented as a matter of benevolence and charity. In the words of one deputy, 'the hapless would not be able to lament without being heeded and consoled with paternal kindness. The Throne and the two chambers are refuges that are constantly open in order to protect innocence as well as misfortune.'[27] This traditional and paternal order adopted different forms at each level of economic knowledge. For economic analysis, it relied chiefly on mercantilist ideas. On a practical level, among deputies and producers, discussions focused on the apportionment of protection: it was to be determined by the respective value of the different interests compounding society. At the lowest and most concrete level, trade policy was equated with submission to state authority and social hierarchy.

The predominant framework of economic analysis was mercantilist. Mercantilism was not a unified doctrine, but a set of common expressions and recurring preoccupations.[28] Different shades of mercantilism co-existed amongst the advocates of restrictive trade policies. François Ferrier, head of customs at the end of the Napoleonic Empire, embodied the most traditional current, which saw the main purpose of external trade in the acquisition of bullion. His audience appears to have been relatively wide, with his treatise *Du gouvernement considéré dans ses rapports avec le commerce* reaching its third edition in 1822. The violent criticisms of liberal economists also point to him as a pillar of protection: the liberal economist Adolphe Blanqui later labelled him the 'Pindar of customs' and 'le Zoile d'Adam Smith'.[29] Ferrier rejected claims that bullion was a merchandise like any other and affirmed that 'a country becomes richer when its bullion augments, because thanks to this augmentation in bullion all the productive faculties of labour generally increase'. Consequently, the administration's policy should consist in maximizing the surplus of the 'balance of trade'.[30] One finds similar emphasis on bullion and the balance of trade in the works of Auguste de Saint-Chamans, *préfet* and later *ultra* deputy.[31]

A second group promoted trade restrictions on the grounds that it maintained or increased the quantity of labour. Its greatest representative was Jean-Antoine Chaptal, the chemist and Napoleon's former minister. In *De l'industrie française*, he asserted that '[a] good customs legislation (...) enriches [France] with a workforce, which, as I have said several times, is the principal source of its riches'.[32] According to Charles Ganilh, a liberal publicist, the goal of trade restrictions on manufactured products was to preserve 'one of the sources of labour'.[33] This group was more moderate in its defence of restrictive measures. Neither Chaptal nor Ganilh explicitly invoked the balance of trade. Both were adamant that high tariffs and prohibitions should only be temporary; Ferrier and Saint-Chamans, by contrast, held restrictions to be indefinitely desirable.[34] In Chaptal's view, unrestricted commerce was the 'true destiny' of nations.[35] Also, traditional mercantilists tended to be politically more conservative, while Chaptal and Ganilh were more liberal. Despite these differences, all can be said to share a mercantilist outlook. They all considered international trade relations as a zero-sum game, stressed the importance of population growth and showed an overwhelming concern for power, the 'inseparable companion' of wealth according to Ganilh.[36] Finally, the establishment of high barriers around a unified national market by the 1814–22 legislation can be interpreted as the eventual triumph of the mercantilist programme, which had remained largely incomplete in France at the time of Colbert.[37]

These mercantilist economics were pre-liberal rather than anti-liberal. Trade restrictions were perceived as natural and required no interventionist ideology. The principle of competition, for instance, was seldom rejected. Rather, advocates of high tariffs and prohibitions claimed that competition at a national level was sufficient, or even that trade restrictions, by equalizing foreign and national prices, 'restored' or made competition 'possible'.[38] Extensive use was made of the British example to justify restrictive policies.[39] The secret of Britain's prosperity, it was widely agreed, lay in the 'solicitude' of the government.[40] According to Chaptal, the prohibitive system was created by Britain. Other countries were entitled to retaliate.[41] Restrictions on imports were also needed to thwart British government and business malpractices, that is, export premiums and the sale of British products below production costs in order to wipe out foreign, especially French, competition.[42]

Deputies and producers also resorted to mercantilist ideas, particularly the 'balance of trade' and the necessity to increase the French stock of bullion. Yet, economic theory only constituted a minor share of discussions at the practical level. The prevailing discourse focused instead on the 'reconciliation of interests', a programme with strong moral, social and political undertones. Deputies' speeches on customs bills almost systematically rejected 'systems' and praised the virtues of a pragmatic, item-by-item approach. The 'systems' were either the 'unlimited freedom of trade', associated with the 1786 Eden treaty with Britain and unsound, 'philosophical' experiments, or the Napoleonic continental system, described as the fruit of cupidity and arbitrary rule.[43] Instead, deputies repeatedly invoked 'wisdom' and 'experience'.[44] Yet one principle was unanimously held in high esteem: 'interest'. It was to determine combinations of tariffs and prohibitions: 'A universal, omnipotent motive, forgivable among private individuals and necessary for the upholding of society, interest, holds the veritable key to calculations.'[45] A distinction was frequently drawn between good and bad interests. The 'public', 'general' or 'national' interest, which conveyed a positive connotation, was constantly opposed to the 'private', 'particular' or 'local' interest.[46]

More important, however, was the widespread use of 'interest' as an aggregate notion to describe economic activities. The three 'general interests' were the three main industries of the kingdom: 'Three main ones can be distinguished: the agricultural industry, the manufacturing industry and the exchange industry or, strictly speaking, commerce.'[47] Two other collective interests, of a slightly different nature, were also often taken into consideration: 'consumers' and 'the State'. The chambers' task was to 'conciliate' or 'balance' these interests. Yet 'conciliating' did not mean that all five interests should be accorded the same amount of solicitude. In Charles Richard's words, 'these different interests should not be treated with the same amount of consideration, because there are those that are fundamental and more important, just as there are those that are secondary and subordinate. If there were truly an opposition between them, it would still be necessary to examine which ones should prevail over others'.[48] In the chambers, debates on trade policy primarily consisted in assessing the respective importance of each interest, determined not only by economic but also social and moral considerations.

It was widely agreed that the financial interest of the State ranked last. Baron Louis, Minister of Finance in 1814, spoke of the 'interest of the Treasury, which, as regards customs, should merely be of secondary importance'.[49] To ignore this principle was equated with despotic, in particular, Napoleonic practices.[50] According to the *Conseil Général des Manufactures*, fiscal duties were characteristic of 'barbaric peoples'.[51] Indeed, customs duties represented only about 5 per cent of the French state's income in the years 1815–20, much below the corresponding British figure.[52] The interest of the State was deemed worthy of consideration only as a matter of national defence, for example, in discussions on the iron tariff.

The consumers' interest was not discarded as unanimously as the Treasury's interest, but most deputies viewed it as secondary. 'As Frenchmen', Duvergier de Hauranne argued, consumers 'should submit themselves to the general interest'; their 'social station' prevailed over their consumer status; 'the sacrifices that each individual makes' were more than offset by the outlets secured for national producers, the increase in production, the higher yield of taxes, and the resulting 'well-being for private individuals and the state'.[53]

Consumers saw their position further diminished by recurrent assertions regarding their inability to perceive the true value of goods. This irrational behaviour was attributed to a flaw in the French character, which customs laws aimed to redress. Deputies and producers repeatedly accused French consumers of being biased in favour of foreign, especially English, products.[54] According to the chamber of commerce of Amiens: 'It is unfortunate that experience has proven and still proves each day a bias, an inexplicable preference, accorded by the French towards foreign goods over those from their own factories. On numerous occasions, it is not without sorrow that we have seen them whimsically embrace foreign goods, which are not as fine and are more expensive than French ones.'[55] Arguments on the wrong done to French producers were occasionally combined with concerns about the nefarious moral effects of foreign products. The deputy Puymaurin thus called for an increase in the tariff on tea on the grounds, first, that imports of tea implied a loss of bullion for France and, second, that tea 'harms the national character, by giving those who drink it frequently the seriousness of Northern men, whereas wine spreads in the soul a sweet gaiety, a hilarity that helps to give the French this amiable and witty character that distinguishes them from other nations.' Misguided consumption was perceived as a threat to national identity.[56]

For most, protection was to be reserved to agriculture, commerce and manufactures. The agricultural interest was generally regarded as the most important. France was repeatedly labelled as 'essentially agricultural'. According to Fornier de Saint-Lary, 'the fertility of the soil', 'the nature of the climate', the variety of French productions, together with 'the robustness of this kind of commerce (...) safe from all the vagaries of fashion' implied that France should give its preference to agriculture.[57] Although they rarely questioned the nominal primacy of agriculture, a number of deputies and publicists retorted that manufactures deserved a larger share of the government's attention, for a variety of reasons: they required more capital; they exported more; they were faced with more uncertainty; they had to overcome a widespread reluctance to innovation.[58]

The fiercest dispute, however, bore on the respective importance of manufactures and commerce. The advocates of commerce were hostile to prohibitions on manufactured products, but they did not resort to arguments about the international division of labour. When they did, they generally contented themselves to point out the impossibility to 'acclimatize' or 'naturalize' an industry.[59] More often they praised 'commerce' as a founding principle of society. According to Magnier-Grandprez, 'it is through commerce that different nations unite; industrial rivalry and collaboration in order to satisfy the needs, tastes and joys of life: commerce is the soul of all societies; a state cannot prosper without it'. 'Merchants' should be considered as 'citizens worthy of special protection'.[60] The defenders of commerce rejected prohibitions on imports of manufactured goods in the name of 'protection', the protection of their own interest. Moreover, they did not hesitate to support trade restrictions in favour of merchants and ship owners, such as the prohibition on imports of colonial products 'by land'.

Conversely, the champions of manufactures attacked commerce and merchants for their 'cosmopolitism': 'a merchant is, by nature, less concerned with the general interest than a manufacturer', because he 'directs his speculations both inside and outside the country'.[61] In contrast, manufactures were presented as truly 'national'. Their defenders compared manufacturers to 'patriarchs' who provided numerous workers with a living. The importance of a branch of manufactures was weighed according to the number of workers it employed. For instance, the figure of 600,000 workers in cotton manufactures was repeatedly used to justify the prohibition on imports of cotton yarns and textiles.[62] The role of manufactures could be expressed through a language of rights. According to the chamber of commerce of Rouen, 'prohibition is a political and social right. From the manufacturer who has spent all his financial means to set up an establishment to the worker who finds, in that same establishment, a means of existence for himself and his family, they all claim, and undoubtedly with good reason, the right to provide exclusively for the consumption of the country in which they live.'[63]

Despite the permanent contest for the ranking of agriculture, manufactures and commerce, contemporaries emphasized the 'solidarity' or the 'harmony' existing between the three interests, giving protection strong organicist undertones. 'Everything is connected in a well organised society', Duvergier de Hauranne asserted, 'the prosperity of one makes that of the other'.[64] The three interests were likened to the three Estates of the *Ancien Régime*. They were also frequently compared to the limbs of the same body or the members of the same family.[65]

The repression of contraband is illustrative, on a concrete level, of the combination of political, moral, social and economic aims pursued by the protection of interests. Customs' disorganization after the 1814 and 1815 invasions had rendered smuggling endemic in many border regions. In 1816, new legislation reinforcing repression was adopted. Customs officials saw their powers as well as their numbers increased. By 1818, there was a total of 3000 clerks and 23,000 officers, making it one of the main branches of the state apparatus and numerically the most important force of public order, before the police or the *gendarmerie*. Penal sanctions were increased and smuggling offences were transferred to *cours prévôtales* and *cours correctionnels*, which ruled without a jury. Finally, the new legislation provided for the search of prohibited textiles throughout the kingdom. Searches, including house visits, were to be conducted by the police, municipal and judicial authorities as well as the customs. Samples of seized textiles were to be sent to a *jury assermenté*, a body sitting in Paris and composed of prominent manufacturers, which ruled on whether or not seized textiles were French.

This repressive legislation was passed enthusiastically by the chambers in 1816. Most adopted amendments had augmented the severity of the government bill. The implementation of prohibitions and tariffs was seen as a political and moral issue, not merely a question of law enforcement. Contraband stemmed from past political errors: 'If it was elevated in our midst to the status of an entire system of commerce, we owe it to our disastrous revolution. It was natural that, in drying up all the sources of loyal industry, the revolution opened up other ones, of an impure nature.'[66] In Cornet d'Icourt's view, the aim of repression was to re-establish morality 'in a country where fatal discords have altered public feeling, in a country where selfishness and greed have made such fatal progress'.[67]

The concrete working of these controls illustrates the various meanings of protection. *Registres d'ordres*, that is, the copies made in each *bureau* of the instructions received from Paris, show that Customs' activity also had a political dimension. Some instructions supplied lists of individuals to be arrested, such as Spanish rebels. Circulars at the *bureau* of Bordeaux in 1822 ordered the seizure of subversive writings or objects, such as copies of a *Vie de Napoléon*, or miniature portraits of the emperor.[68] Liberal newspapers and periodicals were similarly targeted. On 20 May 1823, the *bureau* of La Rochelle was instructed to seize copies of *Le courrier des Pays-Bas*, printed in Brussels, on the grounds that it contained 'improper remarks' about the king and the royal family, and, a week later, the 'periodical entitled *British Press* [which] was signalled as being written in an entirely revolutionary spirit'.[69] Customs were to protect the country from foreign goods, but also from dangerous individuals and ideas.

Each seizure offers an example of how prohibitive laws set into motion a wide range of political, social and moral mechanisms.[70] Bourgogne, a small merchant in the town of Condé, in Northern France, saw all his stock of clothes and textiles seized on the 2 July 1816 by customs officers. He sent a letter to the jury dated 30 August in which he justified the loss of several receipts by the invasions of 1814 and 1815 and went on to describe how the seizure took place:

> I never intended to contravene the will of my King, I was by no means able to suspect that after the declaration I had to make at the customs office at the time of its re-establishment at the beginning of 1815 that I could be obliged to reiterate it, and even that it would be towards me alone in the town of Condé that the customs officials would ask in such an improper fashion and that so as to aggravate the position of a shopkeeper like me with all my resources in my business, they would lie to the extent of claiming in their minutes that I had signed it, whereas that is not at all true because I obstinately refused to do it, given the account they put in their minutes that they had found among my papers a Belgian permit for one hundred and twenty two metres of cloth, whereas I am sure that I never had that document and that if it had been found in my home, it must have been put there by some enemies of my peace of mind.

He then explained that he had refused to sign the minutes himself and customs officers had his daughter sign it. Bourgogne concluded by recalling 'the evident will of our august MONARCH with regard to shopkeepers'. In order to 'corroborate [his] statement', he attached a certificate from the *commissaire de police* of the town, which confirmed Bourgogne's version and testified to the 'terror' of Bourgogne, his wife and his daughter. The seized merchandise was finally returned to Bourgogne.[71] Like all the other defendants, Bourgogne did not question the merits of control. He only called for the protection of commerce and insisted on his own obedience to the monarch in a most deferential tone.

As much 'a foolish reckoning' as 'an immoral reckoning'

The discourse promoting protection permeated most of the public sphere. Whereas smuggling was extensive, public opposition was limited to a handful of writers and publicists. Moreover, far from upholding a coherent alternative economic project, opponents merely voiced disparate criticisms against prohibitions as much on moral and political as on economic grounds.

There are several indications that opposition to prohibitions ran high among the French population. Contraband on a large scale implied a great number of smugglers, as well as a high level of tolerance for smuggling. Prohibitionist writers and customs officials accused juries, composed entirely of citizens, of excessive indulgence towards smugglers.[72] Customs were confronted with riots hostile to the enforcement of trade restrictions, especially in border regions such as Alsace.[73] According to a circular sent to *préfets* in January 1815, 'contraband is given an open and criminal protection in most border communes. (...) There are so many audacious smugglers everywhere simply because they are encouraged by success and find everywhere people who can, with impunity, guide their way, cover up their tracks, provide them with refuge and use arms in their defence.'[74]

In contrast to the prevalence of smuggling, public opposition was confined to a few individuals: important thinkers, such as Antoine Destutt de Tracy, Benjamin Constant, Sismonde de Sismondi or Say, and a number of minor publicists. Moreover, they put forward very moderate claims and only showed a limited interest in economic theory; they upheld contradictory views on the actual effects of prohibitions and on the economic goals to be pursued; finally, they all paid a great deal of attention to the moral, social and political problems raised by prohibitions.

Anti-prohibitionists only pursued limited goals. Say, often described as an early free trader, offers a striking example of this moderation. Like other opponents, he was adamant that prohibitions should not be suddenly repealed.[75] Relying on Smith he considered prohibitions for purposes of national defence acceptable.[76] He even supported educative and temporary protection for countries not as enlightened as Britain: 'Any new application of the power of capital is, in such places, a matter of mistrust or disdain, and the protection granted to a very profitable use for labour and money can become a benefit for the country.'[77]

Furthermore, Say did not argue for the complete abolition of trade barriers. He insisted that customs duties were acceptable as a source of fiscal income.[78] He even claimed that when producers were faced with heavy taxation at home, compensatory duties were necessary to restore fair competition. Since French producers bore a higher fiscal burden than their British counterparts, he argued, France was entitled to tax British products, but not vice versa – a surprising argument given the much higher level of taxation in Britain at the time.[79] In a similar vein, pamphlets hostile to prohibitions never asked for more than their replacement by fairly high customs duties on manufactured products, of '20 to 22 per cent' *ad valorem* according to Charles Tempier who claimed to stand for the 'absolute freedom' of trade. As pointed out by Xavier Audouin, another publicist, the debate was limited to what was 'preferable, either taxes or prohibitions'.[80]

Historians of economic analysis have noticed that French authors in the nineteenth century made a poor contribution to the theory of international trade.[81] French economists favouring a more open trade regime resorted to the theory of absolute advantages, often using Smith's formulation.[82] Yet, they showed little interest in the theory of comparative advantage before the 1850s.

Opponents of prohibitions defended a reciprocal conception of international trade. Say repeatedly asserted that 'products [were] always [exchanged] for other products'; whether the export was a commodity or bullion mattered little, bullion also being, in his view, a commodity. Hence, it was pointless to speak of an 'advantageous' or a 'disadvantageous' balance of trade.[83] Pamphlets merely stressed the dangers of retaliation by other countries.[84] Most opponents underlined the wrong done to consumers. Prohibitions and the 'fiscal administrative regime' were described as causes of 'dearness'.[85] Nevertheless, a number of pamphleteers opposing prohibitions also resorted to mercantilist arguments. Like their adversaries, they invoked the balance of trade and the necessity to maintain and increase the French stock of bullion, but considered these goals more likely to be attained by the reduction of trade restrictions.[86] Opposition to prohibitions did not always stem from adhesion to liberal economic theory.

Nor should opposition to prohibitions be equated with support for 'modernity' or enthusiasm for the factory system. A number of opponents, it is true, argued that prohibitions ought to be repealed because they slowed down the adoption of more economical processes. Others, however, rejected prohibitions on the opposite grounds. According to Sismondi, the multiplication of manufactures rapidly put an end to the 'sacrifices' imposed by prohibitions on consumers, and the eventual consequence of a prohibitive policy was 'the immense and excessive increase in production, disproportionate to consumption.'[87] He did not criticize prohibitions for being inefficient; on the contrary, he accused them of causing overproduction. Like him, through prohibitions, many rejected the spread of manufactures and, more generally, the English model, itself seen as the result of trade restrictions: 'Is it a certainty that England can always be presented as a model to follow if one carefully considers the considerable number of failures that have continually occurred there, the workers' revolts, the breaking of looms, etc ...? Does such a state of affairs stand in favour of its trade policy?'[88]

Non-economic concerns formed an essential part of the opponents' reasoning: Trade restrictions and controls, far from repressing immorality, created and nurtured it. According to Augustin Thierry and Henri Saint-Simon, prohibitions were as much 'a foolish reckoning' as 'an immoral reckoning'.[89] Say accused laws on trade restrictions 'of making a criminal offence an action that is in itself innocent and of punishing people who actually work towards the general prosperity'.[90] Tempier argued that prohibitions fostered 'the frightening spread of immorality'.[91] In Constant's view, 'they create a breeding-ground for men who ready themselves for every kind of crime, by becoming used to law-breaking, and another breeding-ground for men who familiarise themselves with infamy, by living off the misfortune of their counterparts'.[92] Prohibitions were conducive to immorality both on and within the borders. Immediately after the promulgation of a new prohibitive law, 'the value of goods then meets with a great deal of variation and the owners are inevitably engulfed in considerable losses. In order to avoid such losses, they seek to evade this law, they compromise their duties and finally (to adopt common parlance) they compound with their conscience. (...) and this is how public moral principles receive fatal blows, the effects of which we feel nowadays.'[93]

Finally, there was also a political concern: vexations jeopardized basic freedoms. The searches provided for by the 1816 law caused particular anxiety. Audouin pointed out that house visits inevitably occasioned countless administrative persecutions. Even if no prohibited textiles were found, the consequences of a visit were detrimental to a merchant's reputation:

> This operation will create a commotion: in public rumours more lies circulate than actual truths; one is more inclined to believe the former than to look for the latter upon learning that a certain merchant has fallen under suspicion; the flippant man, the idle newsmonger will not say: we were wrong to accuse him, instead they will say, we did not find anything in his house.

And then, Audouin enquired, 'will a special police be created? (…) Will we not see political suspicion follow commercial suspicion?'[94] Constant insisted that prohibitions did not only imply a loss of wealth but also 'for the entire nation, a loss of liberty'.[95] What loomed behind protection according to Tempier was full-fledged tyranny: 'The idea of making the customs protective of commerce does not correspond to an administrative system whose advantages and disadvantages should be analysed. It essentially corresponds to a principle of tyrannical domination and a project of general invasion, of which the customs administrators became the principal agents, perhaps without suspecting the motive behind this protecting competence.'[96]

Echoing the prevailing discourse on the protection of interests, opposition to prohibitions was not only economic either: it had a strong political and moral content. However, it did not correspond to a political faction or party. Opponents were on the margins of the political system: most came from the far left, including many with a republican past or republican tendencies, including Say and Constant, and a few from the far right, such as the *ultra* pamphleteer Charles Tempier.[97]

From the 1820s onwards, however, debates on trade policy underwent a profound transformation, as a result of the combined pressure of economic and political changes. The spread of the factory system and the first cyclical crises, in France and on a wider scale in Britain, provoked new concerns. Two somewhat contradictory anxieties reshaped the meaning of discussions on trade: on the one hand, the dangers of an overly industrial and urban society, namely pauperism and social instability, and, on the other, the fear of lagging behind Britain. Through trade restrictions or their abandonment, contemporaries hoped to confront these problems and master the course of economic change. In the political arena, the final overthrow of the elder branch of the Bourbons and the establishment of the July Monarchy heralded the triumph of liberal ideas. Given the strong ties existing between political and economic representations, the official celebration of liberty as the touchstone of the polity naturally led to the questioning of remaining economic restrictions. Traditional justifications for economic as well as political protection lost their legitimacy. This led to the demise of the protection of interests and the gradual emergence of two competing ideologies, free trade and protectionism.

Economic knowledge also became more autonomous and a new set of economic ideas was diffused throughout society. A new generation of economists (notably Adolphe Blanqui and Frédéric Bastiat), gathered around the new *Société des Economistes*, elaborated and toughened liberal proposals. The chief goal of the group was the swift and complete suppression of trade barriers. Greater emphasis was laid on the material benefits that would accrue from the liberalization of trade. Non-economic considerations remained important; yet, they tended to become implicit or to be derived from the increased material welfare that would result from the suppression of trade barriers. In response to this challenge, the advocates of protection strove to offer new justifications for high tariffs and prohibitions. Under liberal pressure, the balance of trade and other mercantilist ideas lost their legitimacy and gradually waned from discussions. A cluster of new theoretical models, attempting to ground the necessity of protection on scientific laws, were developed and offered to the public in the 1830s. Organicist ideas did not disappear but were subsumed under the economic primacy of the nation.

A major extension of the public sphere accompanied the transformation of ideas on trade policy. Discussions reached beyond the upper layers of society. Press coverage rose continuously. The number of publications dealing with the issue, as well as the number of copies printed, increased significantly. The State played an important part in steering this change: a Ministry of Commerce was established in 1831; chambers of commerce and other economic institutions were overhauled in 1831–32; several public inquiries about specific tariffs and prohibitions, or on commercial legislation in general, were carried out from 1829 to 1838. New actors came to the fore. Industrial sectors created official lobbies such as a *Comité linier* in 1838, or a *comité* for iron in 1840.[98] In terms of representation of the economy and society, these 'interests' gradually superseded the three interests around which previous discussions had revolved. Two national associations, standing for the two ideologies, were founded in 1846: the *Association pour la Liberté des Echanges* and the *Association pour la Défense du Travail National*. These new actors corresponded to a new and more open model of public discussion. Civil society organizations and the state distinguished themselves from each other and acquired more autonomy. Groups representing civil society competed with each other and the state to influence public opinion and enforce certain policies. This change finally affected language and two new words were coined around 1845–46: *libre-échange*, a British import derived from 'free-trade' and *protectionnisme,* which was to be exported to Britain.

Trade policy debates before the emergence of free trade and protectionism were intense but did not correspond to a contest between economic freedom and state interventionism. Trade restrictions were neither the mere fruit of rent-seeking nor tools of national economic policy or development, as they were later interpreted by free traders and protectionists respectively. Rather, economic protection in early Restoration France ensured legitimacy and a concrete expression to a traditional conception of social and political power based on benevolence from state authorities on the one hand, and deference from the masses on the other. The discussion of trade policy was confined to the social and political elite. Within this limited public sphere, protection was underpinned by two main types of economic knowledge: mercantilist arguments on the balance of trade, and organic representations of the French state and society as compounded of interdependent interest, that is, agriculture, manufactures and commerce. Both types were combined to justify protection, in varying proportions according to the level of discussion. While the former type of economic knowledge was predominant on an analytical level, the latter prevailed on a practical level. On a popular level, debates on trade policy were inexistent and protection was equated with state authority. Conversely, the liberal critique of prohibitions and high duties in those years was concerned at least as much with the moral and political dangers of protection as with its economic consequences. Amongst the population, refusal to comply with trade restrictions was equated with rebellion. The adoption of a highly restrictive trade regime in France between 1814 and 1822 offers a compelling example of how economic ideas and policies may be used to assert a form of political and social power – or to contest it. This case also shows that, in order to recover the original meaning of economic debates, it is crucial to take into account the complexity of contemporary social realities and the way in which they interact with economic knowledge.

Acknowledgements

I would like to thank for their comments and suggestions the participants in the conference 'Worlds of Political Economy' in 2002. I am particularly grateful to Paula Beegan, François Crouzet, Pierre Rosanvallon, Emma Rothschild and Claudia Schrag for their support and advice.

Notes

1. For factual accounts of changes in French tariff legislation in the early nineteenth century, see Léon Amé, *Études sur les Tarifs de Douanes et sur les Traités de Commerce* (Paris, 1876), pp. 65–156; Ernest Levasseur, *Histoire du Commerce de la France* (Paris: Rousseau, 1912), 2 vols, II, pp. 107–36; Francis Demier, 'Nation, Marché et Développement dans la France de la Restauration', unpublished PhD dissertation (Paris X: Nanterre, 1991).
2. See, for example, Fernand Braudel and Ernest Labrousse (eds) *Histoire Économique et Sociale de la France, Tome III: L'Avènement de l'Ère Industrielle* (Paris: PUF, 1976), 2 vols, I, pp. 305–46.
3. Demier, op. cit., 3. For a summary of debates on French economic growth, François Crouzet, 'Réflexions sur l'Histoire Économique de la France Contemporaine', in Jean-Pierre Poussou, *L'Économie Française du XVIIIe au XXe Siècle: Perspectives Nationales et Internationales* (Paris: Presses de l'université Paris-Sorbonne, 2000), pp. 21–68. Paul Bairoch, *Commerce Extérieur et Développement Économique de l'Europe* (Paris: EHESS, 1976). See also John V. Nye, 'The Myth of Free-Trade Britain and Fortress France: Tariffs and Trade in the Nineteenth Century', *Journal of Economic History* 51 (1991), pp. 23–46.
4. On the role played by ideas in trade policy debates, see Frank Trentmann, 'Political Culture and Political Economy', *Review of International Political Economy* 5 (1998), pp. 217–51 and 'National Identity and Consumer Politics: Free Trade and Tariff Reform', in Donald Winch and Patrick K. O'Brien (eds), *The Political Economy of British Historical Experience, 1688–1914* (Oxford: Oxford University Press, 2002), pp. 187–214.
5. Typology inspired by Mary O. Furner and Barry Supple, 'Ideas, Institutions, and State in the United States and in Britain: an Introduction', in Mary O. Furner and Barry Supple (eds), *The State and Economic Knowledge – The American and British Experiences* (Cambridge: Cambridge University Press, 1990), pp. 3–39.
6. François Hincker, *Révolution Française et Économie: Décollage ou Catastrophe?* (Paris: Nathan, 1989).
7. Charte of 1814, preambule; see text and comments in Pierre Rosanvallon, *La Monarchie Impossible – Les Chartes de 1814 et 1830* (Paris: Fayard, 1994), pp. 45–64. All the translations henceforth are the author's own.
8. Steve Kaplan, *Bread, Politics and Political Economy in the Reign of Louis XV* (The Hague: Nijhoff, 1976), 2 vols, I, pp. 187–214, 254–65.
9. Pierre Rosanvallon, *L'État en France* (Paris: Seuil, 1990), pp. 202–3.
10. See, for instance, speech by Crignon d'Anzouer, *Archives Parlementaires – 2ème série* (*A.P.*), XXI, Chamber of Deputies (C.D.), 19 March 1818.

11. See, for instance, exchange between André Morellet, the former Abbé Morellet, and Tanneguy-Leveneur, in *A.P.*, XII, C.D., 1 October 1814 and Kaplan, op. cit., I, p. 61.
12. Anne-Marie Piuz, 'Note sur l'Acception Ancienne de Free Trade (16ème-17ème siècles)' in Jűrgen Schneider (ed.), *Wirtschaftskräfte und Wirtschaftswege: Festschrift für Hermann Kellenbenz* (KlettCotta: Nuremberg, 1978), II, pp. 585–97.
13. Melon quoted in Auguste de Saint-Chamans, *Du Système d'Impôt fondé sur les Principes de l'Économie Politique* (Paris: Le Normant, 1820), pp. 259–60; Montesquieu quoted in Louis Tollenare, *Essai sur les Entraves que le Commerce Éprouve en Europe* (Paris: Janet et Cotelle, 1820), p. 5.
14. Archives Nationales (A.N.), F12 633–7.
15. Jean-Baptiste Say, *Traité d'Économie Politique* (Paris: Renouard, 2nd edn, 1814); François Ferrier, *Du Gouvernement Considéré dans ses Rapports avec le Commerce* (Paris: Pélicier, 2nd edn, 1821); Charles Ganilh, *Théorie de l'Économie Politique* (Paris: Deterville, 1st edn, 1815).
16. Tollenare, op. cit.; Xavier Audouin, *Quelques Idées sur les Prohibitions Commerciales* (Paris, 1816).
17. Ferrier, op. cit., pp. 370–1, 449.
18. Richard, *A.P.*, XVII, 13 April 1816.
19. Say, op. cit., I, pp. 170–1.
20. A.N., F18*, II, registers 3 to 5.
21. 1201 pages out of 16,412 bearing on tariffs, based on *A.P.*, XII, XIII, XIV and LXII. The mean of annual means is slightly higher than the arithmetic mean (8.4 per cent).
22. Newspapers consulted: *Le Moniteur, Le Journal des Débats, Journal général de France, La Quotidienne, Le Constitutionnel, La Gazette de France, Le Journal de Paris, Le Courrier Français.*
23. *Le Journal de Paris*, 1 September 1814.
24. Results for 11 of the 12 laws at the chamber of deputies (results not available for the 28 April 1816 law): 139 votes for vs 19 against; 120 vs 22; 105 vs 25; 160 vs 17; 137 vs 21; 139 vs 5; 164 vs 10; 87 vs 0; 134 vs 28; 185 vs 1; 282 vs 54. When results are available for the chamber of peers, they always show even stronger majorities. Results in *A.P.*, XIII–XXXII.
25. A similar consensus in favour of protection existed in the British Houses of Parliament. On protection in Britain, see Anna Gambles, *Protection and Politics* (Woodbridge: The Boydell Press, 1999).
26. M. Kwass, *Privilege and the Politics of Taxation in 18th-century France* (Cambridge: Cambridge University Press, 2000).
27. Dampmartin, *A.P.*, XII, C.D., 1 October 1814.
28. Lars Magnusson, *Mercantilism: the Shaping of an Economic Language* (London: Routledge, 1994), pp. 13–17.
29. In Jean-Baptiste Say, *Œuvres Diverses de Jean-Baptiste Say* (Paris: Guillaumin, 1848), pp. 355–7.
30. Ferrier, op. cit., pp. 206, 376, 572.
31. Saint-Chamans, op. cit., pp. 176–270.
32. Jean-Antoine Chaptal, *De l'Industrie Française* (Paris, 1819), p. 479.
33. Ganilh, op. cit., I, pp. 200–1.
34. Ferrier, op. cit., p. 573; Saint-Chamans, op. cit., pp. 228–33.

35. Chaptal, op. cit., p. 502.
36. Ganilh, op. cit., I, p. 224.
37. Eli Hecksher, *Mercantilism* (London: Routledge, 1994), 2 vols, I, pp. 78–110.
38. Chaptal, op. cit., p. 287.
39. On British trade policy in the immediate aftermath of the Napoleonic wars, see Boyd Hilton, *Corn, Cash, Commerce* (Oxford: Oxford University Press, 1977).
40. Claude Costaz, *Essai sur l'Administration de l'Agriculture, du Commerce, des Manufactures et des Subsistances* (Paris: Huzard, 1818), p. 242.
41. Chaptal, op. cit., pp. 498–9.
42. Saint-Cricq, *A.P.*, XXI, C.D., 18 March 1818.
43. Duvergier de Hauranne, *A.P.*, XVII, 8 April 1816.
44. Magnier-Grandprez, *A.P.*, C.D., XVII, 6 April 1816; Durand-Fajon, *A.P.*, C.D., XVII, 8 April 1816.
45. Dampmartin, *A.P.*, XII, C.D., 1 October 1814.
46. Saint-Aldegonde, *A.P.*, XXI, C.D., 25 March 1818, p. 474; de Serre, *A.P.*, XIX, C.D., 8 March 1817, p. 412.
47. Saint-Géry, *A.P.*, XVII, 8 April 1816.
48. Richard, *A.P.*, XVII, C.D., 13 April 1816.
49. Louis, *A.P.*, XII, C.D., 24 September 1814.
50. Duvergier de Hauranne, *A.P.*, XVII, C.D., 8 April 1816.
51. *Mémoire au Ministre de l'intérieur,* 1819, in A.N., F12 196.
52. John V. Nye, 'Guerre, Guerre Commerciale: les Échanges Franco-anglais Réexaminée', *Annales ESC* 3 (1992), 613–31.
53. Duvergier de Hauranne, *A.P.*, XVII, C.D., 8 April 1816.
54. Héricart-Ferrand de Thury, *A.P.*, XVII, C.D., 13 April 1816.
55. A.N., F12 1941.
56. Puymaurin's intervention in *Journal Général de France*, 10 April 1816; on consumption in France, see Rebecca Spang, 'What's Rum? The Politics of Consumption in the French Revolution' and Leora Auslander 'National Taste? Citizenship Law, State Form, and Everyday Aesthetics in Modern France and Germany, 1920–1940', both in Martin Daunton and Mathew Hilton (eds), *The Politics of Consumption* (Oxford: Berg, 2001), pp. 33–49, 109–28.
57. Fornier de Saint-Lary, *A.P.*, XIII, C.D., 4 October 1814.
58. Cornet d'Incourt, *A.P.*, C.D., XVII, 16 April 1816.
59. Beungot, *A.P.*, XVII, C.D., 9 April 1816.
60. Magnier-Grandprez, *A.P.*, XVII, 6 April 1816.
61. Bouffey, *A.P.*, XII, C.D., 3 October 1814.
62. Delessert, *A.P.*, XXI, C.D., 24 March 1818.
63. Chamber of commerce of Rouen, *Mémoire sur la Nécessité de Maintenir le Système Prohibitif* (Paris, 1814), p. 5.
64. Duvergier de Hauranne, *A.P.*, XXI, C.D., 17 March 1818.
65. A.-L. Ecrement, *Entretiens et Vues sur l'Économie Politique* (Paris-Lille: Bertrand, 1818), pp. 48–9; petition entitled 'Mémoire des manufacturiers de coton de la ville de Paris', in A.N. F12 2502.
66. Dussumier-Fonbrune, *A.P.*, XVII, C.D., 9 April 1816.
67. Cornet d'Incourt, *A.P.*, XVII, C.D., 16 April 1816.
68. Archives des Douanes (Bordeaux), 3B21.
69. Archives départementales de la Gironde, 5P 215.

70. A.N., F12 1973–96 and F12 1997–2003.
71. A.N., F12 1973–74.
72. Ferrier, op. cit., pp. 517–18; letter from the director of customs to the minister of Justice in A.N. BB 18 980.
73. See for instance Archives départementales du Bas-Rhin, P. 319.
74. Archives départementales de la Meurthe-et-Moselle, P. 8.
75. Say, op. cit., I: p. 218; Sismonde de Sismondi, *Nouveaux Principes d'Économie Politique* (Paris: Delaunay, 1819), 2 vols, I, p. 422.
76. Say, op. cit., I, p. 213.
77. Say, op. cit., I, pp. 224–5.
78. Say's note in Ricardo, D., *Des principes de l'Économie Politique et de l'Impôt* (Paris: Aillaud, 1819), p. 107.
79. Say, op. cit., I, pp. 215–16.
80. Charles Tempier, *Essai sur les Avantages qui Résulteraient pour la France de la Liberté Absolue du Commerce* (Paris: Le Normant, 1816), pp. 41–2; Audouin, op. cit., p. 12.
81. Arthur I. Bloomefield, 'Aspects of the Theory of International Trade in France: 1800–1914', *Oxford Economic Papers* 41 (1989), pp. 619–39.
82. Say, op. cit., I, pp. 81–2 ; Sismondi, op. cit., I, p. 418.
83. Say, I, op. cit., pp. 179–200.
84. Anonymous, *Questions Importantes sur les Prohibitions* (Paris, 1817), p. 6.
85. Bérard, *Des Moyens de Réduire à son Minimum le Prix de Denrées* (Paris: Poulet, 1815), p. 12.
86. *Questions*, op. cit., p. 10; Tempier, pp. 35, 49–50.
87. Sismondi, op. cit., I, p. 416.
88. *Questions*, op. cit., p. 11. On negative perceptions of the British economic model, see Gareth Stedman Jones, 'National Bankruptcy and Social Revolution: European Observers on Britain, 1813–1844', in Winch and O'Brien, op. cit., pp. 61–92.
89. Augustin Thierry and Henri de Saint-Simon, *L'Industrie* (1817), in *Œuvres de Saint-Simon et d'Enfantin* (Paris, 1963), 47 vols, vol. 2, p. 73.
90. Say, op. cit., I, p. 211.
91. Tempier, op. cit., p. 17.
92. Constant, op. cit., p. 547.
93. Tempier, op. cit., p. 31.
94. Audouin, op. cit., pp. 70–1.
95. Constant, op. cit., p. 547.
96. Tempier, op. cit., p. 33 (his emphasis).
97. On the complex relation of political economy to liberal and republican ideas, see Richard Whatmore 'The Politics of Political Economy in France from Rousseau to Constant', in Mark Bevir and Frank Trentmann, *Markets in Historical Context: Ideas and Politics in the Modern World* (Cambridge: Cambridge University Press, 2004), pp. 46–69 and James Livesey, 'Agrarian Ideology and Commercial Republicanism in the French Revolution', in *Past and Present* 157 (1997), pp. 93–121.
98. Rosanvallon, op. cit., p. 269.

4
The Political Economy of Empire: Freedom of Contract and 'Commercial Civilization' in Colonial India

S.M. den Otter

> If there be any one political truth proved by a vast mass of experience, it is this, that the interference of legislators for the purpose of protecting men of sound mind against the inconveniences which may arise from their own miscalculations or from the natural state of markets is certain to produce infinitely more evil than it can avert.[1]

The utilitarian and liberal T.B. Macaulay paid this unambiguous tribute to free markets and wise statecraft in response to an imperial issue: controversy over the cultivation of indigo in Bengal. Labourers – primarily indigenous labourers – received cash advances in exchange for contracting to produce crops of indigo, a blue dye and a lucrative remittance crop. Because these indigo contracts were often unprofitable for them, cultivators defaulted on their agreements. This in turn prompted a long-standing and highly contentious debate about freedom of contract in colonial India. Freedom of contract was widely thought in the mid-century to be synonymous with progressive and sophisticated civilizations: complex civil societies were governed by contracts into which individuals freely entered, in contrast to those societies governed by status or kinship ties in which individuals had no freedom to enter into their own agreements. Individual freedom, contract and progress thus became bound up together.[2] But part of this ideology of freedom of contract was also the stipulation that contracts must be kept, or to use contemporary words, that 'the security of expectation' must be ensured. Parties to contract, and civil society more generally, required some assurances that promises would be met.

Colonial law was a critical arena for the deliberation of this balance between uncoerced economic relations and the need to ensure security of expectation. Many early to mid-nineteenth-century observers regarded the close intersection of law and political economy as axiomatic and unassailable, and in particular, they pointed to the commanding fusion of a Benthamite science of legislation and Ricardian economics.[3] A powerful current in legal thinking from the late eighteenth century on had been the notion that law was artificial (rather than rooted in divine authority or innate benevolence, for example), deliberately manufactured to secure the possession and use of property.[4] Law acquired enormous authority to create the conditions of a peaceable and progressive civil society, and a prosperous economy. As the East India Company gained dominance in the subcontinent, law became one of the principal means for the creation of a civil society in India, and was animated by one particularly powerful form of political economy – economic liberalism. Colonial law-making in India, however, was not the uncontested application of one particular form of contemporary political economy. Diverse strands of economic thinking inter-mingled and were variously re-cast in colonial India. Further, there were numerous constraints on law-making which constantly eroded the application of any single economic doctrine. The complexity of indigenous societies, pre-existing patterns of commerce and trade, the weakness of the colonial state, the vagaries of individual administrators, and the power of pressure groups in India and London were just some of the multiple factors that broke apart any unassailable binding of colonial law-making and liberal political economy. Even the most ardent enthusiast for legal revolution in India did not counsel the wholesale suppression of the enormous body of Indian customary law that governed social and economic relationships; from the beginning the East India Company had operated a dual legal system so that indigenous law was not replaced unilaterally. Furthermore, the general presumption towards free trade and laissez-faire was expressed in diverse and nuanced ways in the early and mid-Victorian periods, rather than as an unequivocal celebration of unbridled economic individualism.[5] Many Indian administrators were influenced by evangelical Christian political economy or a Tory paternalism, though more commonly administrators brought to India familiarity with the classical political economy of Smith, Ricardo, Malthus and later J.S. Mill. Malthus and Richard Jones taught political economy at Haileybury, the training school of aspiring Indian civil servants; an impressive cast of political economists was directly involved in either the East India Company or in colonial government: James and J.S. Mill,

William Thornton, John Wilson, among others.[6] Armed with a slight training in political economy, young civil servants went out to India and there made decisions about agriculture, banking, taxation and the labour market. Esoteric theorizing about rent, wages and value appeared there in a very different context.

The language and the arguments of philosophers and political economists who, in the metropole, were establishing the importance of contractual obligation to the economic and moral vitality of modern civil societies, resonated with colonial administrators in India. I explore the currents of thought and practice about political economy which flowed between Britain and colonial India by examining the attempt to entrench in India one of the pillars of economic liberalism in the middle of the nineteenth century, freedom of contract, and to create thereby a free wage labour in agriculture. I consider specifically two attempts by the colonial state to make breach of contract in indigo cultivation a penal offence (first in 1830, and again in 1860). Colonial policies regarding freedom of contract moved between the belief that the state had a primary duty to guarantee security of expectation (this motivated measures to entrench contract relations in India), and the notion that economic vitality and progress came from free and uncoerced interaction between individuals. In addition to these two strands, considerations of equity and fairness, which had long been part of indigenous understandings of obligation, also became part of colonial debate about contract.

The half century of controversy over freedom of contract and indigo production points to how fluid the boundaries between colony, Empire and metropole were in this period,[7] and how this transnational conversation configured in part the thought and practice of Victorian political economy. More influential than an exchange of formal theories of political economy was the transnational flow of information which came out of the actual experience of conquest and colonial rule. In the Empire economic principles were shaped by the specific dilemmas of imperial governance and often of political expediency as the colonial state sought to preserve its tentative dominance. Indigenous subjects also forced adaptations to free market thinking, and thus, the Empire set new patterns for understanding and treating the questions of political economy.

Indigo cultivation

While the indigo trade at least initially embodied aspirations of the East India Company and colonial governments for profitable, vigorous and unrestricted commerce as an engine for civilizing the subcontinent, by the 1840s indigo cultivation was no longer consistently lucrative. As planters struggled under the fluctuations of global trade, they lobbied for state intervention, specifically in their relations with the indigenous cultivators of the indigo plant upon whom the indigo trade depended. By far the most common form of indigo cultivation was by *raiyots* or labourers who had some hereditary entitlement to the land which they worked and who entered into contracts with planters to produce indigo crops on land which they occupied.[8] Most often labourers were given cash advances to purchase indigo seeds to sow and to maintain farming operations. Indian agricultural workers had not enthusiastically taken up indigo cultivation. Cash advances to cover the cost of sowing the crop and maintaining the land and its buildings had been the primary incentive to cultivate indigo; plantation owners rarely extracted payment of debts on cash advances since the debt burden so effectively tied the labourers to cultivate indigo, in spite of their disinclinations. By this arrangement, owners were provided with an unpaid or underpaid labour force.[9]

Planters also used more overt coercion to secure labour. As early as the 1790s the Governor General was sending reports back to London of abuses by indigo planters who used violence to force labourers to cultivate the crop. By 1810 violence had become so widespread that magistrates were instructed to destroy stocks which were kept by indigo planters in their factories illegally in order to detain recalcitrant labourers, and to threaten any planters who beat, imprisoned or intimidated *raiyots* with a withdrawal of their licence.[10] Magistrates were instructed to prevent planters from obliging *raiyots* to accept cash advances in an attempt to bind them to indigo cultivation. Despite these injunctions, abuses by planters continued. Nonetheless, the planters formed a persuasive lobby, and in 1830 Governor General Bentinck peremptorily made breach of indigo contracts a penal offence (Regulation V of 1830).[11] This law made evasion of indigo contracts by the *raiyots* punishable by imprisonment of up to one month for a first offence (two months for a second). Recalcitrant *raiyots* could also be required to cultivate the crop. But within a short time, the other arm of colonial government – the East India Company's Court of Directors in London – had, in some anger, protested against this planter-friendly measure and the penal provision was repealed in 1836.[12]

There matters stood until, 30 years later, a penal law against breach of contract was again introduced, this time in response to a series of sporadic uprisings in Bengal, known as the 'Blue Mutiny'. 'Blue Mutineers' tore up indigo plants, attacked factories or simply refused to cultivate indigo in protest against the often harsh demands of primarily European indigo planters. Within a few months, in response to these localized disturbances and forceful lobbying by indigo planters and some other commercial bodies, the Indian Government passed a draconian temporary law which made refusal to cultivate indigo a penal offence punishable by imprisonment, if labourers had already undertaken to sow the crop. Indigo commercial interests argued that it was only the threat of imprisonment that led to the successful harvesting of the crop that year and saved Bengal from economic calamity, although the investigations of an Indigo Commission in the same year found the law to be remarkably ineffective: many cultivators chose punishment rather than to harvest their indigo crops.

Freedom of contract and the security of expectation

By the mid-nineteenth century, a sophisticated body of philosophical literature on promises and contracts existed and it was in this framework, erected primarily during the Scottish Enlightenment, that legal and political deliberations about colonial law-making were set. David Hume in particular had established the importance of contracts for fashioning a civil society. Keeping one's word was an artificial virtue learned in civil society: people came to see that keeping one's word might secure some expectation that promises made to them might also be kept. For Hume it was not the resolution or will that created the promise but the use of signs or expressions to publicize the resolution because it created a new motive, namely the fear of not being trusted by our fellow citizens in case of non-performance.[13] Adam Smith extended this recognition of the importance of spectators and public witnesses to promises and contract by emphasizing the operation of law. 'Commerce and manufactures can seldom flourish long in any state which does not enjoy a regular administration of justice, in which people do not feel themselves secure in the possession of their property, in which the faith of contracts is not supported by law, and in which the authority of the state is not supposed to be regularly employed in enforcing the payment of debts from all those who are able to pay,' wrote Adam Smith.[14]

This security of expectation was also an important element in early nineteenth-century utilitarian legal and economic thought. Law provided a framework for security of expectation, by creating rules which governed social interaction and produced regularities of behaviour, and all this served to protect the inviolability of property.[15] In his draft Civil Code, Bentham established expectation of the future as an indispensable task of law.[16] J.S. Mill expanded at some length on this Benthamite idea in his *Principles of Political Economy*, arguing that the ability to rely on the fidelity of engagements was essential to a prosperous economy.[17] The centrality of freedom of contract to prosperous civil societies was powerfully advanced by the legal theorist H.S. Maine who in *Ancient Law* argued that societies evolve from status to contract. This narrative was essentially a moral one in which contract was the means by which the virtues of independence, honour, and self-government could be cultivated. This state of modern enlightenment was juxtaposed to primitive societies and the vestiges of these earlier arrangements that lived on in India, all governed by custom, superstition and often despotic kinship ties.

The insistence that contracts would only become firmly planted in India if contracting parties had some expectation that the agreement would be kept appeared over and over again in the heated interchanges between colonial officials and indigo planters. Governor General Bentinck made a vibrant defence of the Benthamite notion of security of expectation when he argued for more punitive measures for breach of contract: 'It is sufficiently manifest ... that most if not all of the evils complained of by the planters are inherent in the system, by which large sums of money are advanced to an indigent population without security to the manufacture or adequate remuneration to the cultivator to ensure the cheerful and honest performance of his contract.'[18] Indigo planters also used the argument of security of performance to threaten wholesale economic disaster if contracts were not enforced, asserting that in the absence of enforced contracts, there was no security for commercial relations, 'and with such insecurity capital cannot materially increase'.[19] Commercial groups not only regarded recalcitrant indigenous labourers as a threat to their economic interest but also colonial government officials, more specifically those guided by paternalistic concerns about the well-being of the Indian population. In this vein, the chairman of the Landholders and Commercial Association warned that, before Europeans would be willing to risk capital investments in India, they would need 'to secure themselves against the caprices of government and they must have security for their advances, and not to be at the mercy of any socialist civilian who thinks himself called upon to redress the wrongs of labour at the expense of capital'.[20] Indeed colonial administrators were not always sympathetic to the aggressive claims of European planters, insensitive as these lobbyists often were to the intricate mingling of private commercial gain and other elements of empire-building.

Ideas of cultural and racial difference permeated administrative and commercial discussions of contractual obligation. Shifting understandings of moral sense and virtue were also implicated, whether moral sense was instinctive as argued by philosophers of the Scottish Enlightenment, or acquired in human society as Bain and Mill argued, and if the latter, whether certain forms of civil society fostered moral sense more than others, and a greater inclination to keep one's word. One of the criticisms of Hindu society made by various Victorian commentators was the weakness of moral sense among indigenous peoples, of the duplicity and capriciousness of the 'native mind'. Accordingly, colonial administrators suggested that non-enforcement of contracts would be 'especially pernicious in this country. If Europeans are to come to India for the investment of their capital the best relation which can be established between them and the natives is surely one of contract, provided the contracts are fair ones.'[21]

In addition to the utility of contract in cementing commercial exchange and safeguarding private property – all these ends were axiomatic in early nineteenth-century political economy – the defence of freedom of contract also took on a pedagogical and moral dimension in the context of Empire. Freedom of contract became an important part of the mission to civilize India, and in the attempt to forge a civil society grounded on virtue and manners (keeping one's word), defenders of contract appealed to the language of classical republicanism. Framing legal measures to enforce contract would not only expedite commercial transactions and secure labour arrangements; it would also bring about a change in manners. Contracts could be a kind of moral education – teaching one to keep one's word.

This emphasis on manners reflected a more widespread belief among colonial administrators that founding British law in India was 'a moral conquest more striking, more durable, and far more solid than the physical conquest which renders it possible'.[22] One pamphleteer, contrasting *raiyots* from Tirhoot with their Lower Bengal counterparts, claimed that: 'the more manly up country ryot would not for a moment stand what the more womanly Bengali absolutely requires before he thinks of performing an agreement'.[23] The effete Bengali depended on coercion in order to consider keeping to a contract. The Lieutenant Governor of Bengal, J.P. Grant, and others in the colonial administration sought to create a respectable, independent and dependable Bengal yeomanry, selling their labour on an open market. Grant described *raiyots* as the 'the free yeomanry of his country and indeed, strictly speaking, the virtual owners of the greater part of the land in the old cultivated parts of Bengal'.[24] He affirmed that special legislation was not necessary to induce Bengalis to keep promises, for 'there is evidence on record given by men of intelligence and experience to show that, if fairly treated, the Ryot will readily act up to his agreement, and that, in regard to Indigo, it is the unprofitableness of the contract which has led to evasion on the part of the Ryot'.[25] This image bore striking parallels to the stalwart and independent economic man upon whom natural prosperity relied who figures so dominantly in metropolitan classical political economy. When Maine introduced a contract law several years later, he proclaimed this universalism by reminding the Governor General and Council that 'contract is the branch of law on which men of all times and races have come most nearly to identical conclusions'.[26] Yet this apparent universalism of classical economic theory was combined with a much more highly particularized idea about cultural and racial difference in the Empire.

Freedom of contract and free labour

Throughout the sixty odd years of controversy over indigo contracts, the nature and meaning of 'freedom of labour' in contract-based societies was extensively debated, not only by colonial administrators both in India and in Britain, but also by European planters, landowners, indigenous labourers, the Bengal intelligentsia, missionaries and various other groups. The category of 'free labour' which was constructed by colonial interventions in indigenous societies exemplified all of the tensions and contradictions of 'free labour' that appeared in the metropolitan context: slavery incorporated negotiation over pay and conditions, and, at the other end of the spectrum, the ostensibly free labour of contracts was often circumscribed and restricted, most visibly in penal enforcement, but in multiple other ways.[27] In the apparently 'free labour' of indigo cultivation, coercion was widespread. Attention to consent accordingly became a significant element in contract law in India even before it did in Britain.[28] Ross, a self-declared Benthamite in Governor General Bentinck's Council, observed in 1830 that labourers 'do not seem to consider the contracts entered into under such circumstances as voluntary on their part and it may therefore be believed that they have little scruple in employing all the means they are said to resort to, in order to evade performance when any advantage can be gained by so doing.'[29] Successive petitions by indigenous cultivators to the Indian Government endorsed Ross's earlier speculation; in the words of Ushruff Mundul and his co-petitioners, indigo cultivators in Jessore and Nuddea districts, 'finding the cultivation of indigo plant very unprofitable, in fact ruinously unprofitable to them, have refused to enter into contracts to cultivate the plant, and therefore the manufacturers have in various ways proceeded to press them, with a view to force them to enter into such contracts'.[30] The Indigo Commissioners who were appointed to investigate the causes of the widespread unrest of 1860 and the efficacy of the 1860 Breach of Contract law found, after interviewing 74 labourers, numerous planters and other Europeans, that kidnapping by indigo planters to secure labourers and coercion to enforce contracts was endemic in some regions. A prevalent form of coercion was forged contracts. The Commissioner of Nuddea Division reported that of the 609 contracts taken to court under the penal law, no less than 42 invoked forged endorsements.[31]

But often coercion was more subtle. Although contemporaries described contracts as free because the labourer could refuse to accept the cash advances offered to them, that freedom was circumscribed in other ways. Many indigo cultivators believed that they had little choice but to accept the cash advances and to continue to cultivate indigo. Investigations by the Indigo Commissioners revealed that many labourers believed that they had inherited debt load from previous generations which had accepted cash advances before them; they often knew little about the degree of their indebtedness to indigo factories. They often had some shadowy knowledge of grandparents taking on obligations which they presumed were still not met. Although cultivators had nominal freedom to choose which crop to cultivate, economic imperatives, in this case debt burdens, bound them to cultivate indigo.

The criticisms of the indigo system in the late 1850s and 1860s which highlighted the economic bondage of the indigo cultivator paralleled humanitarian critiques of slavery and indentured labour.[32] Protests especially in the indigenous newspapers used prevalent images of forced labour and slavery to argue against indigo contracts. The newspaper *Indian Field* reported that contracts made the raiyot 'a slave to the factory with which he has once engaged, and prevent[ed] that fair and open competition, which is the mainspring of commercial transactions'.[33] Here, the *Indian Field* made humanitarian arguments against coercive contracts, but also highlighted another injurious aspect: the contracts prevented the operation of competition, and were thus inimical to a flourishing economy.

For many colonial administrators, local elites and influential Indian lobby groups, freedom of labour and freedom of the market were closely entwined, and the vision of a society in which labourers could sell their labour and their produce in a free market was continually reaffirmed. Labourers could choose to cultivate tobacco, indigo, jute, sugar or any other product, depending on current prices. They invoked the Smithian notion that economies flourished if relationships were uncoerced, if everyone could pursue their own idea of well-being, and if labour were free. The well-being of the labourer did not lie in indigo cultivation, at least under the current regime, but the idea of allowing the market price to determine whether or not a labourer chose to cultivate indigo seemed to be substantiated from the example of Madras, where indigo was profitable and was widely cultivated: labourers voluntarily and readily entered indigo contracts, though indigo was also cultivated extensively without either contracts or advances.[34] Notwithstanding all the ways in which state monopolies, high levels of taxation, and tariffs whittled away at a free market in colonial India, the rhetoric of the free market was pervasive. Even during the most severe famines of the first two-thirds of the century – Madras and Bombay in 1823–24, North West Province in 1860 and Orissa in 1865–66 – the overriding presumption against interfering with the market price of grain was unshakeable, and intervention was limited to public works programmes. It was not until the Orissa Famine that criticism of the application of the classical famine policy to India began to be challenged, although some contemporary political economists offered alternative responses based on the Irish Famines. As early as the 1830s Revd Thomas Chalmers, the evangelical political economist, had argued that laissez-faire famine policies ought not to apply in pre-capitalist societies like Ireland.[35]

The Indigo Commissioners determined that the only possible solution to the impasse between cultivators and planters was to leave indigo to open market forces; if the price of jute or sugar fell in comparison with indigo, the *raiyot* could turn a profit in cultivating indigo.[36] Nature was elevated as the model for a new free and fair market in agricultural labour, as opposed to the unnatural practice of coerced labour exemplified by the old indigo advances and contracts. This vision was not the sinecure of metropolitan liberals and classical economists; indigenous landowners also argued for a free market in agricultural labour.[37] The influential Indian Association opposed a penal law to enforce contracts, not so much out of humanitarian concern for the bondage of labourers but because special legislation would distort the natural market governing indigo production: 'Your petitioners cannot view the contest in any other light than as the natural struggle between labour and capital, and as such, its settlement, they are of opinion, ought to be left to the operation of economical laws, uninterfered with by the government or legislature on any side.'[38] The natural rhythms of a free market in agricultural goods were contrasted with the artifice of indigo contracts which contravened the axioms of political economy: the land, the labour and the risk were the *raiyot*'s; no share in the labour of producing indigo was born by the planter, and yet the *raiyot* received no payment. It, therefore, was not simply colonial governors and administrators or metropolitan political economists who were pressing the utility of the market; numerous petitions from local landed elites and indigenous merchant groups argued against penal contracts not only on humanitarian grounds but out of convictions about the utility of a free market.

Although inconvenient to European commercial interest, labourers' refusal to cultivate indigo without profit showed the kind of market savvy which the British ostensibly hoped to cultivate on the subcontinent. Although the voice of indigenous labourers are not often recoverable, records of interviews with labourers imprisoned under the new penal breach of contract law are a valuable source and demonstrate that market thinking was part of the calculations of some indigenous labourers. Interviewed in July 1860 in Kinshagur Gaol, Astul Mundul of Kanainuggur who had been imprisoned under the penal breach of contract law, said: 'I and five others were sued for breach of contract. We were all cast [imprisoned], but the others managed to get the money together, and thereby got off. I was cast in a sum of 110 rupees for five beegahs and a half. I understood that there was an order that it was optional with us to sow or not to sow, and, as I considered that I was not under agreement, I did not sow. My cattle and property have been sold, and realized only 32 rupees, and I lie in prison for the balance. I heard that my property had been sold from some villagers who came here; I was sent off to prison as soon as the decree was passed against me.' Asked if he would sow indigo upon his release, he replied, 'No, for what with having to give to *aims* and *takidgirs* and what with breaking clods, I am become a fakir, and a dog.'[39] Indigenous custom had long acted to enforce the performance of obligations within local societies, but in addition to stressing the morality of debt repayment, custom governed expectation of a fair price and thus served to reduce the burden on the borrower. In the case of these exploitative contracts with European planters, local leaders did not act to enforce the contracts, and as the preceding quotation indicates, labourers elected not to sow indigo under such exploitative terms. Even early evidence suggests that many zamindars preferred that indigo was not cultivated in their districts because it occasioned the disturbances which became a common form of protest against exploitative contracts.[40] Indigo cultivators saw themselves as working within a market, and knew that they could exercise some power within that market.[41] Planters and merchants also realized this, and accordingly sought protection from the colonial state.[42]

Those cultivators who were imprisoned and refused to return to indigo cultivation became part of a transnational flow of economic ideas. While breach of contract statutes had been introduced in the eighteenth century on the prevalent understanding that free markets could not operate without breach of contract legislation, the indigo disturbances in India highlighted a growing sensibility that labour was most productive when it was voluntary and consensual. Unless labourers worked willingly, even penal breach of contract legislation could not secure a labour supply. By far the majority of labourers convicted under the 1861 penal act elected not to cultivate indigo; they chose either imprisonment or fines. When imprisoned labourers were interviewed in jail about whether they intended to cultivate indigo upon their release, the most common answer was a resounding refusal to plant indigo. The system of indigo contracts which had artificially protected the Bengal trade in indigo by maintaining a cheap supply of family labour collapsed when the colonial government did not renew breach of contract legislation.[43]

The fairness and equity of contracts

Ideas of fairness and equity and their place in a free market were contested and debated in the Empire by both European and indigenous parties. Considerations of equity and fairness and consent were not generally features of freedom of contract thinking in the first part of the nineteenth century.[44] But the indigo debates show how much considerations of equity shaped understandings of freedom of contract in India. Increasing indigenous criticism of aspects of British rule, added to the concerns voiced within colonial elites, questioned how fairness could coexist with freedom of the market. When the Court of Directors of the East Indian Company opposed Governor General Bentinck's new penal law on breach of indigo contracts in 1830, they protested on the grounds of equity. This 1830 law provided for the imprisonment of convicted labourers, but made no provision for the punishment of ruthless or coercive planters. The relative status of the employer and the labourer in contracts was debated vigorously in Britain and India. In Master and Servant legislation in Britain up until 1875 labourers convicted of breach of contract were liable to a penal sentence, whereas employers merely to a civil injunction. But this imbalance was even more striking in the Indian indigo context where in all cases of penal legislation for breach of contract, the employer was not touched by the law. The employer had no obligations and could not be punished either for civil or criminal offences under the law on breach of contract. This was the primary objection of the Court of Directors who chastised the Indian Government for hastily introducing penal legislation in 1830 without first consulting them.[45] They protested that the law said nothing about the obligations of the planter: contracts were in fact not mutual at all. Regulation V of 1830 did empower labourers to appeal to the Zillah Court for an expiration of their indigo contracts, but this was only permissible if the labourer was able to settle any outstanding debts to the planter, and if the planter refused to accept payment, the labourer would have to begin a regular suit. The lack of mutual protection remained one of the most telling arguments against penal legislation for breach of contract. Thirty years later, Sir Charles Wood, Secretary of State of India, echoed the Court of Director's objections: 'the Ryot has been left too long in ignorance of the protection which he might claim against the proceedings of any Planter who has bound him by unreal obligations, and who had enforced them by unlawful means; and further that the Ryot has not been adequately defended against the Native servants of the Factories by the Government and its Officers.'[46] This principle of mutuality was also reflected in the huge disparity in the profit to be gained by the contracts, although the principle was widely recognized that 'No system of trade can be safe or stable where the bargains are not for the profit of both parties ... '.[47]

The inequity of indigo contracts was compounded by the widespread conviction that judicial administration was also prejudicially inclined towards the planters. Both the Indian Reform Society and the newspaper *The Hindoo Patriot* exposed the close interest between Bengal planters and magistrates, noting that in some cases, the same magistrates who had the authority to hear suits against labourers also had pecuniary interests in indigo production.[48] The Indian government had appointed several indigo planters to serve as lay magistrates in the districts of Nuddea and Mooradabad,[49] a politically disastrous decision that was memorialized in popular Bengali folksongs which were widely disseminated by indigenous newspapers.[50] After the demise of the penal law of 1861, the decline of the indigo system was hailed as the victory for the cause of freedom and for equity, although some planters attempted to retain the coercion of the old indigo system by threatening rent enhancement to those who declined to cultivate indigo.[51] A contemporary memorial presented by the signatories – self-described as 'rajahs, zemindars, talookhdars merchants, tradesmen, agriculturalists and other natives of Bengal' – celebrated British protection of equity. 'They have broken up the system of serfage which had taken root for the last fifty years, under the vicious method of Indigo Planting, prevalent in Bengal, have secured the Ryots the equal protection of the Law with their powerful neighbours of the

Factory, and have declared one unvarying standard of justice for the rich and poor, strong and weak, without distinction of country or colour, race or religion.'[52] The fact that great differences of property and profit separated the rich and poor, strong and the weak, in this memorial was not regarded as an inequity by the signatories who were themselves men of property; rather, the inequity was that these economic differences led to a different standing before the law.

That the market itself might introduce coercion or inequity into free contracts was acknowledged, but these inequities were deemed to be less telling and more temporary than if the state intervened. Grant argued that it was quite wrong to represent the indigo disturbances as conflict between capital and labour for both *raiyots* and planters were capitalists: 'The capital of the Ryot is his land, his crops and his cattle, and in very many cases his means of hiring labourers over and above the value of his own bodily labour. The whole cultivation of Bengal is in his hands; and the ruin of this mighty interest would be the ruin of the country. ... As a national interest, the owners and the cultivators of the soil must be ranked second to none in an agricultural country like India.'[53] Grant said nothing about the difference of degree of capitalist enterprise. But on the other hand, he as well as other colonial officials, was aware that the state in framing laws which would facilitate a 'free' market in labour might indirectly sanction coercive labour. This was a refinement on the defence of free labour markets that had come out of the Scottish Enlightenment. Considerations of equity were becoming part of contractual thinking in the mid-century, and these considerations vitiated to some degree an unambiguous defence of the benefits of an unrestricted autonomy in a free market.

The concern with fairness and equity was demonstrated by the lengths to which the Bengal Government went to ascertain that *raiyots* charged under the new law were treated fairly and judiciously, that the legislation was not used to exonerate planter capacity, and that contracts were fair and consensual. The Lieutenant Governor of Bengal, J.P. Grant, sent out a number of circulars and letters of instruction to local commissioners and magistrates ordering them 'to be extremely careful in the execution of the new Law, and in all proceedings connected with Indigo cultivation', and providing very specific instructions on how magistrates were to interpret the new act and how to calculate damages.[54] Grant reviewed decisions by which *raiyots* were convicted, and in numerous cases repealed the convictions or lowered the damages awarded to planter plaintiffs. This degree of executive intervention in the judicial process is surprising, and was justified by Grant on the grounds that too often magistrates were poorly educated, too young and misinformed.[55] But it demonstrates that a paternalistic concern for fairness tempered doctrines of the free market, and a growing awareness that even so-called free labour could have coercive elements.

By the time the legal theorist H.S. Maine arrived in Calcutta as Law Member in 1864 and busily set about to codify contract law for India, notions of equity and fairness dominated the appraisal of his proposed laws. Another member of the Viceroy's Council wrote to Maine that he had opposed Maine's contract law on the grounds that 'the main contracts which ... would be demanded in Bengal are not in themselves equitable contracts. They are contracts between the sick and the poor, between men having the influence of station and position over humble dependents, and I don't view with any favour the legislation that seeks to strengthen the former at the cost of the weaker party.'[56] The Whig Secretary of State for India, Sir Charles Wood, also cautioned Maine that the law on enforcing contract could be 'used as an instrument for bullying the ryot awfully'.[57] Wood wrote: 'I am afraid of all legislation which, however framed, is substantially for the English capitalist against the native land occupier or native producer in some shape or another.'[58] In the metropolis, a group of Tory philanthropists, led by the ninth Earl of Shaftesbury, lobbied effectively against any extension of a penal law enforcing indigo contracts. The *raiyots* were thereby enveloped into the category of 'labouring classes' which were the object of Shaftesbury's reforms, those whom it was unfair to leave to the operation of the market and to the unrestricted freedom of contract. In response, the indigo lobby accused Shaftesbury of the cardinal sin of 'prevent[ing] the free labour of India', although it was the cause of free labour which had led him to urge the abolition of slavery.[59] To them, contractual obligation existed regardless of considerations of equity or fairness: 'what on earth have the "principles of equity" to do with a plain enactment, which says that a man who has had his wages shall do his work, and that if one man prevents his comrades from doing his work, he shall be punished for his interference?'[60]

The principle that free contracts could contain either coercive or inequitable elements had been raised by J.S. Mill who argued in *Principles of Political Economy* that states have an obligation to decide whether contracts are fair and whether they should be enforced. Forcing some promises could be inimical to the public good, even if both parties had freely consented to the contract: 'There are promises by which it is not for the public good that persons should have the power of binding themselves. To say nothing of engagements to do something contrary to law, there are engagements which the law refuses to enforce, for reasons connected with the interest of the promiser, or with the general policy of the state. A contract by which a person sells himself to another as a slave, would be declared void by the tribunals of this and of most other European countries.' And once the state rules that some contracts are inadmissible, questions about all contracts arise: 'Whether, for example, the law should enforce a contract to labour, when the wages are too low or the hours of work too severe: whether it should enforce a contract by which a person binds himself to remain, for more than a very limited period, in the service of a given individual.'[61] Mill established that the state had a role in determining the fairness of contract, and of sometimes curtailing the unfettered freedom of contract. The British economist William Thornton, who wrote extensively about labour in the 1860s and 1870s, regarded the inviolability of contract as an essential right of labour – the state exists 'to secure the person, property and performance of contract'[62] – but he did not regard the state as responsible for determining the fairness of contracts. That was the province of the trade unions which sought, in partnership with capitalist interests, to create fair conditions for labour. And it was labour union agitation that finally brought down penal labour laws in Britain in 1875. In the colonial context, Mill's supposition that the state assumed the responsibility to determine which contracts were fit to be enforced became especially prescient. British claims for dominance in the subcontinent depended on their claims to promulgate justice and equity. Nonetheless, considerations of equity did not deter the colonial government from administering an extensive system of indentured labour in which contracts to labour on plantations in the Caribbean or tea plantations in Assam did not meet the standards of equity set out in the indigo debates.[63] Colonial administrations across the Empire were shot through by contradictions of this sort.

Indigo planters often claimed in their own defence that cash advances and peasant indebtedness had been a feature of pre-colonial economies, and that it would be impossible to remove this long-established custom. However, in practice, local and indigenous moneylenders were obliged by force of local custom and public opinion to desist from harsh and usurious loans. The moneylenders depended on village elders to recover their lands in the absence of an organized judiciary. Colonial administration did not adopt this same flexibility. Nor did it understand obligation in these communitarian terms. In place of the complex and interconnected relationships embedded in local communities, the new contractual relationships existed between individuals and were mediated by a colonial state which was insufficiently attuned to local circumstances. Indigenous critics of colonial policy countered that the British had broken apart traditional organic communities, and in their place erected the impersonal force of contractual obligation, without the latitude or flexibility which characterized pre-conquest and highly localized judicial systems. Romesh Dutt, one of the first economic historians of the subcontinent, argued in 1882 that had the British preserved ancient and self-governing institutions, like the village community, their administration would not have been so overly centralized, and that questions of equity and fairness would have had a more stalwart defence.[64]

Legal scholars, political economists and philosophers were beginning to develop a more nuanced understanding of intention in voluntary agreement, and beginning to recognize that freedom of contract could be compromised not only by duress or fraud but by inequitable power relations.[65] The example of indigo contracts vividly demonstrated how difficult it was to measure or adjudicate whether contracts were freely made, when there was such a gulf between the wealth, power and privilege of the contracting parties, and when the contracts perpetuated these inequalities. By the early 1880s, the idealist philosopher T.H. Green was reframing the ideology of free contracts. Freedom of contract could no longer be regarded as an unqualified boon to civil society; oppressive and inequitable contracts abounded, highlighted by agitation in Ireland by the Land League. Principles of equity and fairness which were central to the controversy around indigo contracts became an important aspect of contractual thinking in Britain, and for philosophers like Green, the prime business of government was not only to uphold the sanctity of contract but also to ensure that contracts, because of the helplessness of one of their parties, were not instruments of oppression.[66]

Transnational exchanges

Although I have argued that colonial administrators were led by the principles of contemporary liberal political economy to create a free market in agricultural labour in India and to translate customary or kinship relationships into free contract relationships, numerous constraints militated against this. The first was a heightened preoccupation with issues of equity and fairness. Racial considerations became a pivotal element in determining the equity of the proposed entrenchment of contract on the subcontinent. The Secretary of State for India Sir Charles Wood consistently warned of the danger of underestimating this: a penal law for contract 'would arm "white" European masters against their "black" servants'. This is not to suggest that humanitarian considerations alone led the colonial state to abandon enforcing indigo contracts: had the system of indigo contracts worked efficiently and not acted as a catalyst for localized protest, considerations of equity may not have been such a dominant feature.[67] There were, however, limits to the colonial state's concern for the equity or justice of contractual relationships: translating relationships into free contracts (whether labour or marriage contracts) did not mean invariably that these relationships became more equitable or fair. These new contracts could be less equitable than communitarian alternatives to contractual obligation which had been such a primary feature of social relations in pre-colonial India.

Second, the colonial state in India was vulnerable to indigenous uprisings and protests. Indigenous protests against the oppressive labour relations of indigo cultivation stretched back to the 1830s, to the revolt led by Titu Mir in Barasat in 1831 and the farazi movement in East Bengal throughout the late 1830s and 1840s. The 'blue mutiny' in west and central Bengal in 1859 and 1860 – the peasant attacks on indigo factories and indigo plants, dramatized in Dinabandhu Mitra's play *Neel Darpan*[68] – effectively pushed the Home Government to force the withdrawal of legislation to criminalize breach of contract.[69] Large-scale refusal to cultivate indigo even though cash advances had been made continued to be a powerful form of resistance. Under the shadow of the recently pacified rebellions of 1857–58, the Bengal government acted swiftly to reaffirm British dominance in the disturbed areas. Upon the first signs of distress, a visible military presence was established, not only to prepare for possible widespread insurrection but also 'to show that we are in every quarter'.[70] The colonial state could not simply set up machinery for accumulation of capital, in this case to protect the profit margins of indigo merchants and planters by guaranteeing them underpaid family labour. Third, the colonial state was not a uniform monolith devoted to spreading the gospel of the free market. Views on political economy within the colonial state varied according to time, place and issue, and colonial archives demonstrate protracted and significant disagreement about the proper degree of intervention into the market economy.

Colonial administrators who had been educated at Haileybury were taught the general theories and principles of political economy and law; instruction on Indian matters, apart from Sanskrit which had very little utility for most civil servants, was minimal.[71] Few civil servants sent out to India in the mid-century had anything more than a superficial training in political economy: 'a few have acquired the first principles of jurisprudence and political economy; most know nothing at all about it, except a few terms and phrases picked up in lectures'.[72] The Tooke Professor of Economic Science and Statistics at the University of London, James E. Thorold Rogers, complained about the infrequent attendance and general lassitude of his students from the Indian Civil Service.[73] Most low-ranking civil servants who went out to India as district officers and local judges and magistrates carried with them a fairly rudimentary knowledge of political economy, and when they appealed to the principles of economic liberalism, they were more often reflecting a pervasive culture of liberal political economy rather than familiarity with high theory. More senior colonial officials were sometimes much more knowledgeable in the formal discipline of political economy; members of Bentinck's council frequently appealed to Bentham. The Treasury economist John Wilson served as Governor-General Canning's Finance Minister in the early 1860s: he supported making breach of contracts a penal offence, and introduced licence and income taxes. But John Strachey as Viceroy Lytton's Finance Minster clearly subordinated any consideration of economic theory to the dictates of whatever the Home Government in Westminster (and indirectly this meant the Lancashire cotton lobby) desired.

Indian nationalist critics of the impact of British rule on the Indian economy engaged with metropolitan economic ideas. A foremost voice was that of Dadabhai Naoroji, a social and political activist and 'first' economist of modern India.[74] Beginning in the mid-1870s, Naoroji examined poverty in India using empirical data on expenditure, national income and standard of living, and concluded that the primary cause of poverty was the colonial economic system. He developed 'the drain theory' to explain how the enormous transfer of income and wealth from India to Britain impoverished India and its peoples, and hobbled industrial development in India. While the force of his argument came from his calculations based on statistical data, he also grounded his drain theory on British political economy, especially J.S. Mill's work. Naoroji did not employ Mill so much to define a theoretical model to explain chronic poverty in India. Rather he used Mill's status and authority to command attention for his own theories, developed fairly independently, and to attempt to persuade a sceptical English audience of the value of his drain theory. Accordingly, he highlighted two of Mill's arguments in *Principles of Political Economy*: first, the demand for commodities is not the demand for labour; and second, 'industry cannot be employed to any greater extent than there is capital to invest'.[75]

The controversy around indigo contracts paralleled the metropolitan debate about master and servant legislation. Although one important distinction was that the Master and Servant acts governed wage labour, and as we have seen indigo cultivators owned their own capital and were thus in a somewhat different position, numerous parallels abound. The themes of freedom, mutuality, fairness and security of performance which cut through the indigo controversy also shaped public discussion of the Master and Servant Acts. By 1865, the tide had turned in Westminster against penal legislation, though it took several more years for these reforms to be enacted.[76] The indigo controversy which was widely publicized in Britain contributed indirectly to this metropolitan reform of the master and servant acts. Because the principles of freedom and fairness were so vividly highlighted in indigo contracts which were widely publicized in Britain, the Indian experience served to highlight those parallel principles which undercut domestic discussion of master and servant legislation. While master and servant legislation continued in India longer than in Britain (primarily in the draconian legislation applied to the tea gardens of Assam[77]), nonetheless the indigo contracts anticipated metropolitan reforms. In this case, the metropolitan centre did not provide the example or prototype for colonial legislation.

By the mid-1860s, there were more challenges to the application of economic liberalism in colonial India. In Act X of 1859 and the ensuing 'Great Rent Case' of 1865 it was ruled that customary rather than market rates ought to determine land rent. Some assumed that this meant that the maxims of political economy simply did not apply to India. Maine opined that 'In India, the question of issue related to rents by custom, and not to rents by competition, and hence all quotations from political-economical writers were entirely irrelevant.'[78] The colonial government circumscribed freedom of contract by ruling against arbitrary rent enhancement but this did not mean, as Maine suggested, that political economy was irrelevant to the subcontinent. On other issues, most disastrously famine relief, other colonial administrators appealed to the principles of economic liberalism to sanction non-intervention in the so-called freedom of the market. Had more thorough reforms of agricultural rents been carried out, the burden of taxation on agriculture been lessened, and more restrictions on free trade in the grain and rice markets been set in place, conditions would not have been so conducive to these famines of the mid- and late century.[79]

The universalism of political economy was challenged by the colonial experience. There was no single uniform body of ideas of political economy that could be transplanted to new colonial territories; rather complex interconnections characterized this transnational exchange. The sometimes contradictory claims of freedom of the market, considerations of equity, as well as a moral defence of contract as the foundation of modern civil society, exemplify how principles of political economy were modulated in response to specific dilemmas of imperial governance. Colonial administrators, metropolitan legal experts, political economists, and government officials made up a transnational exchange. The labourers who refused to cultivate indigo were also part of this transnational exchange for it was their rejection of exploitative contracts which forced the state to examine the equity of contractual obligation in colonial India.

Notes

1. Macaulay, 'Minute No. 30', 13 November 1835 in C.D. Dharker, ed., *Lord Macaulay's Legislative Minutes* (Oxford: Oxford University Press, 1946), pp. 276–7.
2. See H.S. Maine, *Ancient Law* (London: J. Murray, 1861) for an influential statement of this position.
3. H.S. Maine, *Popular Government* (London: J. Murray, 1885), 155. See S. Ambirajan, *Classical Political Economy and British Policy in India* (Cambridge: Cambridge University Press, 1978) and Eric Stokes, *The English Utilitarians and India* (Oxford: Oxford University Press, 1959).
4. See D. Hume, *Treatise on Human Nature* (London: Longmans, 1874), sections 480, 491; G. Postema, *Bentham and the Common Law Tradition* (Oxford: Clarendon, 1989), p. 102.
5. See, for example, B. Hilton, *The Age of Atonement: The Influence of Evangelicalism on Social and Economic Thought, 1785–1865* (Oxford: Clarendon Press, 1988); E.D. Roberts, *The Social Conscience of the Early Victorians* (Stanford: Stanford University Press, 2003); D. Winch, *Riches and Poverty* (Cambridge: Cambridge University Press, 2000).
6. J. Majeed, *Ungoverned Imaginings: James Mill's The History of British India and Orientalism* (Oxford: Oxford University Press, 1992); L. Zastoupil, D. Peers, M. Moir, *J.S. Mill's Encounter with India* (Toronto: University of Toronto Press, 1999) and L. Zastoupil, *J.S. Mill and India* (Stanford, CA: Stanford University Press, 1994).
7. See A. Burton, 'Who needs the Nation? Interrogating "British" History?' *Journal of Historical Sociology* 10 (1997), pp. 227–48; 'From Child Bride to "Hindoo Lady": Rukhmabai and the Debate on Sexual Respectability in Imperial Britain', *American Historical Review* 103, 4 (1998) pp. 1119–46; D. Chakrabarty, *Provincializing Europe: Postcolonial Thought and Historical Difference* (Princeton, NJ: Princeton University Press, 2000), and P. Levine, *Prostitution, Race and Politics: Policing Venereal Disease in the British Empire* (London: Routledge, 2003).
8. Indigo was also grown under *nij*-cultivation in which the land was owned outright by the factory, and the factory employed wage labourers to cultivate indigo. *Nij* cultivation was much less common because production costs for the planter were so much higher: B. Kling, *The Blue Mutiny: The Indigo Disturbances in Bengal, 1859–1862* (Philadelphia: University of Pennsylvania Press, 1966), pp. 29–30.

9. S. Bose, *Peasant Labour and Colonial Capital: Rural Bengal since 1770* (Cambridge: Cambridge University Press, 1987), p. 74. He estimates that in the Nischindapur concern in Nadia, 'out of 865 peasants working 3,300 acres with indigo, a mere 110 acres had no outstanding balances ... unpaid balances mounted over the generations to astronomical figures which no indigo peasant could hope to redeem. Here was a marketing and production mechanism that efficiently and relentlessly attached unpaid labour to indigo cultivation' (p. 48). See Stanley Chapman, *Merchant Enterprise in Britain from the Industrial Revolution to World War I* (Cambridge: Cambridge University Press, 1992), pp. 11–119 for a sympathetic perspective on the agency houses involved in indigo cultivation. See also D. Kumar, *Cambridge Economic History of India Volume II 1757–1930* (Cambridge: Cambridge University Press, 1983). Indigo was also cultivated by labourers who were employed by large indigo concerns and were paid a daily wage.
10. Parliamentary Papers, Circular Letter sent on the 13 July 1810 by Orders of the Governor General in Council at Fort William to Magistrates under that presidency relating to Indigo Abuses, VI (1812–13), pp. 387–9.
11. Regulation V of 1830, repealed by Act X of 1836. Regulation V of 1830 was enacted in response to planter dissatisfaction with existing legislation, notably Regulation VI of 1823 which provided that following an inquiry, a judge could order a *raiyot* who had evaded a contract to produce the crop or could permit a planter a temporary lien on the *raiyot*'s land, but this law was only rarely used. The *Nizam Adawlut* in 1830 gave the opinion that any lien on the *raiyot*'s land on the basis of Regulation VI of 1823 was illegitimate. 3689 criminal prosecutions were brought under Regulation V of 1830, of which 354 were convicted. Oriental and India Office Collection (OIOC) E/4/751 20 June 1837.
12. This was embedded in Act X of 1836. Two clauses of Regulation V of 1830 remained on the books which had some bearing on indigo contracts but they were not often referred to partly because one provision was muddied by subsequent legislation on cattle trespass and because *raiyots* made no recourse to this. A proposal by the Lieutenant Governor of Bengal, Frederick Halliday, to re-enact sections 2 and 3 of Regulation V of 1830 did not succeed.
13. K. Haakonsen, *Science of a Legislator: The Natural Jurisprudence of David Hume and Adam Smith* (Cambridge: Cambridge University Press, 1981), p. 30.
14. Smith cited in D. Winch, *Riches and Poverty* (Cambridge: Cambridge University Press, 2000), p. 98, n. 19.
15. P.J. Kelly, 'Utilitarianism and Distributive Justice', *Utilitas* I (1989), pp. 73–4. This principle re-appeared in numerous mid-Victorian treatises on contract: C.J. Addison, *A Treatise on the Law of Master and Servant* (London: W. Benning, 2nd edn, 1847); J.W. Smith, *The Law of Contract* (London: V.R. Stevens, 1860); Smith, George Manley, *A Treatise on the Law of Master and Servant* (London: H. Sweet, 2nd edn, 1860).
16. 'In order to form a clear idea of the whole extent which ought to be given to the principle of security, it is necessary to consider, that man is not like the brutes, limited to the present time, either in enjoyment or suffering, but that he is susceptible of pleasure and pain by anticipation, and that it is not enough to guard him against an actual loss, but also to guarantee to him, as much as possible, his possessions against future losses. The idea of his security

must be prolonged to him throughout the whole vista that his imagination can measure.' Bentham cited in Postema, *Bentham and the Common Law*, pp. 160–1. See D. Lieberman, 'Economy and Policy in Bentham's Science of Society', in S. Collini *et al.* (eds), *Economy, Polity and Society* (Cambridge: Cambridge University Press, 2000), pp. 109–34; and Bentham in Bowring (ed.), 'Codification Proposal addressed by Jeremy Bentham to All Nations Professing Liberal Opinions or Idea of a proposed all comprehensive body of law, 1822', in *Jeremy Bentham's Works: Papers on Codification* (Edinburgh: Tait, 1843), IV, p. 561.
17. Mill, *Principles of Political Economy* in *Collected Works of John Stuart Mill* (ed.) J. Robson (Toronto: University of Toronto Press, 1986), pp. 109–11.
18. OIOC. F/4/1276/51240 ff 443–61.
19. D. Mackinlay, *British Settlers in India* (London: James Ridgway, 1861), p. 63.
20. Delta, *Indigo and its Enemies* (London: James Ridgway, 1861), p. 15.
21. OIOC. MSS Eur c 179/114/1 ff 79–84: Maine to Sir Charles Wood, 5 November 1863.
22. J.F. Stephen, 'Legislation under the Earl of Mayo' in Sir William Hunter (ed.), *The Life of Mayo* (London: Smith, Elder and Co., 1875), pp. 168–9.
23. Delta, *Indigo and Its Enemies*, p. 47.
24. Grant, 'Minute on the Indigo Commission', paragraph 33 in *Selections from the Records of Govt of Bengal Papers Relating to Indigo Cultivation in Bengal*, Part III, Calcutta 1860.
25. Grant, 'Minute on the Indigo Commission', paragraph 59.
26. Parliamentary Paper, 'Statement of Object and Reasons Accompanying the Draft Contract Bill', XILX (1867–68), p. 686.
27. See R. Steinfeld, *Contract, Coercion, and Free Labour in the Nineteenth Century* (Cambridge: Cambridge University Press, 2001); Stanley Engerman, 'Coerced and Free Labour', *Explorations in Economic History* 29 (1992), p. 18; D. Northrup, *Indentured Labour in the Age of Imperialism, 1834–1922* (Cambridge: Cambridge University Press, 1995).
28. See L. G. Ibbetson, *A Historical Introduction to the Law of Obligations* (Oxford: Oxford University Press, 1999), pp. 233–4; H.T. Colebrooke, *Obligations and Liabilities* (London, 1818) and William Macpherson, *Treatise on Contracts* (London, 1860).
29. OIOC. F/4/1276/51240 ff 246–265: Mr. Ross' Minute, 21 September 1829.
30. OIOC. SP/146/25, item 264. Petition of Ushruff Mundul and Others, ryots of sundry villages in Districts of Nuddea, and Jessore to J. P. Grant, 29 March 1860.
31. OIOC. P/146/41/f 198: Charles Wood to the Governor General, 5 June 1861.
32. According to a memorial by landowners and merchants written upon the death of the penal law in 1861, Grant had vindicated 'the rights as free men of hundreds of thousands of innocent ryots who were toiling under its galling thrawldom [sic].' Mss Eur F 127/38, Petition to Grant.
33. *Indian Field*, 24 July 1858.
34. OIOC. Mss Eur F 127/38 (Papers Relating to Indigo in Madras), J.D. Sim Secretary to the Board of Revenue to J.D. Bourdillon, Secretary to the Government, Revenue Department.
35. Ambirajan *Classical Political Economy and British Policy in India*, ch. 3. See also M. Davis, *Late Victorian Holocausts* (London: Verso, 2000) and S. Sharma, *Famine, Philanthropy and the Colonial State* (Oxford: Oxford University Press, 2001).

Maine noted that the Executive Council barely discussed remedies for the Orissa Famine, this in contrast to the extended discussion in the Executive Council on Maine's proposed article on specific performance in response to indigo contracts: OIOC. Salisbury MSS. IOR Neg 11672. Bundle II, Maine to Salisbury, 22 December 1867.

36. 'Should the prices of other products fall, and the defects of the system be eradicated, we see no reason why the *ryot* and the planter should not meet on fair terms, no compulsion being exerted on one hand, no subterfuges employed on the other, and no special law or protection being necessary for either party ... ', Parliamentary Papers, 'Report of the Indigo Commission', XLIV (1861), p. xliv.
37. OIOC. Mss Eur F 127/38: Petition to Grant from 'We the undersigned rajahs, zemindars, talookdhars, merchants, tradesmen, agriculturalists and other natives of Bengal.'
38. 'Humble Petition of the Indian Association to J.P. Grant, Lieutenant Governor of Bengal', 'Report of the Indigo Commission', p. 210.
39. A beegah is about one-third of an acre.
40. R. Guha, *Elementary Aspects of Peasant Insurgency in Colonial India* (Delhi: Oxford University Press, 1983), A. Yang, *The Limited Raj: Agrarian Relations in Colonial India* (Berkeley, CA: University of California Press, 1989).
41. Jaffe argues that a market-mindedness and ingenuity in navigating market relations had penetrated the English labouring classes by the mid-century: J. Jaffe, *The Struggle for Market Power: Industrial Relations in the British Coal Industry. 1800–1840* (Cambridge: Cambridge University Press, 1991). See C.A. Bayly, *Rulers, Townsmen and Bazaars: North Indian Society in the Age of British Expansion* (Cambridge: Cambridge University Press, 1983).
42. See, for example, *Brahmins and Pariahs: An Appeal by the Indigo Manufacturers of Bengal for Protection against the Lieutenant Governor of Bengal* (London: Ridgeway, 1861).
43. The authority of a political economy of 'natural' and 'free' market relations qualified and constrained the assumption, which Craven and Hay have demonstrated to be so prevalent throughout the British Empire, that coercive law was essential to the creation and replacement of labour: Craven and Hay, 'The Criminalization of "Free" Labour: Master and Servant in Comparative Perspective', *Slavery and Abolition* 15, 2 (1994), p. 80.
44. See, for example, T. Haskell, 'Capitalism and Humanitarianism, Part Two', *American Historical Review* 90 (1985), p. 549. See D.J. Ibbetson, *A Historical Introduction to the Law of Obligations* (Oxford: Oxford University Press, 1999), pp. 233–84 for a discussion of how these considerations became part of Indian contract law at a much earlier point than in Britain.
45. OIOC. P/140/13 Bengal Judicial Proceedings. Governor General to the Court of Directors: 20 November 1832.
46. P/146/40 pp. 280–2. Charles Wood to the Governor General, 8 April 1861.
47. P/146/25 p. 171. A.R. Young for the Government of Bengal to the Commissioner of Nuddea, 14 March, 17 March 1860.
48. *Hindoo Patriot*, 26 August 1858; anon., *A Reply to the Indigo Planters Pamphlet entitled Brahmins and Pariahs* (London: Ridgeway, 1861).
49. Issur Chunder Sing of the British Indian Association to the Secretary of Government of Bengal, 29 August 1857. Parliamentary Papers XLIV (1861),

pp. 342–3. The planters were J. Furlong, R. F. Larmour, and I. Burrell in Nuddea, and H. Deverell G. M. Jackson and J. Watson in Mooradabad.

50. *Bengal Huukaru*, 23 November 1858.
51. Petition of Dil Jhan Mundul and other inhabitants of the Zeminadareer of Mr Hill, Indigo Planter, Nuddea to the Honourable Lieutenant Governor of Bengal, 3 March 1861. P/146/38, pp. 63–4 protesting that Mr. Hill 'who, being prohibited to treat the ryots illegally and unjustly as hitherto, regarding the indigo affairs, has determined to ruin the poor ryots on the pretext of rent cases'.
52. Mss Eur f 127/38; Petition to Grant.
53. J.P. Grant's, Minute in Response to Complaints of Indigo Planters Association regarding his prejudicial conduct around indigo system, 17 August 1860, pp. 10–23, in *Selections from the Records of Government of Bengal Papers Relating to Indigo Cultivation, Part III*, p. x.
54. E.H. Lushington, Officiating Commissioner of the Nuddea Division to Magistrates of Nuddea, Jessore and Barraset, 14 May 1860, pp. 639–42 in *Selections from the Records of Government of Bengal Papers Relating to Indigo Cultivation in Bengal*; A.R. Young, Secretary to the Government of Bengal to Officiating Commissioner of Nuddea, 17 May 1860, p. 641.
55. Grant, for example, strongly chastised one magistrate in Nuddea for failing to determine the validity of claims against ryots, and also for not challenging the inflated claim of damages awarded to the planter who had brought charges against the ryot: A.R. Young, Secretary to the Government of Bengal to the Officiating Commissioner of Nuddea, 16 May 1860, pp. 662–4 in *Selections from the Records of Govt of Bengal Papers Relating to Indigo Cultivation in Bengal.*
56. Mss Eur C 179: Sir E. Perry to Maine, 23 February 1864.
57. Mss Eur c 179 ff 31–32: Wood to Maine, 14 February 1864.
58. Wood to Laing, 16 March 1862 cited in Kling, *The Blue Mutiny*, 192.
59. W.F. Fergusson, *A Reply to the Address of the Rt. Hon The Earl of Shaftesbury to the Rt. Hon Sir Charles Wood on the Proposed Law of Contract for India* (London: James Ridgway, 1863), p. 12.
60. Anon., *Brahmins and Pariahs*, 99.
61. Mill, *Principles of Political Economy*, Book V, pp. 801–2.
62. W. Thornton, *On Labour* (London: Macmillan, 1869), p. 102.
63 See S. Sen, 'Questions of Consent: Women's Recruitment for the Assam Tea Gardens, 1859–1900', *Studies in History* 18 (2002), pp. 231–60.
64. R. Dutt, *The Economic History of India*, pp. 148–9.
65. D.J. Ibbetson, *A Historical Introduction to the Law of Obligations* (Oxford: Oxford University Press, 1999), pp. 233–84. Ibbetson argues that Indian lawyers, notably Henry Colebrooke, had a greater sense of how duress and fraud could constrain the voluntary nature of contractual agreements than British lawyers who developed this dimension of contract theory rather later.
66. T.H. Green, 'Liberal Legislation and Freedom of Contract', p. 19.
67. See P. Mohapatra and R. Behal, 'Tea and Money versus Human Life: The Rise and Fall of the Indenture System in the Assam Tea Plantations', *Journal of Peasant Studies* 19 (1992), pp. 142–72.
68. See Blair B. Kling, *The Blue Mutiny: the Indigo Disturbances in Bengal, 1859–1862*; R. Guha, 'Neel Darpan: The Image of a Peasant Revolt in a Liberal Mirror', *Journal of Peasant Studies* 2 (1974), pp. 1–46.

69. Bose, *Peasant Labour*, pp. 148–51.
70. P/146/25 item 260 for 29 March, 27 March 1860; Government of Bengal to the Commissioner, Nuddea Division.
71. 'Examination of William Epsom, Professor of Law at Haileybury', Reports from the Committee on East India Company Affairs – Judicial. *Parliamentary Papers* (1831–32), XII, 2 July 1832, pp. 128–36.
72. G. Campbell, *Modern India* (London, 1853), p. 266.
73 J. Maloney, 'Political Economy in London University', in A. Kadish and K. Tribe (eds) *The Market for Political Economy* (London: Routledge, 1993), p. 36.
74. See D. Naoroji, 'The Poverty of India' (1876) in *Poverty and British Rule in India* (London: Sonnenschein, 1901), pp. 1–126; S. Ambirajan, 'Dadabhai Naoroji: The First Economist of Modern India', *Research in the History of Economic Thought and Methodology* 16 (1998), pp. 155–78 and A.K. Dasgupta, *A History of Indian Economic Thought* (London: Routledge, 1993); B.N. Ganguli, *Indian Economic Thought: Nineteenth Century Perspectives* (New Delhi: Tata McGraw-Hill, 1978).
75. Naoroji, 'The Poverty of India', pp. 55–6.
76. D.C. Woods, 'The Operation of the Master and Servant's Act in the Black Country, 1858–1875', *Midland History* VII (1982), pp. 93–115.
77. See S. Sen for attempts to introduce breach of contract legislation to the jute industry, *Women and Labour in làte Colonial India* (Cambridge: Cambridge University Press, 1999), p. 38.
78. This ruling effectively weakened whatever sweeping powers the once influential zemindars-planters could exercise over indigenous cultivators, and the discovery of chemical indigo dye further marginalized indigo cultivation.
79. R. Dutt, *Economic History of India* (London: Kegan Paul, 1906), II, pp. 180–1.

5

'A Useful Lesson of Contentment': Pedagogies of Failure in Mid-Victorian Market Culture

Timothy Alborn

According to classical economics, free markets correct themselves. In the standard formulation of Adam Smith, prices and wages gravitate towards their natural level, as producers adjust the supply of goods and workers adjust the supply of labour to meet the demand. This idea that markets are self-correcting was one of the many creeds that Victorians borrowed from the Enlightenment only to be amended beyond recognition by the twentieth century. The reality of recurrent distress from the 1820s forward, combined with the rising influence of Evangelical Christianity, produced the view that economic failure signified divine retribution for original sin (defined with reference to individual sinners or to society writ large).[1] Running parallel with this view was the secular claim, most famously formulated by Ricardo and later popularized through Herbert Spencer's notion of a 'struggle for existence', that failure, by eliminating inefficient economic agents, was an inevitable price of progress.[2] Critics of capitalism countered that the real original sin was the market itself, and complained that the human suffering occasioned by the market's resistance to equilibrium was neither deserved nor inevitable.[3]

The history of Victorian reform and radicalism can be read as a series of efforts to soften or remove the often brutal process of market correction, either by teaching people to behave more closely in accordance with the market's own allegedly natural laws, or by transcending the thrust and parry of unmitigated competition. Two of the most prominent of these efforts included legal reform and the formation of voluntary associations. Although they overlapped, each of these responses intervened in distinctive ways to try to redress the human costs of capitalism. Legal reformers either sought to remodel England's medieval legal procedure so that judges could correct people's behaviour when markets failed to do so; or sought to repeal all remaining obstacles to a truly free market, consigning any subsequent flaws in the system to the realm of divine discontent.[4] Voluntarism supplemented the market with the principle of mutual association, in the process recognizing the insufficiency of the purely atomistic world envisioned by classical economics. The associations themselves ranged from the strictly ameliorative to the wishfully transformative.[5]

Of these two responses to imperfect Victorian markets, legal reform more directly addressed the problem of failure. It did so either by assuming that people who failed were corrigible, and hence could be rescued from their errant ways by suitably stern laws; or by nurturing the growth of capital by insulating it from the occasionally errant behaviour of those whose activities contributed to its formation. In the realm of social welfare, the first set of reformers sought to punish those who failed to secure productive employment in order to teach them the error of their improvident ways, while the second more radically called for the abolition of poor relief altogether. In the realm of personal credit, the first set of reformers advised a sliding scale of sanctions in a quixotic effort to correlate personal blame with future access to credit, while the second argued that creditors and bankrupt debtors should be left alone to sort things out.[6] In the realm of company law, where failure loomed largest because the stakes were amplified, legal reformers debated the relative merits of unlimited vs limited liability. Those who viewed the law as performing a necessary educative function urged that every shareholder in a failed company should be liable for the firm's losses to the last penny of his or her estate, in order to teach investors to be careful when choosing where to put their money and vigilant in overseeing its employment. Those who viewed the law as an adjunct to economic efficiency opted for limited liability, on the grounds that the optimal allocation of capital would occur where firms were free to restrict their obligations to creditors who were willing to take that risk.[7]

In contrast to legal reform, which sought either to exaggerate the effects of failure in order to teach a moral lesson or to prevent failure from standing in the way of unmitigated growth, mutual associations sought either to nip failure in the bud or to ameliorate its effects through the mechanism of social solidarity. The first joint-stock banks in England presented themselves as a more secure foundation for the nation's cash economy owing to their power of combination: numerous small contributions of capital gathered together into a single company would be better able to withstand the vicissitudes of trade than a large number of undercapitalized banking partnerships.[8] The thousands of self-help societies that sprang up in Britain throughout the nineteenth century preached that members' subscriptions would provide a safety net for the stray individuals who failed to keep pace with the economy as it lurched forward.[9] Since they subordinated personal to social agency, such professions of faith in solidarity stood at odds with both of the orthodox strands of legal reform that flourished in the Victorian era. Legal reformers supported them only insofar as they incidentally furthered the goal of economic growth, either by improving the efficiency of capital accumulation (as with joint-stock banks) or by diminishing the burden of poor relief (as with self-help societies).

Nevertheless, advocates of legal reform and mutual association constantly worked side by side during the nineteenth-century, since neither joint-stock companies nor voluntary societies could exist without at least a minimal legal identity. Observing in detail the dynamics involved in such co-operation makes it possible to clarify the distinctive attitudes held by these two groups towards the allegedly self-correcting character of markets. That tensions existed when these groups worked together does not mean, however, that they were incapable of productive labour. The extent to which Victorians successfully responded to the fact of individual failure amidst economic success hinged on a succession of compromises between those who preached individual responsibility and those who nurtured social solidarity.

An especially revealing example of awkward co-operation between legal reform and mutual association concerns the intersection of company law with Christian Socialism in mid-nineteenth-century England. This chapter will focus on two such points of intersection, the Joint Stock Companies Winding Up Acts of 1848–49 and the Industrial and Provident Societies Act of 1852, which shared a common architect in the person of John Malcolm Ludlow. Ludlow was a company lawyer by profession and a leading member of the Christian Socialists who clustered around F.D. Maurice between 1848–54.[10] Although seldom discussed in the context of his socialist thought, Ludlow viewed his approach to failed joint-stock companies very much as an extension of his heartfelt belief in the power of association. He accordingly framed the two Winding Up Acts with the goal of encouraging shareholders to see themselves, even in failure, as members of a community with responsibilities to each other as well as to their creditors. In so doing, he pursued a middle ground between unlimited liability, which treated each shareholder as a personification of the larger firm; and limited liability, which treated the failed firm as so much capital in need of reallocation. The better known

Industrial and Provident Societies Act was the culmination of the Christian Socialists' strenuous efforts over the previous four years to give working-class association a chance. They hoped that a secure legal foundation would provide workers with all they needed to stabilize their often volatile economic surroundings. In framing and promoting the law, Ludlow attracted a wealth of allies, most of whom assumed that it would bring about a very different sort of outcome than he had envisioned. They assumed that the law, far from preventing an imperfect market from forever intruding on workers' lives, would set workers' co-operatives up for inevitable failure, which in turn would teach them to be satisfied with the imperfect, but still efficient, industrial economy.

Ludlow's case is also illuminating because of his close personal and intellectual connections with French company law and associationalism, hence allowing for a unique opportunity to compare the larger themes revealed by his reform efforts in Britain with the resonances such themes evoked in the very different religious, political and economic climate across the Channel. Born in Paris, Ludlow's first encounter with Christian Socialism came from the French Lutheran minister Louis Mayer, who envisioned a 'fraternity of young Christians' who would minister to the poor while teaching the rich about social responsibility. Ludlow also drew from utopian socialists like Fourier, whose critiques of the free market rubbed off but whose secular perspective rubbed him the wrong way. His French upbringing convinced him that only by 'Christianizing Socialism' could truly productive change come about in Britain.[11] Like other British company lawyers, Ludlow was also well aware of the distinctive legal environment which was available for company formation in France. French company promoters could either form a *société anonyme*, which conferred limited liability but required state authorization, or a *société en commandite par actions*, which distinguished between sleeping partners (*commanditaires*) with limited liability and managers (*gérants*) with full liability.[12] Both options struck Ludlow as substantial improvements over the choice (up until 1856) faced by British investors between forming a company by royal charter or private Act of Parliament, which was a more expensive version of the société anonyme, and taking a chance with an unlimited, unwieldy partnership. As with his perspective on utopian socialism, however, he found French company laws to be bereft of the true spirit of association. To him, French shareholders were faceless suppliers of alien capital, not (as he hoped their British counterparts could be taught to think of themselves) active members in a corporate community.

Redeeming investors

The stock market, just coming into its own as something more than a repository of public debt, vied with the Bank of England's discount rate in the 1840s as a leading indicator of the wide deviations from anything approaching 'natural' prices. These deviations had a direct impact on people's lives, both by amplifying the business cycle's wayward effects on human capital, and by bringing financial ruin to shareholders who, as often as not, were fully liable for corporate debt. As share prices ballooned and crashed, and as interest rates fluctuated between 2 and 8 per cent, onlookers scrambled to teach investors how to act in ways that would prevent supply and demand from getting so outrageously out of balance. Free-market thinking was split between those who assumed large companies were both evil and unnecessary for growth; and those who assumed that investors only needed to be provided with better information in order to distinguish sound speculations from bubbles. Personifying the first view was S.J. Lloyd (Lord Overstone), whose name became synonymous with the idea of the business cycle as a sign of divine retribution. William Gladstone translated the second view into practice in the 1844 Joint-Stock Companies Act, which required shareholder registration for all concerns with at least 25 members. Both factions were agreed that shareholder liability should only be limited in special cases like railways, which required permission from Parliament or the Board of Trade – arguing that investors could never be taught to be careful with their money unless all their personal property was at risk.[13]

This defence of unlimited liability, whether in its cynical or optimistic guise, represented the mainstream in Britain into the 1850s, despite a clear contemporary movement in the direction of enabling general limited liability in France and the United States. The only British proponents of limited liability at this time were legal reformers like Bellenden Ker, who bemoaned the waste of time and money entailed by private Acts of Parliament and royal charters, and the Christian Socialists, who hoped limited liability would entice investors to support workers' co-operatives.[14] In addition to their appeals to efficiency and social justice, these reformers presented a number of economic benefits that would come from liberalizing company law. They claimed that it would, among other things, divest excess capital from statutory and chartered companies, repatriate money that was presently being squandered on limited concerns abroad, and reduce Britain's reliance on bank credit. None of these arguments succeeded in changing the system, however, until they were joined in the mid-1850s by politicians who offered a new twist on the old free-market reasoning. Led by Robert Lowe, Palmerston's Chancellor of the Exchequer, the new converts to general limited liability defended it as part of a wider 'freedom of contract' ideology. They blasted Overstone and Gladstone as overly paternalistic and argued that creditors could take care of themselves when lending money to a registered company.[15] The legal reformers' earlier emphasis on efficiency remained central in this new defence, which fuelled Lowe's Companies Acts of 1855–56 and further legislation in the 1860s, which introduced general limited liability into Britain for the first time. The same could not be said about the Christian Socialist concern for social harmony.

A key figure in the debate over company law in the 1840s was Ludlow, who found time to co-draft with Ker two pieces of major legislation – the Joint Stock Companies Winding Up Act of 1848 and an amendment act the following year – while he was tirelessly promoting Christian Socialism. In the voluminous scholarly analysis of Ludlow's writings during this period, virtually no mention has been made to either of these two Acts. A close reading of the legislation, however, and especially of Ludlow's commentary on what he accomplished, reveals striking continuities between the 'working-class' interests of the Christian Socialists and Ludlow's vocation as a company lawyer. The fact that Ludlow was able to move so easily, and with much of the same intellectual equipment, between these two realms reminds us that Victorians tended to use the same moral categories to analyse imperfections in all corners of market culture.[16]

Any doubt about the relevance of the Winding Up Act to Ludlow's socialist commitments should be put to rest by his reference to it, in a treatise intended for company lawyers, as a first step in putting down the 'evil results of the action upon trade of large masses of capital, wielded by bodies responsible only to their purse, which constitute the "industrial feudalism" of the present day – as a great thinker, Charles Fourier, has termed it'.[17] Inadvertently abetting such 'feudalism' in this story, as in so many other law reform agitations, was the Chancery judge Lord Eldon, who had repeatedly responded to the 'large masses of capital' that found their way into his Court by treating them as though they were ordinary partnerships. Ludlow complained that Eldon's habit of requiring every shareholder in a large-scale firm to be party to lawsuits rendered the common-law company 'far less controllable and more dangerous' than chartered corporations, which came with strict legal guidelines that no judge could ignore. In the former case, 'provided a sufficient number of swindlers could keep together, they might violate with impunity any regulation of the deed of settlement, and set at defiance all efforts of their fellow-shareholders to put an end to the partnership'.[18]

Against Eldon and subsequent Equity judges, who essentially hoped that companies would one day go away if they kept ignoring them, Ludlow saw companies as signs of a 'necessary ... revolution in society', and insisted 'that our efforts must be to direct it ... forcibly to good purposes – instead of idly attempting to thwart it, or fancying that it can be thwarted by being excluded from the Court of Chancery'. Gladstone's Act of 1844 had gone part way towards recognizing the need to bring companies under the rule of law, by introducing shareholder registration and allowing third parties to sue a company as a separate legal entity (as opposed to tracking down every 'partner'). It had failed, however, to address suits in which members of a company tried to recover funds from one another; these remained under the jurisdiction of Chancery judges, who showed no new signs of paying attention to them.[19] To Ludlow, this was a telling failure, since it avoided reform at exactly the point where the associative nature of the company was at the fore. The gist of Gladstone's reform had been to rectify the vulnerable status (owing to judicial inaction) of individual capitalists who did business with a common-law company, not to solidify the bonds holding shareholders together.

With little fanfare, Ludlow and Ker obtained the passage of a law, the Joint Stock Companies Winding Up Act (11 & 12 Vict. c. 45), which they designed to force judges to do something about contribution suits when they crossed their path.[20] The law made it easier for shareholders to reduce their prospective losses, or to foil an errant board of directors, by petitioning either the Lord Chancellor or the Master of Rolls 'in a summary Way for the Dissolution and Winding-Up' of a company if they could convince the judge of its insolvency. Creditors who had already initiated bankruptcy proceedings against the company had precedence,[21] but the hope was that shareholders, with a better knowledge of the true state of the company's affairs, would spot problems before things reached that point. Another feature of the Act was that Master of Rolls or Lord Chancellor would 'appoint an official manager ... in consultation with the contributors', who could 'act quickly to marshal and dispose of the assets of the bankrupt company'.[22]

The 1848 Act addressed two issues near to Ludlow's heart: the principle of equal financial responsibility among shareholders and the ability of investors to wind up a concern before it had sunk irretrievably into insolvency. Under the old system, a few of the richest investors in an unlimited firm stood to lose everything in the event of its failure, while the vast majority of shareholders escaped without any loss.[23] The 1848 Act forced more shareholders in a firm to feel the burden of unlimited liability, applying 'the stern Communism of the English Law of

Partnership' by requiring proportional calls to be levied on all shareholders instead of a wealthy minority. Surveying his handiwork in 1850, Ludlow surmised that the new procedures were already starting to teach people 'to feel what are the obligations of partnership, and what engines of ruin and misery are large Companies with unlimited liability'. The only ones left who would be willing to invest in such firms, he predicted, would be 'fools who think they can lose nothing, rogues who know they have nothing to lose, and may gain all, and gamblers, who will stake everything upon the cast of a die'.[24]

If Ludlow was correct in this assessment, the passage of the Winding Up Act raised the stakes surrounding the imminent introduction of general limited liability, by virtually shutting off what had earlier been an important conduit for the 'prudent' investment of surplus capital.[25] But limited liability *per se* was never the primary end that Ludlow had in mind. Rather, as he spelled out in his commentary on the Act, the 'searching reforms' he envisioned would transcend 'mere procedure, however perfect', and 'substitute living men who do their duty ... for the dead complication of wheels and springs in human shape which now form what is appropriately termed the "machinery" of Justice and Government'.[26] Specifically, he proposed the appointment of 'a Minister of Justice' who would possess all the expertise of 'men specially employed on labours for which their previous experience has specially qualified them'.[27] What Ludlow hoped such a minister might accomplish in the realm of company law is evident from a later critique he wrote in 1857 of Equity's continuing refusal, dating back to the early nineteenth century, to take over the management of partnerships unless they had already become hopelessly insolvent. His proposed alternative was a more activist judiciary that would 'interfere for the redress of partnership grievances' and thereby create 'a standard of right and wrong ... which men will work up to more or less'.[28]

Ludlow's vision of a minister of justice exercising benevolent encouragement of active shareholder co-operation was wholly foreign to the aims and effects of the fully fledged company laws that would appear in Britain between 1856 and 1862. When Robert Lowe confronted company law as it existed in 1855–56, he certainly did not intend to replace Gladstone's individualist standard of right and wrong with an associative standard which was equally idealistic in its social aspirations. Instead, he sought to abstract capital from shareholder agency. This, he argued, would entrust capital to those who knew best how to employ it, professional managers and responsible directors of large-scale companies; and it would entrust its oversight to those with the most to lose, the bankers and other financiers who lent money to such firms. Lowe undercut the originative role of shareholders by providing, in his 1856 Bill, a standard form for future company deeds; and Palmerston's Lord Advocate confirmed, in speaking on behalf of the Bill, that its definition of a company was 'a combination in which the stocks and not the partners constituted the principal object'.[29]

In practice, what Palmerston's cabinet accomplished in 1856 was to transplant a variant of the French *société en commandite par actions* onto British soil. Indeed, the Vice-President of the Board of Trade had referred, in the course of his defence of general limited liability in 1855, to the problem of British company promoters registering their firms in Paris in order to protect their British investors from full liability. Twenty such firms had formed as *sociétiés en commandite* in 1852–53 with nominal French gérants who signed over their power of atttorney to British directors.[30] In removing the requirement that directors of otherwise-limited firms bear full liability, Lowe had disposed of the fiction that this provision bore any relation to creditors' security. What was left was the company's paid-up capital, shorn of its investors' full liability, and available for creditors to accept or reject as sufficient collateral. Ludlow, who knew as much as anyone in England about the actual working of *societies en commadite*, was well aware that gérants were 'usually men of straw'; and he echoed Lowe in arguing that 'you want absolutely limited liability' or none at all.[31] Where Ludlow parted with Lowe was in assuming that under such a regime, shareholders – now sans their individual responsibility to shoulder their company's burdens – would need to be taught how to re-envision themselves in an associative capacity.[32] Ironically, French company law appeared to move in exactly this direction in 1856, when it closed many of the loopholes which had led to abuses of the *commandite* form. In 1863, however, French lawmakers scurried to reliberalize their company laws, in order to stem the reverse process of capital flight from France to Britain that had accompanied passage of the countries' respective laws seven years earlier.[33] If there was an area in which Victorian markets seldom failed, it was their capacity to sniff out where the friendliest legal environments resided.

Redeeming workers

While Ludlow was doing what he could to change the way middle-class shareholders cleaned up after their failed ventures, he and his fellow Christian Socialists were devoting ever more time and money to teach the 'science of partnership' to London artisans.[34] They did this through continued propaganda; through the establishment and financing both of individual co-operative workshops and of an umbrella group, the Society for Promoting Working Men's Associations;[35] and finally through efforts to enact legislation that would adapt existing friendly society laws to meet the unique needs of co-operatives. Initially, much of the propaganda came from Ludlow and Tom Hughes, who respectively edited the weekly *Christian Socialist* and the successor *Journal of Association*. Most of the funding for the new co-operatives came from Edward Vansittart Neale, a wealthy lawyer who used up much of his fortune bankrolling such schemes during this period. And Ludlow and Neale led way in the fight for legal reform, through their activities in the Law Amendment Society and Juridical Society, and in their testimony before Richard Slaney's Select Committee on Savings of the Middle and Working Classes.[36]

With infusions of cash from Neale when needed, the Christian Socialists cultivated the formation of co-operative workshops in London between 1850–51, reaching out to tailors, bakers, pianomakers, shoemakers and builders.[37] These all started small, competing for the custom of their respective neighbourhoods, and were based on the recognition that co-operatives could only succeed in 'dethroning undutiful capitalists' by 'successfully competing in a capitalist economy'.[38] Once more than a handful of these societies were up and running, they turned their attention to the problem of co-ordinating the burgeoning movement. Hence emerged the SPWMA in March 1850, confronting the Christian Socialists with their first crisis of leadership. Maurice, the avowed leader of the movement, refused to support the SPWMA until its projected 'central board' of artisan-managers was supplemented by a 'Council of Promoters' composed of four lawyers and five clergymen, who would 'concentrate on the spiritual and ethical aspects' of the movement.[39] It was just as well that so many of these 'Promoters' were lawyers – since, regardless of the workers' need or desire for 'spiritual' guidance, legal expertise was a more tangible and undisputed asset. For the promotion of co-operative workshops to have a large-scale impact, it would be crucial to guarantee their future security from mismanagement, to enable easy and cheap formation and dispute resolution, and to allow for growth beyond the limits of local charity; and British history taught that the only way to achieve these things was by winning special enabling statutes. Just as English judges had tended to ignore the separate legal existence of large-scale companies, they often resisted granting rights to working-class associations until specifically directed to do so by Parliament.[40]

The Christian Socialists' legal experts soon found a forum to publicize their views, when Richard Slaney invited Neale and Ludlow to testify before his parliamentary investigation into the 'savings of the middle and working classes' in 1850. He also invited Ludlow, after the committee had issued its report, to draft the Industrial and Provident Societies Act (15 & 16 Vict. c. 31) based on its findings. This Act called for registration of all societies of workmen 'carrying on or exercising in common any labour, trade, or handicraft' apart from banking and mining, and extended to such societies the right to sue and be sued as a separate legal entity. A crucial feature of the Act, in this regard, was that workers would be able to bring their legal problems before the Friendly Society Registrar, which Ludlow lauded in 1850 as 'a tribunal of their own ... who should settle all disputes'. Clearly, to his mind, this was a substantial advantage over the parallel recourse to Chancery that remained the fate of regular joint-stock companies. Less positively, a clause in the Bill extending limited liability to co-op members did not make it into the final Act, postponing that privilege until further legislation in 1862.[41]

Ludlow and Neale were the first witnesses to testify at Slaney's Committee, which they steered down the path of adapting existing Friendly Society laws to meet the needs of co-operatives. Ludlow called for a 'simple mode of registration, similar to that under the Friendly Society Acts, which has been very extremely used among the working classes, and which is very much liked by them.' Neale praised the cheap start-up costs under the laws, contrasting these with the £40 lawyer's fee for drawing up a deed and the £14 registration fee under the 1844 Companies Act. This was nothing like a charter's £1000-price tag, but it was still 'a serious difficulty' for the 99 Oxford Street tailors he knew who could only spare £200 to get their business off the ground. These suggestions, which grew directly out of the Christian Socialists' practical experiences at the newly formed SPWMA, addressed the need to teach London shop-workers that association was both safe and profitable. Slaney, in contrast, mainly focused on the need to inspire industrialists to establish enlightened factory towns.[42] These agendas overlapped at several points, especially concerning a common advocacy of limited liability as a means of attracting middle-class support for either sort of project. But beneath this surface similarity lay deeper differences, which ultimately got in the way of the Christian Socialists' hopes to relay legal reform into social change.

One divide separating Slaney from the Christian Socialists concerned the scale of their hoped-for co-operative ventures. Slaney valiantly tried to keep the focus of his committee on 'local enterprises ... sanctioned by persons of prudence, and caution, and property, who live near the spot where such enterprises would be carried on'. Ludlow, in contrast, dreamed of 'bringing the 23,000 journeyman tailors of London into one association'.[43] Slaney also set little store in the likelihood that the SPWMA's great social experiment would actually succeed, and consequently invited support for workers' co-operatives on the perverse grounds that their failure would teach workers to be happy with their lot. He told the Mercantile Law Commission in 1853 that he did not expect 'any very great advantage [to] be gained by the association together of a number of operatives to carry on industrial establishments'. This did not mean, however, that they should not be allowed to form. Rather, giving them the chance to fail would 'lead to contentment rather than discontentment', by refuting 'their ideas of the indefinite profits of great capitalists, with regard to which ... they would find they were greatly deceived'. Since Slaney's appeal to contentment was deceptively close to the Christian Socialists' professed desire for social harmony, he managed to extract seeming endorsements from both Ludlow (who admitted that workers' disappointment would 'promote their submission to things as they are') and Neale (who agreed that co-operatives would indeed 'produce a great deal of contentment among the working classes'). Unlike Slaney, however, both went out of their way to play down the chances of failure in a reformed legal environment. Neale insisted that beyond mere contentment, workers would 'get much benefit' from co-operative action, and Ludlow parried Slaney's onslaught of leading questions with glowing stories about the needlewomen, builders and tailors of London whose co-operative efforts had gotten off to such a promising start.[44]

Claiming that failed co-operatives would breed contentment proved to be an ingenious tactic for securing eventual passage of the Industrial and Provident Societies Act, but its very success in that regard boded ill for the aspirations of Christian Socialism. The idea of teaching contentment through failure was especially appealing to the large number of mid-Victorian reformers who were starting to have second thoughts about political economy's capacity to disabuse workers of 'incorrect' economic notions. The *Law Magazine* supported Slaney's report on the grounds that if workers' co-operatives were given the chance to fail, it would 'repress innovation and teach a useful lesson of contentment'. The banker George Norman, who cheerfully predicted that 'a good many mistakes productive of loss to individuals would be made', reasoned that 'a great good will be done, by the attainment of truth through the most telling medium'; and William Rathbone Greg concluded that since workers' hopes for success had been 'so recklessly confirmed by the wild assertions of orators and writers ... nothing but experience will disabuse them of it'. Even John Stuart Mill, who offered one of the most confident mainstream endorsements of workers' co-operatives in his *Principles of Political Economy* (1848), had defended co-operatives a decade earlier on the ground that their failure would 'be an instruction ... in political economy, worth a thousand treatises'.[45]

With friends like this, there was scant room left for enemies of the Industrial and Provident Societies Act. The few people who dared oppose such an imposing phalanx emerged looking either hopelessly pedantic or vaguely paranoid. The Manchester merchant Edmund Potter countered co-operation with a *Times* article urging workers to learn how to apply 'the laws which regulate the difference of their own wages to the case of their masters'. Lord St Leonards conjured the image of 'all the domestic servants in some wealthy neighbourhood' putting the neighbourhood bakers out of business by buying bread from a co-operative store.[46] Hence the Christian Socialists got their Act more or less made to order (with the notable exception of limited liability), but they failed to convince anyone that the societies themselves would actually succeed. At least in the realm of producers' co-operatives, which were at the core of Ludlow's original vision for social transformation, the result was something close to a self-fulfilling prophecy. Most of the producers' co-operatives that the SPWMA helped launch in 1850 ceased to exist within a few years; similar associations did resurface during future economic downturns, but they were no more successful at surviving.[47] Part of the blame for this case of arrested development might be traced to the unavailability of limited liability (although only until 1862), but it mainly stemmed from the fact that most of the putative supporters of the movement were content to remain on the sidelines and watch the new societies struggle against the tide.[48]

As for the SPWMA, it lasted only two more years after changing its name to the Industrial and Provident Societies Union in 1852, largely owing to a growing rift between Ludlow and Neale over the future direction of the co-operative movement. Neale turned his sights to the burgeoning consumer co-operative movement in the North, forming a new Central Co-operative Agency in 1851, which he 'projected as a major wholesaling centre for all of England'.[49] The movement's other leaders soon lost interest in co-operation once it became defined in terms of consumption rather than production. Kingsley and Maurice turned their energies in 1854 to the establishment of a Working-Men's College in London.[50] Ludlow, after two inauspicious decades as a writer and lawyer, served as secretary to the Royal Commission on Friendly and Benefit Societies from 1870 to 74, then took over as Registrar of Friendly Societies under a new law in 1875. Although this position apparently provided him with a perfect opportunity to teach workers how to associate productively, what he discovered in practice was that neither the barebones bureaucracy at his disposal nor his cautious superiors gave him much scope for perfecting the societies' constitutions.[51]

Like his former associates, Ludlow's new job put him in the position of lecturing to (or at) those workers who wanted to associate with one another but did not always go about it in the 'correct' fashion. Maurice and Kingsley patiently corrected student essays at the Working Men's College, and Neale less patiently lectured the directors of the Co-operative Wholesale Society when they refused to live up to his ideals.[52] The difference was that Ludlow, within limits, finally could back up his pronouncements by appealing to the higher authority of the state. As Friendly Society Registrar, he could take his first strides in the 'step by step' evolution of 'a great and prosperous Socialist State' that he had anticipated in a letter to Maurice in 1851. In the same letter, Ludlow had assured Maurice that he was no proponent of 'phalansteries, or parallelograms, or Icaria'.[53] Many outside observers, however, and certainly thousands of friendly society members, might have questioned the extent to which he had managed to inject Christian spirit into government machinery. In the 1850s, he could (and did) legitimately blame others for failing to enforce his expertly honed laws with a human touch. In the 1870s, to a large extent, the parallelograms got the better of him, and this time he was the one who could be legitimately accused of sucking the spirit from working-class association through an overemphasis on routine.

The ambivalent ending to Ludlow's career as a promoter of working-class association needs to be seen in the context of the even rockier career of associationism abroad. In France, the same utopian socialists whose ideas had both inspired and infuriated Ludlow spurred thousands of French workers to form producers' and consumers' co-operatives in the heady years of the Second Republic. Nurtured by a grant of 3 million francs for industrial associations in July of 1848, such organizations initially flourished, but most failed within a few years after the state subsidies dried up and their lack of management experience took its toll. The hardy survivors faced two decades of tenacious repression once Louis Napoleon took over in 1851; his suspicious ministers had little time for their protests that they sought social harmony and not political revolution.[54] It would seem, on the basis of this comparison, that the British orthodoxy of benign neglect accomplished more on behalf of working-class solidarity than the pendulating pattern across the Channel of enthusiastic encouragement followed by repression. That this contrast between France and Britain was also true of much of the rest of Europe is evident from an Austrian economist's claim in 1889 that England was a 'theatre of a gigantic development of associative life, which gives to her labour, her education, her social intercourse ... a pronounced direction'; and argued that, more than anywhere else in Europe, '[t]his union of individual forces ... has become a mighty moving wheel of social development in general and especially in the elevation of the working classes'.[55] By assuming workers' co-operatives would fail, instead of fearing lest they succeed, British legal reformers at the very least ensured their stubborn survival.

Conclusion

Markets, in the course of correcting wages and prices, routinely fail human beings. Once Victorians came to realize the extent to which this was happening around them, they developed what might be termed a pedagogy of failure, as they debated the lessons that statesmen and victims might learn from maladjustment. This chapter has surveyed several contributors to these debates, ranging from people who took failure as a sign that the whole system needed renovation, to those who took it to mean that the market's message was not getting through to enough of its participants, and finally to those who passed all the responsibility for failure along to those who failed. Out of this range of responses emerged a broad consensus: this was the idea that individual failure to survive in the free market was the best way, indeed had perhaps become the only way, people (especially workers, but also middle-class investors) would ever learn a proper respect for the market's 'natural' laws. This consensus retained a vigorous, if narrowly defined, role for Britain's legal and political institutions, without detracting from its leaders' postulation of self-reliance and Evangelical religion as pillars of mid-Victorian society.

Against that consensus, the Christian Socialists tried to argue that people (whether investors or workers) should see failure as a sign that society had been put together in an imperfect manner. Especially considering the condition of England in 1848, they argued, failure should be a spur to reform and not a lesson in contentment. With that in mind, they devoted their substantial legal skills to the tasks of enabling investors to make wise choices and enabling workers to succeed in the experiment of producers' co-operatives. This was a large task, given the primitive status of central governmental institutions and the largely local status of voluntary societies. It proved to be too large, especially because so many of their fellow reformers had set their standard for social harmony at a much lower pitch. Hence when Frederick Furnivall asked John Stuart Mill why he did not support 'the principle of ... community', whereby people with property had a duty to 'hold it in trust for the public or for the poor', Mill responded that 'mankind are not yet prepared' for it.[56] Utopians both in law and economics, the Christian Socialists experienced the futility of carefully filling in blueprints for a future society, only to see their schemes sidetracked by ideologues, misunderstood by well-wishers, and resented by the people they were trying to help. Still, their self-assigned task was not too large to prevent them from introducing significant improvements into the basic governing mechanisms of a still-maturing market society.

By the end of the nineteenth century, the lessons of failure favoured by British social scientists and political leaders moved towards calling for social rather than individual reform, and calling for new service-providing institutions rather than minor adjustments to the existing legal environment. Seebohm Rowntree's poverty surveys, Francis Galton's post-Darwinian ethnographies and L.T. Hobhouse's 'New Liberalism' all defined failure as collective (if at present relatively isolated) pathologies, not individual exceptions to divinely ordained progress.[57] In political application, these collective failures could easily be presented as ever in danger of seeping into the more successful, and more complacent, lives of the middle and upper classes. This conception of shared risk would, over the half-century following New Liberalism, usher in a new political consensus around the idea of shared responsibility for contingent economic and physical disability – culminating in the Beveridge Report (1942) and the Labour Party's sweeping post-war social reforms. The strategy of deriving new forms of social solidarity from perceived common contingencies likewise spread to the United States and other nations in Western Europe over the first two-thirds of the twentieth century.[58]

Although it is true that a second (and mostly unrelated) generation of Christian Socialists participated indirectly in the gestation of New Liberal thought, not much by way of continuity can be asserted between the 'great fact of human partnership' which Ludlow celebrated in 1848 and the 'full membership of a community' which T.H. Marshall invoked a century later in reference to the welfare state.[59] On the face of it, the legal reforms which the Christian Socialists helped to engineer in the 1850s found their culmination in the bureaucratic machinery of mid-twentieth century social insurance programmes. Those programmes, however, lacked anything approaching the spiritual harmony or self-awareness without which solidarity would have been unrecognizable for Ludlow and his colleagues. Resting as it did on an actuarial mandate to dispel the risk of poverty and disease, Beveridgean welfarism had more in common with the Evangelical fear of destitution than with the Christian Socialist fear of alienation.[60] The result was a set of reforms that delivered social services more or less efficiently for several decades, but has in the past quarter century failed to sustain a strong bond between society's most and least vulnerable members. Nor is it a coincidence that Margaret Thatcher's polarizing reforms of early 1980s were followed closely by a stock market boom which produced scandals seldom witnessed in the City of London since the 'manias' of the mid-nineteenth century. Such blueprints for reforms as were submitted by the Christian Socialists in that earlier era of alienated labour and capital remain available for consultation by today's reformers.[61] What is far less certain is whether today's older, but not terribly wiser, market economies are any better prepared for the sustained commitment to community implied in these plans than they were when Mill urged the Christian Socialists to bide their time.

Acknowledgements

The author wishes to thank Donna Loftus, Pat Thane, Donald Winch, the editors of this volume, and the other participants in the 'Worlds of Political Economy' conference for helpful suggestions regarding this chapter.

Notes

1. Boyd Hilton, *The Age of Atonement: the Influence of Evangelicalism on Social and Economic Thought, 1795–1865* (Oxford: Oxford University Press, 1988).
2. G.R. Searle, *Morality and the Market in Victorian Britain* (New York: Oxford University Press, 1998), p. 14.
3. See Marx's 'History of Economic Original Sin', with which he opens his section on 'Primitive Accumulation' in *Capital* (New York: International Publishers, 1967), I, p. 667.
4. See Avner Offer, *Property and Politics, 1870–1914: Landownership, Law, Ideology, and Urban Development in England* (Cambridge: Cambridge University Press, 1981).
5. See R.J. Morris, 'Voluntary Societies and British Urban Elites 1780–1850: An Analysis'. *Historical Journal* 26 (1983), pp. 95–118.
6. Searle, *Morality and the Market*, pp. 168–72, 89.
7. Robert A. Bryer, 'The Mercantile Laws Commission of 1854 and the Political Economy of Limited Liability', *Economic History Review* 50 (1997), pp. 37–56.
8. Timothy L. Alborn, *Conceiving Companies: Joint-Stock Politics in Victorian England* (London: Routledge, 1998), ch. 4.

9. P. Gosden, *Self-Help: Voluntary Associations in Nineteenth-Century Britain* (London: B.T. Batsford, 1973).
10. The most thorough study of Ludlow's theological and social thought and practice is Paul Henry Friesen, 'The Man Behind the Prophet: The Making of John Ludlow and the Fortunes of Christian Socialism in England 1821–1856' (PhD dissertation, University of St. Michael's College, 1995).
11. Torben Christensen, *Origin and History of Christian Socialism 1848–1854* (Aarhus: Universitetsforlaget, 1962), pp. 54–6; Friesen, 'The Man Behind the Prophet', p. 383.
12. Charles E. Freedeman, *Joint-Stock Enterprise in France 1807–1867: From Privileged Company to Modern Corporation* (Chapel Hill: University of North Carolina Press, 1979), chs 2–3.
13. Hilton, *Age of Atonement*, pp. 255–67.
14. It was probably not a coincidence, in this context, that the most famous theological quirk of this generation of Christian Socialism was F.D. Maurice's refusal to countenance the existence of Hell. To the extent that well-punished bankruptcy was the 'Hell of the English', their diffidence regarding the financial suffering of shareholders is not surprising.
15. See Alborn, *Conceiving Companies*, pp. 127–9 and sources cited therein.
16. Hilton and Searle make this point (see notes 1 and 2 above).
17. Ludlow, *The Joint-Stock Companies Winding-Up Act, 1848 ... with an Introduction, Notes, Practical Directions, Notes on Cases, and an Appendix of Forms* (London: V. and R. Stevens and G.S. Norton, 1849), p. xxvi.
18. Ludlow, *The Joint-Stock Companies Winding-Up Act*, 1848, p. xxv. Eldon's leading decision in this regard came in *Van Sandau v. Moore* (1826), which left open the gap created by the repeal of the Bubble Act in 1825. In repealing that Act (which had outlawed unchartered joint-stock companies) without writing a new enabling statute, Lord Liverpool had essentially left the fate of the large-scale company up to the judges. See Ron Harris, *Industrializing English Law: Entrepreneurship and Business Organization, 1720–1844* (Cambridge: Cambridge University Press, 2000), chs 9–10.
19. Ludlow, *The Joint-Stock Companies Winding-Up Act, 1848*, pp. xxvi, xxx–xxxi.
20. V. Markham Lester, *Victorian Insolvency: Bankruptcy, Imprisonment for Debt, and Company Winding-Up in Nineteenth-Century England* (Oxford: Clarendon Press, 1995), p. 223.
21. An Act accompanying 1844 Companies Act (7 & 8 Vict. c.111) had stipulated that 'the bankruptcy of a company could be handled in the same manner as that of an individual'; it 'did not limit the creditors' rights to proceed against individual shareholders': *Ibid.*, p. 223.
22. *Ibid.*, p. 224.
23. See *Report of the Select Committee on Savings of the Middle and Working Classes* (*British Parliamentary Papers* 1850, XIX), q. 36; Ludlow, *The Joint Stock Companies Winding-Up Amendment Act, 1849* (London: V. and R. Stevens and G.S. Norton, 1850), p. xxxii.
24. Ludlow, *The Joint Stock Companies Winding-Up Amendment Act, 1849*, pp. xxx, xxxiii; *Report ... on Savings of the Middle and Working Classes*, q. 29.
25. As it happened, new company laws would provide the option of limited liability to such investors within a decade; and the Companies Act in 1862 included winding-up provisions that brought Ludlow's goals for corporate governance substantially forward: see Lester, *Victorian Insolvency*, p. 226.

26. Ludlow, *The Joint-Stock Companies Winding-Up Act, 1848*, p. lv.
27. *Ibid.*, pp. xlv, xliv.
28. Ludlow, 'On the Mercantile Notion of "the Firm", and the Need of its Legal Recognition' (1857), *Juridical Society Papers* 2 (1863), pp. 57–8, 54.
29. *Hansard's Parliamentary Debates*, 3rd ser., 140 (1856), col. 133; 143 (1856), col. 360.
30. Freedeman, *Joint-Stock Enterprise*, p. 132.
31. *Report ... on Savings of the Middle and Working Classes*, qs. 165, 173.
32. Lowe did not go so far as to retain the feature of the *société en commandite par actions* that forbade shareholders from participating in corporate governance, but neither did he promote shareholder democracy as a likely benefit of his Companies Acts.
33. Freedeman, *Joint-Stock Enterprise*, pp. 135–9.
34. 'Science of partnership' is from Ludlow's article on 'The Great Partnership' in *Politics for the People* (1848; New York: Augustus M. Kelly, 1971), p. 273.
35. I refer to this society below as the SPWMA to conserve space, although it did not last long enough to earn the status of a recognizable acronym.
36. Friesen, 'The Man Behind the Prophet', pp. 352–82; Philip L. Cottrell, *Industrial Finance 1830–1914: The Finance and Organization of English Manufacturing Industry* (London: Methuen, 1980), pp. 48–9; Philip N. Backstrom, *Christian Socialism and Co-operation in Victorian England: Edward Vansittart Neale and the Co-operative Movement* (London: Croom Helm, 1974).
37. N.C. Masterman, *John Malcolm Ludlow: The Builder of Christian Socialism* (Cambridge: Cambridge University Press, 1963), pp. 95–6; Christensen, *Origin and History of Christian Socialism*, pp. 130–42.
38. Friesen, 'The Man Behind the Prophet', p. 358; Christensen, *Origin and History of Christian Socialism*, pp. 131–2.
39. Christensen, *Origin and History of Christian Socialism*, pp. 144–7.
40. Gosden, *Self-Help*, pp. 64–7.
41. *Report ... on Savings of the Middle and Working Classes*, q. 9; Gosden, *Self-Help*, pp. 192–3. See also Simon Cordery, *British Friendly Societies, 1750–1914* (London: Palgrave Macmillan, 2003), ch. 3.
42. Ludlow had earlier diagnosed the 'Condition of England' in terms of the two distinct problems of alienated workers in London and inhumane employers in the industrial North: see 'Labour and the Poor', *Fraser's Magazine* 41 (1850), pp. 2–3.
43. *Report ... on Savings of the Middle and Working Classes*, q. 26; Ludlow, *Christian Socialism and its Opponents* (London, 1851), 54. This sticking point was related to a further dispute regarding the merits of the commandite system, which Ludlow derided as 'Mr. Slaney's special hobby': *The Autobiography of a Christian Socialist* (London: Frank Cass, 1981), p. 195.
44. *Hansard*, 3rd ser., 139 (1855), col. 1919; *Report ... on Savings of the Middle and Working Classes*, qs. 88, 104–5, 245.
45. 'Laws of Partnership and Principles of Co-operation', *Law Magazine* 44 (1850), pp. 212–13; *Parliamentary Papers* 1854 (27), pp. 169–70; Greg, *Essays on Political and Social Science* (London: Longman, Brown, Green, and Longmans, 1853), pp. 435, 433, 453; Mill, *Collected Works* (Toronto: University of Tornto Press, 1967–86), VI, p. 487. On Mill see Donna Loftus, 'Capital and Community: Limited Liability and Attempts to Democratize the Market in Mid-Nineteenth-Century England', *Victorian Studies* 45 (2002), pp. 101–2.

46. Potter, *Practical Opinions against Partnership with Limited Liability* (London, 1855), p. 9; *Hansard*, 3rd ser., 139 (1855), col. 2029.
47. Peter Gurney, *Co-operative Culture and the Politics of Consumption in England, 1870–1930* (Manchester: Manchester Univesity Press, 1996), pp. 150–3.
48. On the exclusion of working-class co-operatives from subsequent Parliamentary inquiries into limited liability (the 1854 Mercantile Law Commission and the Commons debates on the 1856 and 1862 Companies Acts) see Loftus, 'Capital and Community', 103–9.
49. Backstrom, *Christian Socialism and Co-operation*, pp. 32–4.
50. Friesen, 'The Man behind the Prophet', pp. 376–80, 388–92.
51. For an example of Ludlow's difficulties with his superior see Lord Northcote's complaint to Ludlow, 7 May 1876 (Ludlow Papers 11/66, Cambridge University Library), that it was 'impossible for the Treasury, without great inconvenience, to specially authorise classes of societies in such minute terms as you propose ... the distinction is too fine to be drawn in describing the "purposes" of a loan society'. See also Gosden, *Self-Help*, pp. 81, 86.
52. Backstrom, *Christian Socialism and Co-operation*, pp. 6–8.
53. Ludlow to Maurice, April 1851, cited in Friesen, 'The Man Behind the Prophet', pp. 369–70.
54. J.M. Merriman, *The Agony of the Republic: The Repression of the Left in Revolutionary France 1848–1851* (New Haven, CT: Yale University Press, 1978), pp. 67–80.
55. J.M. Baernreither, cited in Martin Purvis, 'Societies of Consumers and Consumer Societies: Co-operation, Consumption and Politics in Britain and Continental Europe *c.* 1850–1920', *Journal of Historical Geography* 24 (1998), p. 148.
56. Mill to Furnivall, 19 November 1850, in Mill, *Collected Works*, XIV, p. 50.
57. See, for example, E.P. Hennock, 'Concepts of Poverty in the British Social Surveys from Charles Booth to Arthur Bowley', in M. Bulmer, K. Bales and K.K. Sklar (eds.), *The Social Survey in Historical Perspective 1880–1940* (Cambridge: Cambridge University Press, 1991), pp. 189–216; George W. Stocking, *Victorian Anthropology* (New York: Free Press, 1988), pp. 92–6; Stefan Collini, *Liberalism and Sociology: L.T. Hobhouse and Political Argument in England 1880–1914* (Cambridge: Cambridge University Press, 1979).
58. This theme is argued for Britain and other Western European countries in Peter Baldwin, *The Politics of Social Solidarity: Class Bases of the European Welfare State 1875–1975* (Cambridge: Cambridge University Press, 1990).
59. *Politics for the People*, p. 273; Baldwin, *Politics of Social Solidarity*, 3. On the late nineteenth century Christian Socialists see, for example, Paul T. Phillips. *A Kingdom on Earth: Anglo-American Social Christianity, 1880–1940* (University Park, PA: Pennsylvania University Press, 1996).
60. On the contrast between 'abstract' (or actuarial) and 'qualitative' mutuality see François Ewald, 'Insurance and Risk', in G. Burchell *et al.* (ed.), *The Foucault Effect* (Chicago: University of Chicago Press, 1991), pp. 203–4.
61. See, for instance, Jonathan Boswell, *Community and the Economy: The Theory of Public Co-operation* (London: Routledge, 1990); David G. Green, *Reinventing Civil Society: The Rediscovery of Welfare Without Politics* (London: IEH Health and Welfare Unit, 1993).

6
'Provident' Political Economy in Indian Forests

E.G. Reisz

India's Victorian British rulers were mostly in little doubt that their rule was beneficent. Historians, however, have increasingly viewed this judgement with scepticism, seeing the Raj rather as a device for extracting the natural and labouring wealth of India and transferring a surplus to British taxpayers. While the harsh judgement of historians does not logically entail hypocrisy on the part of nineteenth-century civil servants, it does create a problem for the student of historical political economy. How should we understand the intentions of a ruling regime whose representatives frequently pontificated about their commitment to developing the wealth of India for its people but whose actions seem entirely at variance with this? Should we see their observations as self-serving propaganda, and concentrate on reconstructing a political economy of praxis, in which the rhetoric of empire is relevant only as an ancillary cultural expression of the hegemony of the real political-economic system? This chapter suggests that the answer should be no, proposing that it is neither possible nor necessary to separate the discourse and practice of political economy in the years after the Rebellion of 1857. It is true that the employment of the political economy of the Raj varied with circumstances, as administrators considered their freedom of action to be restricted by the necessity to preserve local political stability. Moreover, official political economy evolved piecemeal and developed over time. Nonetheless it was strong enough to bind together the disparate groups involved in the administration of the subcontinent, and significant enough to form the central battleground for the internecine struggles which occurred within the bureaucracy. The unifying role played by this philosophy of governance was significant from a sociological point of view, but the reverse is also true; it was through the experience of governing, and indeed through reflexive consideration of the performance of governance, that the political economy of the Raj took shape.

To reconstruct in detail the process by which the political economy of the British administration in India matured as the mixed-race offspring of a liberal education and of a century exercising imperial power, this chapter concentrates on the regulation of Indian forests. Over the second half of the nineteenth century, fragmentary local forest regulation was supplanted by an India-wide system of government control of forest resources through a series of legislative measures and the creation of a forest department. For the Raj and its subjects alike, the apparently obscure area of forestry law was in fact a key factor in the relationship between government and rural communities, as from 1865 the government acquired effective ownership of huge swathes of India's vast forests. By 1881 the Forest Department directly controlled 12 per cent of British India, and had influence over more than half of the rest.[1] Sweeping changes in the permitted use of forest resources brought the state into contact, and often conflict, with many remote communities upon whom British rule had previously had little impact. The state's role increased substantially in villages bordering the reserved forests, as government became entangled in local village affairs, acquired decisive control of the economically significant forestry sector, and compromised customary private property rights. The impact of all this legislation on villagers was so severe that in 1891 at Nagpur, the generally polite Indian National Congress called for the implementation of the Forestry Laws to be rethought, to 'render it less obnoxious to the poorer classes'.[2]

Two principal models exist for understanding forest legislation. Government claimed that appropriation was necessary to conserve forests, since more modest regulation would not protect them, and this analysis has received some support from historians. Richard Grove's suggestion of 'green imperialism' imputed to administrators a visceral enthusiasm to preserve tropical nature. Grove posits that the Indian government was motivated by a desire to prevent deforestation, forming part of a wider physiocratic pursuit of environmental harmony, or 'the attempt to reconcile the human ecological impact with the laws of nature'.[3] However for most historians of India, following and simplifying Ramachandra Guha and Madhav Gadgil, forest regulation was rent-seeking of the most self-evident kind. On this argument, the Indian government restricted and increasingly monopolized access to forest land in order to benefit financially and commercially from its position of control, through 'the production of large commercial timber and the generation of revenue'.[4] On this interpretation, resources which villagers had utilized for years were seized from them purely so that the colonial power could then lease the use-rights back to local communities. The scanty cash surplus of Indian villagers was thus further eaten into by the government, which ultimately diverted some of its revenue to British taxpayers through the Home Charges paid by Calcutta to London and other instruments. Underlying the debate remains a sense, as S. Ravi Rajan puts it, that many scholars consider Grove's argument to be 'a form of British neo-colonial revivalism', though such views are rarely expressed in print.[5] Support for both the conservationist and the rent-seeking analysis can be found in the documents of the Indian government: to oversimplify, British naturalists and scientific enthusiasts were enthusiastic about biodiversity, while the Raj's administrators were keen to secure maximal profits, as several historians have shown. Nonetheless both groups worked together in a broadly harmonious manner for the last 90 years of British administration in the subcontinent. As such, prolonged discussion of which was 'really' the dominant impulse of British governance is something of a distraction. Any such alliance of interests could not survive in an institutional setting as a marriage of convenience alone. Certainly scientific foresters were useful to Calcutta for their practical skills and their claim on the sensibilities of a portion of the British elite. However, their working relationship came to be cemented by a political-economic conception of the world in which there was much upon which both parties could agree.

Mention of the political economy of the British in India instantly brings to mind utilitarianism and liberalism. The intimacy of the relationship between the East India Company and both James and John Stuart Mill makes that inevitable. Less often remembered is the role of Haileybury, the Company's training college, as a centre of the teaching and discussion of political economy in the first half of the nineteenth century.[6] However the manner in which the Indian government came to control so much of India's hardwood resources, competing unfairly with private traders, sat uncomfortably with liberal distaste for government interference in trade. Two methodological approaches have had particular appeal for historians approaching the relationship between governmental practice and theory in India. On the one hand, Eric Stokes, following Elie Halévy's analysis of the development of utilitarian thought, suggested that the experience of governing an empire corrupted a purer British liberalism into a utilitarianism run through with authoritarianism.[7] Though other authors have suggested that Stokes overemphasized the policy overlap between Britain and India, underestimated the extent to which the increasing role of authority in utilitarian thought remained in the eyes of thinkers a concession to pragmatism rather than an intellectual conversion, or ignored the tenuous nature of the commitment of early utilitarianism to liberalism *per se*, his analysis has retained appeal. Homi Bhabha has argued that 'for Mill the boundaries of the national culture are open so long as the voices of dissent remain individual and closed when that culture is threatened by collective dissension'; in other words liberalism can only thrive where there is broad agreement about overriding cultural values, a lesson which Bhabha suggests Mill learned at East India House.[8] Latterly attempts to reconcile theory and practice have concentrated on the increasingly bureaucratic culture of Victorian administration. For many, the value of Grove's 'green imperialism' lies in its 'ideology of command', providing legitimation for the reality of resource extraction, with conservation and forest exploitation acquiring prominence together as the two faces of the same historico-economic process.[9] By emphasizing the special claims made by and for scientific knowledge, this argument can be extended from the eighteenth-century context principally considered by Grove, emphasizing the economy of natural law, to the very different climate of the mid-nineteenth century. (It should be noted in passing that this step has been omitted from much of the historiography, which follows Grove in eliding the differences between the two.) In its invocation of power/knowledge, there is a heavy debt to Foucault in much of this historiography, not always made explicit.

Yet forest policy seems to direct attention to conceptual problems inherent in late utilitarian liberalism, which became obvious when the philosophy was removed from the particular social context in which it evolved. The place of these themes in imperial governance has been explored by Uday Singh Mehta and others writing about 'liberal strategies of exclusion'.[10] It can be argued that the apparent tension between liberalism and imperialism was no tension at all, due to the subjectivity of ideas such as reason and progress. If social ends are regarded as truly subjective, then individuals themselves are the only ones who can maximize their own good. The idea that any government can claim its political economy is based on consideration of the good of each distinct individual seems profoundly flawed. Instead individuals are considered within groups, and governmental perceptions of the interests of the populace may differ substantially from the views expressed by the people themselves.

This was not an abstract philosophical point. When thrown into relief by the colonial environment its effects were glaringly and repeatedly obvious to imperial administrators. Particularly in the absence of a true political process to pursue social consensus, the contrast between the social reasoning of the colonizer and the colonized seemed vast. In order to maintain any semblance of intellectual coherence, the British Raj had to generate a political value system which privileged the value judgements of the colonizer. Crucial in this was the notion of rationality. A capacity for rational thought was understood by economists to be necessary for any individual to be capable of securing his or her own political and economic freedom if protected by liberal policy alone.[11] By extension, incapacity for rationality was sufficient not just to leave an individual needing special protection (or restriction) under the law, but also to render that individual's assessment of value open to question. The fact that so much of the difference could be explained by reference to the differential incentives generated by the politico-economic structures of colonialism was then often allowed conveniently to slip from view. Having created an intellectual system which appeared to respect subjective value but actually undermined those decision-making processes which generated divergent concepts of utility, the Raj was in no hurry to suggest that the intellectual processes of Indians were not so different from those of Britons after all. The almost surreal quality of this intellectual manoeuvre should not distract from an assessment of its political potency. The rapid waning of Mill's authority in the wider British public sphere produced by the expansion of academic political economy in the 1870s was accompanied by a highly successful, if less intellectually rigorous, challenge in the Indian administration from a homespun practical philosophy.

While the logic required to justify the expansion of government economic control was convoluted, the factors pushing the British administration in India towards forest regulation by the 1850s were not in themselves obscure. Deforestation had been a matter of major concern since the 1840s and thought responsible for provoking famines. Forest inspectors had been appointed in Bombay and Madras, and demand for timber for railways was rising, particularly in India. Moreover the loss of habitat and the potential effect on biodiversity were making botanists nervous. Forest conservancy was also becoming increasingly professionalized and foresters increasingly articulate. Germany had possessed a tradition of scientific forestry since the early nineteenth century, complementing France's more statist approach.[12] Germany's technological prowess was already seen by the 1850s in many areas of public life as a threat to Britain's supremacy. Successfully introduced in Burma by the East India Company, the extension of forest regulation to India was a natural move for the Company's Whitehall successor. Forestry fitted within the main tendency of post-Rebellion policy, seeming largely politically unobjectionable. Forest conservation sounded sensible and scientific, had clear financial benefits to the government and to British industry, seemed like public works for the good of all, promised to be self-funding, and involved challenging head-on only forest dwellers and marginal villagers, groups which the government thought it could challenge without courting the disaster precipitated by agricultural land reform.

Uniting these different concerns was the sense that the Raj could distinguish itself from, and oppose itself to, Indian ecological practices, British ideas about which reflected what has been called the 'myth of the environmentally profligate native'.[13] Responses to economic change varied, and might include decisions which reduced the long-term viability of a particular environmental source of revenue, or even of an entire ecosystem. European scientific and administrative experts in this period laid two separate specific accusations of environmental profligacy at the door of agriculturalists. One, which was not confined to non-Europeans but which was addressed also to the sturdy British farmer, was that of ignorance. Indian and other colonial agriculturists were regarded as a particular challenge for those who wanted to change agricultural practices, due to the supposed economic stagnation in which they were believed to have lived for centuries. The second complaint, which partially contradicted the first, was that of improvidence with natural resources, an allegation levelled far less by Europeans at their own countrymen. On the contrary, Europeans understood that rapid environmental change was often the result of economic growth. Domestic disaster would be avoided by exporting the necessity for environmental prudence to other parts of the world. Britain had already cleared substantial tracts of domestic forest by the early modern period, and by the eighteenth century the shortage of hardwood for shipbuilding was becoming acute.[14]

However, amid the industrial revolution there was no enthusiasm to embark upon serious reforestation in Britain. In 1791, Dr Thomas Preston informed the Land Revenue Commission that timber yields were declining, but that 'for Royal Navies, countries yet barbarous are the only right and proper nurseries'.[15] This process could clearly not go on indefinitely. By the mid-nineteenth century Canadian, Indian and Australian forests had been substantially depleted for general land clearance, but more specifically their hardwood supplies were being rapidly eroded for shipbuilding.[16] Teak supplies from India took off after 1812 for shipbuilding, and continued to be used in the plate backing of ironclad ships even after the end of wooden capital shipbuilding in 1861.[17]

Moreover, even while wood was giving way to iron in ships, teak was being used in increasing quantities for the railway sleepers needed for the Indian railway system after 1853.[18] The demand for teak for British warships had been a comparatively minor concern for the Government in Calcutta. By contrast obtaining hardwoods and other timbers for the railways took high priority, since infrastructural growth seemed crucial to securing the political and financial position of the Raj. After 'devastating its own woods', Britain carried out a 'fierce onslaught' on India's forests before realizing that teak supplies were under threat there as well.[19] However it was Indian farmers, especially those practising shifting cultivation, who were singled out for criticism. Shifting cultivation was seen increasingly as, to quote one revenue official in 1847, a practice 'of so wasteful and improvident a nature that it appears to me it ought not to be tolerated except in a very wild and unpeopled country'.[20] The (probably correct) British perception of an expansion in shifting cultivation mid-century gave the lie to the notion of Indian society as static and unchanging, but was rarely conceived in this way.

The charge of improvidence was not a universal conservationist one but rather one specific to particular physical and economic environments. Forests were perceived, as Preston had implied, as an impediment to progress. They prevented land being used for more lucrative purposes. Over a century after Preston, Berthold Ribbentrop, who served as Inspector-General of Forests in India, could still write in 1900 that forests were 'an obstruction to agriculture and consequently a bar to the prosperity of the Empire'.[21] The end could justify the forest-felling means. Above all, then, natives were 'profligate' because their cost-benefit analysis did not match that of Europeans. One suggested explanation for this discrepancy was that non-Europeans were simply incapable of predicting and comparing the impact of various courses of action; that non-Europeans were not capable of rationality, whether because of a lack of education and an inappropriate social context, or whether due to some congenital incapacity. Shifting cultivators were frequently referred to in this way. One official wrote as early as 1820 of one group of *kumri* cultivators that they were 'a miserable class of human beings ... [of] their present state of incivilization ... no melioration can be attempted with a prospect of good resulting therefrom'.[22] The linguistic and cultural differences between some groups of shifting cultivators and surrounding populations led many Britons to describe them in racial terms, remarking on 'non-Aryan' Tamil, Telugu and Kanarese peoples who were 'contributing nothing for the support of themselves and others; indeed, most of them are predatory'. The suggestion emerged that they could be moved into unoccupied parts of Burma rather than leaving them 'pressing into Assam to obtain culturable [sic] lands and a milder climate'.[23] Not all administrators had so little hope, however. In 1858 W. Fisher wrote that while 'want of capital, and the ease with which a man who possesses nothing but a strong knife and a good arm can obtain a living ... will prevent anything but a gradual change ..., I am satisfied that that change has already commenced, and that a more settled mode of life and more regular habits will spring from it'.[24] On this view, while the Mutiny had reduced the optimism of Europeans about how far Macaulay's aspiration to create Indian Englishmen could be extended through the ranks of Indian society, some administrators still hoped that shifting cultivators could be elevated to the tradition-bound but nevertheless preferable level of wider Indian society.

While doubts remained in British minds about the capacity of most individual Indians to exhibit rationality, the solution to 'improvident' forest use could not be a Benthamite alignment of personal and public interests. One question for administrators was whether Indian 'traditions' could be harnessed to good effect. The view that even well behaved villagers were more influenced by social norms than by self-interest was a powerful one. Henry Maine stressed this point in his 1861 *Ancient Law*, remarking that any legal institution in India 'will seldom be found to have entirely cast aside the shell in which it was originally reared'.[25] The common currency of this belief sometimes led to labyrinthine logic. Robertson of the Coimbatore Government Farms was optimistic that Hindus could be encouraged to 'plant groves as acts of merit', a long-standing practice with obvious religious and social significance.[26] In other words Hindus could be persuaded of their political-economic duty by couching it in the kind of appeal to religious sensibility which the British thought Indians found more intelligible. Intriguingly, Robertson himself seems, like many administrators working with small communities, to have dressed up his own more nuanced views to meet the prejudices of his masters. He went on to suggest that the locals themselves agreed that rainfall had been diminishing and thought that tree planting would be a helpful response. Since an appeal to faith in Indian rationality would likely have fallen on deaf Calcutta and London ears, it was not made. Robertson's reference to an apparent 'ancient tradition' was more likely to inspire general British confidence. However this alleged enthusiasm for tradition was thought to lead to reluctance to modernize agricultural techniques, creating the overuse of resources about which British officials were anxious.

A futher reason for Indians neglecting their self-interest, as Europeans perceived it, was the view that non-Europeans applied excessive discounts to future prosperity. The effect of uncertain property tenure on discounting was well-understood, even if its implications in the context of colonial renegotiation of property rights was usually neglected. James Mill's *History of India* had made this point, and although by mid-century it was understood that he had been wrong about indigenous property holding patterns, the theme remained in the literature.[27] Writers were also aware of the difficulties of saving where there was little surplus to begin with. However, socio-cultural explanations were placed alongside economic explanations, suggesting that Indian 'profligacy' was essentially a childlike disregard for the future. In the rubber forests of Assam, Indian franchisees and their tappers secured the latex 'without any regard ... for future supplies, which was of most disastrous consequence, in as far as it induced the men who tapped and collected the rubber to indulge in the most outrageous wholesale destruction of these valuable trees, by either felling them with axes, or, if this was too troublesome, to collect firewood and burn them down'.[28]

In all three cases, political-economic orthodoxy suggested that government had a clear right to intervene. John Stuart Mill had observed that 'the uncultivated cannot be competent judges of cultivation. Those who most need to be made wiser and better, usually desire it least'. In particular, for Mill, there would sometimes be an economic activity, of almost any imaginable sort, 'that the government should take upon itself, not because private individuals cannot effectually perform it, but because they will not'. The course of such failure might be the ignorance of 'uncultivation', or it might be poverty, or an incapacity for collective action.[29] The government, in such cases, would have to act as a capitalist of last resort, supplying the economic rationality which, for whatever reason, was not operating correctly through private channels. Shifting cultivation seemed so clearly wasteful of resources, and so inimical to the development of the institutions of social control (as Fisher had pointed out in his remarks of 1858) that its outlawing raised few dilemmas for liberals attached to the idea of social improvement, and was well underway by the 1840s. Marginal forest communities and particularly shifting cultivators had few allies. Attacks on their privileges posed little threat to the integrity of the state. Instead their unconventional behaviour seemed more dangerous to social stability if left unfettered, and attacks on shifting cultivation proceeded rapidly.[30] Shifting cultivation was also the focus of particular irritation to the British because of its effect on the availability of the forest as a public good. This pattern of resource use benefited a few people, but removed from the population in general the public good benefits which government believed well managed forest might have bestowed.

Public goods were in general an area in which government intervention was thought compatible with laissez-faire principles. A public good, defined as one for which the cost of provision does not depend on the number of consumers who benefit from it, and where it is not feasible to exclude those who do not pay from the benefit of the good, were well-understood by nineteenth-century economists. Adam Smith had acknowledged the existence of such goods, and Mill famously provided the example of the lighthouse later attacked by Ronald Coase.[31] Less well-remembered is the fact that the first example of a public good Mill gave in *Principles of Political Economy* was that of 'a voyage of geographical or scientific exploration'. The forest offered a number of public goods, which classical theory suggested would not be adequately valued by simple market methods, a proposition that appeared to be borne out by the pattern of deforestation. First, even within a classical economic framework, forests did retain a little Romantic mystique. The surgeon-naturalist Dr Alexander Gibson wrote in 1841 to Joseph Hooker, noted botanist and the son of the Director of Kew Gardens, that deforestation in the Deccan, was a matter 'for regret ... for the naturalist'.[32] Botanists still cherished the dream of uniting, if not all the world's species, at least a good proportion of them, in an Eden-like botanic garden.[33] They were not enthusiastic about the loss of biodiversity.

Rousseauan environmentalism cut little ice, however, with an Indian administration which repeatedly expressed concerns about botanic garden budgets throughout the nineteenth century, and which was prepared to concede only small amounts of money for the purposes of establishing its liberal credentials with domestic intellectuals.[34] It is in writings for scientific rather than public or official consumption that references to extinction and species loss primarily occurred, and on its own this argument would not have been sufficient reason to embark on a substantial forest regulation programme. A more effective spur to government commitment to the preservation of biodiversity was the view that currently worthless plants might prove to be profitable. As one Madras Presidency collector put it, it was necessary to conserve 'the value of those forests which if preserved might hereafter become a source of wealth to the people which they now do not dream of'.[35] As with wood supplies, local populations were thought likely to over-discount future gains, concentrating on a material present rather than a hypothetical future.

As a public good, forests interested administrators primarily through their effect on soils and climate. Forests had long been believed to reduce malaria by lowering temperatures.[36] By 1859, when an expensive cinchona importation scheme was being contemplated to supply quinine to India, alternative means of controlling the disease could not be discounted.[37] A more critical concern outside areas of European settlement, however, was desiccation and famine. Already by the 1840s the Raj was concerned about deforestation leading to aridity.[38] In an 1847 despatch, the Government of India was instructed by East India House to investigate whether such a pattern was indeed arising due to land clearance for agriculture, exacerbated by water diversion for irrigation. The Directors observed that 'the subject is one having a strong practical bearing on the welfare of mankind, and we are anxious to obtain extensive and accurate information in regard to it'.[39] After a rash of learned articles, particularly in the Indian press, at the 1850 meeting of the British Association for the Advancement of Science Dr Hugh Cleghorn instigated the establishment of a Committee to consider forest destruction in India.[40]

The argument that forests were a public good justified the acquisition of forests, but climate management was not the key determinant of policy. Hence in 1878, during the debate over the passing of the Indian Forest Act of that year, the Surgeon-General Edward Balfour produced a report *On the Influence Exercised by Trees on the Climate and Productiveness of the Peninsula of India*, arguing that deforestation contributed to mass famines such as that in South India the previous year. The 1878 Act was intended to make good the deficiencies of the 1865 Forest Act by bringing more forest land under the control of the state, but was highly controversial within the Indian administration.[41] Balfour concluded that while rainfall had neither diminished nor become more irregular, the lack of forest cover was resulting in more extreme effects from the same number of unusual weather events, topsoil loss and reduced water retention in the soils.[42] Deforestation was 'depriving the country of its conservative agents', Balfour concluded in a flourish of physiocratic rhetoric, but his colourful words stand out more because of their rarity by this late stage.[43]

Instead policy was driven not by forests as a clear public good but by forests as a source of factors of production for public goods. The first forests where substantial usage restrictions (as opposed to simply the abolition of shifting cultivation or a loose government claim to posses a teak monopoly) were introduced were those of Burma, a major supplier of teak. During the East India Company period, forest control was generally considered an unnecessary expense, despite mounting concerns about desiccation, but the management of teak was an exception to this. Teak, from 'countries yet barbarous', was needed for shipbuilding but demand was exceeding supply. Since the market was meeting the demand by eroding the viability of Burmese forests, resulting in deforestation, government intervention was seen to be necessary. A monopoly system had been introduced in Tenasserim in 1829 but had produced devastation in the teak forests rather than creating the anticipated security of tenure which would create a private incentive to cultivation. By 1839, Dr J.W. Helfer had concluded that 'a continuation of the same system will lead in a short time to the extermination of all available teak forests, and deprive Moulmein of this valuable resource'.[44] There was a brief attempt to extend teak licences sufficiently to make replanting attractive, but this was abandoned in favour of more direct government intervention.[45] Burma acquired a forest conservator for this purpose in the 1840s, and by 1848 the House of Commons had noticed the unusual steps being taken there.[46] In the newly conquered province of Pegu, teak was determined to be government property immediately upon conquest at the end of 1852. By the time of Governor-General Dalhousie's famous memorandum of 1855, usually taken to mark the beginning of Indian forest conservation, government was aiming not merely to claim but to exercise ownership rights over all teak in the province.[47] While internal debate raged about the degree to which administrators should monopolize trade, which was a sensitive subject for the Company, the right of the government to place at the centre of policy its own need for teak, and that of the British state, was hardly disputed by officials.

After 1857 the attempt by government to manipulate, control and monopolize access to wood as a factor of production required more complex reasoning. Although the Rebellion focused British attention on government's essential functions, it also confirmed that attacks on liberties currently enjoyed had to be very thoroughly justified, if only to calm the anxieties of Anglo-Indians themselves. The period which led up to the 1865 Indian Forest Act exemplified both of these processes. That British discourse would be grounded in classical rather than physiocratic economic thinking was established in two 1862 despatches confirming that the government would be adopting a more interventionist policy in Indian forests. The argument of these despatches relied on the ambiguity of liberal statements about the basis upon which the individual possesses rights within the polity. Determining that an Indian, or group of Indians, were 'profligate' implied that they were economically incapable, and legitimated removing their economic rights. However, the despatches deployed this standard imperial line in an unusual way. Sidelining the (by now substantial) literature on deforestation which referred to individual irrationality, the Indian Government suggested that there were in fact 'no conceivable circumstances' under which it would be rational for an individual to pursue forest conservation. 'The length of time required for maturing a growth of timber is so great that no individual can have a personal interest in doing more than realising the largest possible present amount from any forest tract of which he may get possession.'[48] This was a prudent argument for the government to adopt, since the franchisees in Burma and elsewhere had included Europeans who had shown no more inclination than Indians or Burmese to replant felled forest. Yet this line of discussion threatened to raise concerns about the behaviour of business in any laissez-faire context, anywhere. In order to avoid this implication, Calcutta was able to reapportion the blame back to Indians through some intricate argument. Individuals could indeed have very little personal interest in planting the most slow-growing hardwoods, especially teak, unless they were confident that property rights would pass down the family for almost a century. Their interest in replanting softwoods was not much greater because of the propensity for freeriding; softwood use for fuel, household purposes and so on proved difficult for government to control, and was almost impossible for individuals to restrict, even those with secure tenure.

Calcutta implied, though, that in European countries social conventions existed to defend the categorical imperative in these sorts of situations against unscrupulousness, and to secure the well-being of future generations. Social structures should be responsible for ensuring that conservancy was perceived as a moral duty by citizens and business. Communities, though not individuals, did have a rational reason not to discount substantially future benefits when calculating what was in their interest. As the Secretary of State wrote in reply, they ought to 'prevent the destruction of forests, and hand them down in such quantity and conditions as to leave a due supply for future generations'.[49] However the Governor-General continued '... the moral or social restraints that are likely to operate to prevent such a course [destruction] are most especially wanting in India'.[50] This was not due to a lack of community institutions; Maine had drawn attention only the previous year to communal landholding patterns, and J.S. Mill had acknowledged his father's error in neglecting their importance.[51] It was, though, these village communities which increasingly seemed to be responsible for the failures perceived in forest, as opposed to land, management. Not individuals but entire communities were being accused of environmental profligacy.

The racial element of the argument, then, applied at the level of communities as well. Through this tortured logic, the administration was able to suggest that tradition (which the new India Office had made a clear commitment to attempt to respect, however incomprehensible it seemed to the British) was simultaneously rooted in the ancient habits of India, namely poor economic rationality, and plunging India into an unprecedented environmental crisis. The simple explanation for this, that Indian conventions were not sufficient to defend against a rapidly encroaching and increasingly greedy global market for timber or against the economic and social dislocations provoked by British rule, was not mentioned. Instead, with forests as with empire generally, the British were able to argue themselves into a corner where they appeared to be forced to shoulder the burden. 'It requires the stability of a settled administration ... A Permanent Government only can be expected to wait long enough to reap the profit obtainable from articles which it takes eighty or an hundred years to bring to maturity. Permanency, as far as it can be obtained, is therefore of the highest importance in any arrangement for the administration of Forests ... Individuals cannot be relied upon for due care in the management of the Forests.'[52]

Locating moral responsibility for long-term economic planning with social communities rather than individuals was significant in three ways. First, the perceived failure of communities to provide for their people gave imperialism an apparently sensible and indeed moral basis, grounded in racial ideas, without compromising liberal optimism about the perfectibility of any particular individual, or of any group of individuals in general. It was structures, rather than people, which were fatally flawed – a distinction which created a rationale for the policy in the 1860s which would be acceptable to those who found the hardening of racial attitudes distasteful. Second, it was bound into a notion of economic and social behaviour with strongly statist implications. Here, too, is found an explanation for the apparently bizarre dualism in the rhetoric of Britons about many communities in the empire. Imperial subjects were both the sinners and the sinned against: sinners for creating improvident social structures, but sinned against, for being deprived of the environment in which they could acquire the moral skills taught by a benevolent authority, or enjoy its benefits. Finally this exchange is important for the extent to which concerns were raised about the protection of forest resources from European agents.[53] Even while African policy focused on the hopes for 'legitimate commerce', the Indian experience was finding limits to the civilizing capacity of commerce.[54] The Governor-General had been careful to include Europeans in his 1862 remarks, writing, 'whether we deal with natives of the country or European settlers ... we think that the idea of giving a proprietary right in forest to any individual should be abandoned, as the possession of such a right is almost certain to lead to the destruction of the forest'.[55]

On the colonial frontier, detached from the European cultural environment, white business became to colonial administrators indistinguishable in its improvidence from local economic interests. Indeed, shorn of its proper social and legal setting, white capital was seen not simply as no better than indigenous communities, but as an active cause of the sort of social chaos which led to deforestation. Although the Indian government chose not to make this point in these documents, it arose naturally out of this line of logic, and became one aspect of a fear of unfair exploitation which by the twentieth century was institutionalized outside India into colonial policies of indirect rule, 'trusteeship' and protective administration.[56]

A further important line of debate in these documents was the subject of a disagreement between London and Calcutta. Having established that a new forest administration was needed, and having laid the intellectual groundwork for new legislation, the Indian Government suggested that forest administration be transferred to the Public Works Department.[57] This would have the effect of bringing forest administration together with its principal public customer, the railways. Adopting this policy would have been a clear indication that the government would attempt to justify its increasing control of teak through a reference to a public good, although the argument outlined above gave Calcutta scope to justify its control of the forests much more broadly. However, the proposal that the Forests should be transferred to the PWD met with India Office resistance on the grounds that it was an unnecessary change; the creation of a free-standing Forest department (which was done from 1867 to 1878) would secure the interests of forests without the need for upheaval. A second, and more telling, line of argument was that 'the products of the soil naturally come under the Revenue Department'.[58] The Secretary of State acknowledged that to set up a forest department 'an outlay may now be necessary in many instances, and, where necessary, should, I think, be incurred'. However there was a hefty silver lining to the clouds of alleged moral responsibility. He continued, 'I firmly believe that a considerable profit will be derived from the forests, when permanently placed under experienced and careful management ... it is another advantage of a permanent administration that it will look forward with certainty to the repayment of such an outlay in future years.'[59]

Charles Phillimore, the author of the relevant minute rejecting the suggestion of PWD superintendence, was the scion of a family of reforming Indian administrators, and understood that forest conservancy was not being contemplated simply in order to secure teak supplies or to preserve the climate, or even to change the habits of shifting cultivators, desirable as all of those ends seemed. The government had succeeded in producing an argument which appeared to demonstrate that an entire economic sector could not function through the agency of private enterprise, or be regulated by local communities. The only economic actor combining rationality with thought for the future was the government. The rest of the economic terrain was apparently empty, leaving the government as the capitalist of last resort. In short, the government had demonstrated, on principles which owed a great deal to classical economic thought, that its only sensible course of action was the diametric opposite of *laissez-faire*: to nationalize the forests. However the determination of complete market failure did not resolve the question of what government should use its powers to achieve. Faced with a new intellectual playground, Phillimore and Clements Markham embarked upon the two major projects which epitomized British imperial interference in forest markets in the last half of the nineteenth century: the attempt to bring cinchona to India in the 1860s, and to bring South American rubber to India in the 1870s. For Markham, the private sector could not be trusted to run even plantations in a truly rational manner. The laws of supply and demand could apparently be subverted as easily as the necessity of conservation, deprived of a familiar competitive environment. Markham argued that private quinine plantations needed government competition, at least at first, to ensure that they produced for volume, and did not aim simply for price.[60]

Scientist-foresters were never so concerned with maximizing the production of forest products, but the formula which had been hit upon allowed them to work effectively within the administrative structures of British India nonetheless. There remained areas of disagreement. Particularly prior to the 1878 Act, scientists more worried about forest area rather than about hardwood yield remained concerned that climatic concerns would not be addressed by teak conservation. As early as 1850 Dr Robert Wight had pointed out that climate control required the quickest growing trees rather than the best quality hardwood, and that these two aims of forest policy could only be reconciled in a mixed forest.[61] Balfour complained in 1878 that hardwood had won out, and that replanting 'seems not to have had in view the regulation of the rainfall'. Meanwhile many foresters were dissatisfied with the pace of conservation. It is conspicuous that many senior foresters in the 1860s, 1870s and 1880s were German, as the Forest Department had been established on German foundations.[62] The Germans were distinguished by their technical competence and by their enthusiasm for regulation. They voiced, like Gustav Mann quoted above, complaints about native profligacy with as much frequency as any Briton. It was through the condemnation of Indian irrationality that German scientific foresters were able to talk most persuasively to British gentleman-amateur administrators.

This chapter has tried to show that those engaged in the imperial venture in India were united not simply by a British enthusiasm for conquest, but by a complex collection of broadly, if not universally, shared ideas about the nature of a functioning competitive market, and the social and racial ideologies intertwined with the understanding of reason so crucial to a rationalist political economy. The British administration frequently prided itself on standing above the petty squabbles of interest groups, a self-image institutionalized in the later nineteenth century emphasis on the 'competition wallah' and the cult of amateurism by which administrators were supposed to be brilliant but also increasingly detached from Indian society, and even from Anglo-Indian interests.[63] As such it turned the Platonic ideal of a dictatorship of philosophers into a precursor of Lionel Robbins' rational decision-maker, allegedly uniquely qualified by independence from vested interests to reach decisions about ends.[64] However, this emphasis on a detached situation justified a conceptualization of global economic efficiency in which three sets of preoccupation, namely the need for hardwood for government projects, the need for it for imperial business, and an emphasis on the very long term and minimal discounting of future benefits, were portrayed as demonstrably superior. Sound logical reasons for privileging localism, such as the limited abilities of the global market to deliver efficiency benefits to remote nineteenth-century communities, and for discounting future benefits in view of the enormous opportunity cost of forgoing village timber access, were sidelined. In this sense, the language of rationalism was run through with a commitment to the global structures which benefited imperial powers and those with good access to international markets. As Chinua Achebe observed of literature, 'the word universal ... [has been] a synonym for the narrow, self-serving parochialism of Europe'.[65] The use by governmental agents of a language emphasizing self-evident universal truths displaced discussion from ends to means, from politics to technocracy. Gyan Prakash has argued for the enduring importance to Indian society of this approach to science.[66] The importance of this strategy in the sensitive area of controlling the distribution of imperial resources was just as considerable, and it supplied the political basis of the specific policies of scientific interventionism, without which the complaints of both scientists and business could have come to nothing.

Notes

1. Berthold Ribbentrop, *Forestry in British India* (Calcutta: Office of the Superintendent of Government Printing, 1900), p. 121.
2. A. Moin Zaidi (ed.), *Inc, the Glorious Tradition: Texts of the Resolutions Passed by the INC, the AICC, and the CWC*, vol. 1: 1885–1920 (New Delhi: Indian Institute of Applied Political Research, 1987), pp. 66–7, 71.
3. Richard Grove, *Green Imperialism: Colonial Expansion, Tropical Island Edens and the Origins of Environmentalism, 1600–1860* (Cambridge: Cambridge University Press, 1995), p. 481.
4. Ramachandra Guha and Madhav Gadgil, *This Fissured Land: An Ecological History of South Asia* (Delhi: Oxford University Press, 1992), p. 140.
5. S. Ravi Rajan, 'The Ends of Environmental History: Some Questions', *Environment and History* 3, 2 (1997), pp. 245–52, at pp. 247, 250n. 4. There has been similar discussion about Gregory A. Barton, *Empire Forestry and the Origins of Environmentalism* (Cambridge: Cambridge University Press, 2002).
6. William Barber, *British Economic Thought and India, 1600–1858. A Study in the History of Development Economics* (Oxford: Clarendon Press, 1975).
7. Eric Stokes, *The English Utilitarians and India* (Oxford: Clarendon, 1959); Elie Halévy, *The Growth of Philosophic Radicalism* (London: Faber & Gwyer, 1972 [1928]); F. Rosen, 'Eric Stokes, British Utilitarianism, and India', in Martin I. Moir, Douglas M. Peers and Lynn Zastoupil (eds), *J.S. Mill's Encounter with India* (Toronto: University of Toronto Press, 1998), p. 30.
8. Homi Bhabha, *The Location of Culture* (London: Routledge, 1994), pp. 94–5.
9. Richard H. Drayton, *Nature's Government : Science, Imperial Britain, and the 'Improvement' of the World* (New Haven, CT: Yale University Press, 2000), pp. 234–5.
10. Uday Mehta 'Liberal Strategies of Exclusion', *Politics & Society* 18, 4 (1990), pp. 427–54; Uday Singh Mehta, *Liberalism and Empire: A Study in Nineteenth-Century British Liberal Thought* (Chicago: University of Chicago Press, 1999).
11. Mill, *Principles of Political Economy* (1849), Bk V, ch.11, §9; 'The individual ... may be incapable of judging or acting for himself; may be a lunatic, an idiot or an infant ... Freedom of contract, in the case of children, is but another word for freedom of coercion.'
12. S. Ravi Rajan, 'Imperial Environmentalism or Environmental Imperialism? European Forestry, Colonial Foresters and the Agendas of Forest Management in British India, 1800–1900', in Grove *et al.* (eds), *Nature and the Orient*, pp. 334–8; on German forest conservancy, see H. Rubner, *Forstgeschichte im Zeitalter der industriellen Revolution* (Berlin: Dunker & Humbolt, 1967), pp. 103–28. See also John Croumbie Brown, *Schools of Forestry in Germany, with Addenda Relative to a Desiderated British National School of Forestry* (Edinburgh: Oliver & Boyd, 1887) p. 1.
13. R. Drayton, *Nature's Government: Science, Imperial Britain, and the 'Improvement' of the World* (New Haven, CT: Yale University Press), pp. 236–8.
14. Keith Thomas, *Man and the Natural World: Changing Attitudes in England 1500–1800* (London: Penguin, 1983), pp. 192–3.
15. Preston was a doctor of divinity rather than an MD. *House of Commons Journal 1792*, p. 343.

16. J.F. Richards and M. McAlpin 'Cotton Cultivating and Land Clearing in the Bombay Deccan and Karnatak, 1818–1920', in R.P. Tucker and J.F. Richards (eds), *Global Deforestation and the Nineteenth-Century World Economy* (Durham, NC: Duke University Press, 1983); C.A. Bayly, 'The Second British Empire', in Robin Winks (ed.), *Oxford History of the British Empire Vol. 5* (Oxford: Oxford University Press, 1999), p. 69.
17. Robert Greenhalgh Albion, *Forests and Sea Power* (Cambridge, MA: Harvard University Press, 1926), pp. 365–8, 403.
18. John Hurd, 'Railways', in Dharma Kumar (ed.), *Cambridge Economic History of India* vol. 2 (Cambridge: Cambridge University Press, 1983), p. 739. Other woods were also initially used extensively to make charcoal for railway locomotives. Hurd, 'Railways', p. 749.
19. Guha and Gadgil, *This Fissured Land*, pp. 118–19; 'fierce onslaught' was the colourful phrase of a British author, E.A. Smythies writing in 1925 and quoted by Guha.
20. Report by Thomas L. Blane, Collector of Canara, to Board of Revenue, Fort St. George, 31.8.47 §14, in *Madras Board of Revenue Proceedings* 8.11.47, British Library Oriental and India Office Collections, India Office Records (hereafter BL OIOC IOR) P/307/38 pp. 14422–44 at p. 14434.
21. Ribbentrop, *Forestry in British India*, p. 60.
22. Collector of Canara to Govt. of Madras, 13.9.20, quoted in *Bengal Revenue Proceedings* 21.3.71, p. 1958, BL OIOC IOR P/227.
23. Edward Balfour, *The Influence Exercised by Trees on the Climate and Productiveness of the Peninsula of India* (London: India Office, 1878), p. 18, BL OIOC IOR V/27/560/107.
24. W. Fisher to Board of Revenue, Fort St. George, 30 August 1958, in *Bengal Revenue Proceedings* 13.10.58, p. 91, BL OIOC IOR P/66/19.
25. Henry Maine, *Ancient Law: its Connection with the Early History of Society and its Relation to Modern Ideas* (London: John Murray, 1861), ch. 10.
26. Cited in Balfour, *Influence of Trees*, pp. 10–11.
27. James Mill, *History of British India* vol. 1, 1858 edn, (London: Routledge, 1997), p. 210 and p. 210 n. 1 by Horace Wilson J.S. Mill drew on his father's work at *Principles of Political Economy* Bk.1 Ch.7 §6, calling uncertain tenure 'the acknowledged explanation of the poverty of many fertile tracts of Asia'.
28. G. Mann, 'Assam', in Stenhouse, 'Progress Report of Forest Administration in Bengal for the Year 1868–69', p. 56, BL OIOC IOR V/24/1362.
29. J.S. Mill, *Principles of Political Economy* (1849), Bk V, ch.11, §8; §16.
30. Jacques Pouchepadass, 'British Attitudes to Shifting Cultivation in Colonial South India: A Case Study of South Canara District 1800–1920' in D. Arnold and R. Guha (eds), *Nature, Culture, Imperialism: Essays on the Environmental History of South Asia* (Oxford: Oxford University Press, 1998) Passim, esp. pp. 143–4.
31. Adam Smith, *An Inquiry into the Nature And Causes of the Wealth of Nations* (1776) ch.1 pt.3 'Of the Expense of Public Works and Public Institutions'; J.S. Mill *Principles of Political Economy* (1849) Bk.5 Ch.11 §15; Coase pointed out that many English lighthouses had, in fact, been privately run, in his 'The Lighthouse in Economics' repr. in *The Firm, the Market and the Law* (Chicago: Chicago University Press, 1988).

32. Gibson to Hooker 24.3.41, *India Letters* no.211, RBG Kew Archives.
33. John Prest, *The Garden of Eden: the Botanic Garden and the Re-creation of Paradise* (New Haven, CT: Yale University Press, 1981).
34. E.G. Reisz, 'City as Garden: Sharing Space in the Urban Botanic Gardens of Singapore and Malaysia, 1786–2001', in Ryan Bishop, John Phillips and Yeo Wei Wei (eds), *Perpetuating Global Cities: Postcolonial Urbanism in South East Asia* (Singapore: Routledge, 2003).
35. Blane, Report 31.8.47 §13, in OIOC IOR P/307/38 pp. 14422–44 and pp. 14433–4.
36. cf. J.R. Logan, 'The Probable Effects on the Climate of Pinang of the Continued Destruction of the Hill Jungle', *Journal of the Indian Archipelago and Eastern Asia* ser. 1, 2 (1848), pp. 534–6; Charles Irving Smith, William Cullen and Edward Balfour, *On the Influence Exercised by Trees on the Climate of a Country: Being Reports to the Madras Government* (Madras: Reuben Twigg, 1849), printed as *Madras Journal of Literature and Science* 36.
37. Williams, D. 'Clements Markham and the Introduction of the Cinchona Tree into British India', *Geographical Journal*, 128 (1962), p. 431ff.
38. See Grove, *Green Imperialism*, pp. 428–9 for a summary.
39. Indian despatch no.21 of 1847 (7.7.47).
40. Cleghorn had become interested in forest conservancy as an army surgeon in Mysore, where he lobbied successfully for the abolition of *kumri* shifting cultivation in 1847. On the British Association, see Roy M. Macleod and Peter Collins (eds), *The Parliament of Science. The British Association for the Advancement of Science, 1831–1981* (Northwood: Science Reviews, 1981) including Richard Yeo, 'Scientific Method and the Image of Science, 1831–90'.
41. Ramachandra Guha 'An Early Environmental Debate: the Making of the 1878 Forest Act', *Indian Economic and Social History Review* 27 (1990). The 1878 Act was followed by a series of other restrictions bringing the law closer to the original intentions of Brandis, namely for near-complete state control of the forests; Stebbing, *Forests of India*, vol. 2, pp. 468–72. See Akhileshwar Pathak, *Law, Strategies, Ideologies: Legislating Forests in Colonial India* (Delhi: Oxford University Press, 2001) for a critique of Guha's argument that Brandis was in fact espousing a more moderate position on state control, pp. 120–1.
42. Balfour, *Influence of Trees*, pp. 11–12.
43. Balfour, *Influence of Trees*, p. 19.
44. Stebbing, *Forests of India* vol. 1, p. 151.
45. Court of Directors to Government of India, Feb. 1842; Government of India to Commissioner, Tenasserim 7.9.46, reported to Court of Directors 21.10.46.
46. In 1848 Henry Drummond MP asked for all correspondence on Tenasserim forests to be printed for the Commons (PP HC 654, 1847–88 vol. XLVIII:371, *House of Commons Journal* CIII: 394, 929). Drummond, a banker, politician and religious thinker was also a noted eccentric. He was described by Charles Greville in his *Memoirs* as 'quite mad, but very clever' (quoted in Robert Blake, *Disraeli*, revised edn (London, 1998), p. 290). He is less well known as an agricultural reformer. See his preface to the English edition of L. Mounier and Maurice Rubichon, *On the Condition of the Agricultural Classes of Great Britain and Ireland. With Extracts from the Parliamentary Reports and Evidence, from 1833 to 1840* (London: John Murray, 1842).

47. Stebbing, *Forests of India* vol. 1, p. 257.
48. §17 PWD Despatch 75, Governor-General of India in Council to Secretary of State, 1.11.62, p.563, BL OIOC IOR L/PWD/3/10.
49. §5 Revenue Despatch no. 5 Secretary of State to Governor-General of India. 25.2.63, India Office no.679, BL OIOC IOR L/E/3/483.
50. §17 PWD Despatch 75, Governor-General of India in Council to Secretary of State, 1.11.62, p.563, BL OIOC IOR L/PWD/3/10.
51. J.S. Mill, 'Maine on Village Communities', repr. in J.M. Robson, M. Moir and Z. Moir (eds), *Writings on India by John Stuart Mill* (Toronto: Toronto University Press, 1990), p. 223.
52. §5, §6 Revenue Despatch no. 5 Secretary of State to Governor-General of India. 25.2.63, India Office no.679, BL OIOC IOR L/E/3/483.
53. See R.L. Bryant, *The Political Ecology of Forestry in Burma 1826–1993* (London: Hurst, 1997), p.101.
54. Thomas F. Buxton, *The African Slave Trade and Its Remedy* (London: John Murray, 1840), p. 279; Martin Lynn, 'The West African Palm Oil Trade in the Nineteenth Century and the "Crisis of Adaptation" ', in Robin Law (ed.), *From Slave Trade to Legitimate Commerce: The Commercial Transition in Nineteenth-Century West Africa* (Cambridge: Cambridge University Press, 1995), pp. 69–71.
55. §17 PWD Despatch 75, Governor-General of India in Council to Secretary of State, 1.11.62, p.563, BL OIOC IOR L/PWD/3/10.
56. B. Berman, and J. Lonsdale, *Unhappy Valley* (London, 1992), pp. 118,234; E. Bradlow, 'The Evolution of "Trusteeship" in Kenya', *South African Historical Journal*, 4 (1972), pp. 62–3.
57. §27 PWD Despatch 75, Governor-General of India in Council to Secretary of State, 1.11.62, p.567, BL OIOC IOR L/PWD/3/10.
58. Charles Phillimore minutes (9.1.63, 10.1.63) to Revenue Despatch no. 5 Secretary of State to Governor-General of India. 25.2.63, India Office no.679, BL OIOC IOR L/E/3/483.
59. §9 Revenue Despatch no. 5 Secretary of State to Governor-General of India. 25.2.63, India Office no.679, BL OIOC IOR L/E/3/483.
60. See Markham to the Secretary of the Government, Fort St George, 16.1.66, (§28), BL OIOC IOR L/E/5/61.
61. *Proceedings of the Madras Central Committee for the Exhibition of the industry and art of all nations held in London in the year 1851* (Madras, 1853), BL OIOC IOR V/27/601/12, p. 180.
62. Ulrike Kirchberger, 'German Scientists in the Indian Forest Service: A German Contribution to the Raj?', *Journal of Imperial and Commonwealth History* 29, 2 (2001), pp. 1–26.
63. Clive Dewey, 'The Education of a Ruling Caste: The Indian Civil Service in the Era of Competitive Examination', *English Historical Review* 88, 347 (1973), pp. 262–85, at pp. 270, 275, 276ff.
64. Lionel Robbins in his *An Essay on the Nature and Significance of Economic Science*, (London: Macmillan, 2nd edn, 1935), p. 16.
65. C. Achebe, 'Colonialist Criticism', in his *Morning Yet on Creation Day* (London: Heinemann, 1975), p. 13.
66. Gyan Prakash, *Another Reason* (Princeton: Princeton University Press, 1999).

7

Competing Ideas of Freedom: Legal Disputes About Restraint of Trade in Britain and Germany, 1870–1914

Willibald Steinmetz

Introduction: freedom of contract vs. freedom of trade

From the mid-1870s the economies of Western Europe and the United States were characterized by intensified competition and declining prices. Entrepreneurs reacted to this in various ways. An obvious response was close co-operation between rival firms to regulate output, stabilize prices and allocate markets. The aim of such agreements between businesses was the same everywhere: restraint of trade. Their form however differed depending on market conditions and legal provisions. Agreements could take the form of cartels, trusts, holding companies or more informal combinations. Comparative research has shown that legal considerations were particularly important in shaping the behaviour of those pursuing anti-competitive arrangements.[1] This is most evident in the American case, where Federal anti-trust legislation made it difficult for independent firms to combine and was decisive in promoting the consolidation of big managerial enterprises. In Britain, on the other hand, judge-made law proved to be far less effective in curbing informal agreements and therefore gave few incentives for family firms to merge into bigger units. German judges not only turned a blind eye towards informal combinations, as their British colleagues did, but favoured cartelization which developed to a degree unknown in Britain or the United States.

While the comparative history of cartels, trusts and other combinations among businessmen has been studied extensively, there is another, less spectacular but more widely used anti-competitive device which has received little attention from historians: individual covenants in restraint of trade between entrepreneurs and their employees. The rationale of these contracts was to oblige employees not to serve a rival firm or open up a similar business after their employment was terminated. Such covenants in restraint of trade, or non-competition clauses (*Konkurrenzklauseln*) as they were called in German legal discourse, could take on various forms. In most cases employees were only prohibited from using certain trade secrets or customer connections for a limited time and space. Sometimes however the ban extended to an entire industry all over the country and was meant to last for an indefinite period of time. In this case the employee's chance of finding a suitable job after termination of the contract was severely restricted. In the decades before the First World War individual contracts in restraint of trade became a ubiquitous feature of employment relations. Even as the depression subsided, non-competition clauses were habitually inserted into labour contracts and became ever more restrictive. By 1900 in Britain as well as in Germany the custom pervaded all branches of industry, from large chemical and manufacturing concerns to the smallest drugstore or dairy shop around the corner.

From a political economist's point of view individual contracts restraining an employee's freedom to exercise his trade had to be regarded with the same critical eye as collective agreements of any kind, be it cartels or trade unions, which interfered with free competition. However within the liberal paradigm an outright condemnation of individual or collective agreements in restraint of trade was highly problematic, since two competing freedoms were at stake: freedom of trade on the one hand, and freedom of contract on the other. The dilemma was that these agreements used one freedom (freedom of contract) to restrain another freedom (freedom of trade). Both freedoms were seen by liberals as concrete manifestations of their fundamental value, personal liberty. And both freedoms were considered necessary for the proper functioning of markets and economic improvement. Therefore the two freedoms had to be weighed against each other to decide the validity of agreements in restraint of trade. There was no easy solution to the dilemma. English and German economists, judges and politicians, as well as entrepreneurs and employees spent decades pondering the question without ever reaching a satisfactory conclusion.

The debate on agreements in restraint of trade had far-reaching legal implications. In English common law as well as in German private law non-competition clauses and collective agreements such as cartels were initially treated as belonging to the same category, although in fact they had not much in common. Things were further complicated by the fact that trade unions, at least in English law, were also regarded as combinations in restraint of trade. Thus judicial decisions in seemingly trivial employment disputes between, say, a surgeon and his assistant, could act as precedents with serious repercussions for collective labour law and the entire law of unfair competition. Judges and legislators thus had to solve a complex dilemma. Not only were they called upon to reconcile freedom of contract and freedom of trade; they also had to strike a balance between the need to keep the law consistent on the one hand, and the urge to follow considerations of social justice on the other. Whereas consistency demanded a rule was applied regardless of whether it concerned a small handicraftsman or a powerful company, social justice might suggest a more equitable, differentiated treatment. English and German judicial decision-makers reacted differently to this challenge. Until the early twentieth century, English common lawyers followed the first course and preferred consistency. German jurists in the *Kaiserreich* adopted the second course; they let German competition law become more responsive to social demands, but also less consistent than the English common law.

Agreements in restraint of trade, then, are an ideal microcosm for observing the interaction between economic knowledge, legislation and judicial practice. Particular attention will be paid to the way in which arguments derived from political economy were, or were not used in court and legal debates. Did judges and lawyers merely follow the leading economists' precepts, as has been suggested recently for the cartel problem and the German Historical School of economics in the Wilhelmine era?[2] Or is it more correct to assume that legal reasoning, at least in England, took place in a relatively autonomous sphere where economic ideas entered, if at all, only in a haphazard, delayed fashion?[3] Comparing the response to restraint of trade cases in Germany and England will also shed light on more fundamental attitudes towards economic freedom and state intervention.

Legislative measures and economists' ideas

'By the 1870s Britain may well have come closer to textbook conditions of free competition ... than any industrialised state has since managed.'[4] The deliberate abstentionism of the British legislator was a crucial and distinctive factor. Parliament in this respect followed public opinion. Among the ruling elites of the Victorian age the belief that Parliament or the government had the right, even the duty, to regulate economic behaviour had almost disappeared. Even large sections of the working class shared the view that Parliament should keep out of the bargaining processes that went on in the market. Freedom of contract *and* freedom of trade were regarded as supreme public policy. When conflicts between the two principles occurred, a balance had to be found by the courts or the parties to the dispute themselves. The British legislator was reluctant to intervene in these matters and was rarely called upon to do so.

From the eighteenth century on, legislation on trade and industry had more and more assumed an enabling character, setting citizens free to make their own bargains and to work on whatever terms they could achieve. Obstacles to competition such as monopolies were no longer created, the medieval statutes which punished interferences with the distribution of food (engrossing, forestalling and regrating) were repealed in 1772, and existing powers of local guilds to make by-laws against outsiders were abolished in 1835 with the passing of the Municipal Corporations Act.[5]

Legislation affecting labour conformed to the abstentionist stance, at least as far as individual freedom to move and freedom of contract were concerned. What remained of older paternalist regulations, especially the wage-setting powers of magistrates and the apprenticeship requirements, were formally abolished in 1813–14.[6] True, factory legislation created new limits to freedom of contract, but almost all of this concerned minors and women only, not adult men. For this reason (male) politicians and lawyers felt justified in treating factory legislation as an exception to the general rule that English*men* were free to work under what conditions they chose.[7]

By contrast, collective agreements among workmen to raise the price of labour were criminalized by statute in 1799, and by an act of reciprocity similar combinations of employers to suppress wages were outlawed in 1800. But here again, much earlier than in all other European countries, the British legislator retreated from this position step-by-step, so that with the Act of 1871 trade unions, including masters' combinations, were declared not to be unlawful by reason merely that they were in restraint of trade.[8] Legislation on trade unions thus fell back in line with legislation on other aspects of trade. The protracted history of British trade union legislation before and after 1871 is perhaps the only instance where the legislator was repeatedly called upon to secure for a certain group, the workers, by statute what other market participants already enjoyed by a common law jurisdiction committed to *laisser-faire*: the right to pursue their own economic interests in a robust manner, by all peaceful means available, whether individually or in coordination with others. As this became the policy towards trade unions, it was only logical, following the rule of reciprocity, that no serious efforts were made by Parliament to regulate cartels or other (mostly secret) forms of co-operation between entrepreneurs. Nothing comparable to the American anti-trust legislation beginning in the 1880s or the German cartel regulation of the 1920s was enacted in Britain before the 1950s.[9]

British statute law, then, contributed nothing to solve the dilemmas posed by contracts in restraint of trade. If the legislator remained silent, did political economists offer guidance on the question of priority between freedom of contract and freedom of trade? John Stuart Mill and Alfred Marshall reveal two leading approaches at the beginning and end of our period. In his *Principles of Political Economy* (1848) Mill recognized that the main opposing force to competition in mid-nineteenth-century England was no longer a paternalist government which tried to regulate everything, but what he called 'the influence of fixed customs'.[10] 'Customs' here included engagements undertaken voluntarily to comply with certain (unwritten) rules. It is in this sense that Mill criticized the agreements between booksellers against underbidding by intruders. 'In many trades the terms on which business is done are a matter of positive arrangement among the trade, who use the means they always possess of making the situation of any member of the body who departs from its fixed customs, inconvenient or disagreeable.'[11] Here was a politely worded description of what later became known as a cartel. With regard to the labouring classes Mill used the same conceptual opposition between 'competition' and 'custom', but in a more polemical way. For him the efforts of skilled workmen to exclude outsiders and erect strict boundaries around particular kinds of work belonged to a bygone age, the age of old customs, monopolies and illegitimate privileges.[12] The arrangements of trade unionists to close labour markets thus fell under an even stronger verdict than the closing of commodity markets by business cartels. There is no doubt, however, that for Mill both kinds of agreement in restraint of trade were illegitimate and bad.

At the same time, Mill did not believe that these collective agreements could be suppressed by law. The failure of the combination acts were too obvious not to be recognized by Mill. Hence, laws against combinations of workmen fell under the chapter of 'Government Interference Grounded on Erroneous Doctrines'.[13] Mill pleaded for a neutral attitude of the law towards such combinations, except if they used criminal methods such as violence or fraud. It was in the 'best interests of the human race', he said, 'that all economical experiments, voluntarily undertaken, should have the fullest licence'.[14] Translated into legal language this meant that contracts made between the members of such combinations should not be declared void, let alone punishable. Whether they should be enforceable in a court of law, was another matter. But even in this respect, Mill put the onus of proof on those who resisted *laisser-faire*.[15] He was convinced that producers, including workers, knew best what suited them, because they had a direct interest in the matter: 'The persons, or some of the persons, who do the work, are likely to be better judges than the government, of the means of attaining the particular end at which they aim.'[16] In disputes between businessmen or between employers and workmen (and workwomen)[17] contracts should be interpreted as expressing the will of the parties, and the law should give effect to that will, irrespective of the provisions contained in the contract. It was different with consumers: here Mill had serious doubts that they always knew, or had the means of knowing, what was best for them.[18] And it was different in another, more specific case, namely, when someone engaged himself in perpetuity. In this case, he said, the 'maxim of leaving contracts free' should not be applicable without limitations.[19] As an example for this, Mill mentioned marriage, but logically the same reservation would apply for an individual contract in restraint of trade, whereby an employee bound himself not to compete for an indefinite period of time.

A Victorian contemporary consulting Mill's *Principles* would have found good arguments for enforcing contracts in restraint of trade as well as for making them void. On balance, however, Mill was inclined to hold such contracts valid except in extreme cases as, for example, lifelong obligations. It will be shown that English courts followed this line of reasoning up to the famous Nordenfeldt case (1893–94) which became the leading case on contracts in restraint of trade for another generation.

While the House of Lords still deliberated on the Nordenfeldt case, a new leading figure began to dominate political economy: Alfred Marshall. His *Principles of Economics* (1890) was designed to supplant Mill's *Principles* and created a new orthodoxy.[20] Economics was to become a science relying on mathematical models of economic behaviour, though for Marshall institutional change and 'ethical influences'[21] still played an important role. The question of priority between freedom of contract and freedom of trade was addressed in the very first pages of the work. Here Marshall made strong statements in defence of the *reality* of competition against its detractors, while at the same time admitting that the *term* 'competition' had taken on such negative connotations in recent times that it was hopeless to use it any longer in a positive way.[22] His choice of examples reveals Marshall's sympathy with newcomers who were excluded by established groups of producers from making full use of their abilities:

> In many cases the 'regulation of competition' is a misleading term, that veils the formation of a privileged class of producers, who often

> use their combined force to frustrate the attempts of an able man to rise from a lower class than their own. Under the pretext of repressing anti-social competition, they deprive him of the liberty of carving out for himself a new career, where the services rendered by him to the consumers of the commodity would be greater than the injuries, that he inflicts on the relatively small group which objects to his competition.'[23]

There could be no clearer condemnation of non-competition clauses than these sentences. Preventing an individual to develop his or her capacities also meant that the public at large, the nation of consumers, would be deprived of a potentially useful member. Marshall thus reintroduced the concept of public good into the debate on competition. From a legal point of view his statement could only be interpreted as a call to readjust the balance in favour of individual self-made men and the consumers who, in Marshall's opinion, needed more protection than powerful companies or cartels.

Marshall did not elaborate these ideas any further in the rest of his work. He gave no hints as to how his demand for re-establishing free choice for individuals could be reconciled – legally and morally – with the principle of freedom of contract. As an economist, he was more interested in describing what happened in the economy than in formulating ethical or juridical rules. It was his desire for precision which led him to abandon the term 'competition' as 'not well suited to describe the special characteristics of industrial life in the modern age'.[24] Marshall favoured another concept instead, 'Economic Freedom'. This concept, he thought, was more suitable to grasp the fundamental tendency of modern economic behaviour: 'deliberate and free choice'.[25] Yet from a lawyer's point of view this concept had the disadvantage of obscuring the conflict between the two competing freedoms in restraint of trade cases. Having introduced the new concept Marshall dismissed any further discussion of it as lying 'beyond the scope of the present volume'.[26] Marshall's initial strong statement in favour of readjusting the balance in favour of individuals thus remained little more than an opinion without the elaborate reasoning necessary for authoritative entry into arguments in court.

The German debate on freedom of contract and freedom of trade differed from the British in several respects. Scepticism with regard to both principles was widespread in Germany even in the heyday of liberalism during the 1860s and 1870s, and grew stronger towards the end of the century. While parliamentary deliberations on the industrial code

(*Gewerbeordnung*, enacted 1869, extended to the whole *Reich* 1872–73) were still going on, the leading economist of the day, Wilhelm Roscher, ridiculed the expectations of liberal politicians who believed that absolute freedom of trade would immediately lead to harmony and improvement in the economy: 'You will only have to leave a new-born child to his "natural freedom" and it will probably be dead within 24 hours.'[27] When Roscher equated the newly liberalized German economy with a baby, he alluded to the backwardness of German industry in general, but he also had in mind that economic subjects in Germany, producers and consumers, employers and employees, were not used to absolute freedom and would misuse it, if suddenly let free.

In addition to proclaiming freedom of trade (subject to limits imposed by law) in Art. 1, the *Gewerbeordnung* of 1869 also enacted freedom of contract between industrial employers and employees in Art. 105. Here again, economists belonging to the Historical School were convinced that in the present state of the German economy there could be no such thing as real freedom of contract between persons who were in such an unequal bargaining position as employers and workmen. Already in his opening address to the first gathering of the Association for Social Policy (*Verein für Sozialpolitik*) in 1872, Gustav Schmoller demanded that workers should be given the full means to realize freedom of contract, otherwise 'a so-called free employment contract would in reality lead to the exploitation of the worker'.[28] The addressee of such demands was of course always the state – *der Staat,* which in German political discourse comprised the legislator, the government and the bureaucracy and which conveyed a quasi-personal, even god-like vision of this entity. Schmoller tellingly called the state 'the most splendid institution for the education of humanity' – an image which in the 1870s would have been unthinkable for a British economist.[29]

In contrast to Britain, then, the belief that the legislator was called upon to regulate economic behaviour to a certain degree never became extinct in Germany. Whatever the difference of opinion about the desired extent of regulation, there was no controversy among German economists or jurists that, in principle, freedom of contract always had to be subject to certain imperative rules concerning the contract's form *and* contents, and that it was the legislator's task to prescribe such absolute rules. This, again, was an idea which English common lawyers at the time would have treated as absurd.[30] The concept freedom of contract itself had different meanings in English and German legal-political discourse.[31] Freedom of contract in Germany was *per definitionem* a limited freedom.

Schmoller went further than many in his demands for imposing limits on contractual freedom through legislation. Already in 1874 he proposed general prohibitions of very long employment contracts, and of clauses which exempted employers from liability in cases of accident.[32] More generally, he wanted to 'lift the contract to the level of public law' by 'introducing into it certain conditions which in the interest of the whole are indispensable'.[33] Most contemporaries, including juridically trained state functionaries, accepted his general line of argument: that the state via legislation should intervene into freedom of contract in order to protect weaker subjects – in the case of employment relations, the employee.

There were plenty of occasions when this general idea was put into practice. Each time the existing industrial code came to be reviewed, an opportunity arose for pressure groups and political parties to raise controversial issues of employment relations. The same was the case when new codifications were prepared, especially the code of commerce (*Handelsgesetzbuch, 1897*), and the Civil Code (*Bürgerliches Gesetzbuch, 1896/1900*). The need to create a unitary law for the whole *Reich* and the idea of codification itself, which aimed at completeness and demanded discussion of all eventualities, made it inevitable that the *Reichstag*, political parties, interest groups and juridical experts concerned with the drafting of codes had to consider contracts in restraint of trade from various points of view.[34] Here was another difference from Britain where it was more difficult for particular groups to set in motion the machinery of legislation and where, even more importantly, the onus of proof that a statute was necessary always lay on those who demanded the statute.

It was through reforms of existing codes and preparation of new codes that individual employment contracts in restraint of trade (*Konkurrenzklauseln*) became the object of precise regulations which limited freedom of contract.[35] This happened several times, first in 1896, when Art. 133f was added to the *Gewerbeordnung*. An agreement between an industrial employer and his technical and commercial employees, foremen and the like was now valid only if the clause did not limit in an unreasonable way the ability of the employee to advance in professional life, whether in period, space or object. In addition, Art. 133f declared void all agreements of this kind which were made, while the employee was still a minor.

More detailed and far-reaching were the regulations concerning employees in commercial firms in Articles 74–76 of the *Handelsgesetzbuch* of 1897. Here, the same formulation was used as in Art. 133f *Gewerbeordnung*, with the additional provision that any agreement beyond a period of three years was invalid. Further, the employer could not enforce his claims in court if he himself had dismissed the employee, except for a serious ground, or had broken the contract and thus given the employee a reason to leave. If a penalty had been stipulated, the employer could only demand the payment of this penalty, not an injunction against the employee. An employee who had made considerable progress in his career could thus no longer be hindered by his former employer. All agreements contrary to these prescriptions were declared to be void, thus making contracting out impossible.

These provisions of the *Handelsgesetzbuch* had to be interpreted in connection with the general private law as laid down in the Civil Code of 1900 (*Bürgerliches Gesetzbuch*). Of special importance here was Art. 138 which declared any legal transaction void if it offended common morality (*gute Sitten*). This general rule gave German judges a large discretion and enabled them to introduce considerations of equity and social justice in their jurisdiction; in different political circumstances, especially during the Third Reich, Art. 138 and similar general rules became of course highly problematic.

The far-reaching protective provisions of the *Handelsgesetzbuch* for commercial employees excited the envy of industrial employees; hence the new Art. 133f *Gewerbeordnung* came under fire almost at the moment it was put into force. Extensive debates on this issue took place in the *Reichstag* from 1906 onwards. The only reason why a reform could not be achieved was that the *Reichstag* was dissolved two times before the deliberations were finished, but the topic remained on the agenda until the First World War. As this episode makes clear, the dynamics of German labour legislation before 1914 resulted to some extent from its corporatist ideological foundations. German legislation on employment still distinguished between various social groups and professions, and this meant that each time one group of employees was able to achieve a benefit, other groups would claim the same benefit for themselves. On the other hand the dynamics was also created by demands for a unitary codified labour law which began to be aired by left-liberal jurists, the Social Democrats and others.[36] The debates on non-competition clauses contributed to this development. Advocates of an unitary employment law argued that the highest current standard of protection should be made into general law.

For contracts in restraint of trade the standard was set by the law for commercial employees as laid down in the *Handelsgesetzbuch* of 1897. Commercial employees succeeded with additional reforms of its protective provisions. The campaign was led by the influential right-wing

Deutschnationaler Handlungsgehilfenverband (German Nationalist Association for Commercial Clerks)[37] and received support from expert lawyers, especially from the judges of commercial tribunals (*Kaufmannsgerichte*). These were special courts, created in 1904 and functioning as courts of first instance for the adjudication of all disputes between merchants and their employees.[38] The judges and lay members of these courts were occupied with complaints on excessive restraint of trade clauses on a daily basis and therefore had a strong interest in further regulation. Their substantial reform proposals were considered by the *Reichstag* and with some modifications passed into law in 1914.[39]

The most stringent provisions of the new Articles 74–76 *Handelsgesetzbuch* were the following: any competition clause to be valid had to be laid down in writing; the maximum period for which a competition clause would be valid was reduced from 3 to 2 years. To be valid it had also to be shown that the clause was necessary for the protection of a legitimate interest of the employer; if it went beyond this, the court had the right to reduce its range. (By Art. 343 *Bürgerliches Gesetzbuch* the court had also the right to reduce an excessive penalty.) Any clause of this kind was void if the employee earned less than 1500 Marks or was a minor when the agreement was made; the agreement was also void if the principal had demanded a pledge of honour by the employee to enforce it. Finally, the clause was valid only if the employer had agreed to pay the employee at least half of his last yearly income as compensation, and this for each year the restriction lasted. This provision was meant to discourage employers from stipulating non-competition clauses unless they were really necessary for the protection of an essential interest, for example, a valuable trade secret or customer connections.

By 1914 then, certain categories of German employees had achieved an amount of legal protection against non-competition clauses which went much further than anything employees in Britain could hope for under common law. In the field of individual employment law contractual freedom had been suspended to a large extent in order to enable employees to move freely on the labour market. These exceptions to the general law had been introduced with the support of important sections of the legal community and they were also in accord with leading economists' ideas on the illusionary character of freedom of contract in individual employment relations.

With respect to anti-competitive agreements among businesses, especially cartels, the debate among German jurists and economists took a different course.[40] Here, considerations of social policy and consumer protection were superseded by concerns for the conservation of German industry as a whole and its international competitiveness. Voluntary regulation of competition by businesses was regarded as useful for economic peace and sustained development, except in cases where the forcing up of prices could clearly be identified as the unique purpose of such agreements.

Economists were the first to put forward such views. As cartels began to multiply in the crisis years of the 1870s and 1880s,[41] the Austrian economist Friedrich Kleinwächter summed up the dominant position for years to come when he declared that cartels were 'born out of necessity' (in German: 'Kinder der Not') and would bring 'order out of chaos'.[42] Even in the boom years of the later 1890s, when it could no longer be said that the sheer existence of businesses depended on such devices, the argument that cartels were a necessary self-defence against pernicious competition and overproduction remained a standard formula among economists; by this time the number of cartels in Germany had risen to about 260.[43] Gustav Schmoller, resuming the debates on the cartel question in the Association for Social Policy in 1894, proclaimed that cartels were 'a quasi-natural, inevitable institution which aimed at lowering production costs and improving production techniques', that they were a constituent part of modern economic life and 'a development ... which was stimulated by the way in which the social forces of the present age could combine using freedom of contract and the right to associate freely'.[44] This last argument could of course also be used to defend trade unionism against its critics. Hence, by analogy, economists with strong pro-trade union views, like Lujo Brentano, also came to a positive assessment of cartels.[45]

German judges and jurists – by and large – followed these arguments in favour of cartels put forward by the economists.[46] This led them to advocate a policy of *laisser-faire* towards anti-competitive agreements among businessmen. Such agreements were in general upheld and enforced in the courts, the leading case being a decision on a cartel of Saxon wood pulp manufacturers in 1897.[47] Thus, in the same year as the German legislator began an active policy of restricting freedom of contract in restraint of trade matters in favour of certain classes of employees, the courts adopted a policy of non-interference with cartels and similar collective agreements between businesses. The legislator of the *Reich*, as far as cartels were concerned, simply followed the courts and did not enact any significant measures against cartels before the 1920s.

The comparison of attitudes of German and British economists, legislators and lawyers towards agreements in restraint of trade has revealed significant differences. To look only at the outcomes of leading cases, such as the Nordenfeldt case of 1894 and the Saxon wood pulp case of 1897, would suggest apparent similarities: in both cases agreements in restraint of trade between businessmen were upheld. The rationale behind the court decisions, however, points to fundamentally different legislative, cultural and intellectual contexts. The British House of Lords, being primarily interested in the consistency of the common law, decided to enforce the agreement in order to save the principle of freedom of contract against any attempt to weaken it. The German *Reichsgericht* decided in favour of the Saxon cartel for reasons of public policy, derived from economists' arguments stressing the necessity and usefulness of such agreements for the national economy.

In general, German jurists and legislators of the late nineteenth and early twentieth century shared the views put forward by the dominant school of economic thought of the day, the Historical School. Following the economists they treated *individual* contracts in restraint of trade as a matter of social policy, while they regarded anti-competitive combinations of businessmen as a necessary device for strengthening the national economy. By contrast, English common lawyers continued to adhere to the principles of an older political economy for which – in cases of doubt – freedom of contract and *laisser-faire* had priority over other considerations of public policy, and this regardless of the kind of dispute they had under review. Only in the early twentieth century did English courts begin to retreat from this position of strict enforcement by developing distinctions that allowed them to treat restraint of trade cases differently depending on the kind of business and the social situation of the employee.

Economic arguments in judicial decisions on restraint of trade

English case law on contracts in restraint of trade between employers and employees follows the trajectory of Patrick Atiyah's formula of the 'Rise and Fall of Freedom of Contract'. The culminating point in this story are the years around 1900. From the early Victorian era up to the end of the nineteenth century judges became ever stricter in their policy to enforce such contracts, however wide the restriction to which the employee had consented when entering the service. From 1900 to the First World War an inverse movement took place by which the right of the employee to have a fair chance of using his skills and earning a living, as well as the general public's interest in freedom of trade, regained some of their former importance.

Lord Shaw of Dunfermline in *Morris* v. *Saxelby* (1916) described this movement when he interpreted his own and his fellow Lords' judgement of 1916 as a return to the sound principles which had been laid down two hundred years ago by Lord Macclesfield in the first leading case on the subject, *Mitchel* v. *Reynolds* (1711). At the same time Lord Shaw saw this movement as reflecting the evolution of economic thought:

> It may be, and probably is, that jurisprudence has reflected the evolution of economic thought by accentuating at one period freedom of trade, and at another freedom of contract; but the stage of balance and reconciliation which has now been definitely reached is, it may be observed, in truth a reversion to, and a restatement of, the perennial problem set forth in the penetrating judgment of Lord Macclesfield in *Mitchel* v. *Reynolds* ... [48]

That judgement of 1711 had been that general restraints of trade were *prima facie* to be considered bad and therefore void, but that partial restraints were to be upheld if it could be shown that they were justifiable in the interest of the parties and the public.[49] In addition, it had to be shown that the covenantor had received a consideration for his promise not to compete. This decision more or less remained the state of the law throughout the eighteenth and early nineteenth centuries.[50]

From about the late 1830s however, beginning with a decision in the Exchequer Chamber of 1837 (*Hitchcock* v. *Coker*), the tests which were applied to determine the validity of such contracts were more and more weakened. Step-by-step the courts worked their way up to a general presumption in favour of such contracts unless it could be shown that they were plainly unreasonable and not in the interest of the covenantee, that is, the employer who wanted to protect his business. In *Hitchcock* v. *Coker* (1837), the case of a druggist's assistant, a non-competition clause indefinite in point of time was upheld by Tindal C.J. as being not larger than the protection of the employer required, and the question whether there was an adequate consideration for this promise was brushed aside with the argument that it was enough if there was any consideration at all and that it was not the court's business to enquire whether it was adequate or not.[51] Here, the doctrine that the parties themselves were the best judges of their own interests began to gain ground.

The next important step came in the case of *Tallis* v. *Tallis* (1853), a case of dissolution of a partnership in the bookselling trade, in which Lord Campbell C.J. removed the onus of proof that a restraint of trade was reasonable from the plaintiff (the person who wanted to enforce the restraint, in employment disputes the employer) to the defendant (in employment disputes the employee). This he did in the name of a doctrine, now already in full sway, which said that contracts if freely entered into by the parties had to be adhered to.[52]

In the following decades the attitude of judges towards employees became ever harsher. In 1858, Lord Campbell even enforced an agreement whereby a tailor had bound himself to pay his former employers a penalty of £400 if 'after leaving their service' he would carry on business or solicit customers in a specified area, although the tailor had been dismissed without notice and without any reason: 'It is an agreement', Lord Campbell explained, 'that whenever the service is at an end he will not enter into rivalry with the plaintiffs. A convict who is sent to Botany-bay "leaves" England'.[53] In such decisions the doctrine of freedom of contract reigned supreme, no consideration at all was given any more to questions of public interest in freedom of trade or to the right of an individual to the free exercise of his skills.

Although the reasonings of judges in the following decades were in general less crude than Lord Campbell's, the result was always the same: I have not been able to find a single restraint of trade case between 1850 and 1900 which was decided in favour of the employee.[54] In the 1880s and 1890s, the range in terms of space and time which was held to be reasonable for the protection of certain established businesses was more and more extended; even world-wide non-competition clauses were upheld for a former employee of a French champagne business and the British agents of a German chemical concern.[55] While in these cases the firms that demanded the restraint could at least show that they had indeed world-wide business connections, the limits of reasonable argument were definitely passed in a case of a milk carrier who had worked for a dairy business in London's East End and 'agreed' to a clause which not only restrained him from soliciting customers he had served while working for the firm, but also all future customers the firm might acquire afterwards.[56] The reasoning of the Lord Justices of Appeal adjudicating in this case verged on the absurd, when they declared that the defendant (the milk carrier) could have avoided the inconvenience, because 'the whole of the rest of England was open to him'; that his counsels' contention 'that he could not contract not to serve persons whom he did not know to be the plaintiffs' customers is clearly not tenable as the law now stands'; and 'that it was reasonably necessary for the complete protection of the plaintiffs within the meaning of the cases on the subject that the defendant should undertake never to interfere with those who at any time were actually existing customers of the plaintiffs ... .'[57] In addition to extending the range of 'reasonable' protection to established businesses, the courts were also ready to make excessive use of their capacity to 'construe' contracts, that is interpret the language of a written agreement in such a way that what the judges supposed to be the will of the parties (which was usually only the will of one party, i.e. the employer) would be read into it.[58]

The climax of the courts' policy of upholding contracts in restraint of trade by all means was reached with the Nordenfeldt Case (1893–94).[59] This was not a dispute between an employer and his former employee, but a case of a Swedish gun-manufacturer who had sold his business and agreed not to compete with the new proprietors. The contract was held to be valid and enforceable on the well-known ground that businessmen were the best judges of their own interests. What made this case remarkable was that the whole case law on restraint of trade came under review and general considerations of justice and public policy, including economic considerations, were reintroduced into judicial decision-making by the House of Lords.

The decisive statement by Lord Macnaghten which would be quoted over and over again in decades to come was far from unambiguous but went some way to correct the string of decisions that had been found against employees since the 1850s. Lord Macnaghten made it absolutely clear that in cases of this kind the interests of *both* parties *and* the public had to be considered:

> The public have an interest in every person's carrying on his trade freely: so has the individual. All interference with individual liberty of action in trading, and all restraints of trade of themselves, if there is nothing more, are contrary to public policy, and therefore void. That is the general rule. But there are exceptions: restraints of trade and interference with individual liberty of action may be justified by the special circumstances of a particular case. It is a sufficient justification, and indeed it is the only justification, if the restriction is reasonable – reasonable, that is, in reference to the interests of the parties concerned and reasonable in reference to the interests of the public, so framed and so guarded as to afford adequate protection to the party in whose favour it is imposed, while at the same time it is in no way injurious to the public.[60]

Although it cannot be proved that Lord Macnaghten had knowledge of Alfred Marshall's *Principles of Economics*, his statement can be read as a judge's answer to the problem posed by the economist. From the employees' point of view, Macnaghten's statement was progress compared to the earlier jurisdiction which had tended to disregard the interests of employees almost completely. It was also an advance, because the 'circumstances' of particular cases, as for instance the usages in particular trades, now had to be taken back into the picture. The decision in the Nordenfeldt case, although still adhering to freedom of contract, was thus a departure from the policy of enforcing all contracts, regardless of circumstances.

It took several years before the courts began to follow the swing in favour of freedom of trade. Ordinary High Court judges and also county court judges, who, in general, were nearer to the concerns of citizens than the supreme court, were slow in abandoning the policy of strict enforcement of contracts which had been imposed on them 'from above' for half a century. From 1900 to the First World War therefore, there was a string of restraint of trade cases in which the Court of Appeal or the House of Lords reversed decisions of the courts below which were still based on freedom of contract, in order to establish the new doctrine of a just balance between the interests of *both* parties in the dispute. From 1900 to 1914 the change in the way of reasoning also had consequences for the outcome of cases; of the 17 decisions I have analysed for this period nine went against the employers seeking damages or enforcement of non-competition clauses, only seven went in favour of the employers, one county court case ended with an arrangement in court.[61]

One after another the doctrines established in the period between the 1850s and 1890s were now reversed. Wrongful dismissal of an employee was now considered a good ground for him not to be bound any longer by a restrictive agreement.[62] Unusual provisions in non-competition agreements were now scrutinized more carefully; and evidence as to the usages in certain trades was admitted and taken into consideration when the courts decided about what was 'reasonable' protection.[63] Excessive radius agreements were no longer upheld. Thus a ban unlimited in point of space was held to be unreasonable (on appeal) in the case of a former manager of a Taunton cider merchant,[64] and a clause prohibiting a shop assistant who had served customers at the grocery counter not to engage in a similar business within a distance of two miles was held to be 'wider than was reasonably necessary for the purpose'.[65] Finally, the burden of proof was put back on those who wanted to restrain a person in the use of his faculties; in the words of Viscount Haldane, L.C.: 'My Lords, the respondents have to shew that the restriction they have sought to impose goes no further than was reasonable for the protection of their business.'[66] By 1914, a new judicial practice was firmly established which looked at contracts made between employers and employees with a more critical eye than at those made between businessmen.[67]

What exactly brought about this change of attitude is difficult to say. Economic thought may have had some influence, but this is hard to prove. In contrast to German judges who made frequent use of academic works, whether juridical, economic, or social scientist, and quoted them with exact references in their decisions, English judges almost exclusively quoted only one 'authority': the precedents as laid down in the Law Reports.[68] By the turn of the twentieth century English judges themselves began to feel a growing uneasiness that they were forced by that 'authority' to drive the doctrine of freedom of contract to most absurd consequences, as for instance in the above-quoted milk carrier's case. Because the legislator remained silent however, the only agency which could free English judges from this dilemma was the House of Lords. And the Lords themselves, when looking back at the change of attitudes from *Mitchel* v. *Reynolds* (1711) to the First World War, thought it probable that jurisprudence had indeed been responsive to the 'evolution of economic thought'.[69]

German jurisdiction on contracts in restraint of trade from 1870 to the turn of the century took a more erratic course than the English case. This was partly due to the fact that until 1900, when the Civil Code came into force for the whole *Reich*, German private law was founded on different sources and was adjudicated by different courts in various regions of Germany. Roughly speaking, left of the river Rhine and in Baden French law applied, that is, the Napoleonic *Code Civil* of 1804, in Prussia the *Allgemeines Landrecht* of 1794 was in force, Saxony had its own civil code since 1863, and in the rest of Germany a common law based on Roman law was the basis of jurisdiction in civil matters. As far as commercial transactions were concerned, judges had to consult the *Allgemeines Deutsches Handelsgesetzbuch* of 1861 which, in 1897, was replaced by the new *Handelsgesetzbuch*. Finally, in all matters concerning trade and industry, most German states had their own industrial codes until these were replaced by the *Gewerbeordnung* of 1869, extended to the whole Reich in 1872–73. From the turn of the century, when the hierarchy of courts had been regularized and the substantive law unified in most respects, German jurisdiction on the whole became more consistent.

Despite its lack of consistency the general trend of German jurisdiction on non-competition clauses between the 1850s and the 1880s resembled the evolution of English law as far as the outcome of cases was concerned.

In all cases which I have been able to trace for this period the courts decided in favour of employers who had asked for enforcement of the restrictive agreements they had made with their employees.[70] The decisive argument in these cases however was not the wish of judges to give effect to freedom of contract, as in England, but an assessment of the German legislators' intent with regard to the regulation of trade. When German courts decided on the validity of non-competition clauses they asked in the first place whether these agreements were harmful to the general public in the sense that competition in a certain trade *as a whole* would thereby be excluded. In other words, the test was whether private agreements violated a public law regulation which aimed at prohibiting complete or partial monopolies.

Thus, in the case of a traveller for an Elberfeld firm selling haberdashery articles the *Reichs-Oberhandelsgericht* in 1872 upheld a non-competition clause by which the traveller had agreed not to engage in a similar business for a period of five years in the whole area of the German *Zollverein*; the reason given for this extremely harsh decision was that there were no indications that the firm intended to disadvantage the public at large by excluding 'pernicious competition', but that they only wanted to secure their own business against a man who, because of his confidential position, could 'exploit' the knowledge and connections he had acquired in their service.[71] Whether individuals had a right to the free exercise of a certain trade was considered irrelevant.

This was also made clear by the *Reichsgericht* in a decision of 1879 which enforced a non-competition clause by which an employee of an asphalt and tar manufacturer had bound himself not to engage in a similar business for ten years in the whole of Germany.[72] The employee in this case had contended that this agreement offended public morality and the principle of personal freedom. Against this the court held that this argument would only apply, if the employee would be left with no means at all for earning a living.

These judgements of the highest German appeal courts in the 1870s show a complete lack of concern for the rights of individuals, especially employees. The foundation for these decisions was an extremely narrow interpretation of the German legislators' intent as laid down in the *Gewerbeordnung* and other public law regulations concerning trade and commerce. There was only one instance where an appeal court, the Prussian *Obertribunal*, tried to give a different meaning to the text of the *Gewerbeordnung*. Significantly, this was not an employment dispute, but a dispute between two entrepreneurs. In 1876 a divisional court of the *Obertribunal* declared void an agreement, whereby a malt manufacturer who had sold his business had agreed not to compete with the new proprietor within a certain radius.[73] This decision was based on the ground that agreements which prohibited the independent exercise of a certain trade violated Art. 1 and Art. 10 of the *Gewerbeordnung*.

If this decision of 1876 had been allowed to stand, jurisdiction on non-competition clauses would have taken a different course in Germany. The plenary court of the *Obertribunal* however reversed the decision in 1877, affirming the doctrine that the legislator had only intended to prevent exclusive rights of certain persons to exercise certain trades, that is, monopolies.[74] Individual non-competition clauses in the eyes of the court did not violate that intent, because other people remained free to exercise the trade.[75] Technically, this judgement of the plenary court of the Prussian *Obertribunal* was based on an exegesis of the text of the *Gewerbeordnung*. That the court entertained other motives is revealed by explanatory remarks which pointed out the disadvantages of the earlier decision: it would have forced the courts to outlaw non-competition clauses in labour contracts as well; employers would thus be left with no remedy against 'disloyal' behaviour of former employees, and this, the court concluded, could not be considered in the public interest.[76]

In the early 1880s, German academic jurisprudence began to take a more critical look at the case law on restraint of trade. In 1883 Josef Kohler directly attacked a *Reichsgericht* decision of 1880, which had again affirmed the established doctrine and upheld a non-competition agreement unlimited both in time and space. Such decisions, Kohler wrote, were based on an erroneous principle: 'It is not the public interest, not the prevention of monopolies, which should be the decisive argument in such cases, but the protection of the individual against a contractual restraint of his freedom to exercise a trade.'[77] This intervention by an academic lawyer proved to be a turning point for judicial practice as well. The first major decision of the *Reichsgericht* on a non-competition clause in an employment contract after Kohler's critique, a judgement of 1893 in a case of a traveller for an umbrella factory, expressly referred to Kohler's article when it declared void an agreement which was unlimited both in time and space.[78] Contrary to its earlier position the court now held, that the proper limits of such restrictive clauses had to be assessed in each single case, and that only a 'legitimate interest' of the employer had to be protected.[79] The right of the individual employee to work in the trade he had learned was now for the first time clearly affirmed.[80]

In the following years the *Reichsgericht* elaborated these principles.[81] Yet as far as disputes between employers and former employees were concerned, it did not develop any new doctrines of its own. It was different with cases of anti-competitive practices between independent businessmen, but from the late 1890s this case law had only very limited repercussions on the law of non-competition clauses between employers and employees. From the late 1890s the German legislator in agreement with economists' and lawyers' proposals took the initiative in prescribing certain imperative rules for contracts in restraint of trade for those employees who were most frequently subject to them: foremen, supervisors, travellers, confidential clerks and others in industrial firms and commercial employees. By the detailed provisions in these codes the discretion of German appeal court judges to create new doctrines was substantially reduced. There was nothing comparable any more to the law-making power of English supreme court judges in this particular field of law. The reported cases show that the *Reichsgericht* generally endeavoured to give effect to the considerations of social policy which had motivated the legislator. The same can be said to an even larger extent of judges of the commercial tribunals which themselves had been instrumental in the above-mentioned reform of the *Handelsgesetzbuch* of 1914.[82]

Conclusion

The development of case law in England and Germany on individual agreements in restraint of trade took a remarkably similar course as far as results are concerned. From the 1850s to the mid-1890s such contracts were generally enforced in both countries even if they imposed excessive restraints on the employee. From the late 1890s to the First World War, and beyond, courts in both countries were more prepared to consider the legitimate interests of employees, especially their right to earn a living and exercise their skills in the trade they had learned. Employment contracts containing unusual or excessive non-competition clauses were no longer enforced. Not only did this change of judicial policy occur almost at the same time in both countries, it also brought about a dissociation of the law concerning anti-competitive combinations among businessmen (cartels) on the one hand, and non-competition clauses in individual employment contracts on the other. From the late 1890s English as well as German judges viewed such cases differently depending on who the parties of the conflict were – a point which is often overlooked by legal historians who tend to disregard the 'facts' of the cases they deal with.[83]

While the course of justice in both countries thus developed in a broadly similar way, it did so for very different reasons. German and English judges acted in different institutional and intellectual contexts.

In England the common law tradition itself was the supreme authority for judicial reasoning, whether on restraint of trade or other matters. Economic theory, mediated through public opinion, had a certain, if not exactly measurable influence on the guiding principles and presumptions of judges.[84] Shifts of opinion in dominant economic schools could find their way into judicial argument, sometimes with a time-lag, sometimes quickly. The British legislator was clearly the weakest player in the triangle of law, economics and politics: once Parliament had established in free competition in the late eighteenth and early nineteenth century it remained on the sidelines.

In the German case, the State was clearly the strongest player. German economists as well as lawyers looked in the first place to the State. For economists of the Historical School the State – in its legislative as well as administrative capacity – was the first addressee of all their demands; for lawyers and judges the public law regulations and private law codifications of the State were the supreme authority. Economic thought in Germany acted on the judiciary indirectly via influencing the legislative process, in which juridical experts played a central role. Legislation thus brought together the two knowledge communities. Finally, codification in the last third of the nineteenth century – uncontroversial in Germany because of the need to unify German law – provided occasions to discuss all potential legal problems on the political level, as for example, restraint of trade.

The different institutional and intellectual context accounts for the different style of reasoning in German and English courts. References to 'authority' meant different things in both countries: in England judicial precedents, in Germany the legislator's 'intent'. Similarly, the concept of freedom of contract itself had different meanings: in German legal and economic discourse it did not exclude far-reaching limitations imposed by legislation; for English economists as well as lawyers a contract could only be called free, if there was no interference from outside, whether from the State or anybody else.

Attitudes towards state intervention and certain fundamental concepts were thus different in both countries, and these attitudes and concepts were shared by lawyers and economists. Therefore, although the development of German and English justice in restraint of trade cases was similar as to the results, it was different as to their underlying rationale. Whereas in England between the 1850s and 1890s common lawyers justified their *laisser-faire* attitude with a wish to give effect to the free will of the contracting parties, German judges came to the same result by interpreting the will of the legislator. And while between 1900 and 1914 the English House of Lords felt a need to correct the balance in favour of another fundamental individual freedom, freedom of trade, German judges justified their employee-friendly jurisdiction with a concept of social justice which had been advocated by economists of the Historical School and put into practice by the state.

Notes

1. See the classic account by Alfred D. Chandler, Jr., *Scale and Scope: The Dynamics of Industrial Capitalism* (Cambridge, MA. and London: The Belknap Press of Harvard University Press, 1994); cf. also the contributions in Norbert Horn and Jürgen Kocka (eds), *Recht und Entwicklung der Großunternehmen im 19. und frühen 20. Jahrhundert/Law and the Formation of the Big Enterprises in the 19th and Early 20th Centuries* (Göttingen: Vandenhoeck & Ruprecht, 1979).
2. David J. Gerber, 'Law and Economics in Wilhelmine Germany. Examining the Dynamics of the Relationship', in Richard H. Helmholz *et al.* (eds), *Grundlagen des Rechts. Festschrift für Peter Landau zum 65. Geburtstag* (Paderborn: Schöningh, 2000), pp. 865–81.
3. Patrick S. Atiyah, *The Rise and Fall of Freedom of Contract* (Oxford: Clarendon Press 1979), pp. 666–9; and more generally: David Sugarman, 'Law, Economy and the State in England, 1750–1914: Some Major Issues' in id. (ed.), *Legality, Ideology and the State* (London: Academic Press, 1983), pp. 213–66.
4. W.R. Cornish and G. de N. Clark, *Law and Society in England 1750–1950* (London: Sweet & Maxwell, 1989), p. 267.
5. See R.O. Wilberforce, Alan Campbell and Neil Elles, *The Law of Restrictive Trade Practices and Monopolies* (London: Sweet & Maxwell, 2nd edn, 1966), pp. 25–32, and Atiyah, *Freedom of Contract*, pp. 128–30. On patent legislation as an exception to the liberalizing tendency see: Cornish and Clark, *Law and Society*, pp. 275–83.
6. 53 Geo. 3, c. 40 (1813) and 54 Geo. 3, c. 96 (1814); for the opposition against the repeal of this legislation see: Iorwerth Prothero, *Artisans and Politics in Early Nineteenth-Century London* (Folkestone: Dawson 1979), pp. 51–61.
7. For a discussion of this issue see: Jane Lewis and Sonya O. Rose, ' "Let England Blush". Protective Labor Legislation, 1820–1914', in Ulla Wikander *et al.* (eds), *Protecting Women. Labor Legislation in Europe, the United States, and Australia, 1880–1920* (Urbana and Chicago: University of Illinois Press, 1995), pp. 91–124; Willibald Steinmetz, *Begegnungen vor Gericht. Eine Sozial- und Kulturgeschichte des englischen Arbeitsrechts* (Munich: Oldenbourg, 2002), pp. 63–9.
8. 34 & 53 Vict., c. 31. For a complete history of trade union legislation and its interaction with common law jurisdiction on 'conspiracy' and civil liability see: John V. Orth, *Combination and Conspiracy: A Legal History of Trade Unionism, 1721–1906* (Oxford: Clarendon Press, 1991).
9. See W.R. Cornish: 'Legal Control over Cartels and Monopolization 1880–1914: A Comparison', in Horn and Kocka (eds), *Großunternehmen*, pp. 280–305.
10. John Stuart Mill, *Principles of Political Economy, with some of their Applications to Social Philosophy* (Collected Works of John Stuart Mill, vols 2 and 3), ed. V.W. Bladen and J.M. Robson (Toronto: University of Toronto Press, 1965), p. 240.

11. Ibid., p. 243.
12. Ibid., pp. 795–6.
13. Ibid., pp. 929–34.
14. Ibid., p. 934.
15. Ibid., pp. 944–5.
16. Ibid., p. 946.
17. Mill opposed factory legislation as far as it restrained freedom of contract for women: ibid., pp. 952–3.
18. Ibid., pp. 946–7.
19. Ibid., p. 954.
20. I am using the eighth edition: Alfred Marshall, *Principles of Economics: An Introductory Volume* (London: Macmillan, 1938). Cf. Donald Winch: 'Introduction', in id. and Patrick O'Brien (eds.), *The Political Economy of British Historical Experience, 1688–1914* (Oxford: Oxford University Press, 2002), pp. 1–28, p. 12: 'the bible that replaced Mill'.
21. Marshall, *Principles*, p. vi.
22. Ibid., pp. 5, 8.
23. Ibid., p. 8.
24. Ibid.
25. Ibid., p. 9.
26. Ibid.
27. Wilhelm Roscher, *System der Volkswirtschaft* (1868), quoted in Hans-Jürgen Teuteberg, 'Die Doktrin des ökonomischen Liberalismus und ihre Gegner dargestellt an der prinzipiellen Erörterung des Arbeitsvertrages im "Verein für Socialpolitik" 1872–1905', in Helmut Coing and Walter Wilhelm (eds), *Wissenschaft und Kodifikation des Privatrechts im 19. Jahrhundert, Bd. 2: Die rechtliche Verselbständigung der Austauschverhältnisse vor dem Hintergrund der wirtschaftlichen Entwicklung und Doktrin* (Frankfurt: Klostermann, 1977), pp. 47–73, 54.
28. [Gustav Schmoller]: 'Eröffnungsrede Schmollers zur Gründung des Vereins für Sozialpolitik am 8. Oktober 1872 in Eisenach', in id. *Historisch-ethische Nationalökonomie als Kulturwissenschaft. Ausgewählte methodologische Schriften*, ed. Heino Heinrich Nau (Marburg: Metropolis-Verlag, 1998), pp. 67–74, 73.
29. Ibid., p. 70.
30. Cf. Otto Kahn-Freund, 'A Note on Status and Contract in British Labour Law', *Modern Law Review* 80 (1967), pp. 635–44.
31. For a further discussion of this see: Steinmetz, *Begegnungen vor Gericht*, pp. 92–6, and: Willibald Steinmetz, 'Introduction: Towards a Comparative History of Legal Cultures, 1750–1950', in id. (ed.), *Private Law and Social Inequality in the Industrial Age* (Oxford: Oxford University Press, 2000), pp. 1–41, 18–21.
32. Gustav Schmoller, 'Die Natur des Arbeitsvertrags und der Kontraktbruch' (1874) in id., *Zur Social- und Gewerbepolitik der Gegenwart: Reden und Ausätze* (Leipzig: Duncker & Humblot, 1890), pp. 64–130, 103.
33. Ibid., p. 104. For a discussion of Schmoller's and other German economists' ideas on the employment contract see also Martin Becker, *Arbeitsvertrag und Arbeitsverhältnis in Deutschland: Vom Beginn der Industrialisierung bis zum Ende des Kaiserreichs* (Frankfurt: Klostermann, 1995), pp. 162–70.
34. On the codification movement in general see Michael John, *Politics and the Law in Late Nineteenth-Century Germany: The Origins of the Civil Code* (Oxford: Clarendon Press, 1989).

35. For the legislative history of *Konkurrenzklauseln* in detail see Paul Altmeppen, *Die Entwicklung des Rechts der Konkurrenzklausel* (Rheine 1917) (jur. Diss. Greifswald).
36. Cf. Hugo Sinzheimer, 'Über den Grundgedanken und die Möglichkeit eines einheitlichen Arbeitsrechts für Deutschland' (1914) in id., *Arbeitsrecht und Rechtssoziologie: Gesammelte Aufsätze und Reden*, ed. Otto Kahn-Freund and Thilo Ramm, 2 vols (Frankfurt and Cologne: Europäische Verlagsanstalt, 1976), vol. 1, pp. 35–61; Heinz Potthoff, *Probleme des Arbeitsrechtes: Rechtspolitische Betrachtungen eines Volkswirtes* (Jena: Eugen Diederichs, 1912), pp. 88–112.
37. For its position on non-competition clauses see Hermann Schuon, *Der Deutschnationale Handlungsgehilfen-Verband zu Hamburg: Sein Werdegang und seine Arbeit. Abhandlungen des staatswissenschaftlichen Seminars zu Jena, Bd. 13, 3. Heft* (Jena: Fischer, 1914), pp. 137–8.
38. On the use of commercial tribunals (*Kaufmannsgerichte*) see Steinmetz, *Begegnungen vor Gericht*, pp. 303–6, 317–32.
39. For a detailed account of the law of 1914 and the preceding debates see Georg Baum, *Das vertragliche Wettbewerbsverbot (Konkurrenzklausel)* (Berlin: Guttentag, 1914).
40. In addition to Gerber, 'Law and Economics', see Bernhard Grossfeld, 'Zur Kartellrechtsdiskussion vor dem Ersten Weltkrieg', in Helmut Coing and Walter Wilhelm (eds), *Wissenschaft und Kodifikation des Privatrechts im 19. Jahrhundert, vol. 4* (Frankfurt: Klostermann, 1979), pp. 225–96; Siegbert Lammel, 'Das Verbot der Kartelle durch § 138 BGB – eine verpaßte Gelegenheit?', *Zeitschrift für Neuere Rechtsgeschichte* 9 (1987), 51–73; Knut Wolfgang Nörr, *Die Leiden des Privatrechts: Kartelle in Deutschland von der Holzstoffkartellentscheidung zum Gesetz gegen Wettbewerbsbeschränkungen* (Tübingen: J.C.B. Mohr, 1994).
41. Cf. Lammel, 'Verbot der Kartelle', p. 53.
42. Friedrich Kleinwächter, *Die Kartelle: Ein Beitrag zur Frage der Organisation der Volkswirtschaft*, Innsbruck 1883, quoted in Grossfeld, 'Kartellrechtsdiskussion', p. 259.
43. Cf. Lammel, 'Verbot der Kartelle', p. 54.
44. Quoted in Lammel, 'Verbot der Kartelle', pp. 71–2.
45. On Brentano's position in this debate see Hans Pohl: 'Die Entwicklung der Kartelle in Deutschland und die Diskussion im Verein für Sozialpolitik', in Helmut Coing and Walter Wilhelm (eds), *Wissenschaft und Kodifikation des Privatrechts im 19. Jahrhundert, vol. 4*, pp. 206–35, esp. p. 225.
46. Gerber, 'Law and Economics'.
47. RGZ 38, 155. Cf. Nörr, *Leiden des Privatrechts*, pp. 8–9.
48. *Herbert Morris, Ltd.* v. *Saxelby* (1916) 1 A.C. 688, 716.
49. *Mitchel* v. *Reynolds* (1711) 1 Peere Wms 181; E.R. 24, 347. This was the case of a baker who had sold his business and promised to the purchaser not to compete with him within certain limits; the contract was held to be good.
50. Cf. *Homer* v. *Ashford* (1825) 3 Bing. 322; E.R. 130, 537: contract of a clerk and traveller to an ironmonger not to compete for the period of 14 years in certain specified towns – held good; and *Horner* v. *Graves* (1831) 7 Bing. 735; E.R. 131, 284: contract of a dentist's assistant not to compete within a radius of 200 miles; not upheld.
51. *Hitchcock* v. *Coker* (1837) 6 A. & E. 438; E.R. 112, 167.
52. *Tallis* v. *Tallis* (1853) 1 E. & B. 391, 412–13; E.R. 118, 482, 491. Cf. *Benwell* v. *Inns* (1857) 30 L.T. 70.

53. *Murray and another* v. *Close* (1858) 32 L.T. 89.
54. Number of cases seen: 16.
55. *Roussillon* v. *Roussillon* (1880) 14 Ch.D. 351; *Badische Anilin und Soda Fabrik* v. *Schott, Segner & Co.* (1892) 3 Ch. 447.
56. *Dubowski* v. *Goldstein* (1896) 1 Q.B. 478.
57. Ibid., p. 486.
58. Examples: *National Provincial Bank of England* v. *Marshall* (1888) 40 Ch.D. 112; *Mills* v. *Dunham* (1891) 1 Ch. 576.
59. *Nordenfeldt* v. *Maxim Nordenfeldt Co.* (1893) Ch.D. 659 and (1894) A.C. 535.
60. (1894) A.C. 565.
61. *Everett's Stores Ltd.* v. *Vincent*, reported in *Bakers' Record*, 27 Dec. 1912, 5: a case before the Bow county court (London) of a baker's roundsman who, the defence claimed, 'did not properly understand the effect of the agreement when he signed it'.
62. *General Billposting Co., Ltd.* v. *Atkinson* (1909) A.C. 118.
63. *Sir W.C. Leng & Co., Ltd.* v. *Andrews* (1909) 1 Ch. 763: a case of a junior reporter for a Sheffield newspaper who was prevented for the whole of his life to work for another newspaper within a radius of 25 miles around Sheffield. See also: *Mason* v. *Provident Clothing and Supply Co., Ltd.* (1913) A.C. 724, 732–3 (Viscount Haldane, L.C.).
64. *Dowden & Pook, Ltd.* v. *Pook* (1904) 1 K.B. 45.
65. *Pearks (Ltd.)* v. *Cullen* (1912) 28 T.L.R. 371, 372.
66. *Mason* v. *Provident Clothing and Supply Co., Ltd.* (1913) A.C. 724, 733.
67. See *S.V. Nevanas & Co.* v. *Walker and Foreman* (1914) 1 Ch. 413, 421: here the new rule was only suggested by the defendant's counsel; it was expressly formulated by Lord Haldane in: *North Western Salt Co.* v. *Electrolytic Alkali Co.* (1914) A.C. 461.
68. See the illuminating remarks on the language of English judicial decisions in this period by Steve Hedley, 'Words, Words, Words: Making Sense of Legal Judgments, 1875–1940', in Chantal Stebbings (ed.), *Law Reporting in England* (London and Rio Grande: The Hambledon Press, 1995), pp. 169–86.
69. Lord Shaw of Dunfermline in *Morris* v. *Saxelby* (1916) 1 A.C. 688, 716; see the full quotation above (fn. 48). Cf. also Younger J. in *Attwood* v. *Lamont* (1920) 2 K.B. 146 and 3 K.B. 581.
70. For a brief discussion of early cases see: Lammel, 'Verbot der Kartelle', pp. 58–60; unfortunately Lammel does not clearly distinguish between employment disputes, disputes between businessmen and cartel-cases. See also Baum, *Wettbewerbsverbot*, p. 11.
71. Entscheidungen des Reichs-Oberhandelsgerichts 7 (1873), pp. 418, 421.
72. RGZ 1 (1880), 22–23.
73. Entscheidungen des Königlichen Ober-Tribunals 77 (1876), p. 231.
74. Entscheidungen des Königlichen Ober-Tribunals 80 (1877), p. 1.
75. Ibid., p. 31.
76. Ibid., pp. 31–2.
77. Josef Kohler, 'Vertragsmäßige Beschränkung des Gewerbebetriebs', in id., *Gesammelte Abhandlungen aus dem gemeinen und französischen Civilrecht* (Mannheim: J. Bensheimer, 1883), pp. 62–74, esp. p. 74. Kohler in this article also commented on English and American decisions and it cannot be excluded that his knowledge of common law decisions on this subject influenced him in his position.

78. RGZ 31, 97, 98.
79. Ibid., p. 99.
80. Ibid., p. 100.
81. See for example: RGZ 40, 97 (1897); RGZ 53, 156 (1902); RGZ 54, 123 (1903).
82. A useful collection of decisions of commercial tribunals as well as ordinary courts on all levels up to the *Reichsgericht* can be found in Georg Baum, *Handbuch für Gewerbe- und Kaufmannsgerichte* (Berlin: Georg Reimer 1912), pp. 422–6 and 547–87.
83. Lammel, 'Verbot der Kartelle', and Atiyah, *Freedom of Contract*, are cases in point.
84. See on this: Frederick Pollock, *The Genius of the Common Law* (New York: Columbia University Press, 1912), esp. pp. 94–109.

8

Savings-promotion as Economic Knowledge: Transnational Insights from the Japanese Experience

Sheldon Garon

To what extent have states and societies shaped the economic behaviour of their peoples? Could a government or groups, for instance, mould a 'culture of thrift' that values high levels of savings while discouraging 'excessive consumption'? Few Anglo-American economists today consider such questions. Nevertheless, since the early nineteenth century, reformers and governments in numerous countries have actively intervened to promote popular saving. They established savings banks, postal savings institutions and school savings programmes. In the first half of the twentieth century, states mounted intrusive wartime savings campaigns. Although these programmes were first institutionalized in Europe, North America and Australasia, the modern Japanese state also aggressively promoted saving following the Meiji Restoration of 1868. Indeed, during the latter half of the twentieth century, the centre of thrift-promotion shifted to Japan and several rapidly developing economies in East and Southeast Asia.

Encouraging people to be thrifty may not figure in the study of economic thought in Western nations today, but during the nineteenth and much of the twentieth centuries the promotion of saving played an important role in the formation of 'economic knowledge'. Its history helps us understand the emergence, diffusion and contestation of political economy in the following respects. First, discourses and policies concerned with popular saving illuminate some of the complex historical relationships among economics, morality, politics and society. Household saving has been promoted in terms of various imperatives, notably (1) moral: to create virtue and build character, (2) social: to stabilize people's lives and integrate the labouring classes, (3) economic: to generate capital and (4) political: to finance such state projects as war, imperialism and development. These objectives often coincided, and their precise mix has varied over time and across space. It is easy today to dismiss the encouragement of thrift as old-fashioned 'Victorian' morality that runs counter to the modern discipline of economics. But in the world of the nineteenth and early twentieth centuries, the preoccupation with cultivating thrifty citizens was itself a modern manifestation of the rise of capitalism, political participation and nation-states. Morality, political economy and state power interacted to shape each other.

Second, this chapter examines the array of producers of such economic and social knowledge. Thrift was championed by political economists and state bureaucrats, but also by countless actors within the emerging 'public sphere'. The cast of characters featured best-selling authors like Samuel Smiles, clerics, merchants, philanthropic organizations and women's groups. Third, the promotion of saving – like so many other aspects of political economy – developed to a significant degree as the result of the transnational diffusion of economic and social knowledge. This chapter identifies some of the key agents in the process of dissemination. States studied how other states encouraged popular thrift; colonial powers transplanted promotional institutions; transnational Christian organizations preached the gospel of thrift; and prominent moral tracts were translated and read in much of the world. By no means was the process of diffusion unidirectional, flowing from a few European powers to the 'peripheries'. Rather, nations continually learned from each other, and the past two centuries have witnessed a succession of national models of savings-promotion and economic development.

Finally, I present the case of Japan to offer comparative and transnational insights that may be useful in revisiting questions of political economy in European, US and global history. The Japanese were not simply the takers of knowledge from the West, but occasionally the *makers* of ideas. Embarking in the 1870s on investigations of the world's leading models, the Japanese state often adopted these models before many Western nations, and Japanese innovations sometimes became part of transnational policy debates. Moreover, in their unusually thorough study of the latest Western trends – whether British postal savings or European austerity campaigns following the First World War – the Japanese reveal a Western world, now forgotten, when the saver, not consumer, was sovereign. More recently, Japan's success in financing its post-war 'economic miracle' profoundly influenced theories of economic development and the actual policies of emerging Asian economies.

'Organizing Thrift' in Europe

As one banker-turned-historian put it, 'the instinct to save is almost as old as human nature', but 'organized thrift is a more recent development'. Its origins date only to the late eighteenth and early nineteenth centuries.[1] Within a short span of time throughout much of Europe, large numbers of individuals, groups and public authorities began encouraging *all* strata of society to save money – a 'radical innovation', according to one French scholar.[2] In the course of the nineteenth century, governments and reformers actively 'organized thrift' by increasingly elaborate methods.

The initial wave of savings-promotion in the Western world was characterized by the founding of what came to be known as 'savings banks' (Sparkassen, caisses d'épargne, casse di risparmio, etc.). Despite national and regional differences, the early savings banks generally shared the mission of enabling and encouraging the working poor to put aside small savings. In contrast to the existing commercial banks, which catered primarily to merchants and the wealthy, the savings banks accepted small deposits. To encourage children and the very poor to save, clergymen and other philanthropists further created intermediary organizations, such as church-based 'penny banks' or neighbourhood and workplace-based savings associations. These organizations collected mere pennies and deposited them in nearby savings banks. Founders commonly depicted the savings bank as a social or 'moral institution', in the words of the French reformer the Duc de La Rochefoucauld-Liancourt. Its trustees, generally people of means, often donated their own funds to offer depositors higher interest, and they invested the savings bank with the role of educating people in the proper use of money.[3]

The first savings banks appeared during the late eighteenth century in a number of German and Swiss cities, beginning with Hamburg in 1778. They spread rapidly throughout the German states after the Napoleonic wars. Between 1817 and 1838, similar banks sprang up in the Netherlands, France, the Scandinavian countries, the Austrian empire, Italy, Belgium and Spain. Yet it was in Britain that reformers created the most extensive network of savings banks. In England, clergymen and philanthropic women and men founded the first informal savings banks in the waning years of the eighteenth century. During the 1810s, Scotland became a veritable laboratory, as pastors and others established savings banks in a number of rural parishes and then in the cities. England followed suit in the latter half of the 1810s, and by 1820 the British Isles counted nearly five hundred savings banks.[4]

Why did societies become so avid about encouraging thrift two centuries ago? As Daniel Duet observes, the savings bank movement developed in too many places, within too many social structures, and at too many different stages of economic development to reduce the phenomenon to a single explanation. Weber's 'Protestant ethic', for example, is of limited utility. Besides 'frugal Scots' and self-disciplined New England Puritans, we must also reckon with the proliferation of savings banks in the Catholic lands of France, Belgium, Italy and elsewhere. Similarly, although some European scholars relate the emergence of savings banks to the Industrial Revolution, savings banks spread throughout much of Europe during the late eighteenth and early nineteenth centuries – decades before the significant appearance of mechanized industry in most places.[5]

Rather, the origins of 'organized thrift' lay in the interplay of a number of important developments in socio-economic conditions and social knowledge. In several European countries, the living standards of the masses slowly improved to the point that ordinary people attained some margin to save. The growth of wage labour further advanced the propensity to save. Notably the earliest savings banks overwhelmingly drew upon the small surpluses of domestic servants, artisans, sailors and agricultural labourers. As factory labour expanded in the nineteenth century and assertive labour movements challenged the existing order, industrial workers became the major target of these banks.[6] At roughly the same time, middling strata of merchants and professionals expanded, and they joined aristocratic elements in organizing reading societies, moral reform groups and other associations that contemporaries referred to as 'civil society'. Members not only emphasized self-cultivation, but also strove to 'civilize' the working poor by inculcating such habits as thrift and sobriety.[7]

Just as important, the encouragement of saving reflected new ways of thinking about society, economy, the nation-state and the individual. Unquestionably the emerging study of political economy influenced the savings bank movement. In *An Inquiry into the Nature and Causes of the Wealth of Nations* (1776), Adam Smith portrayed saving as vital to the creation of wealth: 'Parsimony, and not industry, is the immediate cause of the increase of capital.' Individual acts of thrift generated macroeconomic development, and they also – unlike increased consumption – improved people's lives, made individuals less dependent on others, and were downright natural: 'The passion for present enjoyment; which, though sometimes violent and very difficult to be restrained, is in general only momentary and occasional.' On the other hand, 'the principle which prompts to save, is the desire of bettering our condition, a desire which ... comes to us from the womb, and never leaves us till we go to the grave'.[8] In his influential *Essay on the Principle of Population* (second edition, 1803), Malthus went beyond Smith to propose an institutional means to 'promote the habits of prudence and foresight'. His 'country banks' would 'facilitate the saving of small sums of money' and 'encourage young labourers to economize their earnings with a view to a provision for marriage'. Like other British political economists, Malthus expounded upon the utility of allowing individuals to make their own economic decisions. The labourer should be able to withdraw his savings 'whenever he wanted it, and have the most perfect liberty of disposing of it ... because the knowledge of possessing this liberty would be of more use in encouraging the practice of saving, than any restriction of it in preventing the misuse of money so saved'.[9] Throughout the nineteenth century and well into the twentieth, economists overwhelmingly favoured the act of saving over consumption in fostering both economic growth and social stability.[10]

Infusing the work of the political economists was a new body of ideas that aimed more at ameliorating social problems than advancing economic development. The early nineteenth-century champions of savings banks in Europe rarely encouraged small saving for the purpose of generating substantial capital. Instead they couched their arguments in terms of improving the lives of the working poor. Enlightenment thought in France and Britain sparked a series of proposals for savings institutions as self-help alternatives to poor relief. As early as 1755, Diderot's *Encyclopédie* included an entry on 'Thrift', in which the author advocated the creation of establishments in every town that would permit labourers and domestics to deposit small sums that would otherwise be dissipated or lost. By providing a secure institution from which depositors could freely withdraw their savings for future needs, these facilities would insure that 'most workers and domestics will become thriftier and more orderly in their lives'.[11] At the height of the French Revolution in 1791, the National Assembly's Committee on Begging seriously considered the establishment of a savings bank in each department of France, reasoning that 'checking poverty is, without a doubt, the urgent work of society, but preventing it is no less sacred and necessary'.[12] English thinkers were particularly concerned about rising Poor Law expenses. In 1797, the philosopher Jeremy Bentham penned a singularly scientific plan for savings banks. As part of a proposal to employ the 'burdensome poor' in Industry Houses, he recommended the institution of 'Frugality Banks'. The poor, he recognized, lacked safe means of deposit and receiving interest, with which they might resist constant 'temptations afforded by the instruments of sensual enjoyment'. Accordingly, Bentham devised an elaborate system in which savings entitled the depositor to an annuity that varied by one's age. In both England and France, proponents depicted savings banks as a 'vaccine' that would eradicate poverty.[13]

In the realm of political thought, too, emerging conceptions of the nation-state and citizenship fuelled the expansion of savings banks in Europe. On one hand, upper-class and middle-class proponents envisioned these banks as instruments for blunting disorderly and revolutionary conduct by the working classes.[14] In a more positive sense, the champions of popular thrift were often political liberals who conceived of saving as an act of citizenship, serving to integrate the humbler classes into the polity. Beginning with the Scottish political economist Patrick Colquhoun in 1806, British reformers repeatedly argued that savings banks would convince the poor that they, like the rich, have 'a stake in the country'.[15] John Tidd Pratt, the barrister who oversaw the operations of the early savings banks, added that 'every person who has vested his savings in the public funds [by depositing in the savings banks] has a stake in the security of the country, ... and will be deterred from compassing the disturbance of his native land by a personal motive ... . He who possesses property in a country is not interested in the stability of the administration for the time being, but in the perpetual stability of universal order and good government'.[16] In France, too, many spoke of the savings banks as an opportunity to transform the people into creditors of the state, imbuing them with a self-interest in stability and patriotism.[17] These arguments reflected the fact that in both Britain and France saving banks redeposited their funds in the national treasuries.

It was no coincidence that savings banks sprang up in Europe, North America and Australia at roughly the same time in the early decades of the nineteenth century. Transnational networks of communication enabled the rapid diffusion of social knowledge, as the pioneers of organized thrift learned from successful experiments in other lands. An 'international movement' is how Daniel Duet describes the widespread introduction of savings banks.[18] British institutions quickly emerged as the leading model, having developed systematically on a nationwide basis. Savings Bank Acts in 1817 set down rules for the management of the new banks and the disposition of their assets in England, Wales and Ireland (extended to Scotland in 1835). After surveying savings banks in England and Scotland, a Swedish treasury official issued an influential report that led to the establishment of his country's first savings bank in 1820. The British model similarly influenced the inauguration of savings banks in the Netherlands, Norway, Finland and Austria. Patrick Colquhoun championed thrift institutions not only in Britain, but also in his letters to American philanthropists who went on to found savings banks in Philadelphia, Boston and New York between 1816 and 1819. The French founders of the Caisse d'Épargne de Paris (1818) – Benjamin Delessert and the Duc de La Rochefoucauld-Liancourt – openly proclaimed their intellectual debt to Britain, where both had spent considerable time. Likewise, in the 1830s, liberal exiles returned to Spain and, influenced by British and French ideas, introduced the country's first savings banks.[19]

Whereas individuals, philanthropic groups and municipalities had taken the lead in founding the first generation of savings banks in Europe, many states seized the initiative in organizing thrift during the latter half of the nineteenth century. The key innovation was the formation of national savings banks – in most cases, postal savings systems. Once again, Britain emerged as the leading model, inaugurating the world's first Post Office Savings Bank in 1861. Independently in 1865, the Belgian government instituted the Caisse Générale d'Épargne et de Retraite (General Savings Bank and Pension Fund). The CGER, which also relied on post offices as branches, attracted more than 80 per cent of the nation's savers and deposits in 1880. Post office savings banks spread rapidly through the British empire, and several European governments conducted investigations of the British model. Between 1876 and 1884, Italy, the Netherlands, France, Austria and Sweden adopted postal savings systems. In the United States, federal officials actively surveyed European models, and they pressed Congress to approve a postal savings system. However, commercial banks and regional interests resisted efforts to adopt what they viewed as a dangerous experiment in European statism aimed at centralizing finances. After four decades of rejecting numerous bills, the US Congress instituted a singularly tepid version of postal savings in 1910.[20]

In the European cases, postal savings proved compelling because of the perceived inadequacy of local savings banks in promoting habits of the thrift among the growing working classes. One British postal official summed up the government's case. The Post Office Savings Bank would greatly increase 'the means afforded to the humbler classes of the country for depositing at interest their little savings'. It would give depositors 'a feeling of perfect security', so they would 'not be exposed, as too often at present, to the risk of peculation.'[21] In Britain and

Belgium, the collapse of prominent savings banks – often resulting from mismanagement and fraud – emboldened political leaders to demand that governments guarantee the security of deposits by setting up state-run savings banks. Moreover, in Britain, France and elsewhere, proponents touted the convenience of post offices, which served smaller communities and were open on a daily basis (unlike the vast majority of savings banks). From a political perspective, liberal forces attacked the paternalism of the local savings banks while trumpeting the efficacy of the post office as a neutral state institution.[22] In 1878, some 34,000 of France's 36,000 communes lacked a savings bank, according to the government's spokesman for postal savings legislation. This state of affairs ran 'contrary to justice because all Frenchmen have a right to equal treatment ... and the little communes whose inhabitants pay their taxes ... are justified in making demands on the State'.[23] In Britain, William Gladstone, as Chancellor of the Exchequer, suggested in 1861 that workers would more readily make deposits at the post office, where they enjoyed 'secrecy', whereas at the savings banks they were compelled to act 'under the immediate view of their local superiors'.[24]

In short, during the middle decades of the nineteenth century, several European states assumed direct responsibility for promoting saving as part of broader programmes to solve social problems and cultivate modern citizens. The objective of national integration also figured in growing efforts by central educational authorities and the national savings banks to inculcate habits of thrift in all schoolchildren, particularly in France and Belgium.[25] When modernizing Japanese leaders after 1868 set out to discover the secrets of Western might, they astutely observed the 'civilized' powers to be obsessed with creating patriotic, hard-working and thrifty citizens.

'An Instrument of the National Economy'

Halfway around the globe, Japan had not participated in the Western world's early nineteenth-century movement to create thrifty people and savings banks. For more than two centuries, the Tokugawa shogunate had largely secluded Japan from the outside world, while permitting limited trade and exchange with only the Dutch, Koreans and Chinese. Then came Commodore Matthew Perry and his 'black ships', forcing the shogun in 1854 to 'open' Japan to commerce and diplomacy with the United States and then the European powers. Almost overnight Japanese officials and scholars embarked upon a spirited study of Western techniques and thought. The embrace of Westernization became state policy following the Meiji Restoration (1868). The new government dispatched growing numbers of officials to survey Western institutions and policies. It also devoted substantial resources to hiring more than 2400 foreign consultants, whose chief job it was to inform the regime of the latest Western trends in military, economic, social, legal and political affairs.[26] Even conservative state officials came to believe that Japan's future lay in the ongoing study of the West's present. Few Japanese leaders regarded such emulation as slavish imitation or an affront to national pride. On the contrary, as Vice Minister of Home Affairs Ichiki Kitokurō would remark, every successful nation was importing 'knowledge' from other countries in the relentless struggle to progress.[27]

By 1909, when Ichiki wrote, savings-promotion had become central to moulding Japan into a modern nation and world power. 'Nothing can be as positive', he remarked, 'and nothing increases the nation's wealth nor contributes to the rise of the nation as much as thrift'.[28] Over the span of 40 years, the Japanese had introduced the basic institutions, organizations, and thinking that would guide the promotion of popular saving throughout the twentieth century. Many of these mechanisms and ideas were directly inspired by Western models, while some represented the modernization of traditional organizations and virtues. Yet the most distinctive characteristics of Japanese savings-promotion developed from a haphazard process of emulation, as well as the decades-long interaction between Western knowledge and indigenous developments.[29]

In retrospect, the new regime made a brilliant decision when Japan became only the third nation (after Britain and Belgium) to institute a postal savings system in 1875. Postal savings became the linchpin of the government's twin programmes to increase household saving and channel the people's wealth towards financing rapid industrialization and national power. However, we should avoid reading that story back onto its creation. The Japanese postal savings system originated as a modest effort to encourage habits of thrift in an era of unsystematic exposure to a range of economic knowledge from abroad.

Far from constituting a top priority of the Meiji regime, postal savings began its Japanese life incidentally. It was born of the nation's serendipitous encounters with foreign models, plus the sheer determination of one official. Maejima Hisoka, who had heavily invested in the mastery of British knowledge, stumbled upon the Post Office Savings Bank while engaged in investigations of other matters. Growing up under the Tokugawa shogun, Maejima had been sent to Edo (Tokyo) to study 'Dutch medicine', including the Dutch language. But after Commodore Perry arrived in a show of force in 1853–54, Maejima switched to studying

English and particularly things British. The Dutch, he was told by one Japanese lord, were 'dull and in decline', whereas Britannia ruled the waves, dominated trade, and was 'peerless among the civilized nations.'[30] In 1870, the new government appointed Maejima to modernize the postal system. Later that year he travelled to England on a year-long mission to renegotiate a government loan with London financiers. There, in his spare time, he surveyed the British post, widely considered the world's leading model. Before long he encountered the Post Office Savings Bank, which had opened shop less than ten years earlier and was already attracting the interest of European governments. Maejima returned to Japan, and, encountering remarkably little resistance, he persuaded government leaders to inaugurate postal savings in 1875. The revolutionary institution of postal savings had slipped into Japan as part (and parcel) of the omnibus model of the British post.[31]

The relative ease with which the Japanese government adopted postal savings was not lost on future generations of bureaucrats, who boasted that their country had assimilated the 'civilization' of the West more quickly than many of the Western powers themselves. France, Austria, Italy and others 'all lagged behind our country', crowed the postal savings official Shimomura Hiroshi in 1910. The French and Germans expended considerable time and resources in studying the British Post Office Savings Bank, he remarked, yet the French did not institute their own system until the 1880s, and the Germans debated the measure to no conclusion in several parliamentary sessions. The Americans had yet to adopt postal savings, Shimomura observed. The Japanese, by contrast, he explained with no apparent sense of irony, introduced postal savings in 'just the time it took to do the translations'.[32]

Indeed, a little transnational knowledge went a long way in late nineteenth-century Japan. Bureaucrats were able to establish the innovative postal savings system because they governed with few challenges from 'society'. No national parliament existed until 1890 to voice objections to the creation of a state-run savings bank, as happened in many Western nations. And in the Japan of 1875, unlike the United States or Germany, few commercial banks and no local savings banks existed to block competition from postal savings.

The highly derivative quality of Japanese emulation shaped the government's early objectives in instituting postal savings. Officials scarcely considered that conditions in agrarian Japan differed greatly from those in industrial England. Nor did they conceive of themselves as a 'late-developing' nation that might adapt Western European institutions to indigenous needs. Whereas British leaders created the Post Office Savings

Bank in part to pre-empt a radical workers' movement and reduce poor relief costs, Japan as yet lacked a significant industrial work force and spent little on relief. While Europeans generally promoted postal savings banks in reaction to the inadequacies of local savings banks, the Japanese state effected postal savings before a single savings bank had opened for business. Most surprising, at a time when the modernizing Japanese regime was desperate for capital, officials initially took no steps to invest postal savings deposits strategically. Rather, postal savings were passively deposited in the First National Bank, a commercial institution.[33]

Instead of selectively borrowing from among Western models, Japanese bureaucrats in 1874 embraced the rationale of Victorian moral and social improvement with nary an adaptation. In the words of a Home Ministry memorandum: 'It is an obligation of Government to encourage the poor to set aside what they can save. Their assets may thus be preserved, themselves protected from misfortune, and their habits improved.'[34] Maejima Hisoka, echoing British rhetoric, informed the public one year later that deposits at the post office would, above all, 'greatly elevate the ways of thrift' among 'the humble folk' (*shōmin*).[35]

The government's initial lack of interest in mobilizing popular savings for national projects was very much related to the state of transnational knowledge in the 1870s. The world of the mid- to late nineteenth century was one in which modernizing economies depended on foreign capital. This held true not only in Europe, North America and Australasia, but also for Egypt, Argentina and Mexico. Japan's oligarchs similarly looked abroad. The regime floated two major loans in London in 1870 and 1873.[36] Moreover, Japanese authorities lacked a blueprint for going beyond Europe's pioneer postal savings systems. The architects of Britain's Post Office Savings Bank had not envisioned the 'small savings' of lower-income people as a key source of capital for the national economy. For the most part, the National Debt Commissioners conservatively invested postal deposits in government bonds and securities.[37] As the world's leading financial centre, Britain was awash in investment capital from other sources.

Although Japanese officials, too, at first promoted saving for reasons of social policy and moral betterment, the objectives of economic growth and nation power soon dominated efforts to spur popular saving. In a momentous political decision, Japanese leaders eschewed all foreign borrowing between 1873 and 1897. They thus defied the conventional wisdom prevalent in other late-developing economies. Officials became haunted by the spectre that Europeans would intervene in Japan's internal affairs if the nation could not repay its debts. They were well aware of such interventions in contemporary Mexico, Egypt and China.[38] In lieu of foreign capital, the Japanese state turned to mobilizing the savings of its entire people. By 1879, Maejima Hisoka was instructing the nation's postmasters to promote postal savings as 'an instrument of the national economy'. Deposits would be used to fight inflation and 'supply capital for industry and trade'.[39]

In addition, Japanese officials became exposed to new types of economic knowledge that went beyond the socially oriented British approach to organizing thrift. Much has been made of the influence of the nation-centred ideas of Germany's 'historical school', notably Friedrich List. His influential treatise, *The National System of Political Economy* (1841), appeared in Japanese translation in 1889.[40] In an institutional sense, however, French models played a more significant role in transforming savings-promotion in Japan, which had already emulated the centralization and bureaucratic structure of the French state. In 1885, Finance Minister Matsukata Masayoshi placed all postal savings deposits under the management of the Ministry of Finance's Deposit Bureau. Henceforth Ministry of Finance bureaucrats would invest the growing pool of postal savings with absolute discretion.[41] Remarkably this system has persisted with few changes into the twenty-first century. The ministry appears to have modelled the Deposit Bureau after its namesake, France's Caisse des Dépôts et Consignations (Bank of Deposits and Consignations). Matsukata had investigated French financial administration during a recent stay in Paris. In the 1850s, the French state had ordered private savings banks to transfer all of their deposits to the bureaucratically managed Caisse des Dépôts, thereby denying the savings banks any control over lending and investment. When the government instituted postal savings in 1881, the Caisse des Dépôts managed those deposits, too. Drawing on this vast central fund, the French state converted the small savings of its people into strategic investments in the nation's economic development, aiming to advance 'the grandeur and prosperity of our country'.[42]

Like their French counterparts, Japanese bureaucrats would invest the expanding assets of the postal savings system in various national projects. The Deposit Bureau funds played a large role in financing government bonds for the Sino-Japanese War (1894–95) and the Russo-Japanese War (1904–05). These monies also funded Japan's imperial interests in the colonies of Taiwan and Korea and in Manchuria and China proper.[43] To stimulate economic development at home, the Deposit Bureau channelled substantial sums to the government's 'special banks' – notably the Hypothec Bank (Nihon Kangyō Ginkō, est. 1896) and later the Industrial

Bank of Japan (Nihon Kōgyō Ginkō, est. 1900). Both were modelled after special banks of the French state. Besides lending to agriculture, these banks also made low-interest loans to modern industries. By 1931, the special banks' loans surpassed the total lending of the zaibatsu-affiliated 'city banks'.[44]

As Japanese postal savings evolved into a vital instrument of national power after 1900, the promotion of saving assumed the form of increasingly aggressive nationwide campaigns. State control of the rapidly expanding pool of small savings gave the central bureaucracy more and more reason to encourage popular saving. Indeed, zealous officials did their best to constrain the development of private savings banks, whose assets were not placed in the Deposit Bureau. To the delight of the Ministry of Finance, the savings banks all but disappeared by the end of the 1920s. In contrast, savings deposited in the post offices soared from 741,000 yen in 1880, to 24,733,000 yen in 1900 and to 201,243,000 yen in 1912.[45] By the 1930s, the Japanese postal system exceeded every one of its Western counterparts both in aggregate deposits and the number of depositors.[46]

Although the state never relinquished its central position in organizing thrift, non-governmental groups assumed important roles in encouraging popular saving after 1900. Particularly active were Japanese Protestants and members of the emerging 'new middle class' – notably educators, health professionals, social workers, journalists and salaried employees in companies and government.[47] These groups not only mediated the importation of Western knowledge on thrift, they were in a sense collectively constituted by currents of social knowledge prevalent in contemporary Europe and North America. Middle-class Japanese voraciously consumed Victorian moral tracts, especially the work of Samuel Smiles. Smiles' *Self-Help* (1859) was translated into Japanese as early as 1871, and it remained a best-seller for decades. The Scottish writer elaborated on the virtues of frugality and saving in *Thrift* (1876), which appeared in Japanese translation in 1906.[48] Smiles popularized the conventional social and economic knowledge of his time: 'The building of all the houses, the mills, the bridges, and the ships, and the accomplishment of all other great works which have rendered man civilized and happy, has been done by the savers, the thrifty; and those who have wasted their resources have always been their slaves.'[49] As the Japanese Protestant social reformer Tomeoka Kōsuke remarked, Smiles' *Self-Help* had transformed much of the world, having been translated into more than twenty languages. Tomeoka was at the time working for the government to propagate the 'diligence and thrift' gospel of Ninomiya

Sontoku, a Tokugawa-era reformer, and he proudly proclaimed Ninomiya's ideas to be 'the Orient's theory of Self-Help'.[50]

Such Western writings appealed to self-styled middle-class Japanese. The traits of diligence and thrift, of course, offered a means to personal advancement. Also, a thrifty middle class elevated its own status by inculcating habits of saving in those below them. This was as true in Japan as it was in England or the Netherlands. Moreover, from the turn of the twentieth century, middle-class Japanese began promoting the Anglo-American ideal of the 'housewife', who controlled family spending and kept household account books (*kakeibo*). Western-style housewives' magazines found a mass market among Japanese during the 1920s, and their emphasis on encouraging household saving continues to the present. Determined to teach ordinary Japanese the habits of thrift, middle-class activists shared much with government officials (who also widely quoted Smiles and Benjamin Franklin).[51] Beginning in the first decade of the twentieth century, well-known Protestants and leaders of women's organizations enthusiastically participated in the state's pervasive savings campaigns.[52]

The advent of 'National Savings'

As Vice Minister of Home Affairs Ichiki Kitokurō noted in 1909, '[w]hile our country has progressed [over the past forty years], so, too, have other countries – nay, even more so.'[53] Japan had learned from Britain, then France. By 1905, Japan had surpassed all European nations in its relentless promotion of saving for the purpose of transforming a resource-poor land into a major military and industrial power. Yet Britain and the other powers were hardly standing still. Governments that had initially encouraged thrift as social policy and moral betterment came to recognize the value of small savings in augmenting national resources. This was perhaps inevitable in Britain and France, where both the postal savings institutions and savings banks (Trustee Savings Banks in Britain) deposited all their assets in government-managed funds. Without particular design, small savings became mountains of cash, which European states – like their Japanese counterpart – could draw upon as they saw fit. France, in particular, provided a mythic lesson after its humiliating loss to Germany in 1871. By 'investing their savings in the National Defense Loan', remarked Samuel Smiles, the French peasantry had financed the indemnity and 'liberated French soil from the tread of their German conquerors'.[54]

The decades leading up to the First World War saw the world's powers engaged in fierce rivalries and military build-ups. The degree to which one's people saved became a common index of relative national strength. To demonstrate their nation's weakness vis-à-vis the other powers, Japanese authorities released cross-national tables that listed Japan's relatively high rates of death, suicide, divorce and imprisonment, while communicating its low level of saving. In 1908–09, according to one table, Japanese saved a mere 5 yen per capita, compared to 172 yen in both the United States and Germany and 110 yen in Britain.[55] In contemporary France, too, publicity posters illustrated 'Total Savings Per Capita in France and Some Other Countries'. A stereotypical American, German, Frenchman and others posed next to different-sized bags of money.[56]

Although it would be too much to claim that a 'Japanese model' reshaped statecraft in Western nations, Japan's success in social mobilization figured prominently in key debates raging within the great powers. Especially in Britain, Japan gathered a cult-like following after the Asian power defeated Russia in 1905. In the wake of their country's recent humiliation in the Boer War, British leaders and thinkers became fixated on national reinvigoration. Japan – their new partner in the Anglo-Japanese Alliance (1902) – offered an engaging model of 'national efficiency'. From Conservative imperialists to Liberals and Fabian Socialists, eminent Britons touted Japan's superior national organization.[57] In 1906, the journalist Alfred Stead published his provocatively titled *Great Japan: A Study in National Efficiency*. Former Liberal prime minister Lord Rosebery wrote the laudatory forward. Britain, noted Rosebery, had 'muddled through', while 'the old State machine creaks on'. Fortunately it was furnished by the 'stimulating example' of Japan, a 'nation determined on efficiency' led by what the British could only envy: a 'directing and vitalizing Government that shall do and inspire great things'. In the remainder of the book, Stead portrayed a Japan where state policies and traditions had moulded a patriotic, frugal people who were prepared to 'sacrifice' for the 'country's good' on the battlefield and at home. Saving for the nation formed one pillar of this 'universal and practical patriotism'. At the time of the Russo-Japanese War, Stead observed, Japanese saved at high rates at post offices and private banks to finance the war: 'The farmer, labourer, the tradesman, and the servant eagerly handed in their savings. The very school-children, hoarding up their small pocket-money ... also carried their offerings to the Treasury department.'[58] Two years later an inspired Rosebery declared that 'thrift is the surest and the strongest foundation of an empire – so sure, so strong, and so necessary that no great empire can long exist that disregards it'.[59]

Obsessed with the 'national efficiency' drives of other powers, the British state soon developed another model for the world – the National Savings Movement. In Japan and France, postmasters and schoolteachers had been deputized to encourage thrift, but no nineteenth-century government had systematically mobilized state and society to promote popular saving. Britain changed all that in the First World War, leapfrogging the Japanese in its statism. Of all the belligerents, the 'liberal' British state imposed the most elaborate nationwide campaign apparatus. Savings drives extracted vast amounts of small savings and funnelled them directly to the national treasury. In 1916, the government established three National War Savings Committees for England and Wales, Scotland, and Ireland, respectively. By the end of 1918, the central committee in England and Wales was co-ordinating the activities of 1840 Local War Savings Committees and 41,301 War Savings Associations (based in schools, workplaces, churches, clubs and neighbourhoods). The myriad volunteers included rural notables, teachers, trade unionists, women's organization leaders, and artists. The state also turned to techniques of mass propaganda to encourage saving – notably posters and advertisements. One could save for the war by making ordinary deposits or buying government securities at the post office or trustee savings banks. But the new savings associations had the advantage of relying on local volunteers to harangue members to buy small-denomination War Savings Certificates on ongoing basis. The levels of national saving soared in the course of the war. By the end of 1917, more than 16 million people held some form of government securities, compared to a mere 345,100 individuals before the war.[60]

Britain's National Savings campaigns introduced not only new modes of organization, but also enduring forms of social and economic knowledge. The act of saving came to be regarded as the patriotic duty of all citizens – on a par with military service.[61] Targeting the working class and others of modest means, the authorities discovered that 'the material wealth of the nation was far more evenly distributed amongst the population than had previously been the case. ... The Savings Movement had revealed to an extraordinary extent how great was the reservoir of Small Investment'.[62] After the First World War, British political leaders, including those from the Labour Party, maintained the National Savings Committee structure. They shifted the focus to encouraging saving to finance the post-war needs of recovery, industrial expansion, housing and social welfare. In 1927, Labour's former Chancellor of the Exchequer Philip Snowden declared the centrality of saving in official economic thinking: 'saving is absolutely necessary, not merely to maintain industry, but to permit of its progressive expansion; and that saving, instead of reducing employment, adds to the volume of employment and increases the consuming power of the community'. Rather than encourage across-the-board consumption, Snowden recommended 'wise spending' because 'spending on things which do not tend to the reproduction of capital and to the constant employment of productive labour is the wasting of national resources. To the extent to which spending is employed in luxuries and extravagance, the country is poorer and the national wealth is reduced'.[63]

The British model of National Savings campaigns spread rapidly during and after the First World War. Within months of entering the war in 1917, the US government launched a British-inspired 'War Savings movement', created a National War Savings Committee and state committees, and introduced small-denomination war savings certificates. Facilitating the process of transnational dissemination was Basil Blackett, a National War Savings Committee leader, whom the British government had dispatched to advise the US Treasury Department on war savings.[64]

State-directed savings-promotion became truly internationalized following the First World War. In 1924, Italian savings bankers convened the first International Thrift Congress in Milan. Attended by delegates from 27 nations, the congress resulted in the establishment of the International Thrift Institute. Later renamed the World Savings Banks Institute, the organization sponsors periodic congresses to this day. Affiliated savings institutions exchanged campaign posters and information about 'thrift propaganda'. Although members included some non-governmental savings banks, many of the principal players represented postal savings systems and government-linked savings banks in Britain, France, Belgium, Japan and several other nations.[65] The British National Savings Committee, itself a member, greeted the first International Thrift Congress as a sign of a worldwide 'growing concern for popular saving'. The First World War had 'caused a considerable displacement of wealth from its former channels, and in its new distribution it has tended to become more elusive and less immediately available for those constructive purposes to which a nation's wealth must be put if the nation is to prosper'. Other nations, the British reported, had frequently consulted the National Savings Committee as they implemented their own programmes to promote popular saving.[66]

The Japanese were among the most enthusiastic emulators of the British savings campaign structure. They, too, subscribed to the era's mainstream economic thought, which regarded savings-promotion and the restraint of consumption as effective tools in the struggle against inflation and unfavourable trade balances. The Japanese government had dispatched teams of bureaucrats to wartime Britain, where they surveyed the extensive programmes of social and economic mobilization. Although one Japanese agency also reported favourably on war savings campaigns in the United States, the Ministry of Finance resolved in 1924 to 'emulate the British system'. This decision was undoubtedly informed by a detailed report on the National Savings Movement that the ministry's financial officer in London had submitted earlier that year.[67]

The Japanese state thereupon launched the Campaign to Encourage Diligence and Thrift (1924–26), its most comprehensive savings drive to date. Despite seemingly anachronistic exhortations against 'luxury' and excessive spending on weddings and funerals, the campaign introduced several British innovations. For the first time, the Japanese government created a co-ordinating agency, the Central Council to Encourage Diligence and Thrift, along with a nationwide hierarchy of campaign committees at the prefectural, city, town and village levels. Like Western governments in the First World War, the government also made unprecedented use of modern media – advertisements, motion pictures, essay contests and radio (inaugurated in 1925). Officials commissioned some of the world's most engaging campaign posters, according to the International Thrift Institute.[68] Equally important, Japanese organizers were inspired by the wartime British and American drives to broaden the social bases of the campaign workers. Whereas previous campaigns had relied on rural notables and the ubiquitous semi-official associations, Japan's interwar campaigns also deputized autonomous women's organizations, urban middle-class groups and diverse religious associations.[69]

After Japan embarked on war against China in 1937 and the Anglo-American powers in 1941, the state mounted a series of savings and austerity campaigns that continued until its defeat in 1945.[70] Not only was Japan pressed to finance its first protracted war, but for the first time the nation had isolated itself from transnational knowledge from Western Europe and the United States. Japan ended up fighting the last war, elaborating on the British National War Savings model of the First World War. In 1938, the Ministry of Finance established the powerful National Savings Promotion Bureau, together with a National Savings Promotion Council comprised of outside experts. Like the Western belligerents, Japanese officials professed to have learned the economic mistakes of the last world war. Accordingly, they effected massive savings campaigns to finance war production and restrain inflation by soaking up the people's rising purchasing power.

Nonetheless, the Japanese and British approaches to war finance soon diverged. Whereas the British and Americans paid for the war effort in large part through taxation, the Japanese relied far less on taxes, preferring to stimulate 'voluntary' saving. In the last two years of the Second World War, taxes financed less than 20 per cent of government expenditure in Japan, but roughly 50 per cent in Britain and the United States. Progressive thought in the Anglo-American countries conceived of taxation as a more equitable and efficient means of extracting popular wealth. In Japan, officials counted on the people's historical trust in postal savings and other governmental financial institutions. Rather than widely purchase war bonds or national savings certificates as in the United States and Britain, Japan's small savers continued to save at the post office, which as before transferred all funds to the Ministry of Finance's Deposit Bureau. By war's end, the Deposit Bureau was purchasing an extraordinary 35 per cent of government debt.[71]

Furthermore, the wartime Japanese state proved more draconian in reducing popular consumption levels. In 1941, legislation effectively compelled all Japanese to join 'national savings associations'. In neighbourhoods, schools and workplaces, representatives of the ubiquitous savings associations shook down members to deposit more and more of their money. In 1944, households saved some 40 per cent of disposable income, in addition to 10 per cent in taxes plus skyrocketing communal exactions. Economists and finance bureaucrats worried that the state would reach a point where it could squeeze no more out of the populace. Yet the people endured each increase in the national savings target without overt resistance. The economists never determined the breaking point. US bombing and Soviet intervention ended the war first.

From 'National Salvation' to the 'Developmental State'

A little more than a year after defeat in the Second World War, the Japanese government resumed its savings campaigns. Renamed the 'National Salvation Savings Campaigns' (1946–49), the drives now aimed at post-war recovery. In 1952, the Bank of Japan and Ministry of Finance established the Central Council for Savings Promotion. This co-ordinating committee stands atop an extensive network of local councils, schools, adult education facilities, voluntary organizations and the media. The Central Council continues to encourage saving today under the new name, the Central Council for Financial Services Information.[72]

The post-war Japanese state was hardly unique in reviving savings campaigns. On the contrary, Japanese thinking consciously reflected world trends in knowledge and policy following the Second World War. In the United States, to be sure, unprecedented abundance permitted thinkers and policy-makers to privilege consumption, not saving, as the engine of economic growth.[73] But the bureaucrats of devastated Japan had their eyes on more comparable European cases. Within the Ministry of Finance, a new mantra was heard: 'whether victor or vanquished', the former belligerents were all engaged in austerity drives to bring about economic recovery. Officials frequently reported on the Soviet Union's New Five-year Plan, as well as savings and anti-inflation campaigns in France, Belgium and the Netherlands.[74] Once again, Japanese officials expressed their greatest admiration for British practices. That nation had won the war, yet

> the British have not chosen the easy path, but rather have austerely maintained wartime controls on the principal daily necessities. ... In the postwar era, they have even rationed bread, which had been freely sold in *wartime*. The British people ... have persevered, wearing extremely old and shabby clothes, and eating small meals. Why must the victorious British maintain harsh lives of austerity? The answer, without a doubt, is that the money and material saved by lives of austerity can be applied, in full, to economic recovery. ... In the near future, free trade will be re-established in the world. These people are in a hurry to establish a favourable position that allows them to strut upon the stage of global economic competition.[75]

The Japanese appear to have got the British case right. The National Savings Committees chugged on, exhorting the populace to 'Keep on Saving' for the post-war needs of reconstruction, industrial development, Cold War defence and the growing welfare state. In words that Japanese bureaucrats constantly uttered about their own country, British leaders urged their 'island nation' to save more and consume less if it were to increase exports to pay for the necessary imports. Labour's Chancellor of the Exchequer Stafford Cripps, was unequivocal in 1949: 'If we consume too many of the goods which we produce ourselves, we cannot export them; and if, in the process, we force up our costs and so our prices, we shall lose our export markets. ... We must therefore limit our internal expenditure. ... It is time for us finally to renounce and to denounce that easy-going get-rich-quick attitude to life.'[76]

As late as the mid-1950s, the Japanese government's determined promotion of high-level saving placed it within the world of economic thought inhabited by most European nations. By the end of the twentieth century, however, Japan's savings-promotion appeared culturally distinctive, even 'Asian'. Clearly it was the Europeans who had changed. In 1978, the British government abolished the 62-year-old National Savings Committees in England/Wales and Scotland, amid growing doubts about their efficacy and the gradual commercialization of the Trustee Savings Banks.[77] Nearly all of Europe's major postal savings systems have recently undergone forms of liberalization that removed their assets from direct state control. Belgium's Caisse Générale d'Épargne et de Retraite, the world's second oldest national savings bank and a symbol of Belgian social solidarity, was sold outright to Fortis, a Dutch commercial bank, in the 1990s. While continental European countries still boast relatively high personal savings rates and generally restrain the growth of consumer credit, they have gradually embraced American notions of the importance of mass consumption to economic growth.

As the Japanese and Europeans diverged, Japanese savings-promotion took on a new life in the world of economic knowledge. Japan increasingly became a model for developing countries, particularly in Asia. Beginning in the 1960s, developmental economists highlighted the role of household savings in financing Japan's post-war 'economic miracle', and they urged developing nations to adopt various savings-promotion measures as means of generating domestic capital.[78] Political scientists soon wrote influential books about the Japanese-style 'developmental state', which strategically invested the people's savings in competitive export industries.[79] The currency of the Japanese model peaked in 1993, when a World Bank team published the *East Asia Miracle*. The study identified high domestic savings rates as key to the remarkable economic growth among the 'High-performing Asian economies' (South Korea, Taiwan, Hong Kong, Singapore, China, Indonesia, Malaysia and Thailand). In their examination of savings-promotion mechanisms, the authors singled out the nations' postal savings institutions for effectively mobilizing household saving.[80]

Within the Asian economies themselves, the Japanese model of state savings-promotion has played a significant part in developmental strategies. South Korea, a Japanese colony until 1945, inherited the metropole's savings campaigns, the ubiquitous savings associations and postal savings. In 1969, the Bank of Korea consciously emulated the Bank of Japan in setting up its own Central Council for Savings Promotion. During the 1970s, Singapore transformed the old British colonial Post Office Savings Bank into a Japanese-style institution that energetically attracted small savings, which the government invested in economic development projects. At the same time, the Central Provident Fund, the government's compulsory savings system began investing its rapidly growing assets in the state's developmental ventures. During the 1980s and 1990s, the Japanese government repeatedly advised Southeast Asian states on methods of expanding postal savings and other savings-promotion mechanisms. And as recently as 2001, the central bank of Malaysia was actively emulating Japanese savings campaigns to the point of translating and distributing Japanese household account books to Malaysian housewives and pocket money books to students.[81] In the realm of culture, the success of Asian states in stimulating popular saving led some Southeast Asian leaders in the 1990s to rhapsodize about essential 'Asian values', among which thrift figures prominently.

Conclusions

The place of saving and savings-promotion in economic knowledge today is far from clear. Few economists and policy-makers in the West any longer believe it desirable or even possible to exhort people to save, although several continental European nations remain wary of excessive consumption and rising personal debt. Within the rising Asian economies following the regional financial crisis of 1997, many express disappointment with the Japanese model. Instead they consider ways of encouraging consumption and a larger home market. However, Asia's state institutions for promoting and investing small savings largely remain intact.

The most fascinating case may be Japan itself. For the past 15 years, the US government and a host of American economists have lambasted Japan for 'oversaving' and maintaining policies that restrain consumption. Joined by some Japanese politicians, foreigners further chide the government for retaining an enormous postal savings system that unfairly competes with commercial banks, soaks up people's savings at relatively low interest rates, and still – after 118 years – permits bureaucrats to arbitrarily invest this vast pool of savings in local construction works and myriad pork-barrel projects. Incredibly, after 12 years of slow growth or no growth, few Japanese have mounted a serious intellectual challenge to the primacy of saving in the economy. Most officials remain convinced that high levels of saving are essential as Japanese families cope with a rapidly aging society and a protracted recession. Nor are they persuaded that the US economy, with its low savings rates and staggering levels of consumer debt, is viable in the long run. Some may judge this mentality as inscrutably 'Japanese'. But Japan, this chapter has argued, may be better understood as a nineteenth-century European nation-state that never got over it.

Notes

Following East Asian practice, Japanese surnames precede given names, excepting those of Japanese authors whose English-language works have been cited.

1. H. Oliver Horne, *A History of Savings Banks* (London: Oxford University Press, 1947), p. 2.
2. Daniel Duet, *Les Caisses d'Épargne françaises et leur Activité: Tradition ou Évolution (1818–1981)*, PhD thesis (Paris: Les Éditions de l'Épargne, 1983), p. 107.
3. Quoted in Daniel Duet, 'Les Caisses d'Épargne françaises', pp. 93–4; also Horne, *History of Savings Banks*, pp. 183–7.
4. Daniel Duet, *Les Caisses d'Épargne* (Paris: Presses Universitaires de France, 1991), pp. 5–6; Horne, *History of Savings Banks*, pp. 80–1.
5. Duet, *Les Caisses d'Épargne françaises*, pp. 66–72, 90.
6. Duet, *Les Caisses d'Épargne françaises*, pp. 69, 71–2.
7. Frank Trentmann, 'Introduction', in *Paradoxes of Civil Society: New Perspectives on Modern German and British History* (New York: Berghahn Books, 2000), pp. 3–4, 13–14, 21–2.
8. Adam Smith, *An Inquiry into the Nature and Causes of the Wealth of Nations*, ed. Edwin Cannan (Chicago: University of Chicago Press, 1976), pp. 359, 362–3.
9. T.R. Malthus, *An Essay on the Principle of Population*, ed. Donald Winch (Cambridge: Cambridge University Press, 1992), pp. 308, 318–19.
10. Robert L. Heilbroner, *The Worldly Philosophers: The Lives, Times and Ideas of the Great Economic Thinkers* (New York: Simon and Schuster, 4th edn, 1972), p. 98.
11. Joachim Faiguet, 'Épargne', *Encyclopédie, ou, Dictionnaire raisonné des Sciences, des Arts et des Métiers*, comp. Denis Diderot and Jean Le Rond d'Alembert, vol. 5 (Paris: Briasson, 1755), pp. 748–9.
12. Quoted in Duet, *Les Caisses d'Épargne françaises*, p. 110.
13. Horne, *History of Savings Banks*, pp. 28–9, also p. 13; Caisse des Dépôts et Consignations, *Le Livret A: Une Histoire de l'Épargne populaire* (Paris: La Documentation Française, 1999), p. 123.
14. Josef Wysocki, ' "Introduction", in Wissenschaftsförderung der Sparkassenorgansation', in Jürgen Mura (ed.), *History of European Savings Banks*, vol. 1 (Stuttgart: Deutscher Sparkassenverlag GmbH, 1996), pp. 11–12.
15. Horne, *History of Savings Banks*, p. 32.
16. John Tidd Pratt, *The History of Savings Banks in England, Wales, and Ireland* (London: C.J.G. & F Rivington, 1830), p. xxi.
17. Antoine Moster and Bernard Vogler, 'France', in Wissenschaftsförderung der Sparkassenorgansation, *History of European Savings Banks*, pp. 76–77.
18. Duet, *Les Caisses d'Épargne*, p. 5.
19. Horne, *History of Savings Banks*, pp. 87–91; Duet, *Les Caisses d'Épargne françaises*, 88–90.
20. See Edwin Walter Kemmerer, *Postal Savings: An Historical and Critical Study of the Postal Savings Bank System of the United States* (Princeton, NJ: Princeton University Press, 1917).
21. F. Hill, in Great Britain and Ireland, Post Office Savings Banks, *Reports, Minutes, and Memoranda from 30th November, 1860, to 13th September, 1861* (London: W.P. Griffith, 1862), p. 33.
22. William Lewins, *A History of Banks for Savings in Great Britain and Ireland* (London: Sampson Low, Son and Marston, 1866), pp. 183–225, 229–31, 236–42;

Guy Vanthemsche, 'Belgium', in Wissenschaftsförderung der Sparkassenorgansation, *History of European Savings Banks*, pp. 31–2.

23. Quoted in Jean-Pierre Thiolon, *Les Caisses d'Épargne* (Paris: Berger-Levrault, 1971), p. 24.
24. *Hansard's Debates*, 3d series, Parliamentary Debates, vol. 162, 8 April 1861, pp. 277–8.
25. Caisse des Dépôts et Consignations, *Le Livret A*, pp. 124–5, 128, 147–8.
26. Hazel J. Jones, *Live Machines: Hired Foreigners and Meiji Japan* (Vancouver: University of British Columbia Press, 1980), pp. 6–7.
27. Ichiki Kitokurō, 'Kokuun no hatten to kinken kyōdō no seishin' [Development of national prosperity and the spirit of diligence, thrift, and cooperation], *Shimin* 4, 7 (1909), p. 8.
28. Ichiki, 'Kokuun no hatten', pp. 10–11.
29. On the unselective nature of Japanese emulation, see D. Eleanor Westney, *Imitation and Innovation: The Transfer of Western Organizational Patterns to Meiji Japan* (Cambridge: Harvard University Press, 1987).
30. Maejima Hisoka, 'Kōsōkon' [Autobiography], in Fukuzawa Yukichi *et al.*, *Fukuzawa Yukichi, Shibusawa Eiichi, Maejima Hisoka*, Nihonjin no jiden, vol. 1 (Tokyo: Heibonsha, 1981), p. 353.
31. Westney, *Imitation and Innovation*, ch. 3.
32. Shimomura Hiroshi, *Tomi to chochiku* [Wealth and saving] (Tokyo: Dōbunkan, 1911), pp. 9–10.
33. Mukai Yurio, 'Ōkurashō yokinbu seido no seiritsu to tenkai' [Formation and development of Ministry of Finance's Deposit Bureau system], in Shibuya Ryūichi (ed.), *Meiji-ki Nihon tokushu kin'yū rippō shi* (Tokyo: Waseda daigaku shuppanbu, 1977), p. 494.
34. Mukai, 'Ōkurashō yokinbu', p. 495.
35. Yūseishō, *Yūsei hyakunen shi* [Hundred-year history of postal services] (Tokyo: Yoshikawa kōbunkan, 1971), p. 158.
36. Edwin P. Ruebens, 'Foreign Capital and Domestic Development in Japan', in Simon Kuznets, Wilbert E. Moore and Joseph J. Spengler (eds), *Economic Growth: Brazil, India, Japan* (Durham, NC: Duke University Press, 1955), p. 185.
37. J.M. Shaw and J.H. Bannerman, *Post Office Savings Bank*, Post Office Green Papers, no. 30 (London: GPO, 1936), p. 6.
38. Ruebens, 'Foreign Capital', p. 185; William L. Langer, ed., *Encyclopedia of World History* (Boston: Houghton Mifflin, 1952), pp. 822, 830–2, 881–2.
39. Mukai, 'Ōkurashō yokinbu', pp. 495–6.
40. Tessa Morris-Suzuki, *A History of Japanese Economic Thought* (London: Routledge, 1989), pp. 60–1; Chuhei Sugiyama, *Origins of Economic Thought in Modern Japan* (London: Routledge, 1994), ch. 8.
41. Mukai, 'Ōkurashō yokinbu', pp. 509–12; Westney, *Imitation and Innovation*, p. 43.
42. Quoted in Thiolon, *Les Caisses d'Épargne*, p. 24; also Moster and Vogler, 'France', pp. 77, 82.
43. Chalmers Johnson, *MITI and the Japanese Miracle: The Growth of Industrial Policy, 1925–1975* (Stanford, CA: Stanford University Press, 1982), 208; Yūseishō, *Yūsei hyakunen shi*, pp. 518, 545.
44. Hugh T. Patrick, 'Japan, 1868–1914', in Rondo Cameron *et al.* (ed.), *Banking in the Early Stages of Industrialization* (New York: Oxford University Press, 1967), pp. 268–70; Juro Teranishi, 'Availability of Safe Assets and the Process

of Bank Concentration in Japan', *Economic Development and Cultural Change* 25, 3 (1977), pp. 451–4, 466–7.
45. Yūseishō, *Yūsei hyakunen shi*, p. 30.
46. *Chokinkyoku tayori*, March 1937, p. 4.
47. David R. Ambaras, 'Social Knowledge, Cultural Capital, and the New Middle Class in Japan, 1895–1912', *Journal of Japanese Studies* 24, 1 (1998), pp. 1–33.
48. See Earl H. Kinmonth, *The Self-Made Man in Meiji Japanese Thought: From Samurai to Salary Man* (Berkeley, CA: University of California Press, 1981), chs. 1–2.
49. Samuel Smiles, *Self-Help* (London: John Murray, 1958), pp. 284–5.
50. Tomeoka Kōsuke, 'Hōtokuki wa tōyō no jijoron nari' [The Hōtokuki is the Orient's theory of Self-Help], *Shimin* 3, 13 (1909), p. 19.
51. For example, Inoue Tomoichi, *Kinken shōrei gyōsei oyobi hōsei* [Encouragement of diligence and thrift: administration and law] (Tokyo: Seibunkan, 1904), p. 1.
52. Sheldon Garon, *Molding Japanese Minds* (Princeton, NJ: Princeton University Press, 1997), chs. 4–6.
53. Ichiki, 'Kokuun no hatten', p. 7.
54. Samuel Smiles, *Thrift* (New York: Harper and Brothers, 1876), p. 132.
55. Inoue Tomoichi, 'Kyūsai jigyo ni tsuki kibo sūsoku' [Ambitions and models for relief work], *Jizen* 4, 3 (1913), pp. 66–8.
56. Caisse des Dépôts et Consignations, *Le Livret A*, p. 167.
57. G.R. Searle, *The Quest for National Efficiency: A Study in British Politics and British Political Thought, 1899–1914* (Berkeley, CA: University of California Press, 1971), pp. 57–60.
58. Alfred Stead, *Great Japan: A Study in National Efficiency* (London: John Lane, 1906), pp. vii–ix, xii, xv, xvi, 29, 135, 161.
59. *The Times* (London), 29 December 1908, p. 8.
60. National War Savings Committee, Annual Report, 1 June 1918, p. 3, in Great Britain, Parliament, House of Commons, House of Commons Sessional Papers, 1918, vol. 14; Annual Report, 2 June 1919, p. 2, in House of Commons Sessional Papers, 1919, vol. 30.
61. 'To the Chairman of the National War Savings Committee', [December 1916], 'Organization File, National Savings Committee: Origin, History and Development, 1915–1916', NSC 7/1, Public Record Office (hereafter PRO), London.
62. Lord Islington, chairman, National Savings Committeee, *Saving*, no. 76 (1922), 305, NSC 3/4, PRO.
63. *Saving* 2, no. 3 (1927), 10, NSC 3/5, PRO.
64. U.S. Treasury Department, War Loan Organization, Savings Division, *War Savings in 1919*, mimeo (January 1919), pp. 2–4; 'War Savings in Great Britain: An Address by Basil P. Blackett, C.B., of the British Treasury,' 27 September 1917, Records of the Bureau of the Public Debt, Records of the War Savings Division, General Files Relating to Liberty Loans and War Savings Bonds, 1917–25, Box 30, British Savings Materials, RG 53, National Archives and Records Administration, College Park, Md.
65. Cassa di Risparmio delle Provincie Lombarde, First International Thrift Congress, Milan, 26–31 October 1924 (Milan: Organising Committee of the Congress, 1925); *World Thrift* (International Thrift Institute), nos 8–9 (1939), 255, Archives of World Savings Banks Institute, Brussels.

66. *Saving*, no. 93 (1924), 374, NSC 3/4, PRO.
67. Ōkurashō rizaikyoku [Ministry of Finance, Financial Bureau], 'Chochiku shōrei ni oite' [Savings-promotion], 26 December 1924, Kinken shōrei, doc. 24, Shōwa zaiseishi shiryō (hereafter SZS), no. 5, Ministry of Finance, Tokyo; for a survey on US campaigns, see Naimushō shakaikyoku [Home Ministry, Social Bureau], Beikoku ni okeru setsuyaku undō [Thrift campaign in US], pamphlet (Tokyo: Naimushō, 1922).
68. *World Thrift*, nos 8–9 (1939), 255.
69. Sheldon Garon, 'Fashioning a Culture of Diligence and Thrift', in Sharon A. Minichiello (ed.), *Japan's Competing Modernities: Issues in Culture and Democracy* (Honolulu: University of Hawaii Press, 1998), pp. 312–34.
70. See Sheldon Garon, 'Luxury is the Enemy: Mobilizing Savings and Popularizing Thrift in Wartime Japan', *Journal of Japanese Studies* 26, 1 (2000), pp. 41–78.
71. Shinju Fujihira, 'Conscripting Money: Total War and Fiscal Revolution in the Twentieth Century' PhD dissertation, (Princeton University, 2000), chs. 1, 3, 4.
72. See http://www.saveinfo.or.jp/e/index.html.
73. See Alan Brinkley, *The End of Reform: New Deal Liberalism in Recession and War* (New York: Vintage Books, 1995), chs. 4, 10.
74. Yano Shōtarō, 'Ōkura daijin rajio hōsō' [Finance Minister's radio broadcast], 12 June 1947, p. 1, Aichi bunsho, Chochiku: Chochiku zōkyōsaku, 2, doc. 21, SZS.
75. 'Jikan chochiku kōen shiryō' [Vice minister's speech, materials], 5 April 1947, Aichi bunsho, Chochiku: Chochiku zōkyōsaku, 2, doc. 1, SZS.
76. 'The Economic Debate: The Danger of Inflation', *National Savings* 7, 2 (1949), pp. 11, 14–15, NSC 3/14; also *National Savings* 6, 3 (1947), NSC 3/13, PRO.
77. See the scathing critique of the National Savings Movement in *Report of the Committee to Review National Savings*, vol. 1, March 1973, p. 457, T 306/12, PRO.
78. For example, Saburo Okita, *Causes and Problems of Rapid Growth in Postwar Japan and Their Implications for Newly Developing Economies* (Tokyo: Japan Economic Research Center, 1967), pp. 9, 25–30.
79. Johnson, *MITI and the Japanese Miracle*; also Meredith Woo-Cumings ed., *The Developmental State* (Ithaca, NY: Cornell University Press, 1999).
80. World Bank, *The East Asian Miracle: Economic Growth and Public Policy* (New York: Oxford University Press, 1993), pp. 41, 218–19.
81. Interview with Hasbullah bin Abdullah (manager, Financial Planning and Savings Unit), Bank Negara Malaysia, Kuala Lumpur, 25 June 2001; Central Savings Promotion Committee, *The Savings Promotion System in Korea*, typescript, March 1979; Richard Lim, *Banking on a Virtue: POSBank, 1972–1997* (Singapore: POSBank, 1997); see also Japanese role in Advisory Committee and Meetings of International Savings Banks Institute Members in the Asia-Pacific Region, in ISBI Regional Office Bangkok – Advisory Committee Meetings (1979–92), Archives of World Savings Banks Institute, Brussels.

9

The Crisis of *Gelehrtenpolitik* and the Alienated Economic Mind: Economists and Politics in Interwar Germany

J. Adam Tooze

By 1914 *Gelehrtenpolitik* was in crisis. Ideal-typically *Gelehrtenpolitik* (literally the politics of academics) can be defined as a strategy of influence which aimed to promote associations of university professors as arbiters of social and economic reality. The ideal of academic independence was contrasted above all with the partisan approach of the emerging political parties. The ideal audience of the *Gelehrten* was an educated middle-class public and an independently minded civil service. This ideal type was never realized even in the heyday of the *Verein für Sozialpolitik* (Association for Social Policy) in the 1870s and 1880s. The *Verein* itself was always an ambiguous entity, both an association of reasoning middle-class associations and a public relations event. However, until the First World War the ideal of *Gelehrtenpolitik* remained an aspiration, a project continually revived in various guises by Brentano, Weber and others.[1]

The evaporation of this ideal is generally seen as initiating a period of hiatus. We are agreed, despite many qualifications, that the key protagonists of the historical school played an important part in German public life in the late nineteenth century. There is also pretty general agreement that, after 1945, 'social market liberalism' provided at least an ideological veneer for the West German *Wirtschaftswunder*. By contrast, the intervening interwar period, is generally viewed as one of confusion and alienation between power, politics and social thought. This was felt most acutely in sociology. Ludwig Marcuse reflecting on Simmel's sociology spoke of the 'powerlessness of thought' (Ohnmacht des Denkens).[2] However, this alienation of the mind was felt as well within economics. Let me pick just two prominent accounts from the sparse literature on economics in interwar Germany.

Harold James in a number of contributions has painted a stark picture of a disassociation between economic thought and practical politics.[3] As a neo-liberal, James argues that the Weimar economy was crippled by excessive taxation and excessive wage demands. This overburdening of the capitalist economy was the dysfunctional result of short-sighted interest group bargaining, which James views as a brutish, inarticulate struggle of material interests. James's study of Reichsbank policy similarly emphasizes its pragmatism. In his words, 'policy was made in a theoretical vacuum'. James does have favourites amongst Germany's economists, notably Weimar's small coterie of embattled 'liberals'. And they were clearly disaffected with the drift of German politics. James is thus led to the conclusion that this was a period in which policy and economic thought developed in opposite, indeed, contradictory directions. As the state became ever more encroaching, the best and brightest economists retreated into disillusioned critique.

The second account comes from Claus-Dieter Krohn. In what is still the most wide-ranging study of Weimar economics, he paints a somewhat more complex picture of economics as a bourgeois ideology in crisis.[4] From a Marxist position he discusses academic economics as an ideology torn apart by its own contradictions. It was unable to provide a real insight into Germany's fundamental economic problems and failed as a guide to government policy. He too has his favourites amongst the economists. He singles out the Kiel school, and in particular Löwe, Colm, Kähler and Neisser as peculiarly penetrating in their macroeconomic analysis of money and the employment effects of technological change. But in Krohn's interpretation they too appear as tragic figures. Not unlike James, Krohn's view of policy-making is simple-mindedly materialistic. In his case it is reduced to a muddled but nonetheless deterministic assertion of the interests of capital. Not surprisingly, therefore, the Kiel group found no audience for their deep insights into the workings of the capitalist system.

About the years after 1933 there is no argument and precious little research. Economics had no role to play in the Third Reich. Much of the literature simply assumes that economic thought stopped in the spring of 1933.[5] And there are, of course, good reasons for this assumption. As Krohn has shown the faculties of economics were devastated by the Nazi seizure of power.[6] In economics 40 per cent of Germany's university teachers were forced into retirement or emigration, and there were no replacements. The project of 'Nazi economics' was stillborn.[7] The Nazi ideologues of the first hour were sidelined. Again policy-making in the Third Reich tends to be analysed, as under the Weimar Republic, as a Hobbesian struggle of all against all. What about the regime's apparently radical policies? Well, they certainly cannot be attributed to the Nazi ideologues of the first hour. Nazi economists such as Feder were sidelined during Hitler's first period of consolidation in 1933–34. And with a wave of the macroeconomic wand, the regime's programmes can be made to appear rather modest. Harold James has even characterized the regime's fiscal and monetary policies as conservative.[8] Schacht's New Plan of 1934 was a product of ad hoc administrative improvisation, little more than an extension of controls first imposed to handle the financial crisis of 1931.

In short, the collapse of the historical school left a vacuum in interwar Germany. Academic economics was left in intellectual disarray. Economic thought became divorced from public life. The enormous, historically unprecedented expansion of state intervention that occurred during the Weimar Republic and the Third Reich was an 'un-reflected' process driven by 'conservative' bureaucrats and avaricious interest groups. Furthermore, this picture of the interwar period, provides a convenient backdrop for a neat interpretation of the post-war era. The *Kathedersozialismus* of the Wilhelmine period, the disillusion and incoherence of the interwar years and the triumphant social market economy of the post-war period succeed one other like thesis, antithesis, synthesis: power and knowledge reconciled.

The thesis of this chapter is that this narrative is fundamentally misconceived. The fading of the historical school was not followed by a hiatus. It did not lead to an antithesis between thought and practice, between economics and politics. On the contrary, the 1920s saw an unprecedented variety and intensity of linkages between economic expertise, politics and the state. This chapter will sketch some of the most prominent strategies through which these linkages were built. And this carries with it a more disturbing implication. The wide-ranging networks connecting economics to politics in the 1920s were not comprehensively disrupted by the catastrophe of 1933. At least one influential group of economists sought and at last found a place for themselves at the very heart of the Nazi regime.

How do I arrive at my very different picture? First of all there is a basic difference of interest. The emphasis in much of the existing literature has tended to be on economists who fit into one or other canon of economic thought, liberal or Keynesian, or on reconstructing elements of contemporary thought that 'make sense' in light of later theorizing. By contrast, I am concerned with those individuals, intellectual currents and forms of knowledge that seem to have 'mattered' at the time. This different interest implies a difference in emphasis and focus. The existing story of disenchantment between politics and economics is based largely on studies of academic economists. And it is undeniable that German university economists suffered a loss of public influence in the interwar period. However, this misses the point that economists increasingly found new roles for themselves outside the academy. Efforts were made to incorporate the academic establishment into these new networks of power and knowledge, but these attempts largely failed. Third, my argument also draws on a different conceptual framework. The decline of the historical school and nineteenth-century *Gelehrtenpolitik* fits rather nicely into the framework provided by Habermas's *Structural Transformation of the Public Sphere*. However, for my purposes this provides an unsatisfactory, purely negative characterization of the period that followed. For positive concepts with which to describe the new connections between economics, politics and power it seems natural to draw inspiration from the rich vein of contemporary social theory. This chapter tacitly draws its inspiration from Weber and Gramsci. The concentration of organized knowledge within bureaucracies, so powerfully described by Weber, was one of the basic forces leading to a reconfiguration of relations between knowledge and power. Gramsci's analysis of the role played by intellectuals in the struggle for hegemony is also crucial. It forces us to keep in mind the 'big political picture' and reminds us of the need to encompass the entire, wide terrain of intellectual activity, 'high' and 'low'.

Habermas blamed the structural deformation of the bourgeois public sphere on the commercialization of culture and journalism, the rise of mass party politics and the increasingly incestuous interaction between organized interest groups and the interventionist state. These developments certainly restricted the aspirations of Germany's Professoriat to an independent political role. The *Verein für Sozialpolitik*, most notably, retreated into academic debate. However, the forces transforming the public sphere also offered new possibilities for engagement by academic economists and their students. This chapter aims to provide a sketch map of this terrain, distinguishing a variety of different strategies and sites of engagement. The three types of adaptation discussed here are: commercialization, partisanship and bureaucratic incorporation. The sites of engagement are economic journalism, the political parties, the organized interest groups and the state.

The strategy of commercialization involved a radical break with the snobbery of the *Bildungsbürgertum*. Instead of insisting on the juxtaposition between the spiritual values of academic science and the materialist logic of profit, commercialization turned economic expertise into a commodity in its own right. Most overtly this took the form of private information services. These enjoyed a degree of prominence between the turn of the century and the early 1920s. The model was American. In the late nineteenth century Roger Babson made a fortune supplying his fee-paying clients with an idiosyncratic business-cycle barometer. In Germany the first commercial supplier of economic analysis was probably Richard Calwer.[9] Ironically, Calwer's public career began as a Social Democratic deputy in the *Reichstag*. As a member of the party's reformist right-wing he developed an optimistic interpretation of the long-run prospects for German capitalism. A final crisis and a revolutionary overthrow were a distant prospect. In the short run, the priority was to make capitalism's turbulent crises manageable. To this end Calwer began in 1900 to publish a series of yearbooks entitled *Handel und Wandel. Das Wirtschaftsjahr*. This later expanded into an annual of world economic information. From 1910 Calwer abandoned parliamentary politics altogether to publish a weekly bulletin entitled *Konjunktur* (Business-cycle).[10] In the pre-war years it was by far the most widely read report on the state of the German economy, regularly finding its way into government files. Calwer found a number of imitators, most notably Moritz Elsas. Both Calwer and Elsas attracted considerable attention during the inflation years since they were able to provide a desperate public with reasonably representative price indices much earlier and much more promptly than the Reich's Statistical Office.[11] In the years of stabilization however, they faced intense competition from a variety of official and unofficial sources. In 1927 the unfortunate Calwer declared bankruptcy and committed suicide. A variety of confidential newsletters survived him into the 1930s. However, none had the pretensions to general economic analysis that distinguished the work of Calwer and Elsas.

Economic analysis in its own right was not yet a viable business. However, it did find a wide audience through the medium of daily newspapers and periodical journalism. The history of economic journalism in Germany still remains to be written. However, there can be little doubt that there was a significant development in the quality of newspaper reporting beginning in the last decades of the nineteenth century and continuing into the interwar period.[12] One study summarized this as the replacement of the commercial section (*Handelsteil*) by the more grandly titled economics section (*Wirtschaftsteil*).[13] The early business pages had featured a fairly arbitrary selection of news and information on individual markets and firms. By the interwar period the economics pages were far more ambitious, far more general in scope and far more politicized. A number of newspapers now aspired to provide comprehensive and regular coverage of financial and commodity markets, banking activity and reports on major industries and the labour market as well as comment on business law. The business affairs of private individuals were translated into the language of the national economy. And with this came politicization. The need to report on the economy as a whole, rather than the state of affairs in individual regions, industries or firms, arose from the need to discuss a succession of burning political issues: the social question, tariffs, the successes or failings of the gold standard, imperial rivalry, fiscal policy, industrialism, cartelization, war finance, inflation and the reparations question. The papers thus exactly mirrored the blurring of lines diagnosed by Habermas between the public and the private. From their original role of recording and advertising private business transactions the papers had developed into a politicized forum for the discussion of the national economy as an object of intervention. This provided a vast new terrain for economists.

The *Frankfurter Zeitung* and the *Berliner Tageblatt* were unquestionably the leaders in this development. However, they were not alone. The increasing breadth and sophistication of economic reporting was noted across the entire range of daily newspapers, both regional and local. By the 1920s the economics editors of the major papers had emerged as figures of considerable prominence and influence. Anton Feiler imposed a distinctive stamp on the economic pages of the *Frankfurter Zeitung* in the early 1920s and was also a member of the National Economic Council (*Vorläufiger Reichswirtschaftsrat*), the corporatist assembly in which all economic interests were represented.[14] Feiler also had excellent contacts in the Reich's Ministry of Economic Affairs. Georg Bernhard, who articulated a liberal position at the *Vossischen Zeitung* and the specialist periodical, *Plutus*, sat alongside Feiler in the Reichswirtschaftsrat. Arthur Norden and Felix Pinner set the tone at the *Berliner Tageblatt* under the congenial direction of the liberal Theodor Wolff. Pinner also enjoyed good Ministerial connections in the early 1920s. Walther Funk gave the *Berliner Börsenzeitung* a right-wing twist. Gustav Stolper made his name at the *Berliner Börsen Courier* before striking out on his own with the weekly *Deutscher Volkswirt*. The standard of reporting set by these economic journalists was high. Both the *Frankfurter Zeitung* and the *Berliner Tageblatt* presupposed considerable knowledge of economic theory. They also assumed a considerable appetite for statistics, which were culled from various official reports, or even collected on the initiative of the newspaper itself. And to take things further, some newspapers cultivated links with academics. Arthur Spiethoff for instance collaborated with the *Frankfurter Zeitung* in compiling a regular business-cycle index.

Whilst the dailies reached out to a large middle-class public, the flourishing undergrowth of weekly, fortnightly or monthly periodicals provided a platform from which to address a more select audience. This was the terrain of men such Albert Hahn, editor of *Die Wirtschaftskurve*, Alfred Lansburgh of *Die Bank*, Gustav Stolper of *Deutscher Volkswirt*, Felix Bendixen, banker and monetary economist, and Moritz Bonn, one-time student of Brentano, sometime advisor to the reparations delegation, professor and hack. Some had PhDs. Some had positions, more or less honorary, in the outer reaches of the University system. However, with or without these formal academic credentials they spoke not as practical men, but as 'experts'. And they successfully carved a place for themselves in the rough and tumble of the new Republican public sphere. Especially during the inflation era it was their publications, along with sporadic interventions of foreigners such as Keynes and Cassel that defined the agenda of public discussion.[15] Bendixen achieved notoriety for his advocacy of deliberate inflation and devaluation. Lansburgh was one of the keenest German advocates of the quantity theory of money and of the need for monetary stabilization. Bonn, along with Feiler, Pinner and Bernhard were key advocates of fulfilment of reparations. Stolper served as Schacht's propagandist.[16] The commercialization and politicization of the press did not exclude economists from the public sphere. Indeed, an economist's technical skills were now a saleable commodity if they were combined with a modicum of literary talent and an appetite for controversy.

Economic journalism turned more or less overtly political speech into a commodity. It was thus a hybrid and complex terrain treading a fine line between the market and the political forum. A more straightforward form of political action was partisan commitment. Before 1914 the unwillingness to subordinate academic authority to the cause of a particular party was one of the central dilemmas of political professors. During the war and its aftermath this dilemma was resolved for a significant number of prominent individuals in favour of overt partisanship. In fact, the number of trained economists who attained high political office is startling in light of James's comments about a theoretical vacuum in policy-making. The most striking cases are Karl Helfferich in the nationalist camp and Rudolf Hilferding on the side of the SPD.[17] Both had established reputations as economists before they took on the thankless job of Reich's Finance Minister. Neither of them stands in particularly high regard amongst historians of economic thought. However, that is a comment on the quality of their economic theories and not on their absence. For better or worse, the fiscal policies of both Helfferich and Hilferding were clearly shaped by their doctrinal views on the question of money. And there were other Ministers with economics training. Probably the most notable example is Dr Julius Curtius, Weimar's Minister for Economic Affairs for almost four years between 1926 and 1929.[18] Apart from these economists turned politicians, there were also a number of prominent academics who abandoned the stance of neutrality for open political commitment in the 1920s. Two outstanding examples on the left were Emil Lederer of Heidelberg and the Berlin agricultural economist Fritz Baade, who took the bold step of declaring open support for the SPD.

Economists also found a new role within the German party bureaucracies. To compensate for its relatively weak backing in the academy, the SPD established the euphemistically entitled Research Office for Economic Policy (*Forschungsstelle für Wirtschaftspolitik*) in the winter of 1925/26. This was headed by Fritz Baade but its most prominent member was Fritz Naphtali, the author of the party's programme for economic democracy. A not dissimilar strategy was adopted by that other upstart organization of outsiders, the Nazi party. In the early 1930s Gregor Strasser established a cluster of expert staffs to help work out an economic policy platform.[19] The most prominent Nazi 'experts' were marginal men such as Feder and Keppler. However in the run up to the seizure of power Strasser's apparatus provided a useful network within which to collect the increasingly wide array of unorthodox economic opinion, advocating proto-Keynesian work-creation.

Apart from the organic intellectuals of the political parties we also need to consider the connections between economic experts and private interest groups. In the period before 1914 the defenders of the academic establishment and the advocates of Sozialpolitik had found themselves under increasingly bitter attack by the heavy industrial lobby. Lujo Brentano came in for particularly heavy criticism. However, the business lobby was not content to pillory its enemies. It also began to look for allies amongst the economists. Different factions of capital drew on different bases of academic support. Trading interests looked to the new Institutes for International and Colonial Economics in Hamburg and Kiel. The young Karl Helfferich was the chief confidant of the Reichsbank and the banking sector. Agriculture for its part found an articulate advocate in Professor Max Sering in Berlin. Professor Schumann (also of Berlin) was an advisor of heavy industry. Prof. Tzkia was a regular consultant for the textiles sector. The consumer goods industries of Southern Germany found support in the new Commercial University of Nürnberg. The precise nature of these relationships varied.

In the case of the Nürnberg, Hamburg and Kiel Institutes, business provided funds for academic research. In other cases the links were of a more personal nature. Helfferich for instance benefited from Professor Knapp's connections with the Berlin banking world. Sometimes there was no more than a general affinity between the work of a right-wing academic, such as Schumann, and the interests of a particular business lobby. In other cases an academic served as a 'reliable' but ostentatiously 'neutral' source of technical expertise in negotiations with government.

An even more direct connection between economic expertise and business interests was created in the archives, literary departments, economic research departments and economic policy bureaux, which flourished in German business organization from the late nineteenth century. The leaders in this field were Germany's great banks.[20] The Deutsche Bank was the first to establish a literary bureau. By the turn of the century this had acquired the grander title of Economics Department and it was imitated across the German banking scene. Schacht began his career in the Dresdner economics office. The main role of these offices was to produce publicity. However, to be credible this publicity needed to be couched in the technical terms of economics. Other large corporations were not far behind the banks. By 1914 Siemens,[21] the steel firm GHH, the large Hamburg shipping lines, Thyssen and most of German heavy industry had economics departments. In the 1920s some of these offices expanded to remarkable proportions. The most notorious was the Volkswirtschaftliche Abteilung (Economic Research Department, referred to colloquially as the VoWi) of IG Farben.[22] Headed by the PhD economist Anton Reithinger, a former employee of the Reich's Statistical Office, the VoWi entertained close relations with political parties and the state apparatus, particularly the foreign office. In fact its ambitious planning documents and promiscuous network of contacts were later to haunt its parent corporation. They formed a major part of the indictment of the IG Farben corporation at the Nüremberg Tribunal, in which the corporation was accused of encouraging Nazi imperialism to further its economic ends. In fact the Department's output is best interpreted as the professional doodling of a new breed of policy experts. IG Farben was by no means exceptional in maintaining such a think tank. Every big German corporation had a similar department providing a mixture of routine statistical functions, board room advice and public relations material.

Germany's business associations provided similar services for the mass of smaller and medium-sized corporations. The association of German mechanical engineering (*Verein deutscher Maschinenbau-Anstalten,*

VdMA) was particularly active.[23] Its research department provided advice on questions of accounting, rationalization, pricing and cartelization for the membership. It studied international markets and compiled authoritative statistics on employment, sales, imports and exports of the mechanical engineering industry both in Germany and worldwide. In 1924 the association created a dedicated economics department to produce more general economic reports. Headed by the liberal economist Alexander Rüstow, formerly of the Reich's Ministry of Economic Affairs, it was to become the most articulate advocate of free trade in the Weimar Republic. After a period of years in which they appeared to be losing the public relations battle, German heavy industry responded in kind. The cartel statistics of the coal and steel industry were beefed up and the Western industrial region banded together to fund an Institute dedicated to studying the economy of the Ruhr. And these are just two examples of a general trend. The associations of the porcelain industry, the paper industry, motor vehicles and retailing all hired economists and statisticians to advance their case in the public relations battle.

The efforts of the business lobby were matched by those of the labour movement. The initiative was taken by Carl Legien the highly energetic leader of the free trade union movement. He personally oversaw the establishment in 1908 of a central statistical office of the socialist trade union movement.[24] And this investment was to provide a rapid pay off. The first official recognition extended to the free trade unions by the Reich's authorities was the agreement with the Imperial Statistical Office to publish the monthly figures for unemployment amongst trade union members. Well into the 1920s these figures were to serve as the most reliable guide to the state of the labour market. The statutes of the new national organization of the free trade unions created in 1919, included paragraph 18 which empowered the national leadership 'to collect statistics useful to the interest of the trade unions, in particular relating to the strength and the performance of the unions, on wage movements and strikes'. Furthermore, the *Allgemeiner Deutscher Gewerkschaftsbund* (ADGB) was authorized to 'collect and make useful agitational material contained in the official publications of the Reich, the Länder and the communes'.[25] The well-oiled bureaucracy of the German labour movement pumped out data on wage agreements, earnings and real incomes in industry, industrial employment, unemployment, short-time working and strikes. In December 1922 a central trade union research department was set-up to process the data and advise the ADGB leadership on issues of economic policy.[26] And as its chief economist the ADGB chose the remarkable émigré Georgian economist Wladmir Woytinski. Throughout the 1920s the trade union movement was able to more than match the propaganda effort of the business community. Unfortunately, however, the labour movement itself became critically divided over strategy during the crisis of the Great Depression. Whilst the research department developed plans for a large-scale programme of work-creation, conservative experts such as Hilferding, remained wedded to the precepts of orthodoxy. The labour movement did not throw its combined weight behind an emergency programme until the spring of 1932, by which time initiative had passed to the nationalist right-wing. Again, it was not a lack of theory but an argument between theoreticians that was to blame.

Economic expertise was deeply embedded in the institutions of the transformed public sphere. Indeed, by the second half of the 1920s the network had become so self-referential that we are justified in referring to it as a system. The functions of corporate economic research, for instance, developed in direct parallel with economic reporting. The original function of bank 'archives' was to monitor press reports on competitors and markets and to produce the banks' own publicity. The output of the research departments, in turn provided the raw material for the financial journalists. As newspaper reporting became more sophisticated the banks themselves branched out into general economic analysis. By the 1920s the largest banks were routinely publishing elaborate accounts of general business conditions complete with charts and business-cycle barometers.[27] The fortunes of the bank and its clients were situated within a broader macroeconomic picture. Correspondingly in the press, the analysis of business accounts was intertwined with general economic analysis. Indeed, the rival forecasts advanced by the bank reports became a matter for comment in their own right. The material produced by the interest groups was similarly self-referential. Economists and statisticians were employed not just to produce technical publicity but also to interpret and criticize expert material produced by the experts working for rival interest groups.

Industries such as steel or coal, whose sheer physical and financial presence gave them political clout, might opt out of this game of expertise. However, for weaker and less homogenous groups statistical aggregation and economic analysis were indispensable. It gave weight and coherence to their demands. For the trade unions, unemployment figures dramatically substantiated the socialist critique of capitalism. In practical terms they helped make the argument that seasonal and cyclical unemployment were 'risks' against which the state should offer insurance. Statistics were also crucial to business groups such as mechanical engineering. By contrast with the heavy industrial lobby mechanical engineering was far from being an obvious industrial category. Indeed, Germany's official trade statistics did not recognize mechanical engineering as a distinct category until the 1920s. The industry's various constituent parts were dispersed amongst other headings, such as metalworking, instruments and machines. It took the organizational and political effort of the VdMA to establish mechanical engineering as an economic and political entity in its own right. Statistics which encompassed the scattered branches of the industry demonstrated that it was in fact one of Germany's most dynamic sectors, employing more labour than heavy industry and producing more output and exports by value. The struggle of interest groups and the production of economic knowledge were not counterposed as James suggests. They were inseparably intertwined.

What role did the state play in this self-referential system of economic expertise? The civil service was a demanding audience. High-level economic politics in the Weimar Republic was a technical business, conducted largely through the exchange of memoranda and expert opinions. The archival files of the period are replete with references to 'Material', that is, statistical data and documents. Statistical 'Material' was what gave substance to the flurry of memoranda exchanged between the Ministries and the interest groups in the aftermath of the stabilization. It was what changed hands in personal meetings between officials, politicians, businessmen and trade unionists. Indeed, encounters between prominent spokesmen that did not involve an exchange of such technical information came to be considered worthless. When powerful men sat down together seriously to settle their differences they did so on the basis of facts and figures. Mere words were the stuff of demagogic, popular politics, which both businessmen and the civil servants regarded with disdain.

This structural shift in the nature of political communication in the Weimar Republic is well illustrated by the argument which raged over wage costs and profitability in the aftermath of inflation.[28] As has often been pointed out, Germany's heavy industrialists enjoyed privileged contacts with the Reich's administration and could obtain personal audiences with even the highest officials and politicians when they so desired.[29] What has not hitherto been noted is the insistence of the Reich's Chancellory that such personal conversations be followed up by an exchange of hard statistical data. Perhaps surprisingly, the files of the Reich's Chancellory reveal that in 1925 the Ruhr industrialists found themselves outgunned by the statistics of the trade unions. While their opponents could support their point of view with large surveys which agreed within a small margin of error with official data, the barons of the Ruhr were able to supply the Reich's Chancellory with little more than anecdotal evidence culled from a handful of factories. By the summer of 1925, the civil servants in the Reich's Chancellory were convinced that heavy industry was deliberately attempting to keep them in the dark.[30] By the autumn, official irritation had risen to such a pitch that the State Secretary in the Reich's Chancellory fired off a personal note to the leading officials of the Reich's association of German Industry challenging their repeated failure to deliver the statistics they had promised. In future, when he was asked to arrange a personal meeting between the industrialists and the Reich's Chancellor, the Reich's leading civil servant would feel obliged to inform his political boss of the industrialists' record of obstruction, since '... these conversations lose all value, if the [statistical] material summarized verbally is not delivered as promised. It is in the nature of economic questions that they cannot be dealt with without numbers. After all, these meetings are not held so as to make parliamentary speeches intended for the masses but to deal practically with the issues'.[31] Weimar state administration thus sent a clear message to even the most well established of interest groups. If they wanted to be taken seriously, they needed to dispose of the expertise necessary to produce and interpret statistics to their advantage.

But the agencies of the state were not merely an audience. They were themselves players in the game of expertise. The entire apparatus of national economic administration, which took shape in Germany for the first time after the First World War, was impelled by a reforming, technocratic ambition. The new national Ministries of Finance, Labour and Agriculture all employed a considerable establishment of PhD economists, many of whom continued to publish in professional journals whilst serving as civil servants. They all compiled unprecedented volumes of statistics and all three also sponsored independent research by academic economists. Even more impressive were the initiatives of the Reichs bank and the Ministry for Economic Affairs.

It may appear counter-intuitive to cite the Reichsbank as an example of the new relationship between economics and politics. Hjalmar Schacht, President of the Reichsbank after 1924, liked to present himself as a cynical, hard-headed pragmatist, immune to the blandishments of economic theorizing.[32] However, to take this at face value, to conclude that policy was therefore made in a 'theoretical vacuum', is to misunderstand the context in which Schacht operated. Schacht's pragmatic position was calculated to distinguish him from the dangerous theories espoused by the

Reichsbank itself only a few years earlier. It also identified him as a bastion of common sense in an environment that was otherwise saturated by the babble of competing ideologies and technical expertise. In the Weimar Republic, however, common sense was not easy to come by. Hjalmar Schacht maintained his position of detachment only through the well-disciplined efforts of a back-room team of economists and statisticians who struggled tirelessly not only to produce their own interpretations of events but also a reading of what everyone else was saying as well.

It should be remembered that Schacht had begun his career as an interest group lobbyist and moved into banking via the research and publicity department of the Dresdner Bank. Under Schacht's leadership Dresdner's Department became the most authoritative institution of its kind before the war. To match the Research Divisions of the commercial banks, the Reichsbank had established its own statistical division in the 1890s under the direction of Karl von Lumm. Its function was 'to supervise the business of the Directorate from a scientific point of view and to make recommendations as necessary'.[33] Its facilities also served as a useful source of patronage with which to encourage willing economists such as Karl Helfferich. Once Schacht became President, the Research Division expanded enormously from a staff of 20 officials in 1913 to 107 by 1929.[34] The head of the Research Division was a member of the Reichsbank Directorate who was exempted from all other administrative duties. This kept the Division in close touch with the major policy issues but released the Director from routine bank business to pursue his investigations with what the bank referred to as 'scientific objectivity'.

The statistics section of the Research Department had the routine task of monitoring the development of Germany's financial sector.[35] The Reichsbank could obtain a supply of information on the Berlin Great Banks as a result of a deal struck in the years before 1914. This required the largest banks to make regular, confidential balance sheet reports to the Reichsbank. During the 1920s this system was tightened up, to provide a wider range of information on a more representative sample of banks. Along with a range of figures on currencies and the Reichsbank's own accounts, the data circulated within the extended bureaucracy of the Reichsbank in monthly bulletins.[36] More general economic information was updated daily. For Germany's financial journalists, the Reichsbank statistics were a staple diet.[37] Each new set of figures unleashed a wave of speculation and comment about the state of business and the development of the general economy.

Besides these routine administrative services, the main function of the Reichsbank statistical department was to provide the Directorate with expertise. The head of the research division met daily with both Schacht and his deputy so as to remain in close touch with the questions concerning the bank's governors and to take instructions for memoranda. The economics division was so much in demand that it was forced to introduce a special shift system so as to ensure that its staff was available for immediate consultation by the Directorate during its evening meetings. Memoranda were routinely requested at 24–48 hours notice. The intensity of consultation is illustrated by the number of research papers submitted each year: 400 in 1926, 800 in 1929.[38] These occasional papers complemented the regular statistical digests and commentaries on the clearing bank reports.

Apart from observing economic events directly, one of the chief functions of the Reichsbank Research Department was to provide the Reichsbank leadership with a running commentary on the plethora of rival representations and interpretations of economic conditions produced by other official agencies, interest groups, economic journalists and academic economists. The Department served the Reichsbank Directorate as a form of counter-expertise, allowing the Directors to navigate with aplomb the increasingly jargon-ridden public discussion of the national economy. One primary task was systematically to monitor the press, particularly for assessments of the bank's own actions. Schacht was obsessed with press comments on his conduct of monetary policy and received bulletins twice daily. Furthermore, the research department reviewed all the submissions of important interest groups. Finally, it provided the bank leadership with regular digests of the most recent publications by academics. Its coverage even included doctoral dissertations relevant to the bank, many of which in fact benefited from Reichsbank assistance in the form of library use or access to confidential statistics.

In dealing with the external world of expertise, the Research Department sought to protect the Bank from inadvertent entanglement in theoretical controversy. The research department looked for consensus in the academic literature and reacted sensitively to signs of disagreement. Controversial subjects like the pros and cons of counter-cyclical monetary policy or the possibility of accurately estimating national income were treated with caution.[39] Wherever it identified controversy, the Research Department advised the Directorate to rely on political rather than 'scientific' judgement. To ensure that no deviant opinions developed within the Research Department itself, senior officials exercised close censorship over the output of the junior analysts. Draft reports were subject to painstaking editing and correction. This is particularly evident when reports dealt with contentious material, such as a memorandum by the VdMA on the problem of manufacturing wage costs. Several drafts were required before senior Research Department officials were satisfied that they had found the 'right' line.[40] In an environment saturated with ideology and riven by theoretical disagreement one could not simply rely on one's instincts. Schacht's common sense image owed much to the labour of experts.

Whereas the Reichsbank invested in the expertise necessary to shield itself from the complexities of Weimar's public sphere, the Reich's Ministry for Economic Affairs (RWM) was more ambitious. After 1925 it embarked on what appears to have been a deliberate attempt to reshape the environment in which economic opinion was formulated. This strategy took the form of two important initiatives: one was the *Enquete Ausschuss*; the other involved the Statistical Office and the Institute for Business-Cycle Research. Neither project has received sustained attention in the literature.

The Ministry's most spectacular intervention in the field of economic research was undoubtedly the clumsily named Committee for the Investigation of the Conditions of Production and Marketing of the German Economy, or *Enquete Ausschuss* for short.[41] The *Enquete* was launched in the summer of·1926 in the trough of Germany's stabilization crisis. It was presented as a response both to the dire situation of the economy and the flurry of demands for economic enquiries from the *Reichstag*, the *Reichswirtschaftsrat* and the *Verein für Sozialpolitik*.[42] Each of these requests had called for a different type of enquiry. And the Ministry bundled them together into a Committee charged with an extraordinarily wide remit to investigate all aspects of Germany's economic situation. However, apart from a wide-ranging research, the Ministry had wider hopes for the *Enquete*. The RWM was not content to simply play the game of expertise. It hoped that a wide-ranging enquiry that enjoyed the support of government, academics and the full range of interest groups might rediscover underneath the shifting sands of partisan debate a bedrock of objective fact and analysis. As Minister Curtius put it in his opening speech, the Committee should aim 'to speak a final word in the battles between memoranda and the day to day struggles of economic interest groups ... without losing itself in particular enquiries and without being influenced by party or by attachment to any interest groups'.[43] The civil servant Walter Grävell, General Secretary to the *Enquete* diagnosed the same general problem '... new paths must be attempted to effectively rein in the increasingly pointed conflict of interests, each supported by comprehensive and well-prepared documentation. To achieve this, objective and generally recognized materials are essential'.[44] In this sense the *Enquete* appears as a last ditch effort to revivify the faded tradition of reformist *Gelehrtenpolitik*. As if to emphasize this continuity, the Ministry made efforts to coax the veteran Lujo Brentano out of retirement.[45] However, his days of struggle were over.

The Committee met on 7 June 1926 under the Chairmanship of Klemens Lammers, a business lawyer based in Düsseldorf, a member of the Board of the Reich's Association of German Industry and since 1924 a Centre Party deputy in the Reichstag. Lammers qualified as a 'practical man'. The Committee consisted of 34 other members, each being supported by a deputy who attended the entire proceedings. The Committee was thus an unwieldy body of 70 members. A third of the full members of the Committee were also members of the Reichstag, though many of them like Hilferding also qualified as 'experts'. Agriculture was strongly represented. By contrast the industrial and commercial lobbies showed only little enthusiasm for the proceedings. The academic input was crucial. There were seven professors amongst the 35 full members, a further two professors served amongst the deputies and two more were retained as permanent advisors to the Committee. The *Enquete* might therefore have functioned as an important interface between the academy, politics and the interest groups. However, from the outset its work was dogged with problems. Already in the first plenary meetings it became clear that there were fundamental differences of conception. These sessions were dominated by members of the so-called Presidium, which had been appointed to manage the *Enquete*. This consisted of Lammers, Hilferding, Prof. Dr Harms and Ministerialdirektor Dr Graf von Keyserlingk. Harms was the Director of the Kiel Institute for international economics. Keyserlingk represented the agricultural lobby.

Hilferding's opening speech was couched in technocratic terms.[46] He insisted on the need to replace dilettantism in economic policy with government based on economic science. He also insisted on the need to organize the enquiry in such a way as to respond to the qualitative changes he believed were underway in contemporary capitalism. Following from his theory of organized capitalism he emphasized the fact that the enormous scale of capitalist organization rendered obsolete the distinction between private business and the affairs of the economy as a whole. Furthermore the new structure of the economy provided resources that should be tapped by the *Enquete*. Information was available en masse within the organizations of private business, but hitherto this had been withheld from the public. Germany had excellent economic journalists, who had hitherto been starved of the necessary material with which to inform public opinion. The Enquiry should make it a priority to get at this raw material. Hilferding was less complimentary about academic economics. In its methods and problems it had stood still since the age of Brentano. Hilferding hoped that the Enquiry would galvanize the discipline, directing it towards problems of immediate practical interest. Properly applied, economics could make a contribution to national productivity similar to the natural sciences.

Hilferding's view of the enquiry was, thus, ultimately derived from his analysis of contemporary capitalism. By contrast other participants viewed the situation in terms of a political and cultural crisis. Lammers, as Chairman, employed the conventional anti-parliamentary language of the right in denouncing the failure of Weimar's constitution to rein in the proliferation of competitive interests. The *Enquete* was to do the work which parliamentarians, suffocating in petty politics had proved themselves incapable of achieving. In Lammers's view 'The committee therefore has before it a task that is neither purely scientific nor economic, rather a task dedicated immediately to the people itself. It is to prove that taking on high responsibility for the whole people leads finally to *Volksgemeinschaft* (national-racial community) and to the subjugation of all under one large unified idea.'[47] Following in this vein, Harms – the head of the Institute of International Economics in Kiel, which provided the academic backbone of the Committee – appealed to the members: 'We leave everything behind us that, outside, binds us both inwardly and outwardly – with one exception: our commitment to conscience and to the will to knowledge. ... community of fate equals community of labour and community of knowledge.'[48] Meanwhile, at the Ministry for Economic Affairs, the senior official Hans Schäffer noted laconically in his diary: 'First plenary meeting (of the *Enquete*) with many endless speeches.'[49] And, the next day, his entry makes clear the Ministry's limited objectives: 'what is the point of the *Enquete*? a.) to show what is going on in some areas b.) to create a public opinion ...'[50]

In the event, the *Enquete* was to disappoint even these limited expectations. When the commission began its deliberations the hope was that it would report within the year. However, it soon became clear that the *Enquete* in fact lacked a clearly defined field of enquiry, an agreed conceptual basis or a practical methodology. A rough and ready division of labour was agreed by dividing the members of the Committee amongst a series of five Sub-Committees. The First Sub-Committee chaired by Harms (Director of the Kiel Institute) had the broad remit of 'economic structure'. The Second Sub-Committee dealt with agriculture under the direction of the Reichstag's member and former Minister Schiele.

Sub-Committee three for industry was the province of Lammers of the Reich's Association. The highly political issue of working time and productivity was to be managed by Prof. Heyde, a member of the Reich's Economic Council. Finally, Hilferding took charge of the fifth Sub-Committee for Money, Credit and Finance. Each one of the Sub-Committees embarked separately on the task of defining its questions and collecting material, leaving open the question of how the various reports would be synthesized into an overview of the German economic situation.[51]

The work of the Committee and its Sub-Committees still await their historian. However, from contemporary reports and post-mortems it is clear that the enquiry soon ran into fundamental difficulties.[52] After side-stepping the basic problem of defining its research programme and the relation of its various components, the Committee embarked enthusiastically on the business of collecting material. However, this presented problems of its own. Amidst the welter of memoranda and expertise circulating in Weimar politics, robust statistics were in short supply. In the early days of the *Enquete*, even the Reich's Statistical Office was able to supply only patchy figures. And business interests proved unhelpful. Originally the Committee had hoped to obtain new information by public hearings involving all the major interest groups. However, this proved impracticable. German businessmen were simply not willing to give public answers to intrusive questions on the state of their business, the organization of their firms and the working of their cartels. The work of the Sub-Committees was therefore laborious and increasingly it had to take place behind closed doors. This in turn soured relations with the press who began to carp about the endless proceedings and the huge amounts of public money being wasted on an enquiry that seemed to be getting nowhere.

Once the *Enquete* turned to the business of drafting reports the more fundamental disagreements re-emerged. Given their heterogeneous membership of politicians, economists and representatives of interest groups, the various Sub-Committees proceeded laboriously to often vacuous conclusions. The conclusions contained in the final reports tended to represent lowest common denominator compromises. By the late 1920s the businessmen who had been originally involved in the enquiry had retired from its proceedings in disgust. The enquiry was effectively high-jacked by academics, in particular by the Kiel Institute.[53] It was even rumoured that Harms of the Kiel Institute was about to replace the disillusioned Lammers as Chairman of the Committee. The increasingly 'academic' character of the debates was blamed for further retarding proceedings. By 1930, three years after the original deadline, the *Enquete* had expanded into a gargantuan semi-professional enterprise. The total cost to the Reich amounted to about 5 m RM. There were 1504 sub-committee meetings and 26 sessions of the presidium. Evidence was taken from no fewer than 6223 expert witnesses. And the enquiry was still far from finished.[54] Nothing of any substance had been published.

Finally, the Reichstag lost patience. In 1929 the Budget Committee slashed the parliamentary grant and the Reich's Ministry followed suit.[55] To ensure a swift end to proceedings the Ministry passed over Harms and chose the retired civil servant Dernburg to wind up the enquiry. When Dernburg set deadlines for completion the response of the academics was a fit of pique, at least according to the gleeful reports in the newspapers. The Professors refused to accept deadlines. The Committee protested that such rules were suited to school teachers and homework, not scientific research. As a result the *Enquete* came to a shambolic end. After years of painstaking enquiry it produced no conclusion, not even a summary volume. It made no recommendations for policy. Its sponsors were left to make what they could of the output of 90 thick volumes of stenographic reports, which began to appear in the midst of the Depression. Rather than providing a comprehensive guide to the state of the German economy and a common reference point for political debate, the *Enquete* was reduced within months to a record of a bygone era, of interest only to historians.

What the *Enquete* did demonstrate was the apparent incompatibility of the diverse aspirations, which had been brought to it. Hilferding had called for an investigation of the structure of organized capitalism. However, German business was in no mood to participate in a nineteenth-century model of public enquiry. There was general agreement on the need for a solid basis of 'objective' facts, for the 'appliance of science'. However, there was equally widespread impatience with the pompous, long-winded and inconclusive style, which had come to be associated with the German academy. By a combination of accident and design the second initiative of the Reich's Ministry, the expansion of the Statistical Office and the creation of the Institute for Business-Cycle Research, emerged as a solution to these dilemmas.[56]

In its policy towards economic research, the RWM (Reichswirtschaftsministerium) organized a deliberate division of labour between the *Enquete* and the Kiel Institute, which were jointly responsible for analysis of economic 'structure', and the Institute for Business-Cycle Research and the Statistical Office, which were to focus on problems of ongoing, short-run cyclical analysis.[57] In the nineteenth century the

Reich's statistical office had been preoccupied with the collection of social statistics. Since the First World War it had been pushed systematically into the field of economic statistics by its parent Ministry, the RWM. In 1924, to speed up this transition the Reich's Statistical Office was placed under the control of Professor Ernst Wagemann. Wagemann had trained as a colonial economist at the Hamburg Institute. During the war he had found employment in the Reich's Food Office where he developed a strong interest in problems of inflation. This led him in the early 1920s into the field of monetary theory. At the same time he held a Professorship at Berlin University and a job as *Ministerialdirektor* at the Ministry for Economic Affairs. Once in charge of the Statistical Office he pushed it rapidly into the field of business-cycle research, ably supported by a staff, which in the early days included Adolph Löwe and Gerhard Colm. The Institute for Business-Cycle Research was established in the summer of 1925. Its immediate purpose was to apply to Germany the new techniques of business-cycle research developed in the United States by organizations such as the National Bureau of Economic Research and the Harvard Committee for Economic Research.[58] In the Berlin Institute, these statistical techniques were harnessed to an original brand of macro-economics. This derived its inspiration from classical economics, in particular the circular flow models of Quesnay and Marx, combined with contemporary developments in monetary macroeconomics, in particular the Quantity Theory as revised by Fischer and Schumpeter.

Institutionally, Wagemann at first hoped to make the Institute into a research academy co-ordinating the research of University academics across Germany. Like Hilferding, Schumpeter and others he was highly critical of the state of University economics. And his worst fears were realized when Arthur Spiethoff, the best established academic business-cycle economist, refused to co-operate with the Institute. Wagemann's plans for a training academy for applied economists and statisticians were rejected by the University of Berlin. And by the late 1920s Spiethoff and Diehl were using the platform of the *Verein für Sozialpolitik* to orchestrate an academic campaign against the work of the Institute. To his frustration, Wagemann found himself embroiled in a tedious rerun of the *Methodenstreit* of the pre-war period.

In contrast with the reluctance of the academy, Wagemann was hugely successful in mobilizing public support for both the Statistical Office and the Institute. The Institute was funded by a complete cross section of both government and interest groups. Industry, banking, commerce, agriculture, socialist and Catholic trade unions, the nationalist associations of white-collar workers, the co-operatives, the Reich's government, the *Reichsbank*, the *Länder* all provided financial support for the Institute. The *Reichstag* voted enthusiastic support and repeatedly increased the budget of the Statistical Office. Even the hard-line Reich's Savings Commissioner was persuaded that investment in better statistics was the key to the rationalization of public administration. The Institute, unlike the *Enquete*, offered its members a confidential arena in which to share information. Nothing was published without the prior consent of the source. And on these terms Hilferding's dream of a new organization of economic knowledge was capable of realization. Corporate Germany opened its account books and personnel files to the Institute. In return the Institute provided confidential reports and US-style business-cycle barometers that were supposed to allow industries such as motor vehicles to predict fluctuations in demand.

And despite the limitations imposed by its business partners Wagemann's establishment was able to publish a completely unprecedented array of numbers. The contrast with the confused and 'academic' *Enquete* was stark. Wagemann's establishment made no concession to the need for academic deliberation. The fortnightly bulletin *Economy and Statistics* began to appear in 1921. The Institute published its quarterly reports with metronomic regularity from the spring of 1926 and in 1928 it embarked on the unprecedented venture of a weekly report. The publications aimed for novelty. They did not shrink from controversial estimates of national income or the balance of payments. The latest results were rushed out and if necessary corrected in later editions. By 1928, the Institute was even issuing predictions of the future level of employment, highlighted in bold at the beginning of each quarterly report. There was no room for personal vanity in the output of the statistical establishment. Most publications were anonymous and the entire output of the Institute was subject to rigorous editing so as to achieve a uniform house-style shorn of academic circumlocution.

The enormous volume of new data and the rapid rate of publication were made possible by a new organization of research. By the early 1930s the Statistical Office had expanded into a gargantuan organization with three thousand staff including more than a hundred PhDs. These personnel were backed up by a battery of Hollerith machines, which enabled the Office dramatically to increase both the speed and refinement of its routine publications, in particular the trade statistics. The Institute, with a staff of at least 30 economists and statisticians by the late 1920s, was the heart of the analytical operation. In deliberate imitation of an idealized image of natural science laboratories Wagemann imposed a novel system of team work. Economists and statisticians were coupled together. More experienced analysts combined responsibility for particular sectors of the

German economy with general responsibility for a particular foreign economy. Veterans of the system recall the unique atmosphere of discipline that prevailed at the Institute. A young economist was faced with a hard choice. The Institute did not offer the prospects for rapid, self-promotion available in the academy or journalism. The work was often routine and set to tough deadlines. However, nowhere else in Germany could a budding economist feast on a similar wealth of empirical material.

There was also no other platform that offered a similar prospect of being read and taken seriously by someone who mattered. The Institute's quarterly reports circulated in their thousands to an enthusiastic audience of private subscribers. The weekly reports were introduced in response to public demand for more regular updates. And the Institute's findings reached a wider audience through the detailed commentary published in the dailies and the periodical press. In fact, the Institute's work was plagiarized so freely that Wagemann considered charging a fee for republication. In the end he opted for free publicity. And the reports were not only bought, they were read both at home and abroad. They were cited in Reichstag debates. 'The Institute' was quoted freely in cabinet discussions. Indeed, cabinet meetings were rescheduled to coincide with the publication of recent batches of official data. For the foreign audience, the Institute produced an English translation of its weekly bulletin. And the ultimate seal of approval was applied by the office of the Agent General for Reparations, which by the late 1920s based its annual report on the German economy almost entirely on data compiled by Wagemann's establishment. The Institute and the Statistical Office had established themselves as truly authoritative arbiters of economic reality.

Conclusion

What conclusions may be drawn from this account? The idea that there was a divorce between economics and public life in the Weimar republic is utterly misguided. In fact the opposite was true. In the age of *neue Sachlichkeit*, economists and statisticians were everywhere, in the papers, in the political parties, advising interest groups of all colours. They laboured behind the scenes to produce the 'technical material' which was the stuff of economic politics. In some cases the experts became players, public figures, politicians in their own right. The result, however, was not more clarity. Rival attempts to define reality through statistical and technical means resulted in bewildering confusion and a generalized erosion of confidence in the possibility of 'objective knowledge'. The agencies of the Weimar state responded in a variety of ways. The Reichsbank reacted defensively, seeking to isolate itself, by means of its own in-house expertise, from the maelstrom of ideology and 'theory'. The Ministry for Economic Affairs sought instead to halt the downward spiral. The attempt to do so by harnessing University economists to the widest array of political and social groups in the *Enquete* was a disastrous failure. It served only to feed the common prejudice that 'academics' were out of touch with reality. By contrast, Wagemann's establishment with its 'un-academic' methods was astonishingly successful, producing both a mass of new material on the German economy, material that to this day sets the standard for economic historians, but also finding a wide and influential readership.

In terms of our historical understanding of the interwar period as a whole this reinterpretation of the Weimar era is significant because it suggests a rather different narrative for the period of the 1930s. The Nazis sought to regulate debate in the press. They did irreparable damage to the University system, which in the long run was to threaten the reproduction of the system of expertise, due to a shortage of new recruits. However, the Nazi accession to power did not destroy the nexus between power and economic expertise so broadly established in the 1920s. The damage done to the Universities mattered little in the short term since they were outside the loop, in any case. The Statistical Office, the Institute for Business-Cycle Research and the Research Department of the Reichsbank all survived the rupture of 1933 more or less unscathed. The statisticians and economists of the business organizations served as the administrative backbone of Schacht's new compulsory organization of German business. The labour movement was destroyed, but the Nazi Labour Front rapidly reequipped itself with an agency for social and economic research, the notorious Arbeitswissenschaftliches Institut (AWI). And Wagemann's Institute was ultimately to attain the very pinnacle of power. By 1942 the Institute was firmly ensconced at the heart of the wartime planning apparatus. Its reports circulated in small, top secret, numbered editions to all the key figures in the war economy. And in 1944, in the final months of the war it received the ultimate accolade. The Institute was allocated the services of a draftsman whose job it was to translate statistical reports into the enlarged type that saved Adolf Hitler the embarrassment of having to appear publicly in spectacles!

Notes

1. For the most succinct discussion of this crisis see D. Krüger, *Nationalökonomen im wilhelminischen Deutschland* (Göttingen, 1983). See also R. vom Bruch *Wissenschaft, Politik und öffentliche Meinung: Gelehrtenpolitik im Wilhelminischen Deutschland (1890–1914)* (Husum: Matthiesen, 1980).

2. David Frisby, *The Alienated Mind: The Sociology of Knowledge in Germany, 1918–1933* (London: Routledge, 2nd edn, 1992), p. 16.
3. H. James, 'What is Keynesian about Deficit Financing? The Case of Interwar Germany', in P.A. Hall (ed.), *The Political Power of Economic Ideas: Keynesianism across Nations* (Princeton: Princeton University Press, 1989), pp. 231–62. The discussion of economics in H. James, *The German Slump. Politics and Economics, 1924–1936* (Oxford: Clarendon, 1986) tells a similar story.
4. C.D. Krohn, *Wirtschaftstheorien als politische Interessen: Die akademische Nationalökonomie in Deutschland 1918–1933* (Frankfurt: Campus, 1981).
5. Without offering substantial justification the studies of both E. Coenen, *La 'Konjunkturforschung' en Allemagne et Autriche 1925–1933* (Paris, 1964) and B. Kulla, *Die Anfänge der empirischen Konjunkturforschung in Deutschland 1925–1933* (Berlin: Duncker und Humblot, 1996) simply stop short in 1933. A major exception to this norm is H. Janssen, *Nationalökonomie und Nationalsozialismus: Die deutsche Volkswirtschaftslehre in den dreißiger Jahren* (Marburg: Metropolis-Verlag, 1998), whose conclusions are complementary to the argument of this essay.
6. C.-D. Krohn, *Wissenschaft im Exil: Deutsche Sozial- und Wirtschaftswissenschaftler in den USA und die New School of Social Research* (Frankfurt: Campus, 1987).
7. C. Kruse, *Die Volkswirtschaftslehre im Nationalsozialismus* (Freiburg: R. Haufe, 1988).
8. H. James, 'Innovation and Conservatism in Economic Recovery: The Alleged "Nazi Recovery" of the 1930s', in T. Childers and J. Caplan eds. *Reevaluating the Third Reich* (New York: Holmes and Meier, 1993), pp. 114–38.
9. On Calwer see Alfred Lansburgh, 'Der Fall Calwer', *Die Bank*, 7 July (1927): pp. 414–16.
10. V. Hentschel, *Wirtschaft und Wirtschaftspolitik im Wilhelminischen Deutschland: Organisierter Kapitalismus und Interventionsstaat* (Stuttgart: Klett-Cotta, 1978).
11. On the Elsas and Calwer indices see C.-L. Holtfrerich, *Die deutsche Inflation 1914–1923: Ursachen und Folgen in internationaler Perspektive* (Berlin: De Gruyter, 1980).
12. The most popular contemporary guide to the economic press was E. Kahn and F. Naphtali, *Wie liest man den Handelsteil einer Tageszeitung?* (Frankfurt: Frankfurter Societäts-Druckerei, 1921 and 2nd edn 1930).
13. F. Wirth, *Die Wirtschaftsteile Deutscher Zeitungen* (Leipzig: Gloeckner, 1927).
14. Information on economic journalists can be gleaned from G.D. Feldman, *The Great Disorder: Politics, Economics, and Society in the German Inflation, 1914–1924* (Oxford: Oxford University Press, 1993).
15. An indispensable guide to contemporary monetary theories is H.S. Ellis, *German Monetary Theory, 1905–1933* (Cambridge MA: Harvard University Press, 1934).
16. H. Müller, *Die Zentralbank – eine Nebenregierung. Reichsbankpräsident Hjalmar Schacht als Politiker der Weimarer Republik* (Opladen: Westdeutscher Verlag, 1973).
17. On Helfferich see J.G. Williamson, *K. Helfferich: Economist Financier, Politician* (Princeton: Princeton University Press, 1971).
18. Significantly for our later argument Curtius's dissertation dealt with Bismarck's abortive plan for a national economic council. J. Curtius, *Bismarcks Plan eines Deutschen Volkswirtschaftsrats* (Heidelberg: Heidelberger

Verl. -Anst. u. Dr., 1919) and his memoirs J. Curtius, *Sechs Jahre Minister der Deutschen Republik* (Heidelberg: Winter, 1948).

19. A. Barkai, *Das Wirtschaftssystem des Nationalsozialismus. Ideologie, Theorie, Politik 1933–1945* (Frankfurt: Fischer, 2nd edn 1988).
20. M. Pohl, 'Gedanken zur Entstehung und Bedeutung der Grossen Bankarchive – zwei beispielhafte Beiträge von 1910 und 1929', *Bankhistorisches Archiv. Zeitschrift zur Bankgeschichte* 2 (1976), pp. 46–52.
21. A VoWi department appears in the Siemens Schuckert Werke organizational chart even before the Second World War. See Wilfried Feldenkirchen, *Siemens 1918–1945* (Munich: Piper, 1995), p. 79.
22. On the VoWi Abteilung see H. Tammen, *Die IG Farbenindustrie AG (1925–1933). Ein Chemiekonzern in der Weimarer Republik* (Fu Berlin PhD, 1978), p. 157 and P. Hayes, *Industry and Ideology. IG Farben in the Nazi Era* (Cambridge: Cambridge University Press, 1987), p. 30.
23. G.D. Feldman and U. Nocken, 'Trade Associations and Economic Power: Interest Group Development in the German Iron and Steel and Machine Building Industries, 1900–1933', *Business History Review* XLIX (1977), pp. 413–45. Their account of the VdMA's statistical activities relies heavily on the VdMA's unpublished internal history, see VdMA Archive, Der Deutsche Maschinenbau.
24. Heinrich Potthoff, *Freie Gewerkschaften 1918–1933: Der Allgemeine Deutsche Gewerkschaftsbund in der Weimarer Republik* (Düsseldorf: Droste, 1987), p. 261.
25. Heinrich Potthoff, *Freie Gewerkschaften*, p. 324.
26. Detlev Brunner, *Bürokratie und Politik des Allgemeinen Deutschen Gewerkschaftsbundes 1918/19 bis 1933* (Köln: Bunder-Verlag, 1992).
27. This was particularly marked in the major bank reviews. For the stir created by the Dresdner Bank's attempts at business-cycle analysis, see *Magazin der Wirtschaft* 4 (1928), II. Hj., p. 1289, pp. 1358–9 and 5 (1929), I. Hj., pp. 571–2 and pp. 894–5.
28. This argument is recorded in the file of the Reichskanzlei Bundesarchiv BA R43I 1135 and discussed in painstaking detail in B. Weisbrod, *Schwerindustrie in der Weimarer Republik. Interessenspolitik zwischen Stabiliserung und Krise* (Wuppertal: Hammer, 1978).
29. Carl Böhret, *Aktionen gegen die 'kalte Sozialisierung' 1926–1930. Ein Beitrag zum Wirken ökonomischer Einflußverbände in der Weimarer Republik* (Berlin: Duncker u. Humblot, 1966), p. 103 ff.
30. The bureaucrats in the Chancellory even found fault – wrongly as it turned out – with the industrialists' arithmetic. See BA R43I 1135 No.181 Bemerkungen zu den anliegendem Material Voegler-Kloeckner, notes for the chancellor, dated June 1925.
31. BA R43I 1136 No. 17 Reichskanzlei to Geheimrat Bücher 8. Okt 1925. BA R 43 I 1136 No. 95 Der Staatssekretär in der Reichskanzlei to Bücher and Kastl 7 November 1925.
32. H. Müller, *Die Zentralbank – eine Nebenregierung. Reichsbankpräsident Hjalmar Schacht als Politiker der Weimarer Republik.* (Opladen, 1973), pp. 18–19.
33. BA 25.01 6344 No. 370 ff. Bericht über die Statistische Abteilung der Deutschen Reichsbank. W.Schmidt June 1939, p. 1.
34. BA 25.01 Reichsbank 6347 No. 325 Stat Abteilung der Reichsbank, Die Arbeitsbelastung der Statistischen Abteilung in den Jahren 1913, 1926 und 1929, 25 March 1931.

35. For a summary of functions see BA 25.01 Reichsbank 6346 No. 189 'Notenbankstatistik', Reichsbankrat Speer, Sonderdruck aus *Bankwissenschaft* VII. Jg Nummer 9.
36. For an overview of routine statistical work see BA 25.01 Reichsbank 6346 No. 221 Stat Abteilung der Reichsbank, Übersicht über die von der Reichsbank regelmässig aufgestellten Statistiken, 10 December 1930.
37. See the discussion of their treatment in F. Wirth, *Die Wirtschaftsteile*.
38. BA 25.01 Reichsbank 6347 No. 325 Stat Abteilung der Reichsbank, Die Arbeitsbelastung.
39. For a collection of such reviews see BA 25.01 Reichsbank 6625.
40. Compare and contrast the first draft of the report in BA 25.01 Reichsbank 6574 No. 467 Stat Abteilung der Reichsbank Sch./Rs. 1. Dez 1931 'Lohnniveau und Arbeitslosigkeit. Kritische Betrachtung zu den "Lohnpolitischen Kurvenbildern zur Krisenlage" des Verein Deutscher Maschinenbau-Anstalten'. With the second draft signed by Reichsbank Sch./Dr. Dej./Ta./Frk. 1. The first draft was highly critical of the VdMA assumptions and conclusions. The second draft is toned down, stresses the multiple causation of depression unemployment and even finds academic support for the VdMA's views in recent publications by Landauer and Mises.
41. As far as I know the only secondary study to discuss the *Enquete* as an episode in the history of German economics is M. Dierkes, A. Knie and P. Wagner, 'Engineers, Intellectuals and the State: Assessing Technology in the Weimar Republic', *Industrial Crisis Quarterly* 4 (1990), pp. 155–74.
42. The *Reichstag* called for more information on which to base trade policy decisions on the 12 August 1925. The *Wirtschaftspolitische Ausschuss* of the *Reichswirtschaftsrat* 22 September 1925 demanded information on price structure to accompany the government policy of price reductions. The *Verein für Sozialpolitik* requested a commission with a submission of the 22 September 1925 to compile objective data with which to settle the hotly contested question of working time. Finally on 3 December 1925 a Centre Party motion passed by the *Volkswirschaftliche Ausschuss* of the *Reichstag* calling for an investigation into the causes of the current economic crisis. In fact, the Ministry had a hand in orchestrating the appeals from the *Reichswirtschaftrat* and the *Reichstag*.
43. AUEAdW *Verhandlungen* Vol. I (Berlin, 1927), 1. Sitzung 7 June 1926, pp. 13–20.
44. See W. Grävell, 'Die Reichswirtschaftsenquete', *Allgemeines Statistisches Archiv*, 16 (1926/27), pp. 357–72.
45. Institut Für Zeitgeschichte (IZG) MA 1559/1 Tb H. Schäffer 28 April 1926.
46. AUEAdW *Verhandlungen* Vol. I (Berlin, 1927), 3. Sitzung 8 June 1926, pp. 58–63.
47. AUEAdW *Verhandlungen* Vol. I (Berlin, 1927), 3. Sitzung 8 June 1926, pp. 48–9.
48. AUEAdW *Verhandlungen* Vol. I (Berlin, 1927), 2. Sitzung 7 June 1926, pp. 22–3.
49. IZG MA 1559/1 Tb H. Schäffer 8 June 1926.
50. IZG MA 1559/1 Tb H. Schäffer 9 June 1926.
51. See the highly critical review of the *Enquete's* methodology by Dr Eduard Rosenbaum of Hamburg in *Wirtschaftsdienst* 11, 31 (August 1926), p. 6.
52. See the annual reports on the *Enquete's* progress in BA 01.01 Film 31648 File 2588 and following.
53. See the reports in BA 62 DAF 3 8787 No. 63 PGZ Nr. 69 22.3.29 and BA 62 DAF 3 8787 No. 51 *Kölnische Volkszeitung* Nr. 365 20.7.1930 'Die Enquete'.

54. The *Enquete* was struggling to provide a comprehensive analysis of the Reich's finance and its industrial investigations had covered only 11 of the 47 industrial sectors originally proposed for study.
55. BA 01.01 Film 31648 2589 No. 352 ff, Ausführungen.
56. For detailed references on the following pages see J.A. Tooze, *Statistics and the German State: The Making of Modern Economic Knowledge* (Cambridge: Cambridge University Press, 2001).
57. IZG MA 1559/1 Tb H. Schäffer 12 May 1926. For the basic distinction between structure and cycle which became extremely popular in the 1920s see H. Wolff, 'Struktur und Konjunktur', *ASA* 17 (1927/28), pp. 205–35.
58. See the discussion in M.S. Morgan, *The History of Econometric Ideas* (Cambridge: Cambridge University Press, 1990).

10

Development and Disease: Public Health and the United Nations, *c.*1945–55

Sunil Amrith

The history of international health can be seen as the history of the transmission of ideas and interventions concerning life and death, illness and reproduction, across borders. The earliest Sanitary Conferences of the nineteenth century aimed to standardize procedures of quarantine and surveillance across the European and Ottoman empires.[1] In the first half of the twentieth century, the international health work of the Rockefeller Foundation and the League of Nations bridged nation-states, colonies, and semi-colonial areas of the world.[2] Since the Second World War, the United Nations' World Health Organization (WHO) has brought into a common institutional sphere the health policies of diverse, post-colonial, political entities.

The underlying theme of this chapter is the shifting relationship between international public health and the imperative of economic development in the early years of the United Nations' history. The UN, I suggest, is an important arena for historians investigating the interface between medicine and 'worlds of political economy'. It is now well recognized that political and economic interests were important in shaping the policies of the WHO in the 1950s and beyond, but this chapter suggests that attention ought to be paid to the more complex interaction of economic and medical ideals and objectives, in explaining the practices of international health.[3]

By the mid-1940s, the idea of Development served as an umbrella for diverse intellectual and political concerns. Development united worlds of public health and political economy, for example, in a shared rhetoric of equality, a belief in rational planning, and a concern with the post-war relationship between the Western powers and the soon-to-be 'third' world, moving towards freedom from colonial rule. Many of these concerns informed the founding principles of the UN, and in particular the philosophy of WHO. The argument of this chapter is that, as the UN made the transition from the realm of ideas and planning to the field of practical interventions, the relationship between public health and political economy was instrumentalized. This process took place within a broader political culture in which – to extend, internationally, Sugata Bose's argument about post-colonial India[4] – the 'instruments' of Development (above all, capital accumulation and industrialization) took precedence over its fundamental 'idioms' or values, in which the objective of improved health conditions had occupied a central position.

Social medicine and international health

When the Constitution of the WHO was finalized at the International Health Conference of 1946, the first issue of the Organization's *Chronicle* grandly declared it to be the 'Magna Charta of Health'.[5] The editorial highlighted the fact that: 'The WHO is the first inter-governmental institution to adopt the term "world" as part of its title.' In so doing, the Organization 'wished to stress the fact, which is becoming increasingly obvious, that problems which are no longer purely national must of necessity be solved not by international action merely, but by world-wide action'.[6] Public health had attained an unprecedented global reach. The juxtaposition of 'world-wide' with merely 'international' health work seemed to signal a departure from the League of Nations and its non-governmental counterparts in the interwar years. First, it suggested the early involvement in the WHO of those parts of the world on the verge of freedom from colonial rule, most notably India and Ceylon. Second, the reference to 'world' health signified a set of principles linking public health to the freedom, security, and rights of individuals as well as States – though governments alone were represented at the WHO. The mention of health within the Charter of the UN, and the subsequent establishment of the WHO, was 'an acknowledgement that social, economic and even political progress is conditional on improvement in the state of health of the people'.[7]

The immediate origins of this post-war language of public health lie, of course, in the political inheritance of the Second World War: the language of the Atlantic Charter, and Franklin D. Roosevelt's Four Freedoms were extended to the sphere of public health. Equally important, however, was the emphatic dominance of social medicine in the minds of the architects of the WHO. Indeed, in many ways, the principles of international co-operation in health after 1945 were a product of a longer dialogue between medicine and political economy in the aftermath of the Great Depression, cemented by the experience of the Second World War.

It is now widely recognized that the global Depression of the 1930s led to a heightened concern with the relationships between disease, nutrition and poverty. In centres of imperial power and tropical colonies alike, the consequences of the Depression threw into stark relief the links between incomes, consumption and susceptibility to disease. Throughout the European empires the 1930s saw an expansion of colonial public health, previously confined to the protection of European soldiers and settlers through the prevention or containment of epidemics, and the maintenance of productive labour in colonies of exploitation. During the 1930s, historians have suggested that British medical officials 'discovered' colonial malnutrition.[8] Across the British Empire, from Kenya[9] to Malaya[10], surveys were conducted on the health of native populations. Colonial public health had always played an instrumental role in allowing economic exploitation; from the 1930s there was an increasing preoccupation with the social and economic *causes* of disease.[11]

On an international level, the Health Organization of the League of Nations began to publish increasingly detailed investigations of nutritional conditions – although the organization's work was largely confined to Europe. The League's report on the relation of nutrition to health, agriculture and economic policy of 1937 highlighted the connections between agricultural depression, urban malnutrition and morbidity. Within both the League and the International Labour Organization (which was concerned with industrial health), an ethos of social medicine was increasingly prevalent, though its scope was limited by the politics of the 1930s.[12] The Depression-era dialogue between public health and political economy, often mediated through the subject of nutrition, had one further element: a number of historians have shown that eugenics was a significant transnational movement by the 1930s.[13] Even whilst its nationalist and fascist proponents deployed the language of eugenics in the service of racial purity, others promoted eugenic ideas as a way to break the links between poverty, health and perceived over-population.

The Second World War galvanized the proponents of social medicine, and gave them a prominent role in planning for a post-war world. Dorothy Porter has suggested that the rise of social medicine can be epitomized by the appointment of John Ryle as the first (and last) professor of Social Medicine at the University of Oxford in 1942.[14] Elsewhere in the world, too, the imperative of re-thinking welfare after the war led to imaginative statements of social medicine: Shula Marks has shown that the South African National Health Services committee of 1944 was significantly influenced by ideas of social medicine which had emerged in the 1930s as a response to the contradictions and stresses of South African industrialization.[15] This new thinking focused upon the impact of social and economic inequalities on the incidence and distribution of disease, and with its potential political remedies. In particular, global inequalities in health were more sharply recognized, in a way that would greatly influence the formation of the WHO.

John Ryle was perhaps the most influential, and widely read, theorist of social medicine in the 1940s. In his seminal work, *Changing Disciplines* – based upon a series of lectures given on social medicine – Ryle drew parallels between socio-economic inequalities within the United Kingdom, and an awareness of global inequalities. 'We know from indisputable statistical evidence', he wrote, 'as well as from the evidence of daily experience in city hospitals and slums and elsewhere, that the opportunities for health and the chances of death in the several social stratifications of the communities and as between occupations are very different ... the attack on social inequalities and hazards has made many striking conquests, but here, too, we are far from our goal even in the more advanced communities ... especially when the coloured races are included.'[16] Global disparities were on an even greater scale. He suggested that medical students in Britain were 'misled' by talk of the 'tropical diseases' that continued to devastate the lives of the populations in Asia and Africa: 'cholera, malaria, plague ... these great endemic diseases of backward populations still prevail in India, China and Africa. Nearly all of them are pre-eminently "social" diseases and due to alterable social causes'.[17]

John Ryle concluded his most important work, *Changing Disciplines*, with an explicit call for the insights of social medicine to be put into practice. 'We cannot ... in a democratic age', he argued – reflecting the egalitarian rhetoric prevalent in both Britain and internationally after the war – 'accept that the mortality at the two ends of the socio-economic scale should long continue to be so sharply differentiated'. 'Possessing the knowledge which we now possess', he concluded, 'is it not the duty of physicians everywhere ... to assume leadership in the struggle for improvement of conditions?'[18]

The rhetoric and prescriptions of social medicine found a receptive audience around the world during the 1940s, emerging in part independently in particular countries, but also gaining strength from the exchange of ideas within the international medical community. The case of India illustrates the influence of social medicine particularly well.

John Ryle himself went on a tour of India in 1944, sponsored by the Rockefeller Foundation[19] – accompanied by a group of progressive doctors, including Henry E. Sigerist of Johns Hopkins medical school, and the Foundation's John B. Grant – 'seeing and hearing at first hand something of India's immensely complex problem'. He concluded that 'no narrow or unrelated planning in the fields of medicine and hygiene and no considered population policy can be expected to affect the situation in the near future. Political, social, agricultural, industrial, and economic developments and educational and political progress are all as urgently necessary as sanitation and medicine to the people's health.' He suggested that 'time must be allowed for historical growth, for self-determination, and for the percolation of what is best and most applicable in the ideas derived from the experience of other nations'.[20]

Ryle's comments echoed the prevalent view amongst both nationalist politicians and government administrators in India at the time. Health, in mid-1940s India, was discussed in the context of 'political, social, agricultural, industrial and economic developments'. The two essential documents setting out plans for independent India's health services – one (the 'Sokhey report'[21]) produced by the Congress party, and the other (the 'Bhore report'[22]) by the late-colonial Government of India – are striking for their use of the international language of social medicine, in which discussions of public health were deeply informed by a particular conception of political economy, and, in practice, a belief in planning. The Sokhey report opens with a stirring extract from Jawaharlal Nehru's autobiography: 'India is a country whose people are poor beyond compare, short lived and incapable of resisting disease and epidemics, illiteracy rampant, vast areas devoid of all sanitary or medical provision, unemployment on a prodigious scale ...' As the report's authors point out, 'the above quotation tersely describes the present health conditions of the country and their causes. The poverty of the people is proverbial.'[23] Thus it was held that the 'root cause of disease, debility, low vitality, and short span of life is to be found in the poverty – almost destitution – of the people.'[24] The underlying philosophy behind this analysis was the increasing realization and concern amongst Nationalists of India's 'proverbial' Poverty, and the association of this impoverishment with the political economy of imperial rule.

The Bhore Commission, appointed by the late-colonial Government of India, and composed largely of members of the Indian Medical Service was, understandably, less willing to direct criticism at colonial rule, writing that: 'it is not for us to apportion responsibility for the sombre realities which face us today'.[25] The Commission nevertheless spoke the language of social medicine. The report expressed its interest in widening the 'conception of disease ... by the inclusion of social, economic and environmental factors which play an equally important part in the production of sickness'. It went on to associate public health firmly with plans for economic development, suggesting that 'unemployment and poverty produce their adverse effect on health through the operation of such factors as inadequate nutrition, unsatisfactory housing and clothing and lack of proper medical care during periods of illness'.[26]

One detects, however, an undercurrent in both reports of an older association between political economy and health: a Malthusian concern with India's rapidly expanding population as the root cause of ill health.[27] References to the 'population problem' are fairly muted in the Sokhey and Bhore reports, but the Congress Party's Planning Committee appointed a separate sub-committee on population. The report on population suggested that over-population 'condemns [the people] to poor nutrition and inadequate safeguards against the rigours of nature or ravages of disease to resist which they are very poorly equipped, whether the disease be acquired or hereditary'.[28] The discussion of population growth is inflected with the language of social reform, phrased in terms of the evils of 'social habits, customs and institutions' such as early marriage.[29] The discussion of population also espoused explicitly eugenicist ideas about the 'quality' of India's population. Quoting from a 1938 resolution of the Congress's population committee, the report says that: 'In the interests of social economy, family happiness and national planning ... family planning and a limitation of children are essential ... a eugenic programme should include the sterilisation of persons suffering from transmissible diseases of a serious nature, such as insanity or epilepsy'.[30] This serves to underscore the diverse currents of thought linking public health with political economy inherited from the 1920s and 1930s. Social medicine was one, in the 1940s particularly influential, school of thought, the origins of which lie within the broader debates about population, eugenics and nutrition in the 1930s. Yet, Malthusian concerns remained strong, and when health and population became the targets of planned policy interventions after 1945 – both in India, and globally – the tensions between social–medical and Malthusian prescriptions became sharper.

In the late 1940s Indian policy-makers across the board believed that the mechanism of rational planning would mediate and resolve any potential conflict over the root causes of ill-health, poverty and over-population. 'Planning is a social activity of the utmost importance', the

Congress committee asserted, 'planning means the careful assessment of the available resources of the country, and their allocation ... all planning must be in the hands of one commission ... drawn from the best scientific, technical and administrative ability of the country'.[31] The vision of public health in post-war India was couched in this language of planning. The Bhore Commission suggested that 'the comprehensive conception of what a community health service should undertake has led to the development of modern health administration, in which the State makes itself responsible for the establishment and maintenance of the different organisations required for providing the community with health protection'.[32] State-directed planned health administration is seen, here, as the culmination of a linear narrative of progress towards a 'modern' health service. The WHO was a manifestation of the extension of this principle to the international plane.

Institutionalizing ideas

The intellectual inheritance of the WHO was deeply shaped by the growing consensus around a set of ideas about health which shaped plans for health services from India to South Africa.[33] However, social medicine was far from a viable prescription for action by an international organization founded in times of great political uncertainty, and given minimal financial resources. Even as social medicine formed the intellectual foundations of WHO, the organization's institutional capacity owed more to another inheritance of the Second World War: the revolutions in military medicine and medical technology. This tension would be particularly pronounced once international health became dependent on the project of economic development for funding and legitimacy.

At the San Francisco conference of 1945, where the charter of the UN was signed, the Chinese and Brazilian delegates to the conference proposed the establishment of an international health organization under the auspices of the UN, to replace the moribund League of Nations Health Organization. Many of the men – they were all men – in the Interim Commission of the WHO had previously been involved with international health work, working with the Rockefeller Foundation and the League. The influence of social medicine was strong. Andrija Stampar, chairman of the interim commission was a Croatian physician who had pioneered the idea and practice of social medicine in the 1920s; in the 1930s he spent three years in China as a consultant to the League of Nations, helping to establish rural health clinics.[34]

Dr Brock Chisholm, of Canada (who went on to become the first Director-General of the WHO) was also an ardent proponent of social medicine. His background as a psychiatrist made him particularly interested in mental and emotional health, and he was instrumental in the holistic definition of 'health' adopted in the WHO constitution.

Perhaps the most interesting illustration of the ideology of the WHO's interim committee can be seen in the process of drafting the preamble to the constitution, which defined the fundamental values of international health for the post-war era. An early draft that Stampar submitted to the committee, from which the final version was largely drawn, begins: 'health is a prerequisite to freedom from want, social security and happiness'. It goes on to argue that health ought to be defined as: 'not only the absence of infirmity and disease, but also a state of physical and mental well-being and fitness resulting from positive factors, such as adequate feeding, housing and training'.[35]

The main amendments to Stampar's draft preamble were in the direction of employing even more directly the language of the UN charter.[36] The final draft opens with the following passage:

> The right to health is one of the fundamental rights to which every human being, without distinction of race, sex, language or religion, is entitled.
>
> Health is not only the absence of infirmity or disease but also a state of physical fitness and mental and social well-being.
>
> Health is an essential factor in the attainment of security and well-being for individuals and nations.[37]

This declaration, which was reproduced almost verbatim in the final Constitution of the WHO, encapsulates the ways in which health came to be defined as part of the shared project of human rights, security and development.

When it came to practical policy recommendations, however, the WHO's Interim Committee ran into dissension. James Gillespie has recently shown how the British and American governments worked, from the outset, to limit the WHO's powers, and to keep the organization small and narrowly focused.[38] Whilst there was consensus around the political principles underlying WHO, expressed in the eloquent Preamble to the constitution, it was more difficult to agree upon the practical implications of social medicine. In particular, Stampar's suggestion that the WHO ought to concern itself with the politics of social security, or social insurance, was rapidly dismissed as 'unhelpful'.[39]

As the International Labour Organization had discovered in the later years of the War, proposals to internationalize social security were unlikely to fare well. The State Department was particularly anxious to de-politicize WHO at a time when a hostile Congress, partly under the influence of the American Medical Association, was searching for reasons not to ratify the WHO's Constitution.[40]

What forms of practical intervention, then, were available to the fledgling WHO? The answer lies in the revolutions in military medicine during the Second World War. Above all, the War saw great breakthroughs in medical technology: the insecticide DDT and sophisticated antibiotic drugs were only the most conspicuous products of wartime medical research. DDT was first deployed during the Egyptian malaria epidemic of 1943–44, under the direction of Fred L. Soper of the Rockefeller Foundation, who had pioneered the technique of vector eradication in Latin America during the 1930s. Timothy Mitchell makes a convincing case that accident and improvisation, and the exigencies of the War and Egyptian politics, played a significant role in the transition of DDT from the laboratory to the field.[41] DDT was soon being sprayed from aircraft in dramatic demonstrations around the world.[42] At the same time, institutions of wartime humanitarian relief set a precedent for the WHO. The United Nations Relief and Rehabilitation Association (UNRRA) was established in late 1943, working in China and Ethiopia as well as liberated Europe, undertaking anti-malarial campaigns, distributing dried milk and X-ray equipment to detect tuberculosis.[43] In the immediate aftermath of the war, the official organizations were supplemented by a massive voluntary effort to vaccinate children against tuberculosis in Central and Eastern Europe, initially launched by the Scandinavian Red Cross societies.[44]

The struggle for health

International health in the 1950s was characterized by massive, concerted disease control campaigns, sometimes styled as disease 'eradication' campaigns, implemented with the large-scale use of technology: DDT, vaccines and antibiotics, but also refrigerators, vans and aircraft. These campaigns, and international health work itself, were justified more and more in terms of their *contribution* to economic development, representing public health as an 'input' or an investment in development. This marked a profound shift from the early post-war years, when public health was discussed in diverse ways, with much attention to the social roots of health and illness, and taking into consideration a complex range of institutional and social changes which might be required to bring about an equitable improvement in health conditions.

The broader historical context is central to understanding the nature of this transition. The circumstances of the late 1940s lent a sense of uncertainty to the early years of development interventions. The rapid development of the Cold War in Europe; the wave of anti-colonial revolutions across the Asian continent; food shortages, and the Communist revolution in China in 1949 militated against any of the UN agencies launching long-term or broadly based programmes of development.[45] Instead, UN agencies emphasized ad-hoc interventions and a piecemeal extension of wartime emergency relief extended to refugees and to women and children. The international climate of the late 1940s was described by one contemporary Brookings Institution report as one of 'uneasiness and insecurity which pervades the world'.[46] In this context, the practice of 'technical assistance for economic development' came to be the dominant framework for the UN's development interventions.[47] There were two fundamental characteristics of the new politics of technical assistance: it would be based upon the exchange and implementation of technology; and its ultimate goal was to bring about 'economic development', which involved 'in particular ... an increase in productivity'.[48]

Undoubtedly, some of this sense of urgency for a rapid and technical evolution of international development can be traced to the imperatives of American foreign policy. The UN programme of technical assistance had a close, if not symbiotic, relationship with the 'Point IV program' of the United States government. In 'Point IV' of his inaugural address, on 20 January 1949, President Truman set forth a 'bold new programme for making the benefits of our scientific advances and industrial progress available for the improvement and growth of under-developed areas'.[49] A memorandum on the 'objectives and nature of the Point IV Program' states clearly that technical assistance 'is now raised to a major role among the instruments for the accomplishment of existing objectives'. These 'objectives' included ensuring a regular supply of raw materials from the 'under-developed' world; securing expanding world markets for US manufactured goods, and the desire for 'good will' in 'areas of strategic economic or military importance'.[50]

Yet, to focus too closely upon the intentions of the United States government and to treat US policies as synonymous with those of the UN is to miss an important part of the international political culture from which technical assistance arose. The historical moment of decolonization also helps to explain why public health came to be defined as an instrument of development, rather than an end in itself. As Sugata Bose has argued in the case of India, the nationalist movement's attainment of centralized State power served to blunt previously vigorous debates about the ends and means of development. In Bose's terms, the 'instruments' of development came to be privileged over its fundamental 'idioms'. Such an analysis serves very well as a description of technical assistance on the international level.[51] The singularity of 'technical assistance' – constituted as a body of experts, outside the political process[52] – can thus be seen as the international counterpart to the drive towards State planning, witnessed across Asia.[53]

Between the late 1940s and the mid-1950s, then, the proponents of international public health had to struggle to maintain the place of health at the centre of the project of technical assistance. For, once it was accepted that public health was an instrument directed towards the ultimate goal of 'development' through capital accumulation, health projects were open to the charge that they hindered rather than advanced that goal. Above all, public health had to defend its position against the neo-Malthusian assault of the theorists of population explosion.

The publication of William Vogt's polemic, *The Road to Survival,* in 1949, was symptomatic of a growing fear of a population explosion.[54] We have seen earlier that such concerns were not confined to Western observers; they had a vocal contingent of support in India and elsewhere in Asia.[55] Concerns about post-war food shortages were central to this discourse of over-population; but another clearly emerging theme was the potential threat posed by international public health interventions. Vogt raised the question of whether it was in fact wise to save people from 'dying from malaria so that they could die more slowly of starvation'; indeed, he went so far as to call malaria a 'blessing in disguise'.[56] This was, perhaps, the post-War incarnation of the late-Victorian use of Malthusian ideas to legitimate the reluctance of colonial states to provide famine relief to starving millions, except that now starvation was the spectre, and public health the potential culprit.[57]

The population issue proved altogether too explosive for the fledgling WHO to be able to take it on directly. Indeed, at one point the issue threatened to tear the organization apart. The issue came to a head at the annual World Health Assembly in 1952. Opening the meeting as a guest speaker, Sir Herbert Broadley – deputy director of the Food and Agriculture Organization (FAO) – put the charge against the WHO quite starkly: 'the more successful you are in reaching your goal', he told WHO delegates, 'the more difficult FAO's task becomes ... more mouths demand more food. Where birthrates continue to advance, as is the case in many countries ... [and] where death rates and human mortality are halved ... we cannot just sit back and let nature take its course. If we do, nature's course will be a very desperate one'. He concluded that 'it will be strange ... if, as the result of this great move forward in health which is being carried out under your inspiration, food shortages and famine are transferred from the under-developed countries of Asia to the industrial countries of Western Europe. And yet, it is no impossible dream.'[58] The speech was clearly designed to appeal to Western fears of a population explosion at their gates, threatening the prosperity of Europe. The significance was greater still, however, because the charge came not from a polemicist for population control, but a senior official of the FAO which – at one level – was in direct competition with the WHO for resources and support.

Yet it was not the American or European delegates, but the representatives of India and Sri Lanka that most forthrightly accepted Broadley's challenge. Sir Arcot Mudaliar, the Indian government's representative, concurred that 'in certain countries the population figures have risen to such an extent that they have constituted the greatest menace to health and welfare ... Under these conditions my Government, through our Prime Minister, Pandit Jawaharlal Nehru, approached the WHO, as it has under the Constitution a right to do, and appealed for some help in the solution of a very difficult problem'.[59] The implication was that the WHO, as the agency responsible for public health, ought to match its health efforts with direct interventions in the field of population control. The Indian government, that is to say, was strongly in support of the population problem being medicalized, and delegated to the WHO.[60]

At the same World Health Assembly, however, the response of the Roman Catholic countries within the World Health Assembly was unequivocal: the WHO had no right to intervene in matters such as birth control. The Belgian delegate, for example, said that 'the problem of over-population in several regions of the world was primarily of an economic and social character, and only secondarily a medical problem ... from the purely medical standpoint, population problems do not require any particular action on the part of WHO at the present time'.[61] The Irish delegate went further, threatening that 'some governments may be forced into a position where they had to withdraw from WHO'.[62] Perhaps surprisingly, given the widespread view that population control was above all an American Cold War agenda, the US delegate to the 1952 Assembly was most hesitant: the population issue, he suggested, was 'a burning and controversial one, one which made headlines ... There were many people in the world who were not enthusiastic about international work, which made it difficult to raise enough funds for the work of WHO and other international organizations, and any untimely statement of that kind would give weapons to such people'.[63]

Faced with the threat of internal disintegration at the very time when its legitimacy was being attacked from without, the WHO retreated almost entirely from the population debate, not to intervene in the field again until the mid-1960s.[64] In 1952 in a confidential letter the Director General, Brock Chisholm wrote to a colleague in the US public health service that 'after exploring every possibility I could think of finding ways to take active measures from this headquarters about population problems, it seems there is no probability of our being able to do anything about it in the near future'.[65]

Debating disease and development

The WHO and its supporters did, however, directly challenge their critics. They did so by translating the idioms of public health explicitly into the language of technical assistance. Charles Winslow – a veteran American proponent of social and preventive medicine – articulated the utilitarian defence of international health programmes most explicitly, through an influential pamphlet, *Cost of Sickness, the Price of Health,* and in his address to the 1952 World Health Assembly. Winslow's speech can be seen as an attempt to reaffirm the fundamental values of international health by adopting a very different set of arguments and justifications. Winslow's ideas can indeed be read as an effort to adapt the 'idioms' of international health to the new practical realities, by trying to articulate in a novel way the specifically '*economic* values of health'.

'Economic values', he said, 'do not provide the only – or even the primary – inspiration for the worldwide campaign for public health'.[66] Quoting Matthew Arnold, he reiterated that the true 'values' of health were in 'diminishing human misery'.[67] Health was a 'fundamental human right' and a global moral imperative.[68] However, and this was his key point, it would be 'easier to obtain the support needed for an effective health programme if it can be shown that such a programme will ... [bring] tangible economic benefits. Prevention is not only better than cure; it is also cheaper than cure'.[69] In his speech to the turbulent World Health Assembly, he observed that 'you and I are not contemplating visions in ivory towers. We are working day by day in a tough and practical world. We can realize our dreams only if we can convince our governments ... that our goals can actually be attained and that their attainment will not put new strains on already strained economies.'[70] He acknowledged that 'we sometimes meet a real challenge as to the essential desirability' of global health programmes. 'Certain population experts', he noted pointedly, 'tell us that there are already too many people in the world'.[71]

Winslow's response was to posit a linkage between public health and economic development, which reversed the commonly understood order of causation. The common, and irrefutable, argument was that economic development would, in the fullness of time, dramatically improve public health in the 'under-developed' world.[72] With more than an echo of Edwin Chadwick, however, Winslow argued that disease caused poverty; that public health was an essential prerequisite without which economic development could not occur. 'In the case of mosquito-borne diseases, the economic returns due to control measures are, of course, particularly striking.'[73] Preventable disease was economic 'waste', inhibiting production and productivity.

> In countries such as China, Egypt and India, where the average expectation of life at birth is in the neighbourhood of 30 years, only 54 out of every 100 children born ever reach the age of 15 and enter the period of maximum economic productivity ... 'Reduction in the death rate in the under-developed areas will mean an increase in human resources available for production in proportion to the population.'[74]

Winslow went further, however, and invoked various attempts to explicitly quantify the economic benefits of health. He cited a British survey from the 1930s suggesting that 'malaria in India involves an economic loss of £80,000,000 a year', and another from Egypt claming that bilharziasis 'decreases the productivity by 33 per cent'.[75] In this, he received cautious support from the pioneering Swedish development economist Gunnar Myrdal, whose speech followed Winslow's at the 1952 Assembly. Myrdal conceded that 'the economic value of health and the price of health, have been given comparatively little thought' in economics; 'our very large literature on capital, depreciation, and interest has never taken ... [the concept of "personal capital"] very seriously'.[76] But he warned that 'the economic value of preventing premature death, to take the simplest case, depends entirely upon whether such an economic development is under way which ensures productive work for the greater number of people we thus keep alive'.[77]

What is particularly striking about Winslow's argument is the way in which it draws upon a language inherited from the radical tradition in medicine's own intellectual history. The attempt to quantify the benefits of public health in order to defend preventive medicine from its critics went back many decades before Winslow's speech at the WHO assembly. In his inaugural lecture to the medical faculty in Zagreb in 1923, Andrija Stampar – an old friend of Winslow's – had argued that 'the exploitation of man for the expansion of material wealth, as well as the awareness of the role which his life and health play in any production, are making people gradually realise that man is the greatest value in the world'.[78] The reckoning of human health and sickness in terms of their economic value was, in the context of the 1920s, a tool to justify radical social medicine in the face of resistance from elite clinicians. Stampar lauded the 'science of the economy of man and the value of organic capital' whilst arguing for 'social medicine' to supersede 'individual therapy'.[79] And Stampar himself was drawing on a social–medical tradition that reflected the evolving outcome of the influence, on medical thought, of Marxian political economy. Thus, when he found himself coming to the defence of international preventive medicine in the early 1950s, Winslow was able to resort to a line of justification with which he was familiar, from his own intellectual and professional involvement in advancing social medicine in the inter-war years.[80] There was, thus, no contradiction between Winslow's use of a seemingly limited, or instrumental, economic justification for public health, and his restatement of the lofty idyll of social medicine: the contribution of international co-operation in health to a more progressive human evolution.[81]

Perhaps the most telling comment which Winslow made, in his attempt to try and reconcile an 'instrumental' argument for international health with its fundamental values, was that:

> From the standpoint of community psychology, the World Health Organization has been wise in choosing for major emphasis during the past two years simple and efficient procedures, such as spraying with DDT, immunization with BCG, and treatment of syphilis and yaws with penicillin, which make it possible to obtain dramatic and immediate results at a minimum cost.[82]

The 'community' in question, here, referred as much to the 'community' of international development policy as to local communities in the under-developed world. This suggests that technology was a major source of strength for an embattled WHO. The need to legitimate public health as a part of technical assistance underpinned the WHO's increasing dependence on medical technology, even when it became clear that the technology had serious limitations. Nowhere do the contradictions in the WHO's position emerge more clearly than in the contrast between the imagery and the reality of the global malaria eradication campaign, launched in 1955.

Malaria eradication

Surmounting the uncertainties surrounding its inception in the late 1940s, public health was imbued with grandeur in the international imagination of the 1950s. In countless publications and feature articles, there was an emphasis on theatricality, and above all on the idea of public health as a great adventure. Malaria control occupied a particularly central place in this narrative.

The heroic account emerges very clearly from the account of Ritchie Calder, a popular science writer who made a 100-day whirlwind tour of Southeast Asia in 1951 to report on the UN's various programmes of technical assistance.[83] Over the course of his journey 'from the jungles of Borneo to the frontier lands between Afghanistan and the Soviet Union', Calder saw public health and medical technology in motion. The images in Calder's pamphlet are replete with technology: an uncertain looking woman with baby being given a yaws injection in Central Java; a floating dispensary taking injections to 'mountain tribes'; a young man armed with DDT, spraying the walls of the 'Temple of the Reclining Buddha'.

Calder's writing on international health for a broad audience also conveys – chattily, almost as 'folk wisdom' – the particular conception of political economy underlying the WHO's mass campaigns of the 1950s. 'One of the concerns of our mission to South-east Asia was with this population problem, and if and how it could be tackled', he writes, and 'no better example can be found than that of malaria-control'.[84] Whereas the more extreme proponents of the population explosion theory argued that a reduction in malaria mortality would exacerbate population growth, supporters of the WHO, like Calder, tried to show that the direct economic benefits of public health campaigns would have a greater, positive impact. 'Following the rout of the malaria mosquito in the Tiger Jungle of the Himalayan Terai', he asserts, 'a million and a half acres of jungle became available for development'[85]; in Chiang Mai, Thailand, the eradication of the malarial mosquito meant that local farmers could 'if they chose, produce a second crop' of rice 'so desperately needed in the Indian subcontinent'.[86]

The example cited above gives some indication of the centrality of technology to the international imagination of public health in the 1950s. Similar instances abound in a range of media ranging from the UN's publicists,[87] to American Cold War propaganda,[88] to the pronouncements of post-colonial governments in the Third World.[89] Everywhere, the focus is not merely on technology but on the direct material gains from its use, and establishing a set of connections between public health and a vision of political economy which revolves around *things*. An injection against yaws allows a canal to be built; spraying a tent with DDT allows another field to be planted. Through such a series of associations, a direct connection is made between a single instant – of vaccination, or the application of insecticide — and the 'national' economy; and from there to 'world' security.

Malaria control projects, then, were at the heart of WHO's struggle for legitimacy and funding in the politics of technical assistance. As the American member of WHO's Executive Board, Henry van Zilde Hyde, wrote to the WHO's director general Brock Chisholm, in 1948: the Organization needed 'some immediate objective that can be understood by the peoples and legislators of the world and which can be defended as an attainable goal. I fail to see any objective that meets the requirements as well as malaria'.[90] When Charles Winslow stood before the World Health Assembly in 1952 and defended WHO against the prophets of population explosion, it was malaria control upon which his argument focused. Malaria control fits particularly well with the framework of technical assistance: it was based on the simple, mass application of technology towards an end that could be justified in terms of its tangible contribution to 'economic development'.

This faith in technology was, however, a paradox of sorts: underlying the image of confidence was a deep fear amongst malariologists, resulting from field experience of malaria projects, that the technology was fallible, and its efficacy fragile. However powerful DDT seemed to be, warnings abounded from an early stage that a number of problems were liable to hinder its mass application, and long-term effectiveness. Malariologists sounded the alarm about the development of resistance to the insecticide, already in evidence at the end of the Second World War.[91] Fred Soper might have thought DDT an 'almost perfect insecticide',[92] but the massive efforts of the UNRRA to eliminate malaria from Sardinia using DDT ended in failure.[93] Despite the use of over twenty thousand men, and hundreds of thousands of pounds of DDT, the mosquito was too well entrenched on the island, and withstood heavily concentrated DDT.[94] Notwithstanding these concerns, the WHO launched malaria control programmes based on the use of DDT across Asia. By 1953, over 46 million people in 13 Asian territories lived in areas 'directly protected' against malaria, though there remained over 224 million 'still to be protected'.[95]

Malaria control using DDT was driven forward, despite evidence of drug resistance and other serious limitations, because the WHO's position depended on it. Knowing that the technology was fallible, the administrators of the malaria programme, at every level from Geneva and New York to the field, worked with a sense of urgency, a desire to finish the job before the DDT ceased to be effective. By 1952, studies began to show the fragility of one of the most publicized successes of DDT: the anti-malaria campaign in Greece. A WHO report suggested that, despite massive spraying, first houseflies and eventually malarial mosquitoes showed resistance to DDT.[96] The fear of developing resistance is clear from reports on malaria control in the Asian region. A 1953 report by WHO states, at first that 'none of the governments reported that the anopheline mosquitoes in their countries had developed resistance to the insecticides'; this is immediately qualified, however, by the admission that 'in Burma. Ceylon, Indonesia, and the Philippines, there were impressions (unconfirmed scientifically) that culicines [mosquitoes] have developed a certain amount of resistance to DDT.'[97]

'To heed the warning from Greece', declared Emilio Pampana – the Venezuelan malariologist and member of the WHO's Expert Committee on Malaria – in 1955, 'means to plan the programme in such a way that house-spraying could be safely discontinued before insecticide resistance develops'.[98] What was needed was a 'new pattern of planning', envisaged in terms of 'huge areas, of total coverage, of great thoroughness of control ... its implementation will require more funds, more trained personnel, greater efficiency of operations, and better systems of epidemiological surveillance than are necessary now'.[99] Pampana's was the opening article in a special issue of the WHO *Bulletin*, designed to make the case for an urgent acceleration of the worldwide malaria programme. By mid-1955, the World Health Assembly had launched a 'global' programme to eradicate malaria. In 1956, the US government committed a substantial amount to support the malaria eradication programme. Yet, less than a decade later, widespread resistance to insecticides and anti-malarial drugs belied the early and dramatic successes of the campaign; in 1963 the US government withdrew its support to the WHO's malaria eradication programme, and by the end of the 1960s, the organization admitted the failure of the campaign.[100]

Conclusion

The story of the malaria eradication programme is often told as a parable of the WHO's failings. The origins of the campaign, and its subsequent failure, have been portrayed as the result of Western dominance over the WHO, and the desire of the US and European governments to use international health as a means of exploiting the resources of the Third World, whilst using the 'dramatic' effects of DDT as a means of Cold War propaganda.[101] Others have analysed the malaria campaign to suggest the dominance over international policy of a very small group of elite scientists: the 'epistemic community of malariologists'.[102] Historians have, indeed, seen the WHO in terms of the 'huge areas, of total coverage ... [and] great thoroughness of control' that Emilio Pampana evoked, hopefully, in 1955.

These interpretations undoubtedly point to important features of the WHO's politics and policy-making in the 1950s, though I believe Packard exaggerates the degree of Western dominance over the WHO. In particular, his interpretation fails to account for the fact that nationalist governments in the Third World might have actively appropriated the technologies of modern governance under the banner of the nation, rather than having it imposed upon them by 'neo-colonial' international agencies.[103] The perspective of this chapter, however, has been quite different. Above all, I have suggested that as a field agency, the WHO was characterized by weakness rather than by strength. This weakness was manifested in the WHO's inability to turn its discourse of social medicine into practice. The practice of international health was, instead, dominated by the 'magic bullet' approach drawn from military medicine. Peter Baldwin has argued, in the case of nineteenth-century Europe, that public health techniques such as mass vaccination or quarantine were the resort of weak rather than strong states; states without the capacity to implement broad-ranging programmes of sanitary reform and medical surveillance.[104] Similarly, I would suggest that whereas historians have interpreted the WHO's reliance on dramatic technology as reflecting its 'hegemony', in fact it was a symptom of weakness.

I have explained this weakness in terms of the interaction between intellectual and institutional history. The WHO's initial moral force and legitimacy came from the compelling vision of social medicine at the heart of its Constitution; a vision that had been shaped through conversations between medicine and economics. In practice, however, within the institutional field of the UN, public health was instrumentalized and directed towards the sole goal of 'economic development', now defined narrowly in terms of productivity and capital accumulation alone. This shift took place within a political culture in which, to return to Sugata Bose's distinction mentioned in the introduction, 'instruments' of Development were privileged over its 'idioms'. I would suggest, finally, that exploring these transformations in the political culture of Development in the 1950s might be a fruitful area for collaboration between economic historians and historians of public health.

Acknowledgements

I am grateful to the Editors, and to Emma Rothschild, for comments on earlier drafts. I am solely responsible for any shortcomings.

Notes

1. N. Goodman, *International Health Organizations and Their Work* (London: J. and A. Churchill; 1952).
2. See the essays in P. Weindling (ed.), *International Health Organizations and Movements* (Cambridge: Cambridge University Press, 1995).
3. The most powerful statement of the 'interest'-based interpretation is R. Packard, 'Visions of Postwar Health and Development and Their Impact on Public Health Interventions in the Developing World', in F. Cooper and R. Packard (eds), *International Development and the Social Sciences: Essays in the History and Politics of Knowledge* (Berkeley, CA: University of California Press, 1997), pp. 93–115.
4. S. Bose, 'Instruments and Idioms of National Development', in F. Cooper and R. Packard (eds), *International Development*, pp. 45–63.
5. 'The Move Towards a New Health Organization', *Chronicle of the WHO* 1, 1–2 (1947), pp. 1–12, 11.
6. Ibid., p. 13.
7. Ibid., p. 3.
8. M. Worboys, 'The Discovery of Colonial Malnutrition Between the Wars', in D. Arnold (ed.), *Imperial Medicine and Indigenous Societies* (Manchester and New York: Manchester University Press, 1988), pp. 208–25; D. Wylie, 'Disease, Diet, and Gender: Late Twentieth Century Perspectives on Empire', in R. Winks (ed.), *Historiography: Oxford History of the British Empire*, vol. 5 (Oxford: Oxford University Press, 1999), ch. 17.
9. See J. Lewis, *Empire State Building: War and Welfare in Kenya, 1925–52* (Oxford: James Currey, 2000).
10. T.N. Harper, *The End of Empire and the Making of Malaya* (Cambridge: Cambridge University Press, 1999), pp. 27–35.
11. M. Vaughan, 'Health and Hegemony: Representation of Disease and the Creation of the Colonial Subject in Nyasaland', in D. Engels and S. Marks (eds), *Contesting Colonial Hegemony* (London: British Academic Press, 1994), pp. 173–201.
12. P. Weindling, 'Social Medicine at the League of Nations Health Organization and the International Labour Office Compared', in P. Weindling (ed.), *International Health Organizations and Movements, 1918–1939* (Cambridge: Cambridge University Press, 1995), pp. 134–53.

13. M. Connelly, 'Population Control is History: New Perspectives on the International Campaign to Limit Population Growth', *Comparative Studies in Society and History*, 45 (2003), pp. 122–47. F. Dikotter, 'Race Culture: Recent Perspectives on the History of Eugenics', *American Historical Review*, 103 (1998), pp. 467–78.
14. Dorothy Porter, 'Social Medicine and the New Society: Medicine and Scientific Humanism in mid-Twentieth Century Britain', *Journal of Historical Sociology* 9, 2 (June 1996), pp. 168–87; D. Porter, 'John Ryle: Doctor of Revolution?', in D. Porter and R. Porter (eds), *Doctors, Politics and Society: Historical Essays* (Amsterdam: Rodopi, 1993), pp. 229–47. See also D. Porter, 'Enemies of the Race: Biologism, Environmentalism, and Public Health in Edwardian England', *Victorian Studies*, 34 (1991), pp. 159–78, on late-Victorian debates on preventive medicine, from which Ryle emerged.
15. S. Marks and N. Andersson, 'Industrialization, Rural Health, and the 1944 National Health Services Commission in South Africa', in S. Feierman and J. Janzen (eds), *The Social Basis of Health and Healing in Africa* (Berekely, CA: University of California Press, 1992), pp. 131–62; S. Marks, 'Doctors and the State: George Gale and South Africa's Experiment in Social Medicine', in S. Dubow (ed.), *Science and Society in Southern Africa* (Manchester: Manchester University Press, 2001), pp. 188–211.
16. J. Ryle, *Changing Disciplines: Changing Disciplines: Lectures on the History, Method, and Motives of Social Pathology* (London: Oxford University Press, 1948), p. 112.
17. Ibid., p. 9.
18. Ibid., pp. 114–15.
19. Rockefeller Archive Centre, New York. Record Group 2 – General Correspondence, 1945, Series 464. Box 306, Folder 2076.
20. Ryle, *Changing Disciplines*, p. 85.
21. National Planning Committee, *National Health: Report of the Sub-Committee*, (Bombay, 1947) [henceforth *Sokhey Report*].
22. Government of India, *Report of the Health Survey and Development Committee*, 4 vols (New Delhi, 1946) [henceforth *Bhore Report*].
23. *Sokhey Report*, p. 37.
24. *Sokhey Report*, p.18.
25. *Bhore Report*, vol. 2, p 1.
26. *Bhore Report*, vol. 1, p. 17.
27. On the history of the discourse of 'over-population' in India, I am grateful for discussions with Sarah Hodges, and for a chance to see drafts of her forthcoming work on: 'Governmentality, Population and the Reproductive Family in Modern India.'
28. National Planning Committee, *Population: Report of the Sub-Committee* (Bombay, 1947), p. 8.
29. *Sokhey Report*, p. 18.
30. *Population: Report*, pp. 6–7. On the history of eugenic thought in India, see: B. Zachariah, 'Uses of Scientific Argument: The Case of Development in India, c. 1930–1950', *Economic and Political Weekly*, 29 September 2001.
31. *Sokhey Report*, p. 218.
32. *Bhore Report*, vol. 1, p. 21.

33. Cf. J. Jackson, 'Regime Theory, Epistemic Communities and International Health Decision-Making', unpublished PhD, University of Wales, Aberystwyth (1997), who sees the group of men who drafted the WHO's Constitution as an 'epistemic community' with shared assumptions.
34. See M. Grmek (ed.), *Serving the Cause of Public Health: Selected Papers of Andrija Stampar* (Zagreb: Andrija Stampar School of Public Health, 1966).
35. World Health Organization Interim Commission, 'Minutes of the Technical Preparatory Committee for the International Health Conference', p. 61, Annex 10, Annex 9, p. 58.
36. Szeming Sze stated that 'at the New York conference ... somebody, I think it was Dr H.S. Gear of South Africa, improved the wording of the text': Sze, 'WHO: From Small Beginnings', *World Health Forum*, 9, pp. 28–34, esp. p. 33. Professor Shula Marks (personal correspondence) was kind enough to fill in some of the details of Dr Harry Gear's story, and his involvement with the South African social medicine experiment of the 1930s.
37. Interim Commission, 'Minutes', p. 61, Annex 10.
38. J. Gillespie, 'Social Medicine, Social Security and International Health, 1940–60', in E. Rodriguez-Ocana (ed.), *The Politics of the Healthy Life: An International Perspective* (Sheffield: European Association for the History of Medicine and Health Publications, 2002), pp. 219–39.
39. Ibid.
40. Ibid.
41. T. Mitchell, 'Can the Mosquito Speak?', in *Rule of Experts: Egypt, Techno-politics, Modernity* (Berkeley, CA and Los Angeles: University of California Press, 2002), pp. 19–53.
42. T. West and G. Campbell, *DDT and Newer Persistent Insecticides* (London: Chapman & Hall, 1950).
43. G. Woodbridge (ed.), *UNRRA: The History*, vol. 3 (New York: Columbia University Press, 1950).
44. See S. Amrith, 'Plague of Poverty? The World Health Organization, Tuberculosis and International Development, c.1945–1970', unpublished MPhil. dissertation (Cambridge, 2002), ch. 1.
45. For an argument on similar lines, see S. Litsios, 'Malaria Control, Rural Development and the Post-War Re-ordering of International Organizations', *Medical Anthropology*, 14, pp. 255–78.
46. Quoted in A. Iriye, *Global Community: The Role of International Organizations in the Making of the Contemporary World* (Berkeley, CA: University of California Press, 2002), p. 40.
47. UN, *Technical Assistance for Economic Development: Plan for an Expanded Co-operative Programme Through the United Nations and the Specialized Agencies* (New York: United Nations, 1949).
48. UN, *Technical Assistance*, p. 3.
49. UN, *Technical Assistance*, p. 9.
50. 'Objectives and Nature of the Point IV Program', 19 March 1949, *Foreign Relations of the United States [FRUS], 1949*, Volume I, 'National Security Affairs, Foreign Economic Policy' (Washington DC: US Government Printing Office, 1976), p. 783.
51. S. Bose, 'Instruments and Idioms'.

52. Adopting here Partha Chatterjee's characterization of post-colonial Indian planning, 'Development Planning and the Indian State', in P. Chatterjee (ed.), *State and Politics in India* (New Delhi: Oxford University Press, 1997), pp. 271–97.
53. The birth of technical assistance coincided with the end of a trend Gunnar Myrdal associated with the immediate post-colonial years in Southern Asia: in the earliest years of post-colonial State-building, 'everything, including the broadest issues, was debated'. In all South Asian countries, there was an 'intense interest in arguing and making explicit fundamental goals for society'. G. Myrdal, 'Spread and Impact of the Ideology of Planning', *Asian Drama: An Inquiry into the Poverty of Nations* (London: Allen Lane/Penguin, 1968), ch. 15.
54. William Vogt, *The Road to Survival* (London: Victor Gollancz, 1949).
55. Matthew Connelly makes this point very convincingly, in 'Population Control is History'.
56. Vogt, quoted in S. Litsios, 'Malaria Control', p. 264.
57. Cf. M. Davis, *Late Victorian Holocausts: El Nino Famines and the Making of the Third World* (London: Verso, 1999), p. 33.
58. Sir Herbert Broadley, *Official Records of the World Health Organization [OR]*. No. 42. Fifth World Health Assembly, Geneva, 5–22 May 1952, pp. 61–2.
59. *OR*, no. 42, p. 90.
60. WHO Archives, First Generation files (WHO.1), GH/12, Rajkumari Amrit Kaur to Brock Chisholm, 25 January 1952.
61. *OR*, no. 42, pp. 234–5
62. Ibid., p. 235.
63. Ibid., p. 206.
64. Cf. Litsios, 'Malaria Control'.
65. WHO.1, GH/12, Brock Chisholm to Paul S. Henshaw, 21 January 1952.
66. C.-E.A. Winslow, 'The Economic Values of Preventive Medicine', *Chronicle of the WHO* (1952), pp. 191–202.
67. Ibid., p. 191.
68. C.-E.A. Winslow, *Cost of Sickness and the Price of Health* (Geneva: WHO, 1952), p. 9.
69. Ibid., p. 10.
70. Winslow, 'Economic Values', p. 191.
71. Ibid., p. 196.
72. This was the sequence of events posited, for example, in one of the classic texts of development economics: W.A. Lewis, *The Theory of Economic Growth* (London: George Allen & Unwin, 1955), ch. 6.
73. Ibid., p. 192.
74. Winslow, *Cost of Sickness*, p. 12.
75. Ibid., p. 15.
76. Gunnar Myrdal, 'Economic Aspects of Health', *Chronicle of the WHO* (1952), p. 203.
77. Ibid., p. 211.
78. Andrija Stampar, 'On Social Medicine', Inaugural Lecture, Medical Faculty, Zagreb, 1923, in Grmek (ed.), *Serving the Cause*, p. 93.
79. Ibid.

80. Winlsow's *The Conquest of Epidemic Disease: A Chapter in the History of Ideas* (Princeton, NJ: Princeton University Press, 1943), for example, is a classic of social medicine.
81. Winslow, 'Economic Values', pp. 200–1.
82. Winslow, 'Economic Values', p. 193.
83. Ritchie Calder, *West Meets East* (London: News Chronicle, 1952): WHO Library, Historical Collection: WA 530.1 52CA.
84. Calder, *West Meets East*, p. 5
85. Ibid., p. 9.
86. Ibid., p. 12.
87. See, for example, WHO's first official history: *First Ten Years of the WHO* (Geneva, 1958); also, the special issue of UNESCO's *Courier* on world health, May 1958, vol. 11, no. 5.
88. A good example is the pamphlet, *Technical Co-operation in International Health* (Washington DC: Technical Co-operation Administration, 1956); also, A. Deutsch, *The World Health Organization – Its Global Battle Against Disease* (Public Affairs Committee, pamphlet no. 265, 1957)
89. For example, the images in the Government of India's annual *Indian Health Statistics*. [London School of Hygiene and Tropical Medicine: Reports Collection.]
90. WHO.1, 400-1-13, H. van Zilde Hyde to B. Chisholm, 25 July 1948.
91. See, for example: P.A. Buxton, in *Transactions of the Royal Society of Tropical Medicine* 38, 5 (1945), p. 377.
92. Mitchell, 'Can the Mosquito Speak?' p. 47.
93. Ibid.
94. Ibid.
95. F.J. Dy, 'Present Status of Malaria Control in Asia', *Bulletin of the World Health Organization* 11 (1954), pp. 725–63, esp. p. 727.
96. G.A. Livadas and G. Georgopoulos, 'Development of Resistance to DDT By Anopheles Sacharovi in Greece', *Bulletin of the World Health Organization*, 8 (1953), pp. 497–511.
97. F.J. Dy, 'Present Status of Malaria Control in Asia'.
98. E.J. Pampana, 'Changing Strategy in Malaria Control', *Bulletin of the World Health Organization*, 11 (1954), pp. 513–20, esp. p. 518.
99. Ibid.
100. For a narrative history, see: G. Harrison, *Mosquitoes, Malaria and Man: A History of the Hostilities Since 1880* (London: J. Murray, 1978).
101. R. Packard, 'Malaria Dreams: Postwar Visions of Health and Development in the Third World', *Medical Anthropology* 17 (1997), pp. 279–96, esp. p. 292.
102. J. Jackson, 'Epistemic Communities'.
103. Cf. G. Prakash, *Another Reason: Science and the Imagination of Modern India* (Princeton, NJ: Princeton University Press, 1999).
104. P. Baldwin, *Contagion and the State in Europe, 1830–1930* (Cambridge: Cambridge University Press, 1999).

11
Economic Knowledge and Managerial Power at the United Nations: A Comparative View

John Toye and Richard Toye

In the early 1960s, the UN economist Hans Singer expressed doubts about the creativity of the UN in the field of political economy. He did not think that the UN Secretariat could be called a major producer of new ideas. 'Creation was not a congenial job for a Secretariat; it could even be dangerous. Traditionally, the Secretariat tried not to run too far ahead of possibilities and not to bring matters up until states had more or less agreed. It wanted to avoid friction, rifts and disputes, and this pacifying role was quite a legitimate one for the Secretariat. Its job, on the whole, was to record and register changes in climates of opinion and to apply new and agreed solutions to international problems.'[1]

This reference to the possibilities of danger and to the need for pacification reminds us that creative ideas, in the field of political economy, as in other areas, may prove inconvenient to the sponsors and managers of international organizations. This is because they may be in conflict with the organization's pre-established goals or doctrines. Creative ideas that provoke such conflicts may be described as 'bureaucratically dysfunctional'. Yet the UN has in fact produced and disseminated a number of such ideas. This chapter explores why, on occasion, such 'dysfunctional' creativity proved possible at the UN, in broad contrast to the experience of the League of Nations and the World Bank. We argue that this was in part a response to the more divergent interests of its sponsors and in part a product of looser editorial control by the UN's research managers. We further argue that creativity that is dysfunctional from the bureaucratic or managerial point of view may in fact be functional from the point of view of the broader public good.

In the two decades between 1945 and 1964, economists working within the UN brought about a major shift in ideas concerning the relation of international trade and finance to economic development. The economic aspects of the UN system, as it was designed, were broadly based on an American blueprint (albeit with significant British input). The central principle behind this blueprint was that, just as collective action was necessary to maintain security in the military sphere, so nations needed to work together to solve the international economic, social and humanitarian problems which themselves tended to undermine world peace.[2] The fundamental causes of these problems, it was believed, could be eradicated by the creation of a world economy based on multilateral, non-discriminatory trade and payments regimes. This in turn would facilitate a high degree of international economic specialization, unleashing forces which would help develop 'backward' countries, thus increasing the prosperity both of the world as a whole and of all its constituent national parts.[3] Consequently, a return to freer trade and payments should be the chief objective of international economic policy, provided that adequate safeguards against mass unemployment were built in to the international economic arrangements.

By 1964, a powerful challenge to this orthodoxy had been mounted by a group of economists operating within the UN, the very organization that had been established to implement the orthodox view. This group had deployed arguments suggesting the existence of systematic economic forces that diminished the benefits that underdeveloped countries gained from trade and from foreign investment. It had also designed a package of interventionist measures that constituted 'a new trade policy for development' and rallied support for a new international organization to put them into effect.[4] In other words, the UN did not merely disseminate or implement an existing set of ideas, but actually helped develop a new set. That is to say, it had a role as an intellectual actor.

International public organizations as intellectual actors

That international public organizations sometimes operate as intellectual actors is startling. The role of an international bureaucracy may extend to the collection and dissemination of available knowledge, if this helps it in the discharge of its functional responsibilities. That the production of novel ideas should be one of its functions would come to most people as a surprise. An organization that does such a thing could well be viewed as going into competition with universities, institutes, think tanks and consultancy firms, but without having the necessary advantages, either of human and physical infrastructure or, perhaps more importantly, in terms of the structure of institutional incentives. 'Universities and think-tanks can out-perform the UN in research', according to Michael Edwards, because they are 'without the combination of high costs and low levels of innovation that characterises organisations lacking both market discipline and social pressures to reform'.[5]

Nevertheless, in the twentieth century, national governments did increasingly become a locus of the creation of economic knowledge. This went beyond the gathering and presentation of economic statistics. Statistics, as the word implies, had long been the province of the state. In the years between the two World Wars, by contrast, some statisticians became unusually inventive, creating new empirical representations of novel economic concepts. In Germany, Ernst Wagemann's theoretical work inspired the Statistical Office to use census data to produce an input–output table, quite independently of Wassily Leontief.[6] In the United States, Lauchlin Currie and Martin Krost, while on the research staff of the Federal Reserve Board, made pioneering estimates of the effects of government fiscal changes on the national income – as early as 1937–38.[7] These examples could be multiplied. In step with national governments, international organizations moved from statistical collection to the quantification of new macroeconomic concepts. The League of Nations moved on from collecting balance of payments statistics in the early 1920s to producing innovative studies of trade and the business cycle in the late 1930s. This transition was undoubtedly hastened after the Great Crash, when it seemed to many that academic economists had little that was useful to contribute to the formation of economic policy.

Yet the economic justification for the state becoming an intellectual actor was, and is, problematic. Admittedly, knowledge is a public good, and the market, if left to itself, will tend to supply too little of it to achieve maximum welfare. The force of this argument is to justify public intervention to boost investment in new knowledge. However, it does not entail that the new knowledge must be produced in a public sector institution. If individuals tend to under-invest in their health and education, this is not a sufficient justification for setting up public hospitals and schools, because a better outcome might result from giving private schools and private hospitals a public subsidy. Similarly, if knowledge is under-supplied, it might be better for public sector institutions to subsidize its private production, rather than to produce it themselves.

Some international public institutions have, nevertheless, wanted to be intellectual actors, rather than just investors in the production of knowledge. As will be suggested later, in the field of economic and social development, perhaps the foremost contemporary repository of this ambition is the World Bank. The economic justification advanced for it is that only by producing knowledge in-house can its benefits for the institutions' functional operations be secured.[8] Partly, it is argued, this is a matter of being able to ensure that outside researchers undertake the research agenda that the institution in question wants them to undertake. Partly it is that, in the absence of in-house champions of specific pieces of research, potentially useful research will not get noticed and will not in fact be used. While there is doubtless merit in these arguments, they look only to the advantages of doing research in-house, and these advantages always need to be balanced against the potential difficulties.

What then are the drawbacks? For the answer to this, one must turn from the economics of public goods to the sociology of bureaucracy. Weber argued that modern bureaucratic organizations would increasingly replace patrimonial ones. He claimed that they are formally the most rational means of exercising control over human beings, because their goals are set by their sponsors and are implemented by bureaucrats who remain politically neutral. In making this claim for the efficiency of modern bureaucracy, Weber simply assumed that bureaucrats' assigned formal roles are always congruent with their actual motives and orientations. However, this is not necessarily so: officials may don their organizational masks, but they do not easily or frequently become them.[9] Weber's ideal type needs to be modified to take account of the fact that people inside bureaucracies can rebel against the machine-like expectations of formal rationality.[10] Experience forces us to confront the fact that 'defiant bureaucrats' exist, who 'engage in behavior that is from the perspective of organizational goals and procedures irrational and dysfunctional'.[11]

A modified Weberian theory of bureaucracy asserts that, inside all public organizations, authority stands in potential tension with power. Authority is hierarchical, and is formally delegated from the pinnacle of the Executive Secretary (or other like role) downwards in a very precise manner. Power – the ability to make others act as one requires – may be distributed differently. It will be exercised from above only to the extent that those in authority at the top have the resources of power – personal leadership skills, access to information, incentives and sanctions – with which to motivate, control and appropriate the efforts of those below them in the hierarchy. This potential tension sets the scene for the outbreak of power struggles between superiors and subordinates, as the former seek to conjure up from the latter the activity that will support the goals of the organization (which are derived from those of its sponsors), and as from time to time they meet resistance.[12] Maintaining the congruence of power with authority is a quite onerous task that heads of bureaucracies often fail to perform.

This is especially so in international bureaucracies. Here control by sponsors is weaker than in the national case, because the conflicting interests of the multitude of country sponsors permanently dilute it. This is partly a matter of a lesser ability to determine clear and consistent objectives. It is also because divergent interests of sponsors can reduce the resources of power available to those in high authority in international organizations; requirements of geographical balance in recruitment, or the diplomatic consequences of disciplining officials of particular nationalities, deplete the normal armoury of sanctions that high officials can deploy against subordinates who engage in dysfunctional behaviour.

Within an international bureaucracy, the in-house research function presents a special case. Intellectual originality and creativity are achievements that, almost by definition, cannot be commanded, sometimes not even by their authors. Original research, when produced, may turn out to be congruent with the objectives that an international bureaucracy and its sponsors are seeking to fulfil. Yet it also has the potential to be dissonant with those objectives. In that case, therefore, its authors, because of the peculiar nature of their specialized expertise, run a particularly large risk of becoming, in the course of defending their research procedures and results, 'defiant' bureaucrats. The political neutrality required of a Weberian bureaucrat may turn out to be at odds with the intellectual disinterestedness that must discipline the good researcher. Ideally, researchers should have no personal stake in the results of their enquiries. If they are researching, for example, whether trade liberalization does or does not stimulate economic growth, or whether commodity prices are set to rise or fall, they should have no vested interest in reaching a particular conclusion.[13] When the organization that employs them aims to persuade external agents of the truth of certain propositions, and researchers willy-nilly have such a personal stake, this threatens to damage the integrity and quality of their work. Thus in-house intellectual activity will be constantly in danger of being to some degree distorted by managers' success in imposing their organizational goals.

International bureaucracies still wield some incentives and sanctions, even if to a lesser degree than national bureaucracies. International officials who are researchers on political economy resemble their colleagues in that all are wholly dependent on their organization's managers for their material rewards, so they may face disincentives to coming up with results that top managers find unhelpful to their goals, even if the results that they produce are intellectually sound. Similarly, they may face incentives to certify propositions as valid knowledge when their top managers find it helpful to their goals, even if the propositions are not valid. The independence that is the only safeguard for intellectual honesty will be lacking, when the internal power struggle favours the top management. This does not of course imply that intellectual honesty must always be lacking: it may or may not turn out to be consistent with an international organization's goals.

However, the significance of this potential drawback is amplified as soon as we recognize that international public institutions do indeed at times identify with and defend certain doctrines of political economy. They are often required to do so by the governments that are their members and their main financial sponsors. The defence of an organization's core doctrines can be managed in several different ways. One is to design the research agenda in a way likely to support the consensus, for example, by not devoting resources to researching topics that were regarded as marginal, or potentially antagonistic to it. Another is for top managers to vet carefully high profile research output, and to edit out unwanted messages.[14] Another is the self-censorship of the researchers, who can usually guess where the limits of acceptability lie. Even when top managers try to avoid shooting the messengers that bear bad, but accurate, tidings, it will not be every staff member who will venture to put that restraint to the test.

The League of Nations and the United Nations compared

Within this general understanding of how the sociology of international bureaucracy impacts on political economy research, it is necessary to take account of different international organizations' varying characteristics. Here our primary focus is on the United Nations Organisation. In order to point up the specific characteristics of the UN in this regard, it will be useful to begin by indicating some contrasts with its predecessor organization, the League of Nations. The particular characteristics of their sponsors influenced the modalities of operation and intellectual focus of both organizations. In the case of the League, its sponsoring governments were predominantly European countries, and among them the already industrialized France and Britain played the leading role. This influenced the intellectual agenda of the League's economic research, which was largely concerned with the problem of economic crises, the nature of business cycles and the international transmission of economic depressions. The UN had a wider membership, one that not only included the United States, but also and increasingly developing countries including many ex-colonies. This influenced the UN to turn towards the study of issues of economic development policy in the late-1940s and 1950s.

The League of Nations Economic Intelligence Service (EIS) was the institutional predecessor of the United Nations Department of Economic Affairs (DEA), and there was considerable continuity of personnel. The DEA also inherited an intellectual perspective, as it evolved in the latter years of the League. With the financial assistance of the Rockefeller Foundation after 1933, the EIS had devoted much of its effort to analysing the phenomenon of the business cycle, and especially to the problem of the international transmission of economic depressions. Its Director, Dr Alexander Loveday, had seen it as his and the Service's mission to elucidate the mechanisms by which the contagion of economic depression was spread from nation to nation, and thereby to educate nations into more co-operative behaviour in the international economic sphere. Even so, it was clear by 1939 that rational persuasion alone would not be sufficient to achieve this.[15]

On the positive side, the League had been able to attract European economists of much creativity, such as Bertil Ohlin, Gottfried Haberler, Jan Tinbergen, J.J. Polak and Tjalling Koopmans. Their work on the causes of depression, the generation of business cycles and the mechanisms transmitting depression was undertaken at a high technical and professional standard. Under the auspices of the League, they had produced pioneering publications in this field.[16] Tinbergen's work on profit and investment cycles was marked by a strong quantitative basis in statistics, most remarkably his innovative use of the new methods of applied econometrics. Polak's work demonstrated quantitatively how depressions originating in the United States were transmitted to the smaller and more passive European economies.[17]

However, on the negative side, the League's pre-war business-cycle research was deficient in two important ways to meet the emerging needs of the post-war international economic scene. First, it stood apart from the new macroeconomics of Keynes's *General Theory* (1936).[18] The League's senior external adviser on its business-cycle work had been Dennis Robertson, who was a strong critic and persistent opponent both of *The General Theory* and of the work of Keynes's disciples.[19] Admittedly, Robertson's supervision of the League's research was superficial, as he willingly admitted.[20] Nevertheless, it was clear that his influence meant that Keynes's advice was not sought.[21] The intellectual distance between the EIS researchers and Keynes was increased by Keynes's highly critical review of the first volume of Tinbergen's 1939 League study, dealing with statistical methods. Keynes pointed out numerous deficiencies in the novel econometric methods that it presented and defended – criticism made harder to absorb because not all of it was well founded.[22]

Keynes made many telling points, though. He questioned how applicable multiple correlation methods were to economic data; he raised the issue of omitted variable bias; he noted that key variables in the business cycle – such as the state of confidence – were non-measurable; and that the data used for investment and saving were unreliable and inconsistent. Additionally, both Keynes and Kahn charged that the League's work gave little help in the practical problems of economic policy. Their own policy conclusion that mass involuntary unemployment was avoidable by state action brought a wholly new dimension to the idea of international economic policy co-ordination. Yet the League economists embraced it only with great timidity and many qualifications before 1943.[23]

The lesson that the UN DEA carried into the post-1945 world was the imperative need for nations to co-ordinate their economic policies, rather than to act independently, following short-run national interest. The UN therefore continued the League's interest in international co-ordination to avoid depressions, albeit with a new Keynesian emphasis. An UN expert group produced a report on *National and International Measures for Full Employment* in 1949. Nicholas Kaldor was the lead author. The policy measures that the UN expert group proposed were, however, a matter of contention between Britain and the United States. United States' political and economic opinion was not persuaded that full employment could be pursued as a sole objective of economic policy, and the UN report was criticized from the American side for its 'academic naivety' and 'extreme Keynesianism'. [24] To move on from this impasse, the second Secretary General of the UN, Dag Hammarskjöld guided the organization to re-direct its research efforts into the economic development field.[25]

The League had normally used (invited) visiting scholars to produce research in the form of independently authored monographs. The UN's use of the device of the expert report was a new departure, moving on from the League's later practice of seeking reports from 'special delegation' with a couple of outside academic advisers.[26] The expert report had the advantage of quickly gathering up research contributions from around the world and of involving more researchers from a wider range of countries. It was certainly speedier, and was seen as helping to build a constituency of world opinion behind policy recommendations. It was nevertheless more superficial. Gottfried Haberler, for example, seems to have doubted that the use of expert reports was an improvement. He preferred the League's approach to research, and paid tribute to 'that remarkable group of economists at Geneva', who 'supported by a very small budget (compared with the sums at the disposal of international agencies in the post-war period) ... produced a most impressive collection of analytical and statistical documents dealing with the many problems of international trade, economic development, commercial, financial and monetary policies, while at the same time advising many governments on their economic problems.'[27]

The UN followed the tradition of the League in producing an annual *World Economic Report*, which in the mid-1950s even reverted to the old title, *World Economic Survey*. It was, however, regarded as much inferior to the League's Surveys. The 1948 edition was heavily criticized by Austin Robinson, who rubbed salt into the wound by contrasting it unfavourably with the earlier work directed by J.B. Condliffe and James Meade of the EIS.[28] The problem that Robinson identified was that the UN *Report* lacked 'an architect': there was no single individual designing and editing it for policy relevance and intellectual coherence.

Significantly, in the early years of the UN Secretariat, tight central editorial control was something more honoured in the breach than in the observance. Alexander Loveday, drawing on his experience of the League, had harsh words to say in 1956 about the failure of UN administrators to exercise sufficient editorial control over their research output:

> The most glaring weakness in certain offices today is the lack of editorial courage and decision. Certain editors ... seek a weak and flabby compromise between the divergent views of politically minded social scientists rather than scientific objectivity. As a result each document is liable to lack substance and to reflect somewhat dimly a number of preconceived views instead of views based on ascertained facts, and the whole documentation is liable to lack unity of design.[29]

Loveday was here promoting the simple Weberian view of international organizations as politically impartial instruments of sponsoring governments. He interpreted failure of impartiality as a problem of managerial character, rather than one of lack of managerial resources and power. He also saw no difficulty in reconciling 'editorial decision' with 'scientific objectivity', although in fact the League economists had their own reformist agenda.[30] This suggests that he cultivated a somewhat arid and rationalistic perspective on international bureaucracy. The understanding demonstrated elsewhere in his writings of the human factor in bureaucratic life did not extend to its role in producing 'defiant bureaucrats'. It is worth noting that he had been earlier described as 'completely League-minded and completely divorced from the reality of planning'.[31]

The ideal of 'objectivity' that was inherited from the League was reinforced in the UN by Cold War politics. The justification for the Secretariat itself to undertake research in-house was that the research required objectivity, which could not be expected either of the UN political organs themselves or of national research institutes in member states. However, this justification brought with it very narrow limits on the type of research that the Secretariat could undertake. Any research that involved much in the way of value judgements that might be politically controversial was deemed unsuitable, and other methods of producing it – often involving outside experts taking the formal responsibility – had to be found. The research produced by the UN Secretariat thus tended to be highly factual and non-controversial. The main problem that it faced was how to achieve meaningful international comparisons of national data. It was generally agreed throughout the first 20 years of the UN that the Secretariat should not 'preach a doctrine' in its publications, and should not be asked by member states to do so.[32] Doing so would have undermined the basic legitimacy of producing research in-house.

However, the pursuit of objectivity carried with it a heavy disadvantage. Although many UN Secretariat research publications – precisely because they were relatively objective – were potentially useful, they were at the same time politically anodyne. They were compilations of statistical data arrayed comparably across countries and across time. Some combined such statistics with analyses of the current economic scene based on them, striving always to be objective. But once the format for a research publication of this type was designed and the methods of collecting, processing and analysing the data were determined, the work of its regular production became progressively more repetitive and dreary. There was consequently a serious problem of maintaining the morale of the officials who were researchers because, while they had to be creative people to do the work at all, relatively little of their creative energy was called for by their allotted task.[33]

Sagging morale quickly became a problem, and, to maintain morale, UN officials in research departments were often permitted, and sometimes positively encouraged, to find other outlets for their creative talent. Many wrote signed articles in the organization's own journals, or published research in outside academic publications. Even Executive Secretaries took this path. As Janez Stanovnik recalled:

> [Gunnar] Myrdal retired shortly before 1960, but during the last of his stay in ECE [the UN Economic Commission for Europe], he already did not have much interest in ECE because things were all retrogressing or stagnant. ... And he decided to write a book. So Myrdal wrote *International Economy*, which I think is a marvellous piece of work. This he wrote during his last couple of years.[34]

The frustration of much of the researcher's creativity by the Secretariat's pursuit of objective research often spilled over into a battle for editorial control of publications between the administrative chiefs of the organization and individual research directors. The heads of administration needed to defend themselves against complaints from UN member states, which were acutely sensitive to any perceived criticism of them, by establishing the claim that Secretariat research was objective. For this claim to succeed, however, they needed to maintain a tight central editorial control over research publications. This was something that caused internal conflict and power struggles, since it was highly unpopular with researchers. To maintain it therefore required great managerial stamina, something that was often lacking.

Loveday's conclusion that firm editorial control was necessary for an international organization's research group to achieve work of the highest quality is one that can be turned on its head. We are inclined to entertain the alternative possibility that the tight editorial discipline that he recommended, and the imposition of a 'unity of design', would have withered any original thought that managers saw as dysfunctional in organizational terms. If this was so, the flourishing of economic heterodoxy – and the paradoxical appearance of interesting and novel arguments for protection within the UN Secretariat – may have depended precisely on the absence of tight editorial control.[35] This can be seen with reference to the origins, within the UN, of the Prebisch–Singer thesis on the terms of trade between industrial and primary-producing countries.

The origins of the Prebisch–Singer thesis

Hans Singer's assessment of the creative potential of the UN Secretariat quoted at the start of this chapter was that it was limited. He was sure that the UN had played an educational role, one that not only circulated ideas but also facilitated the acceptance of new policies. The UN was a forum for a vast range of international contacts between governments, and between governments and technical experts. The process of repeatedly stating government viewpoints in meetings on a multi-faceted economic and social agenda, and then negotiating the wording of agreed resolutions, created a climate of shared opinion about the nature of problems and the kinds of multilateral solutions that might be feasible. To the economically literate, some of texts agreed by the UN diplomats might have seemed rather silly, but the process aired proposals that, despite at first seeming wild and utopian, were often eventually accepted by states. According to this view, the Secretariat, just as the World Bank has done in more recent times, acted more as a 'transmission belt' than as a catalyst of new ideas.

Although this hypothesis is a powerful one, there are some good reasons for thinking that the UN has, at times, played a more creative role than Singer's comments suggest. In this section we explore an example of UN creativity in political economy by reference to Singer's own work. Singer played an important part in the major shift in ideas concerning trade and economic development described at the start of this chapter. This episode is by no means the only example of intellectual creativity by economists in the UN, and our focus on it here should not be misread to imply that it was.[36]

The Prebisch–Singer thesis asserted that the net barter terms of trade between primary products and manufactures have been subject to a long-run downward trend. It has been much disputed and continues to be controversial after more than fifty years. The continuing significance of the thesis is that it implies that, barring major changes in the structure of the world economy, the gains from trade will continue to be distributed unequally (and, some would add, unfairly) between nations exporting mainly primary products and those exporting mainly manufactures. Further, inequality of per capita income between these two types of countries will be increased by the growth of trade, rather than reduced. This could be, and has been, taken as an indicator of the need for both industrialization and tariff protection.

It might seem odd – given the potential pressures on UN economists outlined above – that the UN should be the cradle of such a controversial doctrine, one that lent itself so readily both to the economic nationalism of the underdeveloped countries and to the polemics of the Cold War. Ironically, it was the UN managers' own eagerness to disclaim responsibility for the doctrine that brought one (but only one) of its authors into the limelight. Moreover, the UN managers' failed stratagem for distancing the UN from the Prebisch–Singer doctrine had the unintended consequence of making the world organization itself appear as a nursery of economic radicalism.

The publication dates of the first two works in English that expounded the thesis were nearly simultaneous. In May 1950, the English version of *The Economic Development of Latin America and its Principal Problems*, by Raúl Prebisch of the UN Economic Commission for Latin America (ECLA), appeared under the UN's imprint. In the same month Hans Singer of the UN DEA published an article, 'The Distribution of Gains between Investing and Borrowing Countries', in the *American Economic Review*. However, Prebisch is frequently credited with having formulated the declining terms of trade thesis before Singer did.[37] Other authors have held that Singer discovered the thesis independently and simultaneously.[38] This second view was indeed that held by Singer himself.[39] However, careful examination of the events surrounding the UNECLA conference in Havana in May 1949 reveals that Prebisch did not discover independently that the terms of trade of primary products were secularly declining, but relied wholly on the previous work of Singer. Before he became aware of Singer's UN data, Prebisch never explicitly stated the thesis that Latin America's terms of trade had been subject to long-term decline, as opposed to the sharp short-term decline that he noted in 1934.[40] The false impression that he had made the discovery (either first or simultaneously) was the consequence of political tensions between the developed and the underdeveloped countries that had welled up at Havana, and the way in which the top administrators of the UN secretariat responded to those tensions.

We have established this case in detail elsewhere.[41] The episode shows, to begin with, the truth of Singer's later proposition that 'Creation was not a congenial job for a Secretariat; it could even be dangerous.' Singer, in a research study prepared at UN headquarters in New York, had shown a new result, that the terms of trade of primary commodities had experienced a substantial secular decline. The UN Sub-Commission on Economic Development, which held its third session from 21 March to 11 April 1949, discussed Singer's study on *Post-War Price Relations*. The study's conclusion, that 'the under-developed [countries had] helped to maintain ... a rising standard of living in the industrialized countries, without receiving, in the price of their own products, a corresponding equivalent contribution towards their own standards of living',[42] was likely to prove profoundly controversial. While it appealed to the underdeveloped countries, it appealed not at all to the developed. Accordingly, the Sub-Commission accepted, somewhat grudgingly,

Singer's statistical evidence, but rejected the lessons that had been drawn from it. Its report said that

> The Sub-Commission is constrained to point out that the study under review contains certain conclusions in regard to the price relationship between developed and under-developed countries which, in its opinion, do not represent a correct picture of the actual position. As a result of the discussion, the Sub-Commission agreed that while the document contained an adequate study of relative price trends of primary commodities and manufactured goods, it was necessary to broaden the scope of the study into that of the terms of trade between under-developed and industrialized countries, including prices and quantities traded, and in extending it, to cover the most recent movements in these fields.[43]

It seems plausible to suggest that the Sub-Commission used the fact (which Singer himself had acknowledged) that the picture presented by the study was in some ways incomplete as an excuse for disclaiming its radical conclusions. Likewise, as will be seen, the UN secretariat would be eager to distance itself from the similarly dramatic conclusions subsequently reached by Prebisch.

The second point is that the UN system did in this instance work as a 'transmission belt' for ideas – as Singer later suggested. In preparing for its 1949 conference the fledgling ECLA lacked the statistical infrastructure to discharge one of its primary tasks, to survey the common economic and technical problems of the region. This provided the cue for statistical help from UN headquarters in New York. During the preparations for the conference, Singer's study of the terms of trade was transmitted to ECLA by three different channels between December 1948 and April 1949. An early version arrived in December 1948, but does not seem to have been followed up. The second transfer was via Gustavo Martínez Cabañas and Francisco Coire[44] to Prebisch before the latter arrived at the ECLA office in Santiago, and this was the critical route. At Martínez Cabañas's prompting, Prebisch 'latched onto the terms of trade idea', in the words of Victor Urquidi,[45] and meshed it with his own framework of thought in April/May 1949. The additional data he requested from New York (the third route) arrived too late to be useful.

It can therefore be said that, although some governments and the upper echelons of the UN Secretariat were hostile to Singer's ideas, the system nevertheless transmitted them to other UN organs, with some rather dramatic effects. Moreover, the 'transmission belt' role was not merely a neutral one, for the effect of the transmission was to stimulate further creativity. For although Prebisch relied wholly on Singer's data for his own claim about the decline in the terms of trade, his *explanation* for the decline was significantly different from that offered by Singer.[46] In this instance, the UN's 'transmission belt' role also allowed it to function as a catalyst.

Finally, it will be seen, in relation to Prebisch's ideas, that the UN secretariat's own attempts to avoid being associated with radical ideas could have unintended consequences. Prebisch's proposed introduction to the Latin American *Economic Survey* was a rhetorical *tour de force*, which repeated, in more dramatic terms, Singer's conclusion that underdeveloped countries were helping to maintain a rising standard of living in industrialized countries without receiving any equivalent compensation: 'The enormous benefits that derive from increased productivity have not reached the periphery in a measure comparable to that obtained by the peoples of the great industrial countries. Hence, the outstanding differences between the standards of living of the masses of the former and the latter and the manifest discrepancies between their respective abilities to accumulate capital.'[47]

When he presented his work at the ECLA conference in Havana, it received the acclaim of the delegates of the Latin American countries.[48] However, what was music to the ears of the delegates of Latin American countries would have displeased the industrial countries, especially the United States. This fact appears to have caused some consternation among high UN officials in New York, who were anxious to distance the UN from what Prebisch had written. Accordingly, after the Havana Conference was over, his report was submitted to the Secretary-General as an 'essay' commissioned in the process of 'fostering research' – rather than, as had originally been planned, as the introduction to the *Economic Survey*.[49] It was then proposed to the UN Publications Committee to break the rule that authors of UN publications should not be identified by name. This course of action was designed to ensure that Prebisch took 'credit (and responsibility) for the report ... in order to emphasize that the views expressed ... were those of the author and not those of any UN organ'. The proposal was presented 'as an exceptional one, unlikely to recur but in the present circumstances very desirable'.[50] Prebisch's long-held suspicion that no international organization would feel very comfortable with the viewpoint of the under-developed countries was thus confirmed.

The UN's tactic backfired. The Spanish original had been issued in May 1949, but, as Celso Furtado has noted, it was some time before both this, and the English translation, were eventually published in New York by the UN, being circulated, as he put it, 'with the slowness characteristic of official documents'.[51] Meanwhile, however, a Portuguese translation of the Spanish original, undertaken at Furtado's own urging, was published in Brazil in September 1949. It is at this point that the history of Prebisch's enormous influence began, spreading out from Brazil eventually to become worldwide.[52] The publication of the English version of *The Economic Development of Latin America and its Principal Problems* merely strengthened that effect in North America and Europe. The main result of identifying the author was that the polished and polemical Prebisch rapidly gained greater recognition in Europe and North America as a 'UN economist' than did the more under-stated Singer whose original terms of trade study was published anonymously, as was normal, and who published under his own name only in academic journals. Senior UN officials' attempted to distance themselves from Prebisch by identifying him as the author of the views to which the developed countries took exception. In so doing, they unwittingly heightened his prestige. This example shows how UN managers did react negatively to a radical idea created by its own economists that they judged to be in bureaucratic terms dysfunctional, and tried to distance the UN from the idea. In spite of this, though, the system in this case acted as a 'transmission belt' for an idea between different UN departments and agencies, and – inadvertently – ended up promoting the idea extremely effectively to the wider world.

The case of the Prebisch–Singer thesis demonstrates that the economists working for the UN could, at least sometimes, operate as original and even radical intellectual actors in the field of political economy – in spite of the strong pressures to avoid this inherent in its constitution as a public bureaucracy. A note of caution should, however, be added: this may have been possible at the time under discussion because the UN was still in its rather chaotic initial period. Singer, upon arrival in New York, was left pretty much to his own devices, to an extent that would not have been so likely later on in the UN's evolution.[53] Thus it may well be that, after the McCarthy years when the UN came under political pressure because of allegations of (American) communists in its ranks, the UN's high officials succeeded in tightening their control over the DEA and its publications. It would have been easier to do so at the centre of the UN system, whereas outlying organs such as ECLA continued to enjoy greater intellectual freedom. If this is so it would help to explain why ECLA's *Economic Surveys* continued to be original and intellectually stimulating, whereas the *World Economic Surveys* produced by the DEA remained worthy but rather sterile – in spite of the fact that many of the latter were produced under the direction of Michal Kalecki, who was undoubtedly a more talented economist than Prebisch. All this said, we are still left with the surprising fact that the UN did articulate and disseminate an economic idea that was potentially politically explosive.

Economic knowledge and managerial power at the World Bank

It is the rise of the World Bank to its current position of contested intellectual dominance in the development field that has provoked renewed interest among historians in exploring the intellectual contribution of the UN. This way of putting the comparison acknowledges the de facto separation of the Bank (and the International Monetary Fund) from the UN which took place in 1946–47.[54] The Bank's pursuit of intellectual dominance has fully developed only during the last 25 years. It was the failure of the UN's attempt to negotiate a new international economic order in the 1970s that prompted the Reagan, Thatcher and Kohl administrations to turn to the Bank (and the IMF) and to fashion them as instruments of influence over economic policy in developing countries.

In terms of the institutional restraints on creative research, the World Bank had originally started by defending the doctrine of sound finance and had little use for its few economists.[55] Even this commitment to a limited doctrine required some editorial control, however. An early example of the Bank's urge to control occurred in 1955, when it held up the publication of Tinbergen's *The Design of Development* (which it had commissioned) for three years because the then President objected to Tinbergen's support for a mixed private and public economy.[56] Then, in the 1980s, the Bank formulated a stronger and more elaborated doctrinal stance at the behest of the US, West Germany and Britain, whose governments favoured the spread of economic policies that became characterized as the 'Washington Consensus'.[57] This consensus set up the more extensive doctrinal boundaries that were subsequently defended by the Bank.

A notable example of Bank research having to be conformable to management objectives is its research on the debt crisis. Compared with the academic literature of the day,[58] World Bank researchers made more optimistic predictions in 1981 about the future availability of private capital flows to already indebted developing countries. In this, they supported the view of the Bank's then President, Robert McNamara, that the debt problem was manageable and would not obstruct economic growth. Moreover, as the debt crisis worsened, the Bank fell well behind academic opinion on the need for debt relief. The Bank's chief economist, Stanley Fischer, candidly acknowledged the reasons for this. Discussing a World Bank conference that took place at the beginning of 1989, he commented:

> It was clear to the participants in this conference ... as it had been clear to many much earlier, that growth in the debtor countries would not return without debt relief. But the official agencies operate on the basis of an agreed upon strategy, and none of them could openly confront the existing strategy without having an alternative to put in place. And to propose such an alternative would have required agreement among the major shareholders of the institutions. So long as the United States was not willing to move, the I[international] F[inancial] I[nstitution]s were not free to speak ...[59]

An anecdote from the 1980s illustrates both this constraint and how 'defiant bureaucrats' tried to circumvent its effects. Gerald K. Helleiner has recalled how

> a UN professional group, the one on African finance and debt, was put together with the full cooperation of a vice-president of the World Bank, precisely because he could not, within his constraints, get from the Bank a strong public declaration of the need to act on African debt. ... We decided that ... an expert group [of the UN] including a private banker or two, was the way to go. And the World Bank man, Kim Jaycox, was really supportive and told us that he could not do this and that he could not get a Bank study done that would say what an independent group could say that needed to be said.[60]

The short and controversial career of Joseph Stiglitz as Chief Economist of the World Bank from 1997 to January 2000 is recent evidence of the constraints on Bank research.[61] He wanted to broaden the original Washington Consensus of ten policy thrusts (fiscal and exchange rate reform, trade and financial liberalization, privatisation and de-regulation, among others), by adding improved financial sector regulation, competition policy and technology transfer policies. He also suggested multiplying the objectives of development policy, by adding a sustainable environment, democratization and a more egalitarian income and asset distribution.[62] He did not then question the idea that it was the Bank's job to promote a consensus of some kind on development policy; he merely wanted to move away from a narrow version of neo-liberalism. He also began an internal campaign against the deflationary policies recommended by the IMF during the Asian financial crisis.

The US Treasury Department under Laurence Summers was unhappy with Stiglitz's intellectual ambitions, and made his departure from the Bank a condition of US support for James Wolfensohn's second term as President. Stiglitz submitted his resignation in November 1999. Further US pressure, this time to change the draft of the *World Development Report 2001*, led to the resignation of the report's independent editor-in-chief, Ravi Kanbur, in the following year.[63] After leaving the Bank, Stiglitz moved from modifying the Washington Consensus to rejecting the Bank's drive to promulgate a development formula as such:

> Opposition to globalisation in many parts of the world is not to globalisation per se ... but to the particular set of doctrines, the Washington Consensus policies that the international financial institutions have imposed. *And it is not just opposition to the policies themselves, but to the notion that there is a single set of policies that is right.* This notion flies in the face of both economics, which emphasizes the notion of trade-offs, and of ordinary common sense.[64]

Stiglitz's sudden conversion suggests that, while in the Bank, he was constrained to agree that the role of the Bank is to provide the developing world with 'the single set of policies that is right', an idea that he condemned as flying in the face of common sense as soon as he left. It seems that even 'rebels within' cannot escape from the institutional imperative to preach a doctrine, and that the United States will act to reinforce this imperative when it thinks it is necessary. Kaushik Basu, reviewing Stiglitz's recent book, confessed to being persuaded that in subtle ways the big powers do indeed take control of the major international organizations, using them to defend ideas and policies compatible with their interests. As he went on to explain:

> This is not hard because ... [while] economics has had some major successes [it] remains woefully inadequate on many of the most important issues that confront policy makers. In these latter areas, it is easy for myths to develop. By repeating certain propositions sufficiently often, they can be made to sound like facts, and given the credibility of economics in other areas, most people treat them as facts. This creates scope for subversion, feeding people with 'facts' that are convenient to some.[65]

In such circumstances of tight editorial control linked to strategic objectives, it is not surprising that, when the World Bank's role as an intellectual actor was evaluated, little evidence was found for the originality of the ideas directly emanating from it. Even in the area of economics that concerns its own operations most closely, namely the economic appraisal of projects, the Bank did not pioneer new methods.[66] However, despite failure to originate key ideas or methods in development economics, the Bank's power to propagate ideas is well attested in the media and in university graduate-level syllabi. The Bank has also become 'the single most important external source of ideas and advice to developing-country policymakers'.[67] The example of the World Bank seems to show that international public organizations can become powerful propagators of ideas, if they invest sufficiently in the mechanisms of intellectual propagation. Yet it is almost impossible for them, especially when those in high authority in the organization can command the resources of power, also to operate successfully as creative intellectual actors in areas where their managers are already committed to maintaining an economic doctrine.

Conclusion

A comparative view of economic research in the League of Nations, the United Nations and the World Bank presents three contrasting experiences of the relation between the creation of economic knowledge and managerial control. The League's economic work did not antagonise its sponsors. Its managers maintained tight editorial control, but nevertheless it succeeded in generating some pioneering work, even while keeping its distance from Keynes. This may be because the League's economic research seemed to have very little policy relevance, especially after the failure of the World Economic Conference of 1933 and the subsequent preparations for war. After the war, the UN sponsors were more numerous and diverse than those of the League, and perhaps not surprisingly proved more difficult to satisfy collectively. UN managers now recruited economists directly into the organization and yet, contrary to the ideal-typical view of bureaucracy, they had greater difficulty establishing control over their work. The UN's looser editorial control over economic research allowed its economists on occasion to produce creative new ideas that were dysfunctional in terms of the organization's bureaucratic objectives (as in the Prebisch–Singer case). When, after 1980, the industrial countries built up the World Bank as a counterweight to the UN, the power exercised by sponsors was related to their capital contributions, which gave a few industrial countries a heavy leverage. The Bank succeeded in pleasing these sponsors, maintained a tight editorial control, but its economic work has not been judged as particularly creative.

The paradox that dysfunctional organizations can be creative in the field of political economy and functional ones can be sterile need not, perhaps, be too disturbing. What is good for organizations (including international ones) cannot be assumed to be good for those who work for them, or for the wider society in which they operate. What is dysfunctional for them may be functional on a broader view. To achieve the compliance of participants with the goals of their organization is not necessarily an unmitigated good. Sometimes conflict within organizations may promote desirable values and legitimate interests on a grander scale. There may be more to life than the triumph of a particular bureaucracy, however elevated.[68]

Notes

1. 'Economic Trends', in *Annual Review of United Nations Affairs 1960–1961*, pp. 68–103, esp. pp. 97–8.
2. See, for example, Public Record Office, London (henceforward PRO) FO 475/3 U131/12/70 (Press release dated 15 December 1944 of a speech by Leo Pasvolsky on the Dumbarton Oaks proposals).
3. Geoffrey L. Goodwin, *Britain and the United Nations* (London: Oxford University Press, 1957), p. 278; Cristobal Kay, *Latin American Theories of Development and Underdevelopment* (London: Routledge, 1989), p. 5.
4. John Pincus, *Trade, Aid and Development. The Rich and Poor Nations* (New York: McGraw-Hill Book Company, 1967), pp. 76–8, 126–34, and Harry G. Johnson, *Economic Policies Towards Less Developed Countries* (London: George Allen and Unwin Ltd, 1967), pp. 48–52.
5. See Michael Edwards, *Future Positive: International Co-operation in the 21st Century* (London: Earthscan, 1999), p. 180.
6. J. Adam Tooze, *Statistics and the German State, 1900–1945: The Making of Modern Economic Knowledge* (Cambridge: Cambridge University Press, 2001), pp. 199–207.
7. William J. Barber, 'Government as a Laboratory for Economic Learning in the Years of the Democratic Roosevelt', in Mary O. Furner and Barry Supple (eds), *The State and Economic Knowledge: the American and British Experiences* (Cambridge: Cambridge University Press, 1990), pp. 111–14.
8. Lyn Squire, 'Why the World Bank Should be Involved in Development Research', in Christopher L. Gilbert and David Vines (eds), *The World Bank: Structure and Policies* (Cambridge: Cambridge University Press, 2000), pp. 108–33.
9. Lloyd I. Rudolph and Suzanne H. Rudolph, 'Authority and Power in Bureaucratic and Patrimonial Administration: a Revisionist Interpretation of Weber on Bureaucracy', *World Politics*, 38 (1979), pp. 195–227 esp. p. 207.

10. Weber believed that the specific nature of bureaucracy 'develops the more perfectly the more bureaucracy is "dehumanised", the more completely it succeeds in eliminating from official business love, hatred, and all purely personal, irrational, and emotional elements that escape calculation'. (H.H. Gerth and C. Wright Mills (eds), *From Max Weber: Essays in Sociology* (New York: Oxford University Press, 1946), p. 215).
11. Lloyd I. Rudolph and Suzanne H. Rudolph, 'Authority and Power', 209.
12. Javed A. Ansari, *The Political Economy of International Economic Organization* (Boulder, CO: Rienner, 1986), pp. 143–4.
13. In defining the criteria of the 'good researcher', we do not suggest that bad researchers, who fail to meet these criteria, cannot be found in academia as well as elsewhere. Our point is that good researchers face an additional hazard in the bureaucratic context.
14. For a detailed case study of such vetting at the World Bank, see Robert Wade, 'Japan, the World Bank and the Art of Paradigm Maintenance: *The East Asian Miracle* in Political Perspective', *New Left Review*, 217 (May–June 1996), pp. 3–36.
15. See N. De Marchi (with the co-operation of Peter Dohlman), 'League of Nations Economists and the Ideal of Peaceful Change in the Decade of the Thirties', *History of Political Economy*, 23 (1991), Annual Supplement, pp. 143–78.
16. For example, G. Haberler, *Prosperity and Depression* (Geneva: League of Nations, 1937; 3rd edn, London: George Allen and Unwin Ltd, 1964); J. Tinbergen, *Statistical Testing of Business Cycle Theories*, 2 vols (Geneva: League of Nations, 1938–39).
17. Jean Jacques Polak, 'International Propagation of Business Cycles', *Review of Economic Studies*, VI, 2 (1939), pp. 79–99.
18. Richard Kahn complained of this in relation to Haberler's *Prosperity and Depression*; see his review 'The League of Nations Enquiry into the Trade Cycle', *Economic Journal*, 47, 188 (December 1937), pp. 670–9.
19. Paul Mizen, Don Moggridge and John Presley, 'The Papers of Dennis Robertson: the Discovery of Unexpected Riches', *History of Political Economy*, 29 (1997), pp. 573–92, esp. pp. 575–6. Gordon Fletcher, in his biography *Understanding Dennis Robertson. The Man and His Work* (Cheltenham: Edward Elgar, 2000), does not mention Robertson's connection with the League and later with the UN, but he does explore very fully the nature of Robertson's professional and personal conservatism.
20. Dennis Robertson to Alexander Loveday, 14 June 1939, League of Nations archive, Geneva.
21. Tinbergen later recalled: Loveday 'sent me to England to discuss my work with [Henderson and Robertson]; interestingly enough, not with Keynes'. Jan R. Magnus and Mary Morgan, 'The ET Interview: Professor Jan Tinbergen', *Econometric Theory*, 3 (1987), pp. 117–42, esp. p. 125.
22. John Maynard Keynes, *Collected Writings*, Vol. XIV (London: Macmillan St Martin's Press, 1973), pp. 285–320. For a review of this controversy, see Don Patinkin, 'Keynes and Econometrics: On the Interactions between Macroeconomic Revolutions in the Inter-War Period', *Econometrica*, 44, 6 (1976), pp. 1091–123, esp. pp. 1094–6; and Robert Leeson, ' "The Ghosts I Called I Can't Get Rid of Now": The Keynes-Tinbergen-Friedman-Phillips

Critique of Keynesian Macroeconomics', *History of Political Economy*, 30 (1998), pp. 51–94.

23. Anthony M. Endres and Grant A. Fleming, *International Organizations and the Analysis of Economic Policy, 1919–1950* (Cambridge: Cambridge University Press, 2002), pp. 46–7.
24. Charles P. Kindleberger, 'Economists in International Organizations', *International Organization*, 9 (1955), pp. 338–52. See also Henry C. Wallich, 'United Nations Report on Full Employment', *American Economic Review*, 40 (1950), pp. 876–83.
25. For a discussion of this shift, see John Toye and Richard Toye, *The UN and Global Political Economy: Trade, Finance and Development* (Bloomington, IN: Indiana University Press, 2004), ch. 4.
26. For example, the League's Delegation on Economic Depressions, appointed in 1938, included two academic economists, Bertil Ohlin and Oskar Morgenstern. See Endres and Fleming, *International Organizations*, p. 46, n. 38.
27. Haberler, *Prosperity and Depression*, p. v.
28. Austin Robinson, 'Five Economic Surveys', *Economic Journal*, LIX (1949), pp. 629–38. For Condliffe and Meade, see Neil De Marchi, 'League of Nations Economists and the Idea of Peaceful Change in the Decade of the Thirties', *History of Political Economy* 23, Annual Supplement (1991), and Susan Howson, 'James Meade', *Economic Journal*, 110, 461 (2000), pp. 122–145. Dennis Robertson introduced Meade to Loveday in 1937, and Meade wrote the Surveys for 1937–38 and 1938–39.
29. Alexander Loveday, *Reflections on International Administration* (Oxford: Clarendon Press, 1956), p. 309.
30. Endres and Fleming, *International Organizations*, pp. 252–7.
31. R.W.B. Clarke diary, 12 March 1946, R.W.B. Clarke Papers, 25, Churchill College, Cambridge.
32. Loveday, *Reflections*, p. 294.
33. Ibid., pp. 99–101.
34. Oral history interview with Janez Stanovnik, 7–8 January 2001, pp. 73–4, in the Oral History Collection of the United Nations Intellectual History Project, The Graduate Center, The City University of New York.
35. 'Surely the most interesting examples of UN creativity in the last decades have been those where editorial control has *not* been exercised: e.g. the World Employment Programme, the Human Development Report, and even UNICEF' work on adjustment. In contrast, where editorial control has been strict, the result has been uninteresting and has often failed.' Private communication from Yves Berthelot, former Executive Secretary of UN ECE.
36. For other examples see Toye and Toye, *The UN and Global Political Economy*.
37. Joseph L. Love, 'Raúl Prebisch and the Origins of the Doctrine of Unequal Exchange', *Latin American Research Review* 15 (1980), pp. 45–72.
38. Kay, *Latin American Theories*, p. 32.
39. John Toye and Richard Toye, interview with Singer, 12 May 2000.
40. Prebisch did, however, use the phrase 'persistent fall in the international prices of our exports' in the 1943 outline of his unpublished book, according to Edgar J. Dosman, 'Markets and the State: Theory and Practice in the Evolution of the "Prebisch Manifesto" ', *Revista de la CEPAL/CEPAL Review* 75 (2001), pp. 27–33.

41. John Toye and Richard Toye, 'The Origins and Interpretation of the Prebisch-Singer Thesis', *History of Political Economy*, 35 (2003), pp. 437–67.
42. United Nations, *Relative Prices of Exports and Imports of Under-developed Countries* (Lake Success, NY: UN Department of Economic Affairs, 1949), p. 126.
43. United Nations, *Post-war Price Relations in Trade between Under-developed and Industrialized Countries* (UN document no. E/CN/Sub.3/W.5, Lake Success, New York: UN Department of Economic Affairs, 1949), p. 12.
44. Martínez Cabañas was Executive Secretary of ECLA. Coire was head of the Latin American section of the DEA in New York.
45. In an interview with Tom Weiss for the UN Intellectual History Project.
46. See Toye and Toye, 'Origins'.
47. Raúl Prebisch, *The Economic Development of Latin America and Its Principal Problems* (UN document no. E/CN.12/89/Rev. 1, Lake Success, NY: United Nations, 1950), p. 1.
48. Mateo Magariños, *Diálogos con Raúl Prebisch* (Mexico: Banco Nacional de Comercio Exterior/ Fondo de Cultura Económica, 1991), p. 130.
49. Gustavo Martínez Cabañas to Trygve Lie, 9 October 1949, Letter of Transmittal printed in Prebisch, *Economic Development*.
50. H.E. Caustin to A.D.K. Owen, 12 October 1949, UN Archive, New York, DAG-17 Box 33; see also Magariños, *Diálogos*, p. 129.
51. Celso Furtado, *La fantaisie organisée: Le développement est-il encore possible?* (Paris: Publisud, 1987), p. 80.
52. Its first incarnation was in Spanish, as UN document E/CN.12/89, dated 14 May 1949. It appeared in *El Trimestre Economico* 16, 63 (July–September 1949), pp. 347–431. At the instance of Furtado, it was published in Portuguese in the *Revista Brasileira de Economia* in October 1949. It was re-published in Spanish in Santiago in April 1950, and again in English later in 1950 in Lake Success, NY, as UN Document no. E/CN.12/89, Rev.1. Its subsequent publication history until 1986 is to be found in United Nations, *Raúl Prebisch: Un aporte al estudio de su pensiamiento* (UN document no. LC/G.1461, Santiago de Chile: CEPAL, 1987), p. 52.
53. Leaving staff to their own devices continued in UNCTAD in the 1970s. 'UNCTAD was relatively weak in numbers of quality professional staff, and a large portion of its staff appeared to be dross. Among those who were active, sometimes they were publishing a lot and were doing so because they had been so misplaced in the organization that they had no clear mandate as to what they were supposed to be doing. They weren't led well. So people like Gary Sampson and Sandy Yeats and Dani Rodrik, at that time, were able to do things sometimes that were quite interesting.' Interview of Gerald Helleiner by Tom Weiss for UN Intellectual History Project, Toronto, 4–5 December 2000, p. 60.
54. The story of the Bank's successful resistance to the ambitions of the UN Economic and Social Council is told in Devesh Kapur, John P. Lewis and Richard Webb, *The World Bank. Its First Half Century, Volume One: History* (Washington DC: Brookings Institution Press, 1997), p. 1168. The similar story for the IMF is in J. Keith Horsefield, *The International Monetary Fund 1945–65. Twenty Years of International Monetary Cooperation*, International Monetary Fund (Washington DC: 1969), vol. I, pp. 124, 145–7 and vol. III, pp. 215–18.

55. In its early years, the Bank's most distinguished economist was Paul Rosenstein-Rodan, who had contributed one of the seminal works of the new sub-discipline of development economics in 1943: 'Problems of Industrialisation in Eastern and South-Eastern Europe', *Economic Journal*, LIII (1943), pp. 202–11. His sojourn at the Bank between 1947 and 1954 was a contentious and unhappy one, and after many conflicts with the management, he left for academic life at MIT.
56. Jan Tinbergen, *The Design of Development* (Baltimore, MD: Johns Hopkins Press for IBRD, 1958). His account of the publication delay, and the reasons for it, is given in Jan R. Magnus and Mary S. Morgan, 'The ET Interview: Professor J. Tinbergen', *Econometric Theory*, 3 (1987), pp. 117–42, esp. pp. 134–5.
57. See John Williamson, 'What Washington Means by Policy Reform', in John Williamson (ed.), *Latin American Adjustment: How Much has Happened?* (Washington DC: Institute for International Economics, 1990).
58. See J. Eaton and M. Gersovitz, 'Debt with Potential Repudiation: Theoretical and Empirical Analysis', *Review of Economic Studies*, 48 (1981), pp. 289–309.
59. I. Diwan and I. Husain, *Dealing with the Debt Crisis* (Washington DC: World Bank, 1989), p. v, cited in Beatriz Armendariz and Francisco Ferreira, 'The World Bank and the Analysis of the International Debt Crisis', in John Harriss, Janet Hunter and Colin M. Lewis (eds), *The New Institutional Economics and Third World Development* (London: Routledge, 1995), pp. 215–29, esp. p. 226.
60. Interview of Gerald K. Helleiner by Tom Weiss for the UN Intellectual History Project, Toronto, (4–5 December 2000), 45.
61. Ha-Joon Chang (ed.), *Joseph Stiglitz and the World Bank. The Rebel Within* (London: Anthem Press, 2001), pp. 1–16. Stiglitz's own account of his experience in the Bank is given in Joseph Stiglitz, *Globalization and its Discontents* (London: Allen Lane, 2002).
62. Joseph E. Stiglitz, 'More Instruments and Broader Goals: Moving Towards the Post-Washington Consensus', in Ha-Joon Chang (ed.), *Joseph Stiglitz and the World Bank: the Rebel Within* (London: Anthem Press, 2001), pp. 17–56.
63. These two episodes are chronicled in Robert Wade, 'Showdown at the World Bank', *New Left Review*, Second Series No. 7 (2001), pp. 124–37.
64. Stiglitz, *Globalization and its Discontents*, p. 221, with emphasis added.
65. Kaushik Basu, 'Globalization and the Politics of International Finance: The Stiglitz Verdict', *Journal of Economic Literature*, XLI, 3 (2003), pp. 885–99, esp. pp. 892–3.
66. It was slow to adopt the discounted cash flow and the shadow pricing techniques, according to the Bank's historians, E.S. Mason and R.E. Asher, *The World Bank since Bretton Woods* (Washington DC: Brookings Institution, 1973), p. 257.
67. M. Gavin and Dani Rodrik, 'The World Bank in Historical Perspective', *American Economic Review Papers and Proceedings*, 85 (1995), pp. 329–34. See also Nicolas Stern and Francisco Ferreira, 'The World Bank as an "Intellectual Actor" ', in Devesh Kapur, John P. Lewis and Richard Webb, *The World Bank: Its First Half Century 2: Perspectives* (Washington DC: Brookings Institution, 1997), pp. 523–610.
68. Rudolph and Rudolph, 'Authority and Power', pp. 226–7.

Index

The Healing Within:
Medicine, Health and Wholeness
A generational transaction

by

Robin Price

Institute for Cultural Research

The Institute for Cultural Research,
PO Box 13,
Tunbridge Wells,
KENT TN3 0JD
England.

ICR Monograph Series No.23

ISSN 0306 1906
ISBN 0 904674 11 8

Printed by The Russell Press Ltd.,
Gamble Street, Nottingham NG7 4ET